The Meaning of Religious Freedom in the Public Sphere

The Meaning of Religious Freedom in the Public Sphere

Pablo Muñoz Iturrieta

◥PICKWICK *Publications* • Eugene, Oregon

THE MEANING OF RELIGIOUS FREEDOM IN THE PUBLIC SPHERE

Copyright © 2020 Pablo Muñoz Iturrieta. All rights reserved. Except for brief quotations in critical publications or reviews, no part of this book may be reproduced in any manner without prior written permission from the publisher. Write: Permissions, Wipf and Stock Publishers, 199 W. 8th Ave., Suite 3, Eugene, OR 97401.

Pickwick Publications
An Imprint of Wipf and Stock Publishers
199 W. 8th Ave., Suite 3
Eugene, OR 97401

www.wipfandstock.com

PAPERBACK ISBN: 978-1-5326-3970-8
HARDCOVER ISBN: 978-1-5326-3971-5
EBOOK ISBN: 978-1-5326-3972-2

Cataloguing-in-Publication data:

Names: Iturrieta, Pablo Muñoz, author.

Title: The meaning of religious freedom in the public sphere / by Pablo Muñoz Iturrieta.

Description: Eugene, OR : Pickwick Publications, 2020 | Includes bibliographical references and index.

Identifiers: ISBN 978-1-5326-3970-8 (paperback) | ISBN 978-1-5326-3971-5 (hardcover) | ISBN 978-1-5326-3972-2 (ebook)

Subjects: LCSH: Freedom of religion—United States—History. | Catholic Church—Political activity—United States—History—21st century. | Democracy—Religious aspects. | Democracy—Religious aspects—Christianity.

Classification: BR516 .I86 2020 (print) | BR516 .I86 (ebook)

Manufactured in the U.S.A.   02/25/20

In any question concerning man and the world,
the question about the Divinity is always included
as the preliminary and really basic question.
No one can understand the world at all,
no one can live his life rightly,
so long as the question about the Divinity remains unanswered.
Indeed, the very heart of the great cultures
is that they interpret the world
by setting in order their relationship to the Divinity.

—Joseph Ratzinger

Contents

Abbreviations | ix

Introduction | 1
1. Religion and the Public Square in a Secular Age | 7
2. History, Definitions, and Foundations of the Right to Religious Freedom | 75
3. Religion: History and Meaning of an Uncertain Concept | 140
4. Hanna Arendt's Notions of Freedom and the Public Square | 204
5. Religious Freedom and the Public Realm | 228
   Conclusion: Religious Freedom from a New Perspective | 257

Bibliography | 279
Index | 295

Abbreviations

BNR   Jürgen Habermas. *Between Naturalism and Religion*. Cambridge: Polity, 2008.

DH   Vatican Council II. *Declaration on Religious Freedom* (*Dignitatis Humanae*). Boston: Daughters of Saint Paul, 1965.

Eph. Thomas Aquinas. *Super Epistolam ad Ephesios Lectura*. 8th ed. Rome: Marietti, 1953.

FTHD David Schlinder. "Freedom, Truth, and Human Dignity." *Communio* 40 (2013) 208–316.

HC   Hannah Arendt. *The Human Condition*. Chicago: University of Chicago Press, 1958.

HR   Henry Babcock Veatch. *Human Rights: Fact or Fancy?* Baton Rouge: Louisiana State University Press, 1985.

Io.   Thomas Aquinas. *Super Evangelium S. Ioannis lectura*. Rome: Marietti, 1972.

IPRR John Rawls. "The Idea of Public Reason Revisited." *UCLR* 64:3 (1997) 765–807.

JC   Rainer Forst. *Justification and Critique*. Cambridge: Polity, 2014.

JF   John Rawls. "Justice as Fairness: Political Not Metaphysical." *PPA* 14:3 (1985) 223–51.

MS   Charles Taylor. "The Meaning of Secularism." *HR* 12 (2010) 23–34.

NPS   Richard John Neuhaus. *The Naked Public Square*. Grand Rapids: Eerdmans, 1984.

PL	John Rawls. *Political Liberalism*. New York: Columbia University Press, 2005.
RPS	Jürgen Habermas. "Religion in the Public Sphere." *EJP* 14:1 (2006) 1–25.
RRS	Chales Taylor. "Why We Need a Radical Redefinition of Secularism." In *The Power of Religion in the Public Sphere*, edited by E. Mendieta and J. VanAntwerpen, 34–59. New York: Columbia University Press, 2011.
SA	Charles Taylor. *A Secular Age*. Cambridge, MA: Harvard University Press, 2007.
SCG	Thomas Aquinas. *Summa contra Gentiles*. Rome: Herder, 1934.
Sent.	Thomas Aquinas. *Scriptum super Libros Sententiarum Magistri Petri Lombardi*. Paris: Lethielleux, 1929.
SL	Giorgio Agamben. *Il Sacramento del Linguaggio*. Roma: Laterza, 2008.
S. Th.	Thomas Aquinas. *Summa Theologiae*. Leonine edition 4–12. Rome: Propaganda Fide, 1882–1906.
TC	Rainer Forst. *Toleration in Conflict*. Cambridge: Cambridge University Press, 2013.
Trin.	Thomas Aquinas. *Super Boetium de Trinitate*. Leonine edition 50. Paris: Cerf, 1992.

Introduction

GLOBALIZATION, IMMIGRATION, DANGER AND wars, the many possibilities that allow people to seek a new life away from their countries of origin, and many other factors, have contributed to create multicultural societies. This "multiculturalism" stands for the existence of a plurality of "cultures" within society, cultures which, as Rainer Forst notes, represent more than just "lifestyles."[1] These communities define themselves through a shared history, shared conceptions of value, and shared language and descent. They are marked by deep agreements when it comes to an ethical perspective on life: they agree on the contents, the forms, and the sources of the good life. More importantly for our topic, such cultures are often distinguished by a specifically religious component. It is this religious component, and all it entails, that has been perceived as in danger of being erased from public life, with the consequent result of depriving these cultures of one of their most essential elements.

Religion is considered to touch on people's deepest convictions, the structure of modern, and even secular, society, and the possibility of peaceful coexistence of nations and communities.[2] At the same time, there is increasing fear that religion is being subtly relegated to one's own private life, under the pretext of the plurality of religious doctrines and worldviews. One often hears that either religion must be tamed by restricting its access to public power, or that in the name of neutrality and equality no religious reasoning may be used in the political sphere, as it may be coercive to other worldviews. There is also the idea that religion is a "transhistorical" and "transcultural" feature of human life, essentially distinct from "secular" features such as politics and economics, and has a peculiarly dangerous

---

1. Forst, *Toleration in Conflict*, 522.
2. Cf. Beek, Borght and Vermeulen, *Freedom of Religion*, 1.

inclination to promote violence.³ At the same time, we have the reality of pluralism of "religions" and worldviews in contemporary Western societies. Thus, the rise of secular liberalism has been the occasion for a novel and worldwide discussion on religion, religious freedom, and the place and role of religion in the public sphere.⁴

Religious freedom is also being challenged by new questions: the ban over the use of the niqab, veil or burka, and whether it should be considered as an act of Muslim belief; church adoption services for same-sex couples; Satanism as a religion, or Scientology Church as a church; whether the use of drugs during a cultural ritual can be regarded as a manifestation of belief; or whether female circumcision falls within the ambit of the freedom of religion; or whether Muslims, because of their faith, should have the right to marry more than one woman. There are also conflicts about religious symbols and dress in public life, such as at school and government offices, the financial funding of religious education, and the acceptance of secular values imposed by the government on the people. Combined, these make the meaning of religious freedom in the twenty-first century uncertain, and for that reason it is necessary to clarify the meaning of religious freedom in order to offer an answer that will settle these seemingly never-ending discussions.

A central social aspect present in all human rights is that when and where they have been claimed, it has been because the individuals concerned suffered from, and protested against, forms of oppression or exploitation that they believed disregarded their dignity as human beings.⁵ Yet, in order to argue in favor of the religious freedom of citizens and their institutions, it is important to first clarify the terms of the debate. We are challenged, then, to deepen our understanding of the fundamental value of religious freedom, for this will contribute to the definition, or redefinition, of laws that establish a balance between this freedom and the demands of a public order.

The terms employed in the expression "freedom of religion" or "religious freedom," sometimes even understood as tolerance, have not been duly criticized, with the exception perhaps of those who advocate that "freedom of conscience" is a term wide enough to include religious

---

3. For a criticism of this idea, see Cavanaugh, *Myth*, 3.

4. As José Casanova has shown, during the 1980s, religious traditions around the world began making their way out of the private sphere and into public life, causing what he calls the "deprivatization" of religion in contemporary life. Thus, religious institutions are challenging dominant political and social forces, raising questions about the claims of entities such as states and markets to be "value neutral," and straining the traditional connections of private and public morality. See Casanova, *Public Religions*.

5. Cf. Forst, *Justification and Critique*, 38.

protection. As much as I agree on and defend the existence of the civil right to freedom of religion as one of the most important human rights, the reader will be startled to hear that my goal here is to challenge the concepts themselves. The reason is that it will hopefully result in a stronger and clearer notion of religious freedom, of what it means and entails, in order to argue better in cases that truly belong to issues of "religion," and which should be distinguished from other manifestations that are wrongly considered under the banner of "religion."

Even though much has been written on religious freedom, there seems to be no agreement on what is meant by "religion," which is especially observed when it comes to clarifying the role of religion in the public square. Thus, before we can claim before the state that we have the right to freedom of religion, it is of the utmost importance that we understand what we mean by religious freedom. There seems to be confusion in the way the expression "religious freedom" has been used, either by the fact that the term "religion" is unclear in its content, or because there is no agreement on what is meant by "freedom," or what the public square is about. Thus, the central theme of this book is to elucidate the meaning of religion and freedom in discussions related to religious freedom and the place of religion in the public square. I will explore in which ways these notions are being employed and whether the use of both religion and freedom are coherent uses.

In order to do so, I will present two relevant contemporary topics in the first two chapters: the debate on the place of religion in the pluralistic and secular liberal state, and the debate and justification of religious freedom. The analysis of these debates and justifications will aim at revealing the use these authors make of the notions of religion, freedom, and the public square.

In order to understand our world, and ourselves, it is always helpful to become critical of the terms and concepts that we are using, for that may be the reason why certain debates seem to never end. Perhaps we may have been asking the wrong questions, or using concepts that are too uncertain to even be employed in a debate. At the same time, I propose an approach that tries to avoid contemporary deadlocks, debating as a philosopher who is aware not only of the difficulties that have arisen in modernity concerning religion, but also of the different approaches regarding the place of religion in society. Even more, I will approach this topic by trying to define the terms of the debate, a task that belongs above all to philosophy. In the following chapters of this book, then, my method will be to proceed with a verbal inquiry into the notions of religion and freedom, and their relationship to the public square, in order to see whether it is possible to find an understanding of these notions that may help us overcome the contemporary debates. As a result, a new meaning will be offered on the notion of religious freedom, which will help clarify its place in the public square. This will be done in order to salvage the development from an impasse into which it has been sidetracked due to the use of distorted concepts.

Even though the aim of this book is a concrete and narrow one, it touches upon many current debates and philosophical fields of inquiry. Thus, it is necessary to take an interdisciplinary approach, for the issues dealt with in this book are deeply related to political philosophy, ethics, legal philosophy, metaphysics, philosophy of religion, anthropology, sociology, history, linguistics, and even theology. The approach, however, will remain strictly philosophical, venturing sometimes in other areas in order to clarify and introduce the problems here presented.

In chapter 1, after offering a brief account of the origins of secularism in the West, I will introduce some of the solutions provided by John Rawls to the problem of the place of "religion" in the pluralistic secular liberal state. It will be followed by a challenging view on secularism by Richard John Neuhaus. Then, I will consider the work of José Casanova, Jürgen Habermas, and Charles Taylor on the place of religion within the secular, contemporary context. I will pay special attention to the use these authors make of the notions of "religion" and the "public square." It will be shown that they do not employ a clear notion of religion, for in most cases the term "religion" is employed as meaning a dogma or comprehensive view, or as a way of arguing in the public political forum (for example, religious arguments as contraposed to secular arguments). At the same time, the public square is conceived sometimes as a monolithic reality, to which religion, understood as a dogma, should have or has limited or no access to.

In chapter 2, I will briefly present the history of religious freedom, tolerance, and some of the contemporary debates and justifications of religious freedom, in order to again explore the ways in which the notions of freedom and religion are employed. It will be shown that the right to religious freedom has historically been understood mainly in two ways: first, as (religious) tolerance, or as the justification against religious intolerance, and second, as freedom of conscience. The problem here is that none of these two understandings are able to offer a clear notion of religious freedom. Regarding contemporary approaches to justify religious freedom, there is a lack of clarification on what is meant by freedom and religion, and therefore it is difficult from these perspectives to establish guidelines on the practice of religion in society and the place of religion in the public square.

Chapter 3 will be focused on the notion of "religion." "Religion" has meant different things throughout history. In order to find an appropriate notion, then, one that will help us overcome the difficulties found in contemporary debates on religion in the public square and religious freedom, it will be necessary to do a verbal inquiry into the notion of "religion." Thus, this chapter will offer a genealogy of the concept of religion in the West, in order to find an appropriate meaning of the term. This will also allow us to understand how the authors treated in chapters 1 and 2 have arrived at the notion of religion they employ in their argumentations. A problematic understanding of religion has grave consequences for the understanding and meaning of religious freedom. I will start this inquiry by presenting the meaning and use of religion in Greek and Roman thought. I will also introduce here the work done by the Italian political philosopher Giorgio Agamben on the oath as a juridical and religious institution in Greek and Roman thought which gave origin to the religious and the law. Then, I will present Thomas Aquinas's notion of religion as a moral virtue, which gathers a constellation of acts: devotion, prayer, oaths, vows, tithing, etc. I will also investigate, from Aquinas's perspective, the connection between the virtue of religion and the public square. It will be followed by a historical presentation on the invention of "religion" as a category in modernity, when, for the first time, "religion" was employed to mean an interior disposition, and reducible to belief. This section will also mention some of the ways in which the concept of religion as a category has been employed in colonial contexts outside the West. Finally, contemporary uses and definitions of religion will be presented, which will make it clear that the term "religion," as it has been employed in contemporary debates, should be dropped entirely if one is willing to overcome the impasse present in contemporary discussions.

Chapter 4 will deal with Hanna Arendt's notion of political freedom, that is, freedom as the stage for virtue. I will also explore here the meaning of the "stage" Arendt refers to, that is, her understanding of the public square, and how it differs from notions of the public square presented in chapter 1. The goal of this chapter, then, will be to find a new insight into the notion of freedom and the public sphere in order to avoid many of the dilemmas that current debates on the place of religion in the public sphere encounter, and also in order to gain a better understanding of what is meant by religious freedom.

Chapter 5 will stress the fact that there is a need to adopt a new perspective on religious freedom and the place of religion in the public square, a perspective which avoids unnecessary dichotomies (such as religion versus secular, private versus public, religious or dogmatic reasoning versus secular reasoning). Given that there is a seeming inability in contemporary debates to clarify what is signified by the word "religion," the notion of religion as a category ought to be dropped, for it not only prevents clarifying what falls into the realm of religious freedom and what does not, creating unnecessary debates, but also creates a false problem regarding its place in the public square, for "religion" as a category is not related to actions, and therefore does not have a proper setting or settings for its appearance. Thus, this chapter will show how Hannah Arendt's notion of freedom as a stage for virtue and Aquinas's notion of religion as a virtue offer a unique perspective to help us elucidate contemporary issues on religious freedom and the place of religion in the public square, as well as helping us reach a coherent understanding of religious freedom. For that reason, defining the terms used in the expression "religious freedom" will help us clarify what we are arguing for when we argue in favor of this right. Aquinas's notions of religion and of its various deviations (vices) will also offer us a valuable guideline insofar as the public is concerned. This criteria will help us distinguish actions that properly belong to the realm of religious virtue from those that can be considered irrational, and therefore banned; it will open up space for discussion on arguments that bear on the ethics of citizens; and it will help guide public discussions about beliefs and religious practices, on what does belong to religious virtue as such, and what belongs to different realms such as conscience, cultural practices, etc. At the same time, religion taken as a virtue has commonalities with modern concepts such as public allegiance, civic obligation, justice, public virtue, and a host of other concepts and practices that modernity categorizes as political. Thus, rejecting the religious freedom of citizens will inevitably have negative consequences on political institutions. I will also address in this chapter the issue of religious freedom as a human right in light of the new understanding of religion as a virtue.

In the conclusion, the new perspective on religious freedom offered on this book will be considered in light of a few contemporary court cases and laws that make it evident there is a problematic understanding of religion, religious freedom, and the public square. Thus, contemporary cases regarding religion and religious freedom will be presented in order to test the new meaning offered in this book, as well as in order to compare the results with some of the contemporary theories presented in the first two chapters. This will help us see whether this redefinition of religious freedom signifies a new development and a better solution to contemporary debates.

I hope that by the end of this book it will be clear that this redefinition of the concepts used in debates regarding religious freedom and the place of religion in the public square is meant not to subvert a fixed position, but rather it is offered as carrying forward new developments that will allow us to overcome the impasse into which contemporary discussions have been sidetracked.

CHAPTER I

Religion and the Public Square in a Secular Age

SECULARISM IS ONE OF the characteristics of liberal democracies. However, Richard John Neuhaus denounced in his *The Naked Public Square* (1984) that the separation of religion from politics brought about by ideological secularism had gone too far. Thus, political philosophers have had to deal not only with the problem of pluralism of religious groups, but also with the place and role of religion in a secular setting in order to avoid an extreme separation between religion and politics.

There is no doubt that religious groups have become a huge concern not only for those interested in political theory and philosophy, but also for those involved in political practices as well. There has been a radical shift in reconsidering the relationship between politics and religion, which, as Maria Pia Lara notes, might be due to two major contributions in the academic world: the publication of Charles Taylor's *A Secular Age*, and Habermas's assertion that we must learn to live in a postsecular world, especially by taking into account the existential force of religious belief. Their works, as a consequence, have triggered a revision of theories about secularization, about the prevalence of religion in the life of modern communities, and about the need to establish the possible dependence of politics on religion.[1] One cannot avoid these questions when dealing with religious freedom from a philosophical perspective.

In this chapter, then, I will present the work of some relatively recent and contemporary influential philosophers from various parts of the world that have dealt with the problems that have arisen regarding pluralism, secularism, and the place of religion in public life, and whose work has triggered a revision of theories about secularization. These philosophers

---

1. Cf. Lara, "Postsecular," 72. For Taylor and Habermas, especially see Taylor, *SA*; Habermas, *RPS*.

are Richard John Neuhaus (Canada/USA, 1936–2009), John Rawls (USA, 1921–2002), Jose Casanovas (Spain, b. 1951), Jürgen Habermas (Germany, b. 1929), and Charles Taylor (Canada, b. 1931). These authors have been more than just academic philosophers. Most of them have in fact become important political actors and contributors. Thus, it is important to see how they view the place and role of religion in our contemporary pluralistic societies, how they define or what they mean by religion, which role they grant to religious institutions and associations, and what their view are regarding religious discourse, as all these issues have an impact on the understanding of religious freedom.

In the first place, I will offer a brief account of the origins of secularism in the West. In the second place, I will offer an analysis of John Rawls's attempt to construct a neutral framework for social cooperation that was accommodating of diverse religious views. In the third place, I will present a challenging view on secularism, that of Richard John Neuhaus, who denounces a separatist interpretation of the First Amendment of the U.S. Constitution, leaving the public square "naked", that is, "bare" of religious speech. In the fourth place, I will present the challenges to the "secularization thesis" and the notion of Postsecularism. In the fifth place, I will analyze José Casanovas's definitions of "secularism" and "secularization," as an introduction to the contemporary setting of the discussion. In the sixth place, I will present Jürgen Habermas's views on religion and the public square within a "postsecular" age. And finally, I will present Charles Taylor's positive analysis of "secularism" as the response of the democratic state to the fact of religious pluralism.

Origins of Secularism in the West

In the West, a key question was how the Church—and after successive splits, the various churches—would relate to states and politics, and how the states would deal with it. The church developed the doctrine or notion of distinct powers in different spheres, even though historically there have been many different doctrines and notions on the subject, as well as many instances in which the Pope and the monarchs of Europe didn't live up to the notion of distinct powers.[2]

---

2. For a good account on the relationship between the state and the church from its origins in our Western civilization, see Wiker, *Worshipping the State*, 25–100. For a historical example on the failure to respect the distinct powers, and the political criticism that it ensued, see Falkeid, *Avignon Papacy*.

Later, the Protestant Reformation would bring an intensification of the relationship of religion to politics. The one hundred and fifty years of interstate war, the "religious wars" that wracked Europe through the fifteenth and early sixteenth centuries, were also wars of state-building. In fact, they were more political than religious wars, caused by princes and kings using religious differences, and using the multitude of churches created by the Reformation, as political tools to advance their own ambitions as builders of nations-states.[3] These wars expanded secular power even when fought in the name of religion. In fact, the conclusion of these wars in the 1648 Peace of Westphalia is often cited as the beginning of not just a secular state system in Europe, but it is also claimed as the beginning of modern international relations, understood as a matter of secular relations among sovereign states. However, The Peace of Westphalia did not make states secular. It established a practice rooted in the principle of *cuius regio eius religio*, so that what followed was a mixture of migration, forced conversion, and legal sanctions against religious minorities. Thus, European states after the Peace of Westphalia were still primarily confessional states with established churches. Even though the European path to relatively strong secularism was not a direct one from the Peace of Westphalia, it was shaped by struggles against the enforced religious conformity that followed the 1648 treaties.[4]

This new kind of secular regime came to light within two important founding contexts: that of France and The United States of America.

Secularism (*laïcité*) in France has become not simply a policy choice but a part of its national identity. Modern France is the paradigm of what Tore Lindhom terms "strident laicism."[5] While this type of laicism may want to give an appearance of tolerance and neutrality, laicist politics tend to be intolerant against public manifestations of institutionalized religion, acting as if illiberal policing of religion were mandatory for a religiously neutral state. The French doctrine of *laïcité* was the product of a struggle against a powerful church and priestly authority that continued through the twentieth century.[6]

---

3. On the secular causes of these wars, see Wiker, *Worshipping the State*, 118–20; Cavanaugh, "Wars of Religion"; Cavanaugh, *Myth*, 123–81.

4. Cf. Calhoun, "Rethinking Secularism," 41. Nevertheless, Calhoun concedes that "the Peace of Westphalia produced a division of the international from the domestic modeled on that between the public and the private, and it urged treating religion as a domestic matter. Both diplomatic practice and eventually the academic discipline of international relations would come to treat states as externally secular. That is, they attempted to banish religion from relations between states" (p. 44).

5. Lindholm also includes Turkey as an example. Cf. Lindholm, "Justifications of Freedom of Religion," 45–46.

6. This struggle, José Casanova argues, is central to what has made Europe particularly secular. See his Casanova, *Public Religions*. This might be one of the reasons why

It took a form of militant secularism, and positioned itself as a dimension of social struggle and liberation. As Taylor notes, the strong temptation was for the state itself to stand on a moral basis independent from religion. Then, the notion stuck that *laïcité* was all about controlling and establishing the place of religion in society.[7] Even though laicism signifies just the absence of any official state religion, it gives the appearance of an official state religion. It is also a fact that laicist governments have tended to persecute those advocating for public manifestations of religion, and grant no place to religion as an institution in the public square. If and when the public square is an open place for individuals, no institutions as such can appear there; however, individual members of institutions (religious and others) can bring in ideas from their religious culture only insofar as they do so as representing a given institution. Thus, the laicist liberal state is about individuals abstracted from their institutional and relational soils.

Secularism in the United States originated in a completely different context, and has different characteristics than the French version of the secular. In its origins, there was in the United States, with the exception of a few Deists, a strong Christian presence manifested in a variety of Protestant denominations, which later included Catholics, and moved even beyond Christianity and religion. At the beginning, however, the positions between which the state was to be neutral were all related to Christian, Protestant, denominations. This is the reason why there was a First Amendment: "Congress shall make no law respecting an establishment of religion or prohibiting the free exercise thereof."[8]

The primacy of Christianity in society and its political life was upheld until at least the end of the nineteenth century. Thus, in interpreting the law, judges of the Supreme Court may have well argued that one could invoke the principles of Christianity in making a court decision, since the First Amendment forbade only the identification of the federal government with any Christian (and in fact Protestant) church. Since at the time all the churches were variations of Christian Protestantism, Taylor argues that that may be the reason why the word "secularism" did not appear in the early decades of American public life, for a basic problem had not yet been faced.[9] After 1870, however, there ensued a battle between those who wanted to maintain existing Christian features in the American

---

Europe panics over Islam. For a summary on how French secularism developed, and its present situation, see Bourdin, "Religious Freedom"; Baubérot, "Place of Religion."

7. Cf. Taylor, MS, 27.
8. United States, *Constitution*, 47.
9. Cf. Taylor, MS, 26–27.

Government, on one hand, and those who wanted a real opening to all other religious groups and also to those non-religious. This included Jews, and also Catholics who saw the American version of Christianity as excluding them. Thus, Taylor notes, it was in this battle that the word "secular" first appeared on the American scene as a key term, and very often in its polemical sense of non-religious, or antireligious.[10]

Later on, in the well-known Supreme Court case *Everson v. Board of Education* (1947), the Supreme Court decided two things of momentous consequences for the advance of the secular cause. First, it stated that the First Amendment's Establishment Clause ("Congress shall make no law respecting an establishment of religion") demanded the erection, using Jefferson's terminology, of "a wall of separation between the church and the state."[11] Second, it decided that the Establishment Clause, as newly interpreted by Justice Back, could now be applied by the federal government to the states, so that the federal government could use all its powers to enforce this separation. Thus, the reformulation of constitutional doctrine as separation of church and state, which has given rise to so many controversies, ended up embodying a kind of secularism in the United States Constitution, which, in the original intention of not adopting an established church, meant to protect religious differences and helped to create a sort of marketplace of religious groups in which faith and active participation flourished.[12] Thus, by setting the two religion provisions of the First Amendment in opposition to each other, the Supreme Court's decision has undermined the religious freedom both provisions were designed to serve. The consequences have been denounced as a campaign of the Supreme Court to privatize religion.[13]

---

10. Cf. Taylor, MS, 26–27. It should be noted that Taylor uses the word "religions," instead of religious groups. For more on this polemic, see Smith, *Secular Revolution*. See also Wenger, "God-in-the-Constitution."

11. This advanced a novel and highly secularized interpretation of the Establishment Cause. The phrase comes from Jefferson's letter to the Danbury Baptist Association on January 1, 1802. However, as Neuhaus notes, the First Amendment's religious language does not contain any clauses at all. It is a declarative sentence with two participial phrases: "Congress shall make no law respecting an establishment of religion or prohibiting the free exercise thereof." Cf. Neuhaus, "New Order," 13–17.

12. As Harold Berman has noted, "although the first amendment is usually said to provide for the separation of church and state, in fact it does not contain the word 'church' but speaks instead of 'religion'; and it does not contain the word 'state' but speaks instead of 'Congress.'" See Berman, "Religious Freedom," 149. For more on this, see Wiker, *Worshipping the State*, 251–52, 90–94; Dreisbach, *Religious Autonomy*; Jeffries Jr. and Ryan, "Establishment Clause"; Bradley, "Judicial Experiment," 17.

13. Thus, in the 1960s, the Warren Court worked out the implications of *Everson* more thoroughly, especially in its decisions striking down prayer in public schools (*Engel v. Vitale*, and *Abington School District v. Schempp*). However, there is disagreement

Thus, countries that provide for separation of religion and state do so in different formats and to different effects. While Europe's trajectory was state churches followed by militant *laïcité*, in the United States secularism took place originally as the product of a strong practice of religious pluralism.

John Rawls and the Philosophical Problem of Religious Pluralism

It is a fact that most countries in the West can be politically characterized as representing diverse forms of secular liberalism. While this process of secularization was taking place, the world also experienced the phenomena of globalization and mass migrations, a process that is long from being finished, and which has resulted in a more diverse presence of religious groups. This means that now we should think not only of secular, but also of pluralistic societies marked by the presence of a plurality of views, both religious and nonreligious. For that reason, in order to establish the place and role of religion in this new secular and pluralistic setting, political philosophers had to rethink new ways in which religion could fit within the new context. In this section, I will address specifically the way Rawls dealt with the issue of pluralism, especially when it comes to different religious views competing for their presence and influence in the political sphere.

John Rawls (1921–2002) is considered by many to be one of the most important political philosophers of the twentieth century and a powerful advocate of the liberal perspective.

John Rawls and other liberal political theorists have made pluralism a basic premise of their theories of justice. In response, Rawls affirmed the principles of neutrality and equality, so that no religious reasoning may be used in the political sphere, as it may be coercive to other worldviews. Thus, appeals to metaphysical and philosophical concepts of nature or with thick value content surely seem too uncertain, or at least too contested or contestable, a basis for ethical and political consensus.[14] Instead, in order to provide an answer, Rawls offered the notions of "overlapping

---

on whether this "privatization" project of the U.S. Supreme Court still holds. According to Gerard Bradley, it has been in decay in the last 20 years. On the other hand, Mary Ann Glendon states that, since 1984, the Court has generally continued a six-decade-long trend toward confining religion to the public sphere. For a list of these cases that took place after 1984, the year in which the judicial project of creating an extreme separation of church and state reached its zenith, see Bradley, "Public Square." See also Glendon, "Naked Public Square," 35.

14. Cf. Rawls, *PL*, 224–25.

consensus" and "public reason" as the solution to the problem of religious pluralism in the liberal secular state.

A few years after presenting his *A Theory of Justice* (1971), Rawls realizes that the project would never be feasible by reason of the different views present in our liberal and pluralistic societies.[15] For that reason, in his "Justice as Fairness: Political not Metaphysical" (1985), Rawls presents his conception of justice not as true, but as one that can serve as a basis of informed and willing political agreement between citizens viewed as free and equal persons.[16] Then, in his *Political Liberalism* (1993), Rawls takes into account what he views as incompatible, yet reasonable, pluralistic comprehensive doctrines: "How is it possible that there may exist over time a stable and just society of free and equal citizens profoundly divided by reasonable though incompatible religious philosophical, and moral doctrines?"[17] Thus, he presents his political conception as reasonable, with a practical end: that it may be shared by citizens coming from different comprehensive doctrines as a basis of reasoned, informed, and willing political agreement.[18] His notion of reasonable pluralism, expressed as an "overlapping consensus," is the foundation, then, of a political consensus. Finally, in his "The Idea of Public Reason Revisited" (1997), Rawls presents what he considers the best statement of his views on public reason and political liberalism, especially regarding the compatibility of public reason with religious views.

Here I will limit my presentation to Rawls's work on the pluralism present in liberal societies, and how religion may be accommodated in this plural and secular context. Firstly, I will present Rawls's idea of an "overlapping consensus;" secondly, Rawls's idea of "public reason;" and finally, I will make an evaluation of Rawls's proposal.

Rawls's Idea of an "Overlapping Consensus"

Rawls intended to construct a framework for social cooperation that was neutral and accommodating of diverse philosophical and religious views.

---

15. A development has been noted within Rawls's work, which some even argue includes substantial changes in his vision of justice and of political liberalism in view of pluralism in society. Thus, in his *A Theory of Justice* (1971), Rawls presupposes a particular conception of the good and the person. He later realizes that, because of the pluralism present in our liberal society, his project is not realistic, for the principles of justice would never be accepted by the majority of the people, and that is when he introduces the idea of political justice and political liberalism.

16. Cf. Rawls, JF, 230.

17. Rawls, *PL*, xviii.

18. Cf. Rawls, *PL*, 9.

Thus, the central idea of Rawls's *Political Liberalism* (1993) is his notion of the "overlapping consensus." This idea, according to him, is "the most reasonable basis of social unity available to us."[19] He states:

> Such a consensus consists of all of the reasonable opposing religious, philosophical, and moral doctrines likely to persist over generations and to gain a sizable body of adherents in a more or less just constitutional regime, a regime in which the criterion of justice is the political conception itself.[20]

Rawls conceives the idea of an "overlapping consensus" in his search of a conception of justice that would be acceptable by anyone accepting the essentials of a democratic regime. Now, he states that "a modern democratic society is characterized not simply by a pluralism of comprehensive religious, philosophical, and moral doctrines but by a pluralism of incompatible yet reasonable comprehensive doctrines."[21] For Rawls, a reasonable comprehensive doctrine is that which "does not reject the essentials of a democratic regime."[22] Thus, the fact of reasonable pluralism requires a political, not metaphysical, foundation for political consensus:

> Once we accept the fact that reasonable pluralism is a permanent condition of public culture under free institutions, the idea of the reasonable is more suitable as part of the basis of public justification for a constitutional regime than the idea of moral truth. Holding a political conception as true, and for that reason alone the one suitable basis of political reason, is exclusive, even sectarian, and so likely to foster political division.[23]

In the context of pluralism, then, political liberalism must work out a political conception of political justice that is acceptable to all. Now, since comprehensive conceptions cannot be held unanimously by citizens who are free to exercise their reason, they cannot be the locus of a common political good. Thus, Rawls proposes that "the political conception must employ, instead of that good, political conceptions such as liberty and equality together with a guarantee of sufficient all-purpose means."[24]

Rawls views modern liberal democratic society as a state in which the citizens hold not just different, but also irreconcilable comprehensive

---

19. Rawls, *PL*, 134.
20. Rawls, *PL*, 15. This notion was introduced in his Rawls, *Theory of Justice*, 387.
21. Rawls, *PL*, xvi.
22. Rawls, *PL*, xvi.
23. Rawls, *PL*, 129.
24. Rawls, *PL*, xli.

doctrines. By a comprehensive doctrine he understands a doctrine which "covers all recognized values and virtues within one rather precisely articulated system.... Many religious and philosophical doctrines aspire to be both general and comprehensive."[25] Thus, when citizens are fundamentally opposed in their understanding of religious, philosophical, and moral matters, the basis for political unity, stability, and justification in such a society could not be a shared understanding in these matters. Nevertheless, Rawls holds that pluralism in itself is "reasonable." Therefore, it is possible to find a fundamental consensus among these differing comprehensive doctrines upon which a political order can be unified, stabilized, and justified, a consensus on shared political, as opposed to comprehensive, values.[26]

In this context of reasonable pluralism, Rawls presents political liberalism as the only workable basis for a just political order in a free society. He affirms:

> The problem of political liberalism is to work out a conception of political justice for a constitutional democratic regime that the plurality of reasonable doctrines—always the feature of the culture of a free democratic regime—might endorse. The intention is not to replace those comprehensive views, nor to give them a true foundation.[27]

According to Rawls's historical analysis, "the exercise of reason under the conditions of freedom" was the cause of reasonable pluralism. Religious division, for Rawls, is in fact a healthy sign of human freedom. For Rawls the fact of reasonable pluralism is not a historical fate we should lament.[28] He offers what he considers a definitive historical explanation of the fact of reasonable pluralism in the form of a narrative account of the progress of man's political history, beginning with the political institutions that developed in the wake of the "wars of religion" following the Protestant reformation. Once human reason was set free to work without threat of coercion, it began to multiply comprehensive doctrines, culminating in the peaceful reasonable pluralism of contemporary liberal democracies.[29] This, according to Rawls, is an unequivocal good, resulting in greater political justice and liberty. He states:

25. Rawls, *PL*, 13.
26. Cf. Rawls, *PL*, 143.
27. Rawls, *PL*, xviii.
28. Cf. Rawls, *JF*, 5.
29. Rawls states: "The historical origin of political liberalism (and of liberalism more generally) is the Reformation and its aftermath . . . ." For a summary of Rawls's account of this historical development, see Rawls, *PL*, xxii–xxv.

> For this reason, political liberalism assumes the fact of reasonable pluralism as a pluralism of comprehensive doctrines, including both religious and nonreligious doctrines. This pluralism is not seen as a disaster but rather as the natural outcome of the activities of human reason under enduring free institutions. To see reasonable pluralism as a disaster is to see the exercise of reason under the conditions of freedom itself as a disaster. Indeed, the success of liberal constitutionalism came as a discovery of a new social possibility: the possibility of a reasonably harmonious and stable pluralist society.[30]

Unity in belief, according to Rawls, is not something to be desired, for it can only be maintained by the oppressive use of state power. He affirms:

> In the society of the Middle Ages, more or less united in affirming the Catholic faith, the Inquisition was not an accident; its suppression of heresy was needed to preserve that shared religious belief. The same holds, I believe, for any reasonable comprehensive philosophical and moral doctrine, whether religious or nonreligious. A society united on a reasonable form of utilitarianism, or on the reasonable liberalisms of Kant or Mill, would likewise require the sanctions of state power to remain so. Call this "the fact of oppression."[31]

According to Rawls's view, for a just society to be even possible, one has to construct principles of justice that are not only theologically, metaphysically, and morally neutral, but also completely detached from these realms altogether, detached, in short, from the politically divisive question of truth. Otherwise, any theory of justice having distinct, even if implicit, metaphysical, moral, or theological presuppositions is bound to be unacceptable to anyone not holding those presuppositions. It is just the concept of the reasonable that suffices for the aims of political constructivism.[32]

Now, the kind of pluralism that Rawls advocates through his "overlapping consensus" is not the result of a moral compromise in order to avoid greater evils. It is not merely tolerable, merely strategically appropriate, or merely politically useful, but is seen as, necessarily, morally good. The justification of the "overlapping consensus," however, must come from citizens themselves. Thus, Rawls invites each citizen to affirm this conception of the good from within his own comprehensive conception of the good. He states:

---

30. Rawls, *PL*, xxiv–xxv.
31. Rawls, *PL*, 37.
32. Cf. Rawls, *PL*, 113.

> An overlapping consensus, therefore, is not merely a consensus on accepting certain authorities, or on complying with certain institutional arrangements founded on a convergence of self or group interests. All those who affirm the political conception start from within their own comprehensive view and draw on the religious, philosophical, and moral grounds it provides.[33]

Since the pluralism present in society would make it impossible, according to Rawls, to reach a consensus based on truth, his idea of an overlapping consensus is in itself "truthless," for it focuses strictly on a political conception of justice. However, Rawls still expects the citizens to accept it for moral reasons:

> Thus, to repeat, the problem of political liberalism is to work out a political conception of political justice for a (liberal) constitutional democratic regime that a plurality of reasonable doctrines, both religious and nonreligious, liberal and nonliberal, may endorse for the right reasons.[34]

This means that Rawls's consensus is in itself freestanding, that is, inherently groundless, for the proper foundation and justification for the political conception of justice is each citizen's particular comprehensive doctrine.[35] How is it possible that such a freestanding, political conception of justice be effected? Rawls states:

> We start then, by looking to the public culture itself as the shared fund of implicitly recognized basic ideas and principles. We hope to formulate these ideas and principles clearly enough to be combined into a political conception of justice congenial to our most firmly held convictions.[36]

By public culture, Rawls means a political culture, where one can find fundamental ideas from which a public justification of justice can be expected. He affirms:

> Since we seek an agreed basis of public justification in matters of justice, and since no political agreement on those disputed questions can reasonably be expected, we turn instead to the fundamental ideas we seem to share through the public political

33. Rawls, *PL*, 147.
34. Rawls, *PL*, xxxix.
35. Rawls states: "A political conception of justice is what I call freestanding when it is not presented as derived from, or as part of, any comprehensive doctrine." Rawls, *PL*, xlii.
36. Rawls, *PL*, 8.

culture. From these ideas we try to work out a political conception of justice congruent with our considered convictions on due reflection. Once this is done, citizens may within their comprehensive doctrines regard the political conception of justice as true, or as reasonable, whatever their view allows.[37]

Thus, these basic ideas and principles will be indisputably appropriate for a political conception of justice, for they will be publicly shared and thus universally accessible. Religion, on the other hand, since it is considered by Rawls to be a comprehensive doctrine, will never work as the unifying element in contemporary liberal democracies. Its only role will be to assist citizens in their affirmation of the political conception, as it may provide a religious, theological, or moral ground.

In the formation of this "overlapping consensus," citizens come together from their own comprehensive views or perspectives, in order to offer public reasons that aim to unify citizens in the ideal of political justice.

John Rawls's Idea of Public Reason

As seen above, the "overlapping consensus" is reached as a result of public discourse. Now, in order to take part in this public discussion, Rawls introduced the idea of "public reason" as a requirement for public discourse. In trying to attain an "overlapping consensus," one may only employ "public reasons," which are the basis of political cooperation and just judgment between competing claims. Rawls developed this idea on Lecture VI of his *Political Liberalism* (1993), and later in his "The Idea of Public Reason Revisited" (1997).

Public reason is, according to Rawls, the ability of a political society to formulate its plans, in an order of priority and of making its decisions accordingly.[38] However, not all reasons are public reasons. He states:

> Not all reasons are public reasons, as there are the nonpublic reasons of churches and universities and of many other associations in civil society. In aristocratic and autocratic regimes, when the good of society is considered, this is done not by the public, if it exists at all, but by the rulers, whoever they may be. Public reason is characteristic of a democratic people: it is the reason of its citizens, of those sharing the status of equal citizenship. The subject of their reason is the good of the public: what the political conception of justice requires of society's

37. Rawls, *PL*, 150–51.
38. Cf. Rawls, *PL*, 212–13.

basic structure of institutions, and of the purposes and ends they are to serve.[39]

Thus, the idea of public reason does not apply to all political discussions of fundamental questions, but only to discussions of those questions in what Rawls refers to as the public political forum. Regarding the public political forum, Rawls states:

> This forum may be divided into three parts: the discourse of judges in their decisions, and especially of the judges of a supreme court; the discourse of government officials, especially chief executives and legislators; and finally, the discourse of candidates for public office and their campaign managers, especially in their public oratory, party platforms, and political statements.[40]

Distinct and separate from this three-part public political forum is what Rawls calls the background culture, which includes the culture of churches and associations of all kinds, and institutions of learning at all levels, especially universities and professional schools, scientific and other societies, as well as voters and activists.[41] As Rawls defines it:

> This is the culture of civil society. In a democracy, this culture is not, of course, guided by any one central idea or principle, whether political or religious. Its many and diverse agencies and associations with their internal life reside within a framework of law that ensures the familiar liberties of thought and speech, and the right of free association. The idea of public reason does not apply to the background culture with its many forms of nonpublic reason nor to media of any kind.[42]

Public reason, then, only belongs to the public political forum. Rawls also states that "in a democratic society public reason is the reason of equal citizens who, as a collective body, exercise final political and coercive power over one another in enacting laws and in amending their

---

39. Rawls, *PL*, 213. He also states: "Among the nonpublic reasons are those of associations of all kinds: churches and universities, scientific societies and professional groups. . . . This way of reasoning is public with respect to the members but nonpublic with respect to political society and to citizens generally" (p. 220).

40. Rawls, IPRR, 767.

41. In *PL*, the public forum was taken to include citizens in their capacities as voters and activists. In *IPRR*, however, Rawls draws a very different line around the public forum. Rawls, then, backs off from his earlier insistence that public reason applies to citizens *qua* citizens.

42. Rawls, IPRR, 767-68.

constitution."[43] According to Rawls, fundamental questions and the questions of basic justice are to be settled only by political values, and therefore public reason imposes limits on the arguments that are to be employed in the public square. He states:

> This means that political values alone are to settle such fundamental questions as: who has the right to vote, or what religions are to be tolerated, or who is to be assured fair equality of opportunity, or to hold property. These and similar questions are the special subject of public reason.[44]

Public reason does not limit one's personal deliberations about political questions, or the reasoning about them by members of associations like churches or universities. However, Rawls states:

> The ideal of public reason does hold for citizens when they engage in political advocacy in the public forum, and thus for members of political parties and for candidates in their campaigns and for other groups who support them. It holds equally for how citizens are to vote in elections when constitutional essentials and matters of basic justice are at stake.[45]

Note how Rawls holds that "public reason" and political discourse should exclude "comprehensive doctrines" such as religious belief systems.[46] Even more, religion is seen as an evil "to be tolerated," and only political values can settle this fundamental question. The reason is that, for Rawls, principles of justice and fundamental issues are sustained within a liberal society by an "overlapping consensus" of political (that is, non-comprehensive) beliefs among people of different comprehensive views.[47] Thus, when considering constitutional essentials and matters of basic justice the citizens

---

43. Rawls, *PL*, 214. He also states: "A citizen engages in public reason, then, when he or she deliberates within a framework of what he or she sincerely regards as the most reasonable political conception of justice, a conception that expresses political values that others, as free and equal citizens might also reasonably be expected reasonably to endorse." Rawls, IPRR, 773.

44. Rawls, *PL*, 214.

45. Rawls, *PL*, 215. For Rawls presentation of the ideal of constitutional essentials, see Rawls, *PL*, 227–30.

46. For Rawls, a view is 'comprehensive' if it comprises an over-arching philosophy of life. Comprehensive doctrines are not necessarily religious, but religious belief is the paradigmatic example.

47. Cf. Rawls, *PL*, 226.

of a constitutional democratic regime should only deploy arguments that all citizens may be reasonably expected to endorse.[48] He also states:

> The point of the ideal of public reason is that citizens are to conduct their fundamental discussions within the framework of what each regards as a political conception of justice based on values that the others can reasonably be expected to endorse and each is, in good faith, prepared to defend that conception so understood. This means that each of us must have, and be ready to explain, a criterion of what principles and guidelines we think other citizens (who are also free and equal) may reasonably be expected to endorse along with us. We must have some test we are ready to state as to when this condition is met.[49]

Rawls also distinguishes "public reason" from "secular reason" and "secular values." These, according to Rawls, are not the same as public reason, for a secular reason is reasoning in terms of comprehensive non-religious doctrines, and therefore it is too broad to serve the purposes of public reason.[50] Instead, "liberal political principles and values, although intrinsically moral values, are specified by liberal political conceptions of justice and fall under the category of the political."[51]

Public reason, according to Rawls, supposedly gives those with mutually opposed worldviews sufficient common ground and reasons for the adoption of public policy or legislation.[52] However, this entails that those who hold non-overlapping reasons must be barred from resort to what are considered "nonpublic" reasons. Rawls considered that no such belief would ever possess the free and willing allegiance of everyone in a democratic society. Therefore, for the sake of peace and justice, the truth claims of comprehensive doctrines must not enter the arena of political contest and debate. Now, this, according to Rawls, should not be seen as a political compromise, for the way to incorporate one's comprehensive doctrines is by affirming the ideas of public reason from within one's own reasonable doctrines. He states: "Citizens affirm the ideal of public reason, not as a result of political compromise, as in a modus vivendi, but from within their own reasonable doctrines."[53]

---

48. Cf. Rawls, *PL*, 224.
49. Rawls, *PL*, 226.
50. Cf. Rawls, IPRR, 780.
51. Rawls, IPRR, 775–76.
52. Cf. Rawls, *PL*, 137.
53. Rawls, *PL*, 218.

The institutional exemplar of public reason is the Supreme Court. In fact, "public reason is the sole reason that the court exercises."[54] Thus, justices have no other reason and no other values that the political.[55] Rawls argues that this limitation should be embraced not only by courts, but also by legislators and proponents of public policy, including citizens. He states:

> In discussing constitutional essentials and matters of basic justice we are not to appeal to comprehensive religious and philosophical doctrines—to what we as individuals or members of associations see as the whole truth. . . . As far as possible, the knowledge and ways of reasoning that ground our affirming the principles of justice . . . are to rest on the plain truths now widely accepted, or available, to citizens generally. Otherwise, the political conception would not provide a public basis of justification.[56]

Nevertheless, Rawls softened his position regarding the place of religious discourse in the public sphere. He conceded in his "The Idea of Public Reason Revisited" (1997) that there is not an absolute bar on all reference to "non-public reasons." After being criticized from many fronts, Rawls modified his position so that religion is not totally excluded.[57] There he introduces the idea of the "proviso." According to Rawls, to engage in public reason is to appeal to one of the political conceptions when debating fundamental political questions. However, this requirement still allows one to introduce into political discussion at any time one's comprehensive doctrine, religious or nonreligious, provided that, in due course, one give properly public reasons to support the principles and policies our comprehensive doctrine is said to support. This requirement is what Rawls refers to as the "*proviso.*"[58] Thus,

---

54. Rawls, *PL*, 235.

55. Regarding the justices' use of reason, Rawls affirms: "The justices cannot, of course, invoke their own personal morality, nor the ideals and virtues of morality generally. Those they must view as irrelevant. Equally, they cannot invoke their or other people's religious or philosophical views. Nor can they cite political values without restriction. Rather, they must appeal to the political values they think belong to the most reasonable understanding of the public conception and its political values of justice and public reason. These are values that they believe in good faith, as the duty of civility requires, that all citizens as reasonable and rational might reasonably be expected to endorse." Rawls, *PL*, 236.

56. Rawls, *PL*, 224–25.

57. He affirms: "It contains a number of new ideas and alters greatly the nature of the role of public reason. In particular, I stress the relation of public reason and political liberalism to the major religions that are based on the authority of the church and the sacred text, and therefore are not themselves liberal." Rawls, *PL*, 438.

58. Cf. Rawls, IPRR, 776.

when a comprehensive view (either religious or nonreligious) is advanced in the public political forum, it must be accompanied by an adequate "secular" or "public" reason for the policy advocated. He states:

> Reasonable comprehensive doctrines, religious or nonreligious, may be introduced in public political discussion at any time, provided that in due course proper political reasons—and not reasons given solely by comprehensive doctrines—are presented that are sufficient to support whatever the comprehensive doctrines introduced are said to support.[59]

> What we cannot do in public reason is to proceed directly from our comprehensive doctrine, or a part thereof, to one or several political principles and values, and the particular institutions they support. Instead, we are required first to work to the basic ideas of a complete political conception and from there to elaborate its principles and ideals, and to use the arguments they provide.[60]

In the end, even if religious arguments are not completely barred, they are not given any importance at all, since they should be backed by "political reasons," which are the only ones that really matter in the public square.

Evaluation of Rawls's Proposal

A valuable contribution that Rawls has made to political theory is the attempt to generate an "overlapping consensus," a consensus which is born out of a vision of the political ordering of society as a cooperative as opposed to a competitive enterprise. Rawls also introduced the notion of "public reason," that is, the discourse by which judges, government officials, and candidates for public office argue in the political forum.

It is also important to note that, in Rawls's later work, his concern is not the exclusion of only religious discourse from public debate, or to replace those comprehensive views, but that no comprehensive doctrine of whatever kind, including religious, can form the basis for political decisions regarding the use of coercive public power.[61] This is what Rawls refers to as "political liberalism," distinct from liberalism or secularism taken as a

---

59. Rawls, IPRR, 783–84.
60. Rawls, IPRR, 777–78.
61. Rawls explicitly distances himself from what he calls anti-Christian "Enlightenment Liberalism" and advocates a political form of toleration and autonomy that is not necessarily committed to a conception of the individual agent as a skeptical self-reflexive subject who removes himself from any particular tradition. Cf. Rawls, *Law of Peoples*, 146, 52, 76.

comprehensive view. This is the reason why, in order to participate in public deliberation about the common good, religiously motivated actors must "translate" their reasons for advocating a particular policy, so that they be accepted by all citizens, because in a pluralistic democracy not all share the same views, even if they are reasonable. Thus, according to a favorable view of Rawls's theory, reasonable citizens may ground their political views in their comprehensive doctrines, and they may even employ religious or otherwise nonpublic reasons in public justification. This is the reason why he introduced the idea of the "proviso," so that religion is not totally excluded. However, in special circumstances, as when citizens are making coercive decisions on constitutional essentials and matters of basic justice, they will be bound by a duty to support only those policies that can in fact be justified by public reason only, and therefore, they will either translate their arguments or restrain their reasoning. Nevertheless, this also means that while religious views may be the basis of individual political convictions, they are excluded from the public political forum on these special cases. Thus, citizens *qua* citizens are free to justify their political views in terms of whatever religious or secular worldviews they choose, except when they come to the public political forum regarding coercive decisions. I will return to this last point at the Conclusion of this book, as it has direct implications on current debates on religious freedom.

Now, the question is whether Rawls's overlapping consensus can fulfill its required task of providing a theoretical basis for a free, just, and stable political order in a milieu of ideological pluralism. This has been contested by many, and various circumstances have been identified by which Rawls's model of overlapping consensus does not work.[62] Here I will mention some of the issues one can identify within Rawls's exposition.

Rawls's intention in introducing his ideas of "overlapping consensus," "reasonableness," and "public reason," aimed at providing a widely consensual and generally accepted statement of the appropriate terms of political order in contemporary constitutional democracies. However, his theory has received much criticism, even from authors writing from within the liberal tradition. Thus, Rawls's theory, rather than functioning as a criterion determining which perspectives constitute the overlapping consensus in support of political liberalism, has instead become the subject of intense criticism and disagreement. At the same time, Rawls's exposition does not account for the existence of an emerging antiliberal consensus.[63] This lack of consen-

---

62. See, for example, Kozinski, *Religious Pluralism*, 25–26; Neal, "Hostile"; Bretherton, *Contemporary Politics*, 50–52.

63. Cf. Finnis, "Telling the Truth," 123.

sus, then, contradicts Rawls's claim that his political liberalism would lead to a just, stable and well-ordered society.

Rawls's idea of "public reason" has also been at the center of an intense and often highly critical reaction, generating a substantial critical literature. It is striking that such criticism comes especially from a wide variety of religious perspectives and worldviews, even though the doctrine of public reason is intended to be easily acceptable by anyone holding a reasonable comprehensive doctrine, including religious ones. Rawls's depiction of a public reason requirement for public discourse has been seen by many as an effort to persuade religious believers to embrace political liberalism, while at the same time marginalizing or privatizing religion.[64] Even some authors representing comprehensive liberalism have rejected Rawls's move to presenting liberalism as merely political, and have instead advocated a more robust reaffirmation of comprehensive liberalism as the appropriate framework for contemporary public life.[65]

As mentioned above, in order to participate in public deliberation about the common good, religiously motivated actors must "translate" their reasons for advocating a particular policy. Although the need to translate a comprehensive doctrine into public reasons, according to Rawls's later position, applies only to decisions that involve the coercive use of force to achieve public ends, it is difficult to see, as Bretherton notes, how this does not affect most areas of public policy, as it ultimately rests on appeal to law and the threat of coercion.[66] At the same time, and in favor of Rawls, it is important to avoid misunderstandings, and note that the demand to translate religious reasons into public reasons does not mean that religion is reduced to the realm of private opinion. Rawls's central concern is to establish how those with differing conceptions of the good life can live together in a polity and provide justifications for the use of coercive political force in terms that are acceptable to one another. The problem, however, is that not all religious institutions and traditions have developed a strong philosophical foundation so as to show the reasonableness of their theological doctrines, as the Catholic tradition has done.[67] Many religious groups, including some Christian denominations, are not equipped to offer secular reasons for their beliefs and opinions regarding public policy.

Rawls's exclusion of religious discourse from political life relates directly to the issue of conflict, for Rawls seeks to avoid particular kinds of

---

64. See Wolfe, *Natural Law Liberalism*, ch. 1.
65. Cf. Neal, "Political Liberalism," 244.
66. Cf. Bretherton, *Contemporary Politics*, 65–66.
67. This is, in fact, what Thomas Aquinas intends to do in many of his works.

conflict in politics, specifically over questions of ultimate meaning. However, trying to avoid conflict is not a realistic stance, as conflict is inevitable, and political decisions are necessarily contested. Any process of deliberation is often conflict-ridden. History has proven that questions of ultimate meaning cannot be forever avoided, and addressing these questions necessarily involves highly contested debates over the vision of the good. At the same time, conflict is not in and of itself bad; as Bretherton notes, it can be creative, and disagreement can clarify what is important and enable better judgments to be made.[68] What seems to be really needed, then, is a politics that can engage in a pluralistic approach over questions of ultimate meaning and can acknowledge the fact that many communities and traditions contribute in their own way to the common good.

Another problem with Rawls's approach is that it excessively narrows the range of what constitutes public deliberation.[69] Iris Marion Young argues that political dialogue requires a plurality of perspectives, speaking styles, and ways of expressing the particularity of social situations as well as the general applicability of principles. She points out that other, more tradition-specific forms of communication, such as greeting, rhetoric, and storytelling can contribute to public deliberation.[70] Besides these, we can also add embodied witness and symbolic action or gesture, such as a hunger strike, a march for a cause, or an act of charity, all of which are often a powerful contribution to public deliberation.

Regarding Rawls's use of past events, he bases his political theory on an eminently debatable interpretation of history and contemporary political reality. Rawls seeks to attain a rationally derived overlapping consensus in response to an imagined threat, that religion is the primary or most dangerous source of chaos and violence in the political sphere.[71] Liberalism is then seen by Rawls as what made peace and civility of the social order possible after the "wars of religion" in the seventeenth century.[72] Therefore, it is thought that in order to maintain the social order, religion cannot be allowed to enter the public domain, lest chaos and violent disorder once again hold sway.

---

68. Cf. Bretherton, *Contemporary Politics*, 50.

69. Cf. Bretherton, *Contemporary Politics*, 52.

70. See her critique of public reason on Young, *Politics of Difference*.

71. The "religious wars" that wracked Europe through the fifteenth and early sixteenth centuries were more political than religious wars, caused by princes and kings exploiting religious differences, and using the multitude of churches created by the Reformation as political tools to advance their own ambitions as builders of nations-states. See Wiker, *Worshipping the State*, 118–20; Cavanaugh, "Wars of Religion"; Cavanaugh, *Myth*, 123–81.

72. See Rawls, *PL*, xxv–xxvi.

This is the reason why Rawls also considers that religion is something to be tolerated.[73] However, arguments based on religious reasoning have not been adequately shown to be so seriously divisive in a liberal democratic order as to justify restrictions.[74] While it is true that there is a diversity of such comprehensive doctrines, mainly religious, it is not even a fact that this diversity is necessarily a cause of conflict, as Rawls argues.[75] Rawls's evident fear of such conflict leads him to construct a liberalism that deals with religious pluralism by demanding that the comprehensive be treated as the private. The consequence is that what he understands by "religion" must be tolerated and privatized in the name of justice.

Rawls claims that the subject matter of political liberalism is the question of "how is a just and free society possible under conditions of deep doctrinal conflict with no prospect of resolution?"[76] The solution offered is that, "to maintain impartiality between comprehensive doctrines, it does not specifically address the moral topics on which those doctrines divide."[77] However, a well-ordered, stable, and morally based democratic government is simply not possible in the midst of this "deep doctrinal conflict." It will be impossible to not address, one way or another, those moral topics that supposedly divide.

Rawls also argues that "holding a political conception as true, and for that reason alone the one suitable basis of public reason, is exclusive, even sectarian, and therefore likely to foster political division;"[78] and insists that, "politics in a democratic society can never be guided by what we see as the whole truth."[79] Neal challenges public reason on the grounds that it seems mistaken to require the citizen to avoid stating claims of truth as truth.[80] Vallier tries to clarify this aspect of Rawls's theory:

> The denial of truth objection typically targets Rawlsian political liberalism, which many believe requires that citizens not appeal to their truth claims in public life. But Rawls permits truth

---

73. Cf. Rawls, *PL*, 214.

74. As Vallier shows, writing from a liberal perspective, these arguments are too inconclusive to justify restricting the freedom and equality of religious citizens. See Vallier, *Liberal Politics*, 72–77.

75. It would be wrong to just center one's attention on the dangers that religion poses to society while ignoring the equal or greater danger posed by secular causes. See Wolterstorff, "Role of Religion," 78, 80.

76. Rawls, *PL*, xxviii.

77. Rawls, *PL*, xxviii.

78. Rawls, *PL*, 129.

79. Rawls, *PL*, 243.

80. Cf. Neal, "Hostile," 156.

> claims so long as *the fact that citizens' claims are true* is not used as a justification for coercion. . . . His point is that citizens' truth claims do not ground political authority over others, even if those claims are correct.[81]

Thus, from Rawls's perspective, it is not truth as such that is at the heart of acceptable lawmaking, governance, and responsible citizenship, but a notion of justification that is at least partially detached from truth. However, one's political judgments, lawmaking, and deliberations about the most important matters should precisely be aimed at, and guided by truth, for the question of truth cannot be avoided, theoretically or practically, in political philosophizing regarding fundamental political issues. For example, in cases where religious accommodations are concerned, it is true claims about the good of certain religious practices, especially those that have an impact in the public square, that justify accommodation regarding a certain coercive law or mandate. In this way, Rawls denies that deep truth claims, such as religious doctrines, have any intrinsic and necessary connection with politics.

Rawls considers that pluralism was caused by the free exercise of reason. He therefore advocates this free exercise of reason not just as our condition, but as something good for society, so that no comprehensive doctrine be imposed on those who do not agree with it. However, Rawls seems to miss the fact that doctrines are indeed taught and imposed when possible by the state for social cohesion, and in order to unite politically, and these doctrines are not necessarily religious, or not religious at all, especially regarding policies from contemporary liberal governments. Rawls also conceives pluralism as a permanent state which should not be overcome, and this is also problematic. He affirms, for example, in *Justice as Fairness: A Restatement* (2001):

> We may also suppose that everyone recognizes what I have called the historical and social conditions of modern democratic societies: (i) the fact of reasonable pluralism and (ii) the fact of its permanence, as well as (iii) the fact that this pluralism can be overcome only by the oppressive use of state power. These conditions are a shared historical situation.[82]

What about the possible disappearance of pluralism in contemporary societies? If this were to happen due to a nationwide unification of society on one comprehensive doctrine, why would it necessarily require the

---

81. Vallier, *Liberal Politics*, 66.
82. Rawls, JF, 197.

oppressive use of state power? For Rawls, "a continuing shared understanding on one comprehensive religious, philosophical, or moral doctrine can be maintained only by the oppressive use of state power."[83] He insists:

> Thus I believe that a democratic society is not and cannot be a community, where by a community I mean a body of persons united in affirming the same comprehensive or partially comprehensive, doctrine. The fact of reasonable pluralism, which characterizes a society with free institutions, makes this impossible.[84]

Rawls is extending his theory to a contingent future, and theorizes based on an imaginary problem, making that which is contingent, religious pluralism, into that which is necessary, and which therefore should not be overcome. Why is it that, according to Rawls, "the question the dominant tradition has tried to answer—that of 'the one reasonable and rational conception of the good' has no answer"? Why is it that "no comprehensive doctrine is appropriate as a political concept for a constitutional regime"?[85] Instead, one should make a distinction. On the one hand, we have the prudential judgment that, in light of the fact of religious and philosophical pluralism characterizing contemporary liberal democracies, it would be unjust at this time to ground the coercive power of government upon the unshared particularities of a group's comprehensive doctrine. On the other hand, it does not follow as a consequence that there is "no answer" to that most fundamental of political questions, the question of the possible existence and intelligible identity of the good. Thus, Rawls's vision of pluralism may become an obstacle for religious freedom, for what he excludes is any religious comprehensive doctrine that does not conform to his understanding of the inferior and thoroughly privatized and de-politicized place of religious belief and obligation in the political order.

Finally, Rawls considers "religion" to be a comprehensive doctrine, the cause of wars and strife, and therefore an evil that may only be tolerated in society, but not given a voice in the public political forum. His seems to be a very deficient view of what "religion" entails, as it leaves aside in its understanding a number of actions that are considered religious. At

---

83. Rawls, PL, 37.

84. Rawls, JF, 3. He also states: "While no one is expected to put his or her religious or nonreligious doctrine in danger, we must each give up forever the hope of changing the constitution so as to establish our religious hegemony, or of qualifying our obligations so as to ensure its influence and success. To retain such hopes and aims would be inconsistent with the idea of equal basic liberties for all free and equal citizens." Rawls, IPRR, 782.

85. Rawls, PL, 135.

the same time, while arguing in favor of pluralism, and the reasons why no coercive decision must be made on any comprehensive doctrine, religious or not, Rawls fails to define what he means by "religion" itself. This is a serious problem, as he is attempting to define the place that should be granted to religion and religious discourse in the public sphere. One cannot argue in favor of a certain position without first establishing the meaning of the notions one employs.

Richard John Neuhaus and the Naked Public Square

As Craig Calhoun affirms, ideas of the secular concern not only the separation of religion from politics, but also the separation, or relation, between religion and other dimensions of culture and ethnicity.[86] According to Richard John Neuhaus, in his *The Naked Public Square* (1984), this very separation has gone too far.[87] Neuhaus published the book in a context when the majority of Americans came to think of America as a secular society (no matter how religious they might have themselves been). For Neuhaus, this is a mistaken assumption, the assumption that because the United States does indeed have a secular government, it therefore is and always has been a secular civil society.

Neuhaus's analysis on his *The Naked Public Square* is important for our topic, since it deals specifically with the relationship between religion and politics. According to him, they have always been constantly getting quite mixed up with one another because both, religion and politics, contend for dominance over the same territory. For Neuhaus, both are political in the sense of being engaged in a struggle for power, and both are religious in the sense of making a total claim upon life. Religion, in fact, is seen by Neuhaus as dealing "with the ultimate meanings and obligations in the whole of life."[88]

This struggle is not new. What is relatively new, however, is the naked public square. Neuhaus states: "The naked public square is the result of political doctrine and practice that would exclude religion and religiously grounded values from the conduct of public business. The doctrine is that America is a secular society. It finds dogmatic expression in the doctrine of

---

86. Cf. Calhoun, "Rethinking Secularism," 45.

87. See Neuhaus, *NPS*. Richard John Neuhaus (1936–2009) was a Canadian born, American by citizenship, author of an extensive list of books and articles on religion and public affairs. He was one of the most influential figures in American public life from the Civil Rights era to the War on Terror.

88. Neuhaus, *NPS*, 131.

secularism."[89] He also thinks that "secular humanism has had a pervasive and debilitating effect upon our public life. Without ever having to put them to a vote, without ever subjecting them to democratic debate, some of the key arguments of what is properly called secularism have prevailed."[90]

On this section on Neuhaus's views on politics and religion, I will present especially his notion of the public square, the notion of public reason, the question of why it is dangerous to leave religion aside from public debates, and the solution he offers to the problem of secularization. I will conclude with some comments on his views.

The Public Square

The "public square," or "public space," expressions which Neuhaus uses interchangeably, have to do, for Neuhaus, with "public reason" and "public business." The public square, for Neuhaus, comprises not only the public political forum or political arena, but also other aspects of culture, such as institutions of learning, and the "mediating structures" of our personal and communal existence (such as the family, one's neighborhood, churches, and voluntary associations).[91] Neuhaus also talks about the elementary and secondary school system as being the most important public square for most of a country's children,[92] and refers to other mediating structures as being public as well: "There is a great deal that is public but not in the ordinary sense of the term political. Family life, work, learning, and entertainment all have public dimensions of interaction, not only interaction with other individuals but also with other communities."[93]

Public Reason and Religion

Neuhaus argues that Christian truth, if it is true, is public truth, for "it is accessible to public reason. It impinges upon public space. At some critical

---

89. Neuhaus, *NPS*, vii. In his book, Neuhaus argues that this political doctrine is demonstrably false and the dogma of secularism exceedingly dangerous.

90. Neuhaus, *NPS*, 25.

91. He states, for example: "These structures—family, neighborhood, church, voluntary association—are the people-sized, face-to-face institutions where we work day by day at our felicities and our fears." Neuhaus, *NPS*, 28. And that "the phrase 'public square' evokes images of the political arena with its partisan games and intense debates over public policy." Neuhaus, "Lewis in the Public Square," 30.

92. Cf. Neuhaus, *NPS*, 137.

93. Neuhaus, *NPS*, 28.

points of morality and ethics it speaks to public policy."[94] Thus, Neuhaus is very critical of the idea that religion is something between an individual and his God, and that because each person is free to worship the God of his choice, religion is the business of church and home and has no place in public space. Yet, he notes that this conception is legally and politically supported by a notion of the "separation of church and state" that is understood to mean the separation of religion and religiously based morality from the public realm.[95] Religion, in the supreme court's meaning, has become radically individualized and privatized, just a synonym for conscience. Neuhaus affirms: "Thus religion is no longer a matter of content but of sincerity. It is no longer a matter of communal values but of individual conviction. In short, it is no longer a public reality and therefore cannot interfere with public business."[96] By "interfering with public business," a wording that may sound problematic, Neuhaus means that the role of religion is to help give moral definition and direction to public life and policy.[97]

The major problem that follows if religion is left aside, according to Neuhaus, is that a public ethic cannot be established unless it is informed by religiously grounded values. An establishment of a public ethic would not be democratically legitimate without such an engagement of religion. He states: "The reason for this is that, in sociological fact, the values of the American people are deeply rooted in religion."[98] Neuhaus, in fact, gives great importance to the value of tradition. He affirms that "the understanding that public discourse, especially public moral discourse, must be shaped by and rooted in tradition is neither liberal nor conservative."[99] Then he adds: "The American experiment is severely and unnaturally crippled if the religiously grounded values of the American people are ruled out of order in public discourse."[100] Thus, politics, culture, tradition,

---

94. Neuhaus, *NPS*, 17.

95. Cf. Neuhaus, *NPS*, 20. See also: "In recent decades, separationism has provided the legal rationale for the sanitizing of the public square. As we have seen, this sanitizing of public space, while programmatic in nature, has not been subjected to democratic debate or vote" (p. 26).

96. Neuhaus, *NPS*, 80.

97. Cf. Neuhaus, *NPS*, 59.

98. Neuhaus, *NPS*, 21. Neuhaus's argument is centered on the pervasive religious understanding of the Founders as the ground for the laws they instituted. Thus, political laws depend on the moral law, which pointed to the Author of the moral law. This understanding was developed with arguments of reason that are accessible to all people, they belong to "public reason," and have had an inescapable public significance in the life of the United States.

99. Neuhaus, *NPS*, 47.

100. Neuhaus, *NPS*, 51.

and religion are all interconnected. Neuhaus has repeated tirelessly that politics, in fact, is in large part a function of culture, and at the heart of culture is religion. Neuhaus affirms:

> In this connection "religion" is meant comprehensively. It includes not just those ideas and activities and attitudes that we ordinarily call religious, but all the ways we think and act and interact with respect to what we believe is ultimately true and important. There is nothing frightfully original in this way of connecting politics, culture, and religion.[101]

Thus, in *The Naked Public Square*, Neuhaus charges that the United States, while calling itself a democratic society, is systematically excluding the values of the majority of its citizens from policy decisions. To rule religiously grounded moral viewpoints out of bounds in public life not only does injustice to America's "incorrigibly religious" citizenry, but also saps the very foundations of the American democratic experiment. From Neuhaus perspective, then, the problems stem in large part from the philosophical and legal effort to isolate and exclude the religious dimension of culture. Thus, the result is that only the state can lay claim to compulsive authority over all institutions in societies; yet, only religion can invoke against the state a transcendent authority and have its invocation seconded by "the people" to whom a democratic state is presumably accountable. Thus, for the state to be secured from such challenge, religion must be redefined as a private, not public, phenomenon. In addition, because truly value-less existence is impossible for persons or societies, the state must displace religion as the generator and bearer of values. And this is the reason why Neuhaus denounces that the separation of religion from all dimensions of culture has gone too far.

Vulnerability of the Naked Public Square

According to Neuhaus, the religious evacuation of the public square cannot be sustained, either in concept or in practice. He states:

> When religion in any traditional or recognizable form is excluded from the public square, it does not mean that the public square is in fact naked. This is the other side of the "naked public square" metaphor. When recognizable religion is excluded, the

---

101. Neuhaus, *NPS*, 27.

vacuum will be filled by ersatz religion, by religion bootlegged into public space under other names.[102]

Thus, Neuhaus claims that the public square will not and cannot remain naked. If it is not clothed "with the 'meanings' borne by religion, new 'meanings' will be imposed by virtue of the ambitions of the modern state."[103] That is, religion will be replaced by dogmatic secularism, for a public square from which religion is banished will not long remain naked. He states:

> The truly naked public square is at best a transitional phenomenon. It is a vacuum begging to be filled. When the democratically affirmed institutions that generate and transmit values are excluded, the vacuum will be filled by the agent left in control of the public square, the state. In this manner, a perverse notion of the disestablishment of religion leads to the establishment of the state as church.[104]

> Whatever the rationale or intention, however, the presupposition is the naked public square, the exclusion of particularist religious and moral belief from public discourse. And whatever the intention, because the naked square cannot remain naked, the direction is toward the state—as—church, toward totalitarianism.[105]

According to Neuhaus, the reason why the naked public square cannot, in fact, remain naked is in the very nature of law and laws. He states:

> If law and laws are not seen to be coherently related to basic presuppositions about right and wrong, good and evil, they will be condemned as illegitimate. After having excluded traditional religion, then, the legal and political trick is to address questions of right and wrong in a way that is not "contaminated" by the label "religious." This relatively new sleight-of-hand results in what many have called "civil religion." It places a burden upon the law to act religiously without being suspected of committing

---

102. Neuhaus, *NPS*, 80.

103. Neuhaus, *NPS*, vii. The modern state, however, is probably not the only danger to the public square. We can mention the ambition of capitalist groups, agencies, sects, and radical movements, or the materialistic values of the marketplace. We are also witnessing a partial taking over by the media industry, such as the culture being imposed by Hollywood, the music industry, etc.

104. Neuhaus, *NPS*, 86. Neuhaus also affirms: "This 'vacuum' with respect to political and spiritual truth is the naked public square. If we are 'overthrown,' the root cause of the defeat would lie in the "impossible" effort to sustain that vacuum" (p. 85).

105. Neuhaus, *NPS*, 89.

religion. While theorists might talk about "civil religion," the courts dare not do so, for that too would be an unconstitutional "establishment" of religion.[106]

This is a problem inherent in the notion of a secular society. As Neuhaus affirms, without a transcendent or religious point of reference, conflicts of values cannot be resolved; there can only be procedures for their temporary accommodation, for conflicts over values are viewed not as conflicts between contending truths but as conflicts between contending interests.[107] Therefore, the naked public square is an impossible project, and even if it were possible, he argues that the naked public square is not desirable. He states the reasons:

> It is not desirable in the view of believers because they are inescapably entangled in the belief that the moral truths of religion have a universal and public validity. . . . Even if one is not a believer, the divorce of public business from the moral vitalities of the society is not desirable if one is committed to the democratic idea. In addition to not being desirable, however, we have argued that the naked public square is not possible. It is an illusion, for the public square cannot and does not remain naked. When particularist religious values and the institutions that bear them are excluded, the inescapable need to make public moral judgments will result in an elite construction of a normative morality from sources and principles not democratically recognized by the society.[108]

Thus, the notion of a secular society compels political actors to pretend to be more morally handicapped than they are. It is argued that this is the price to be paid for a pluralistic society. For Neuhaus, the price is too high. At the same time, he states:

> What is meant by "pluralism" in such arguments is frequently indifference to normative truth, an agreement to count all opinions about morality as equal (equal "interests" to be accommodated) because we are agreed there is no truth by which judgment can be rendered. The result is the debasement of public life by the exclusion of the idea—and consequently of the practice—of virtue.[109]

---

106. Neuhaus, *NPS*, 80-81.
107. Cf. Neuhaus, *NPS*, 110.
108. Neuhaus, *NPS*, 86.
109. Neuhaus, *NPS*, 111-12.

This kind of dogmatic pluralism has to be rejected, for "when pluralism is established as dogma, there is no room for other dogmas. The assertion of other points of reference in moral discourse becomes, by definition, a violation of pluralism. Pluralism, relativity, secularization—all come to be much of a piece."[110]

Issues arising in the field of education vividly illustrate Neuhaus's point that a public square from which religion is banished will not remain naked for too long. According to him, the most important public square for most of a country's children is the elementary and secondary school system. Neuhaus believes that it is hard to think of any public settings from which religion has been more rigorously excluded, or where secularism is more dogmatically promulgated. He states: "I am far from convinced of the spiritual imperative of classroom prayer in public schools, but there is no disputing the fact that its elimination was a further step in the 'secularizing' of public institutions."[111]

The consequences of militant secularism are not to be taken lightly, Neuhaus affirms. In fact, he argues that the great social and political devastations of the twentieth century have been perpetrated by regimes of militant secularism, notably those of Hitler, Stalin, and Mao. This, according to him, suggests that the naked public square is a dangerous place: "When religious transcendence is excluded, when the religious square has been swept clean of divisive sectarianisms, the space is opened to seven demons aspiring to transcendent authority."[112] Thus, he states:

> The notion of the secular state can become the prelude to totalitarianism. That is, once religion is reduced to nothing more than privatized conscience, the public square has only two actors in it— the state and the individual. Religion as a mediating structure—a community that generates and transmits moral values—is no longer available as a countervailing force to the ambitions of the state.[113]

That is the reason why, according to Neuhaus, secularism not only attacks individual religious belief, but especially and above all it attacks religious institutions. He affirms:

> Individual religious belief can be dismissed scornfully as superstition, for it finally poses little threat to the state. No, the

---

110. Neuhaus, *NPS*, 148.
111. Cf. Neuhaus, *NPS*, 137.
112. Neuhaus, *NPS*, 8.
113. Neuhaus, *NPS*, 82.

chief attack is upon the *institutions* that bear and promulgate belief in a transcendent reality by which the state can be called to judgment. Such institutions threaten the totalitarian proposition that everything is to be within the state, nothing is to be outside the state.[114]

The Future of the Public Square

Neuhaus offers some guidance on how to fix the problem of the naked public square, as it is not the right solution to the debate on the place of religion in public life. He argues that one has to enter the public square not as an anonymous citizen but as a "moral actor,"[115] "as a person shaped by 'other sources' that are neither defined by nor subservient to the public square."[116] This, he argues, is something that must be insisted upon against those who view compromise as the antithesis of moral behavior, and against those who claim that moral judgment must be set aside before entering the public square.[117] The reason, he states, is that:

> The public square is not a secular and morally sterilized space but a space for conversation, contention, and compromise among moral actors . . . compromise is an exercise of moral responsibility by persons who accept responsibility for sustaining the exercise that is called democracy.[118]

For that reason, moral claims are not an intrusion, an imposition upon a presumably value-free process. We should not accept the view that states that here we have an instance of moral judgment versus value-free secular reason. On the contrary, Neuhaus affirms, "we have rather an instance of moralities in conflict." And he continues:

> The notion of moralities in conflict is utterly essential to remedying the problems posed by the naked public square. Those who want to bring religiously based value to bear in public discourse have an obligation to "translate" those values into terms that are as accessible as possible to those who do not share the

---

114. Neuhaus, *NPS*, 82.
115. Neuhaus, *NPS*, 125.
116. Neuhaus, *NPS*, 128.
117. Cf. Neuhaus, *NPS*, 125.
118. Neuhaus, *NPS*, 128.

same religious grounding. They also have the obligation, however, to expose the myth of value-neutrality.[119]

It is important to note, then, that even Neuhaus insists that there is no such a thing as a value-neutral public square, those offering religiously based values should "translate" their religious arguments in order that they be accepted by all others, an approach similar to Rawls's "proviso."[120] Neuhaus also argues that even if there were a resurgence of a publicly potent religion, we need to look for quite unprecedented ways of relating politics and religion. He states: "The question is whether we can devise forms for that interaction which can revive rather than destroy the liberal democracy that is required by a society that would be pluralistic and free."[121] Thus, he argues in favor of a polity in which no one will be excluded, even those that do not share a particular religious covenant.[122]

Some Comments Regarding Neuhaus's View

The Naked Public Square (1984) appeared at a time marked by the conflicts that erupted over specific issues such as abortion and school prayer, and over the larger question of the role of religion in American public life. Neuhaus was certainly convinced that the moment had come for men and women of faith to make themselves heard in deliberating and setting the conditions under which they order their common lives together.[123] Neuhaus argued that this is what democratic politics really meant. In the American constitutional order people do that through debate, elections, and representative political institutions. The problem, as he saw it, was that in fact it is only the judiciary that deliberates and answers the really important questions.

Even though the question of religion in the public square has not been settled, Neuhaus's book offered a useful introduction to the extraordinary complexities and ambiguities that surround the issue of religion in public life, and in a way established a subtle and nuanced base for further debate. Here I offer a few comments regarding Neuhaus's exposition.

Even though Neuhaus argues in favor of a place for religion in the public square, he is not precise when it comes to defining the meaning of the "public square," or "public space," expressions which he uses interchangeably.

---

119. Neuhaus, *NPS*, 125.
120. See Rawls, IPRR.
121. Neuhaus, *NPS*, 9.
122. Cf. Neuhaus, *NPS*, 52.
123. Cf. Glendon, "Naked Public Square," 34.

In spite of that, we can gather from the examples that he offers that the public square, for Neuhaus, comprises not just the public political forum, but also the "mediating structures" of our personal and communal existence: family, neighborhood, churches, voluntary associations, educational institutions, and places of work, all of which have public dimensions of interaction with other individuals and with other communities. Thus, for Neuhaus, the public square is more than just the political arena. For that reason, Neuhaus is critical of a shriveled definition of "public" that equates "public" with the "political," and further equates the political with the governmental.[124] At the same time, public reason, for Neuhaus, is related to truth, and in that sense Christian truth is public truth, he argues, for it is accessible to public reason, and in its moral and ethical aspects, it speaks to public policy.[125]

Neuhaus also relates politics to religion in the sense that, according to Neuhaus, politics is largely a function of culture, and religion is at the heart of culture. Neuhaus holds a comprehensive notion of religion, for, according to him, religion encompasses all of the aspects of one's own life, including politics. As a consequence, religion cannot be restricted to purely personal concerns; it has public—and therefore political—implications. This is the reason why Neuhaus argues that it is neither reasonable nor legitimate for Americans to be told they can only enter the public arena if they agree to check their deepest beliefs at the door of public spaces. However, he also affirms that religious reasons and values should be included in public debates only as long as they could be "translated" into secular terms. Thus, Neuhaus attaches to religion a cultural function, so that religion be present or should be present in the public square in the sense that it informs values to the formation of a public ethics through laws and public policy. Yet, Neuhaus definition of religion is too vague to justify its use as a category: "Religion" is meant comprehensively. For Neuhaus, "it includes not just those ideas and activities and attitudes that we ordinarily call religious, but all the ways we think and act and interact with respect to what we believe is ultimately true and important."[126] Religion, in Neuhaus's own definition, includes so many things that it may end up meaning just anything one believes is "ultimately true and important," regardless of its morality. Thus, anything might fall under the category of religion, since Neuhaus is not clear on what counts as "religion" and what does not. This

---

124. Cf. Neuhaus, "Lewis in the Public Square," 30.

125. Cf. Neuhaus, *NPS*, 17.

126. Neuhaus, *NPS*, 27. Benjamin Berger argues, for example, that "law shapes religion in its own ideological image and likeness, while notionally confining it to discrete dimensions of human life." See Berger, "Law's Religion," 284.

is not helpful at all when trying to establish the meaning of religious freedom, or the proper place of religion in the public square.

Nevertheless, Neuhaus has made a valuable contribution with the notion of the naked public square and the idea that it cannot remain empty. It, according to Neuhaus, may become the prelude to totalitarianism, for the state will be the agent left in control of the public square. Yet, even though his interpretation of the danger of the "naked" public square is possible, there is more than just the possibility of the state taking a totalitarian control of our institutions. There are also the interests of corporations (such as banks and multinational businesses), the power of the media and the manipulation of information, the film and music industry, etc., that can and do play a role in contemporary society. Yet, Neuhaus's warning still holds that if religion is reduced no nothing more than privatized conscience, the disestablishment of religion will lead to the establishment of the state as church. Maybe one of the reasons why Neuhaus is so insistent on the dangers of the state becoming totalitarian is because: "The public square is not limited to Government Square. At the same time—and for reasons that may be nearly unavoidable—government impinges upon all public squares,"[127] he states.

One of the solutions that Neuhaus proposes in order to fix the problem of the naked public square, is that one has to enter the public square not as an anonymous citizen but as a "moral actor." However, while it is true that person should be "shaped by 'other sources' that are neither defined by nor subservient to the public square,"[128] the political actor is not reducible to a moral agent.

While Neuhaus believed that it is wrong to ban religious discourse from the public square just because it is religious, he also thought that religious discourse should not be privileged in the public forum. At the same time, religious discourse should be made available to those who do not share the same religious background. Thus, while denying a neutrality of values in the public square, Neuhaus comes up with the concept of "translation": Religiously based values, in order to bear in public discourse, have to be "translated" into terms that are as accessible as possible to those who do not share the same religious grounding.[129] Neuhaus also insists that expressions of religious conviction in the public arena must be accessible to nonreligious perspectives and accountable to public reason. He suggests that it is not legitimate for those who are religious to expect to have their views accepted in the public sphere on the ground of special revelation or

---

127. Neuhaus, *NPS*, 28.
128. Neuhaus, *NPS*, 128.
129. Cf. Neuhaus, *NPS*, 125.

private understanding. Religious certainties must be translatable into public arguments. Neuhaus, in fact, appealed to non-theological language in order to demonstrate that religious concerns could be brought to bear on public matters. This idea of "translation" will resonate and find a place in the exposition of John Rawls, Charles Taylor, and Jürgen Habermas.

It is also interesting to note that Neuhaus was an early rejecter of what he calls "the dogma of the secular Enlightenment that, as people become more enlightened (educated), religion will wither away; or, if it does not wither away, it can be safely sealed off from public consideration, reduced to a private eccentricity."[130] It was Habermas who, like Neuhaus, many years later challenged the widely called "secularization hypothesis,"[131] that as nations become more modern, they also become less religious.

Neuhaus was a staunch defender of religious freedom, and, according to him, this is what will prevent the public square from falling pray into totalitarian control. Thus, he accorded great importance to religious institutions, for, according to him, "the secular wisdom can put up with religion that is private, individualistic, subjective," but not with religion that claims a public character.[132] The reason is that, as he states:

> The historic enemies of democratic disorderliness, such as Hitler and Stalin, make their most determined assaults not against religious belief as such but against the institutions of religion. It is the institutions that must be constrained or destroyed in order to make thoroughly secular sense of the social order.[133]

Finally, according to Neuhaus, the separation of church and state cannot require the segregation of religion from public life. This would be a serious mistake. At the same time, its working-out in public policy is bound to be complicated too, by reason of the secular character of the liberal state, as well as by the plurality of religious groups that claim certain public influence. For that reason, Neuhaus states that in a pluralist society like ours, people of minority religious groups—or no religion at all—need to have ironclad assurances that their views and values will be respected by the religious majority.[134]

A lot has happened both in the world and in scholarship since the publication of Neuhaus's *The Naked Public Square* (1984). For that reason,

---

130. Neuhaus, *NPS*, 86.
131. Cf. Habermas, RPS.
132. Neuhaus, *NPS*, 190.
133. Neuhaus, *NPS*, 190.
134. Neuhaus has expressed particular concern for Jewish sensitivities on this point.

it is important to see in the following sections of this chapter what other subsequent authors have had to say when dealing with the place of religion in a secular context, taking also into account that Neuhaus's opposition to secularism is directed to ideological secularism, rather than to political secularism.[135]

The "Secularization Thesis" and "Postsecularism"

As mentioned in the previous section, Neuhaus was critical of the idea that "as people become more enlightened, religion will wither away."[136] He was not alone in noting that the secularization thesis was not viable any more from a sociological and philosophical perspective.

Thus, in response to the criticism, one term increasingly used to name the contemporary conditions and possibilities of the relationship between religion and politics is that of the "postsecular." This term was born as a revision of the "secularization thesis." The classic secularization thesis identifies modernization with secularization and sees secularization as an inevitable outcome of processes of modernization.[137] Bryan Wilson describes the secularization thesis as the process whereby "religious institutions, actions and consciousness, lose their social significance."[138] Thus, the secularization thesis posited a fundamental incompatibility between modernity and religious adherence. The empirical basis of the thesis, however, has increasingly come into question. As Casanova affirms: "It is the postulated intrinsic correlation between modernization and secularization that is highly problematic."[139] Peter Berger, a former leading advocate of the secularization thesis, writes: "The world today, with some exceptions . . . is as furiously religious as it ever was, and in some places more so than ever. This means that a whole body of literature by historians and social scientists loosely labelled 'secularization theory' is essential mistaken."[140]

The view that secularization follows upon modernization, has been challenged by Neuhaus, Charles Taylor, Jürgen Habermas, Herman Lübbe,

135. Cf. Reno, "Neuhaus," 7. Especially note: "He was convinced that an ideological secularism (as opposed to a political secularism) undermines liberalism and over the long haul cannot sustain a free society."

136. Neuhaus, *NPS*, 86.

137. Examples of these processes of modernization are industrialization, urbanization, specialization, and bureaucratization. See Bretherton, *Contemporary Politics*, 10–11.

138. Wilson, *Religion in Sociological Perspective*, 49.

139. Casanova, "Rethinking Secularization," 13.

140. See Berger, *Desecularization*, 2.

and others. Lübbe even speaks of a modernity that resists secularization; he states:

> The expectation that modernisation marginalises religion is falsified by the fact of actually existing societies which combine both—in other words, which are, according to all criteria relevant in the study of cultural evolution, both ultramodern and permeated, even in its public and political life, by a living religious culture. The most conspicuous and politically significant example of such a society is the United States.[141]

Political philosophers came to acknowledge that, against the assumptions of the secularization thesis, religion has always played a prominent role in public and political life, even in contemporary Europe. With the exception of France and the USA, churches have been in fact incorporated into the state through a variety of forms of establishment. Churches have also been involved in the delivery of welfare services, and the formation of the different welfare systems and policies regarding poverty has been directly shaped by differences in belief and practice between different religious traditions. Even within supposedly secular institutions such as prisons, the military, and hospitals, chaplains have continued to have an established and often prominent role.

At the same time, however, even if religion never really went away, we are currently going through a period of deconstruction and reconstruction in which perennial questions about the relationship between religious and political authority are being asked again and previous settlements renegotiated, as Bretherton notes.[142]

In the following sections, then, we will see how Jose Casanovas, Jürgen Habermas, and Charles Taylor view secularism, how they have challenged the "secularization thesis," how they explain "religion" and what place they grant it within the public sphere.

José Casanovas's Definition of Secularism and Secularization

José Casanova (b. 1951) is one of the world's top scholars in the sociology of religion.[143] His work is of great value for our topic, as we are trying to find

---

141. Lübbe, "Religion and Politics," 60.
142. Cf. Bretherton, *Contemporary Politics*, 14.
143. Casanova is a professor in the Departments of Sociology and Theology at Georgetown University and senior fellow at the Berkley Center, where his work focuses on globalization, religions, and secularization.

the appropriate meaning of "religious freedom" within the context of liberal and secular societies. In this section, I will present a very helpful analytical distinction offered by Casanova on the notion of "secularism," which allows one to also have a better understanding of what is meant by "secularization" and "postsecularism," and the place of religion within these settings.

Secularism, Secularization, and Postsecularism

According to Casanova, there are three connotations in which the terms secularism, secularization, and postsecularism are being employed. This classification will be helpful when presenting Habermas's and Taylor's views on these notions.

In his "Exploring the Postsecular: Three Meanings of "the Secular" and their Possible Transcendence,"[144] Casanova offers a synoptic and incisive discussion of the multiple and contested meanings of secularity and secularization, constructing a typology of the different ways in which they have been and can be understood, to which he correlates a range of senses in which, in turn, the postsecular may be thought of.

The first meaning of the "secular" is that of "mere secularity," that is, living in a secular age where being religious is a normal viable option. This is the broadest possible sense of the term "secular," which is derived from the medieval Christian theological transformation of the Latin term "saeculum." Thus, the Augustinian use of "secular" is very similar to the modern meaning of a secular political sphere, that of the constitutional democratic state and of a democratic public sphere, which is neutral with respect to all worldviews, religious as well as non-religious, according to Casanova. The secular is a neutral space that can be shared by all who live in a society that is not religiously homogeneous or multicultural. These societies usually have different and sometimes even competing conceptions of what is "sacred" and what is "profane," and this in fact the situation in late antiquity.[145] Regarding "secularization," the medieval Christian theological meaning of the term means to "make worldly," to convert religious persons or things into secular ones. According to Casanova, it is from this new theological perspective of medieval Christendom that the modern meaning of "secularization" emerges.[146]

---

144. Cf. Casanova, "Exploring the Postsecular."

145. Cf. Casanova, "Exploring the Postsecular," 28.

146. Cf. Casanova, "Exploring the Postsecular," 29. The process of secularization, however, follows two different dynamics, according to Casanova. He states: "One is the dynamic of internal Christian secularization which aims to spiritualize the temporal

It is in this broad sense of the term "secular" that all modern societies are secular and are likely to remain so for the foreseeable future, Casanova states.[147] In this context, if secularism were to be transcended, the "postsecular" could only mean a re-sacralization of modern societies within a sacred immanent frame, something that must be viewed not only as empirically unlikely but as practically impossible.[148]

The second meaning of the "secular," is what Casanovas calls "self-contained secularity," "when people are simply 'irreligious,' that is, devoid of religion and closed to any form of transcendence beyond the purely secular immanent frame."[149] In this case, the experience of living without religion is seen as a normal condition. Thus, in contemporary western societies, religion has become but one among many possible and permissible moral and cognitive orientations within the "immanent frame" of modern society and subjectivity. The social and moral orders are understood as purely immanent secular orders, devoid of transcendence, and thus functioning "as if God would not exist."[150] Since secularity is without religion, it tends to become increasingly the default option, even naively experienced as natural, and no longer in need of justification. Corresponding to this version of secularity, if it were to be transcended, one can think of a concept of "postsecularism" that would suggest something like "secularization in reverse," that is, individuals and society moving away from irreligiosity towards religion; as Casanovas puts it: "individuals as well as societies becoming religious again, undergoing processes of religious revival, which would reverse previous secular trends."[151]

Finally, the third meaning of the "secular" is a "secularist secularity," or secularism as stadial consciousness of secularity by a philosophy of history

---

and to bring the religious life of perfection out of the monasteries into the secular world.... The other different, indeed almost opposite, dynamic of secularization takes the form of laicization. It aims to emancipate all secular spheres from clerical-ecclesiastical control and in this respect it is marked by a laic-clerical antagonism. Unlike in the Protestant path, however, here the boundaries between the religious and the secular are rigidly maintained, but those boundaries are pushed into the margins, aiming to contain, privatize, and marginalize everything religious, while excluding it from any visible presence in the secular public sphere, now defined as the realm of *laïcité*, freed from religion." See also Casanova, "Secular, Secularizations, Secularisms," 56.

147. Cf. Casanova, "Exploring the Postsecular," 30.

148. Cf. Casanova, "Exploring the Postsecular," 30. According to Casanova, this is not the intended meaning of "postsecular" in Habermas.

149. Casanova, "Exploring the Postsecular," 30.

150. This is probably best exemplified by Taylor, *SA*.

151. Casanova, "Exploring the Postsecular," 31. He notes once again that Habermas does not appear to use "postsecular" in this second meaning of the term.

that hypostatizes secularization as a universal process of human development, the teleological movement which culminates in the abandonment of childish belief and the ascension to mature unbelief. This notion of the secular is the one identified with the "secularization thesis" mentioned above, and which has been challenged by many contemporary philosophers and sociologists. In this case, to be secular means to have been liberated from "religion" as a condition for human flourishing and as a result of modernization. Thus, to be secular is to be modern, and by implication, to be religious means that one is not yet fully modern. Present modern secularism is then seen as superior over other supposedly earlier and therefore more primitive religious forms of understanding and of interactions.[152] Casanovas sees that Europeans, for example, usually experience their own secularization as a natural consequence of their modernization, that is, as a natural outcome of becoming modern. Yet, Casanovas challenges this notion of secularization, in that it does not happen automatically as a result of processes of modernization, but rather needs to be mediated by some other particular historical facts, as for example when the absence of religion is seen as the meaningful result of a quasi-natural process of development and emancipation.

As a consequence, and taking into account the secularization thesis, "postsecular" would imply abandoning or at least questioning the modern secularist stadial consciousness which relegates "religion" to a more primitive, more traditional, now surpassed stage of human and societal development. It is this sense of the "postsecular" that was born as a revision of the "secularization thesis." This is, as it will be seen below, what Habermas means by postsecular, that is, as opposes to the secularization thesis.[153]

It is important to note, then, that all these three senses of the terms secularism, secularization, and postsecularization are taken by reference to the religious life of citizens, or the lack thereof.

Secularization

Within the process of "secularization," Casanova also notes that one needs to distinguish between three different connotations of the term in order to speak meaningfully about it.[154] Thus, he distinguishes between secular differentiation, religious decline, and religious privatization.

152. Cf. Casanova, "Exploring the Postsecular," 32.

153. Habermas opposes his concept of the postsecular to this understanding of secularity, inasmuch as secularist secularity is an ideology that relegates "religion" to a primitive stage of human development. Cf. Calhoun et al., *Habermas and Religion*, 10.

154. Cf. Casanova, "Exploring the Postsecular," 34–35; Casanova, "Rethinking Secularization," 7–8.

The first connotation of secularization, that is, as secular differentiation, makes reference to the differentiation of the secular spheres (state, economy, science) from religion. It is usually seen as an emancipation or liberation of the secular from ecclesiastical institutions and religious norms. In this respect, Casanova affirms, both the religious and the secular are reciprocally and mutually constituted structures which first emerge with modernity.[155] It is important to keep this point in mind, as it will be seen later in chapter 3 that the notions of "religion" and the "secular" are both "twin" notions born out of modernity as being opposed to each other.

A second connotation of the term "secularization" refers to the decline of religious beliefs and practices in modern societies. This is often postulated as a human universal developmental process. Casanova notes that this is now the most widespread usage of the term in contemporary academic debates on secularization.[156] Yet, as mentioned above, the "secularization thesis" is being strongly challenged, and its proponents will probably decline as time goes on, since, while societies are becoming more modern, religiosity is not disappearing.

Finally, the third connotation of "secularization" has to do with the privatization of religion, usually understood both as a general modern historical trend and as a precondition for modern liberal democratic politics.[157] Religion is allowed as long as it remains in the private sphere, which results in a purely secular square, as Neuhaus strongly denounced.

This analytical distinction, Casanova argues, allows one to have a better view of what secularization means, in order to account for different patterns of secularization, in all three meanings of the term, across societies and civilizations.[158] This distinction is also useful when talking about the place granted to religion in the public political forum, for both notions of religion and the secular, as will be seen later, were inventions of modernity employed to indicate a total separation: where there is one, there is no room for the other.

Taking these distinctions and meanings into account, Casanova asks whether we are still secular, or we are witnessing the emergence of a postsecular world society, where religiosity will make its presence felt once again. He argues that the European secular development is not a universal norm for the rest of the world. As the rest of the world modernizes, people

---

155. Cf. Casanova, "Exploring the Postsecular," 34.

156. Cf. Casanova, "Exploring the Postsecular," 34.

157. Casanova put into question the empirical as well as the normative validity of the privatization thesis in his Casanova, *Public Religions in the Modern World*.

158. Cf. Casanova, "Exploring the Postsecular," 35.

are not becoming more secular like the European model; instead, people are becoming more religious. Even more, they are becoming simultaneously both more secular and more religious, which then puts into serious question the secular/religion dichotomy. What is important here, then, is that Casanova shows that the simultaneous secularization and lack of religiosity in Europe is rather exceptional, and therefore not the norm to analyze the problem on the place of religion in the public sphere. As he states, "the old theory that explained Europe's secularity in terms of its modernity is no longer plausible."[159]

Yet, even though the theory is no longer plausible, one could challenge the examples and division Casanova proposes between the European model and the rest of the world, as they do not seem to be completely satisfactory. Even though secularism is more accentuated in Europe, it does not mean that only in Europe people are becoming more secular. In the United States and Canada, one also hears of complaints regarding "the empty church."[160] In Latin America, even when a large sector of the population has tended to be religious, most governments are shaped after a very secular model, and secularism is on the rise.[161] At the same time, one can observe different forms of religious revival in Europe. It is a fact that new patterns of immigration are changing the religious demography of Western liberal democracies such that there is greater and deeper religious diversity.[162] These changes in religious demography have led to new moments emerging within existing patterns of relationship within the contemporary context. Thus, one should better speak of a simultaneous process of secularization and modernization, as well as simultaneous processes of religiosity and lack of religiosity in individuals, which varies across different regions around the world.[163] However, as Casanova points out, the most interesting thing about secularization in Europe is not whether it is an empirical reality, but that the secularization thesis was so internalized that both the non-religious and religious believers viewed it as normal. In that case, "the secularization of Western European societies can

---

159. Casanova, "Exploring the Postsecular," 45.

160. See, for example, Reeves, *Liberal Christianity*; Reeves, *Organized Religion*.

161. See Williams, "Emergence."

162. Casanova acknowledges that one of the most significant consequences of the new global patterns of transnational migration has been a dramatic growth in religious diversity in the United States and Western Europe. See Casanova, "New Religious Pluralism."

163. Casanova would agree to this I believe. He states, for example, that: "In the historical processes of European secularization, the religious and the secular are inextricably bound together and mutually condition each other." Casanova, "Exploring the Postsecular," 10.

be explained better in terms of the triumph of the knowledge regime of secularism than in terms of structural processes of socioeconomic development, such as urbanization, education, rationalization, and so on."[164]

The result, then, is to tend to think that if a nation is more modern and secular, it therefore should be less religious, or that no place or role should be granted to religion in public life. This, however, is a myth, the result of interpreting religious and sociological conditions from a secular model, the secularization thesis, and not from what is actually happening in the Western world. Casanova puts it in a clear way:

> The most interesting issue sociologically is not the fact of progressive religious decline among the European population since the 1950s, but the fact that this decline is interpreted through the lenses of the secularization paradigm and is therefore accompanied by a 'secularist' self-understanding that interprets the decline as 'normal' and 'progressive'—that is, as a quasi-normative consequence of being a "modern" and "enlightened" European. The secularization of Western European societies can be explained better in terms of the triumph of the knowledge regime of secularism, than in terms of structural processes of socio-economic development.[165]

Casanova's valuable insights on secularism and secularization are confirmed by the work of Habermas and Taylor, both of whom took into account the existential force of religious belief and concluded that the secular model does not work in explaining contemporary political and social reality of Western democracies.

Jürgen Habermas on Religion in a "Postsecular" Age

The German philosopher Jürgen Habermas (b. 1929) is one of the most influential philosophers in the world.[166] On the topic of religion, Habermas has taken a nuanced position that continues to develop. In this section, I will

---

164. Casanova, "New Religious Pluralism," 63.
165. Casanova, "Rethinking Secularization," 15.
166. Bridging continental and Anglo-American traditions of thought, Habermas has engaged in debates with thinkers as diverse as Gadamer and Putnam, Foucault and Rawls, Derrida and Brandom. His extensive written work addresses topics stretching from social-political theory to aesthetics, epistemology and language to philosophy of religion, and his ideas have significantly influenced not only philosophy but also political-legal thought, sociology, communication studies, argumentation theory and rhetoric, developmental psychology and theology.

present his views on religion and religious discourse in the public sphere, and then will offer some comments regarding his position.

Habermas on Religion and the Public Sphere

In his *Theory of Communicative Action* (1981),[167] Habermas treated religion primarily from a sociological perspective, as an archaic mode of social integration. Since around the year 2000, however, he has taken a new interest on the role of religion in politics, on the one hand, and the relationship between religious and philosophical modes of discourse, on the other. It was in this later period that Habermas questioned the widely called "secularization hypothesis," that if religion mattered, it was because of its influence in the past, a survival out of step with the dominant patterns of progress, and that the modernizing of a society causes the decline, and eventually the disappearance, of religion in that society. Rather than defend this established view, Habermas discredited the functional understanding of religion, taking up issues that posed challenges to his previous theory, and led him to make innovations and to restructure its fundamental assumptions.[168]

It is in this context that Habermas started employing the term "post-secular" in order to indicate the renewed visibility of religion in contemporary culture and the need for a model of law and politics in which religious arguments are not excluded. In his account, the term seeks to account for, and positively demand, a change in mindset among those who previously felt justified in considering religions to be irrelevant.[169] Habermas's use of the term, however, still maintains that the secular, and in particular the secular state, is something that religious groups must conform or adapt to or be in conflict with. Thus, Habermas's work can be seen as addressing a set of political and legal issues, related to the conditions for mutual coexistence of secular and religious communities, and under conditions of what John Rawls has called "reasonable" pluralism.[170] Habermas states:

> As long as religious traditions and organizations remain vital forces in society, the separation of church and state in the context of a liberal constitution cannot result in a complete

---

167. See Habermas, *Communicative Action*.
168. Cf. Calhoun et al., *Habermas and Religion*, 2; Wolterstorff, "Engagement," 93.
169. See Habermas, RPS.
170. However, as Bohman states, contrary to Habermas's previous view of pluralism, which he shared with Rawls, "postsecurlarism" implies that religious pluralism is no longer simply a constraint upon the possibilities of democracy. Cf. Bohman, "Postsecular Global Order?," 179.

elimination of the influence that religious communities may have upon democratic politics.[171]

Habermas realized that in order to shape forms of social organization and solidarity democratically, one has to recognize and hear the voices of all citizens, which includes those of a religious background. Thus, meaning drawn from religious faith could be translated into terms accessible to those without such faith and on the basis of reason.[172] Religion, for example, is a crucial source for convictions at the heart of notions like human rights. Or, as Maria Herrera Lima states, at this later stage of global modernization, religions may provide some resources to counter the lack of solidarity and other deficiencies of a consumer and success-oriented society.[173] Liberal democracies, however, seem to prevent this from happening. Habermas states:

> The starting point of the discussion is the assumption that citizens in a democracy should offer each other reasons for their political stances. The problem is that liberal constitutions exude an air of paradox in this regard. Although they are designed to guarantee all religious communities an equal freedom to participate in civil society, they simultaneously shield the public bodies that make collectively binding decisions from religious influences. The same persons who are expressly authorized to practice their religion and to lead a pious life are supposed, as citizens, to participate in a democratic process whose results must remain free from any religious "contamination." The laicist answer to this problem is to banish religion from the public arena entirely. But as long as religious communities play a vital role in civil society, censoring the voices of religious citizens already at the source of the democratic process is inconsistent with the spirit of a liberal constitution.[174]

171. Habermas and Mendieta, "Postsecular World Society?," 12.

172. Eduardo Mendieta and Jonathan VanAntwerpen, affirm, for instance: "In recognition of the fact that religion has not withered away under the pressures of modernization, Habermas has increasingly stressed the importance of cultivating a 'postsecular' stance, an approach that both reckons with the continuing global vitality of religion and emphasizes the importance of 'translating' the ethical insights of religious traditions with a view to their incorporation into a 'postmetaphysical' philosophical perspective. The postsecular stance looks to religious sources of meaning and motivation as both a helpful and even indispensable ally in confronting the forces of global capitalism, while underscoring the crucial difference between faith and knowledge." See Mendieta and VanAntwerpen, *Power of Religion*, 4.

173. Cf. Herrera Lima, "Anxiety of Contingency," 49.

174. Habermas, "Reply to My Critics," 371. See also Habermas, "Political," 23–24. There he affirms: "Although a liberal constitution is designed in such a way as to guarantee all religious communities equal scope for freedom in civil society, it is, at the

That means that states cannot claim to protect religious freedom, while at the same time requiring that, in the public arena, religious citizens abstain from making statements based on their faith. This motivated Habermas to presents himself as a defender of religious freedom in his "Religion in the Public Sphere" (2006), especially in relation to the growing pluralism of contemporary secular societies. He states:

> The constitutional freedom of religion is the appropriate political answer to the challenges of religious pluralism. In this way, the potential for conflict at the level of citizens' social interaction can be restrained, while at the cognitive level deep-reaching conflicts may well continue to exist between the existentially relevant convictions of believers, believers of other denominations, and non-believers. Yet the secular character of the state is a necessary though not a sufficient condition for guaranteeing equal religious freedom for everybody.[175]

Secularism, for Habermas, will ensure that no religious group be denied religious freedom. Yet, it is the neutrality of the state towards competing world views that is for Habermas the institutional precondition for guaranteeing equal freedom of religion for all. The secular character of the state is not enough, because if there were no restrains on religious reasons whatsoever, one would open the parliaments to the battle on religious beliefs, and governmental authority may thus become the agent of a religious majority that asserts its will, violating the democratic procedure.[176] For Habermas, this restrain on religious reasons does not apply to the political public space in general, as in Rawls. Habermas defines the public sphere, in its ideal form, as being "made up of private people gathered together as a public and articulating the needs of society with the state."[177] He also distinguishes between the informal and the formal public sphere. The "informal political public sphere" is the space of organizations and citizens, while the "formal political

---

same time, supposed to shield the public bodies responsible for making collectively binding decisions from all religious influences. Those same people who are expressly authorized to practice their religion and to lead a pious life in their role as citizens are supposed to participate in a democratic process whose results must be kept free of any religious 'contamination.' Laicism pretends to resolve this paradox by privatizing religion entirely. But as long as religious communities play a vital role in civil society and the public sphere, deliberative politics is as much a product of the public use of reason on the part of religious citizens as on that of nonreligious citizens."

175. Habermas, RPS, 4.

176. Habermas, RPS, 11. This, according to Habermas, is the conclusion explicitly drawn by Nicholas Wolterstorff, who does not wish to subject the political use of religious reasons to any restraints whatsoever.

177. Habermas, *Structural Transformation*, 176.

public sphere" is the realm of parliaments, courts, ministries, administration, and other political institutions. According to Habermas, it is only in the formal political public sphere that citizens should refrain from religious language, and employ only secular reasons. He states:

> The consensus on constitutional principles, which all citizens must mutually assume their fellow citizens share, pertains also to the principle of the separation of church and state. However, in light of the aforementioned objection it would be to overgeneralize secularization if we were to extend this principle from the institutional level and apply it to statements put forward by organizations and citizens in the political public sphere. We cannot derive from the secular character of the state a direct obligation for all citizens personally to supplement their public statements of religious convictions by equivalents in a generally accessible language.[178]

Nevertheless, beyond the institutional threshold separating the informal public sphere from parliaments, courts, ministries, and administration, only secular reasons count, according to Habermas.[179] All that is required of religious persons, in Habermas's own words, is:

> The epistemic ability to consider one's own faith reflexively from the outside and to relate it to secular views. Religious citizens can well recognize this 'institutional translation proviso' without having to split their identity into a public and a private part the moment they participate in public discourses. They should therefore be allowed to express and justify their convictions in a religious language if they cannot find secular 'translations' for them.[180]

Religious citizens, then, should make an effort so as to make their arguments easily understood by all those not sharing their beliefs. At the same time, and in this he also distances himself from Rawls, in cases where it is not possible for a citizen to express his views in any other way than through religious arguments, he will be allowed to express his religious views in the political sphere without the need for a translation into secular arguments. Yet, the proper language of the formal political public sphere is that of secular arguments. The reason is that the neutrality principle in all deliberations preceding a vote is one of the cores of democracy. Thus,

---

178. Habermas, RPS, 9.
179. Habermas, RPS, 9.
180. Habermas, RPS, 9–10.

"all enforceable political decisions must be formulated in a language that is equally accessible to all citizens, and it must be possible to justify them in this language as well."[181]

According to Habermas, in postmetaphysical philosophy "only 'public' reasons count, that is, reasons that have the power to convince beyond the boundaries of a particular religious community."[182] Thus, "religious contributions have to be translated into a generally accessible language, however, before their content can enter into the deliberations of political institutions that make legally binding decisions."[183] He speaks of "the autonomy of a universally shared reason," and that postmetaphysical philosophy employs a "generally accessible language."[184] Postmetaphysical philosophy, according to Habermas, does not presume "to decide what is true or false in religion;" it "leaves the internal questions of the validity of religion to disputes within rational apologetics."[185] Thus, "an institutional filter should be established between informal communication in the public arena and formal deliberations of political bodies that yield to collectively binding decisions."[186] For the state to remain neutral between competing worldviews, "one must," according to Habermas, "accept the translation proviso as the price to be paid."[187] At the same time, secular citizens "are obliged not to publicly dismiss religious contributions to political opinion and will formation as mere noise, or even nonsense, from the start."[188] The reason why in the formal public sphere one should leave aside all religious reasoning is that "the principle of separation of state and church obliges politicians and officials within political institutions to formulate and justify laws, court rulings, decrees and measures only in a language which is equally accessible to all citizens,"[189] for this is what neutrality requires.

---

181. Habermas, RPS, 12.

182. Habermas, *BNR*, 245.

183. Habermas, "Reply to My Critics," 371. See also Habermas, "Political," 25–26. Habermas states: "According to this proposal, all citizens should be free to decide whether they want to use religious language in the public sphere. Were they to do so, they would, however, have to accept that the potential truth contents of religious utterances must be translated into a generally accessible language before they can find their way onto the agendas of parliaments, courts, or administrative bodies and influence their decisions."

184. Habermas, *BNR*, 139.

185. Habermas, *BNR*, 245.

186. Habermas, "Political," 26.

187. Habermas, "Political," 26.

188. Habermas, "Political," 26.

189. Habermas, RPS, 5.

Habermas's notion of translation relies on Rawls's notion of translation: that citizens are obligated to reciprocally render their arguments in terms accessible to each other, and to make their best efforts to understand each other on the basis of what is common to their thought. Habermas also added the idea of complementary learning processes, an idea that goes beyond mere translation, for citizens may gain semantic content from, and possibly even be changed, by their interactions with other citizens. Thus, for Habermas, there is potential for the bridging of other divides through practical reason, while at the same time he takes the differences between religious and secular reason as being more profound.

Habermas also highlights the importance of the dialogue between philosophy and religion. He acknowledges that among philosophers there is a judgmental attitude implicitly expressed by a waning of philosophical interest in possibly undiscovered treasures from religion. If dialogue is to occur, this waning of interest must be overcome. No dialogue can occur, he states, if the philosophical side declares that the epistemic status of religious convictions is that they are simply irrational.[190] According to him, philosophy must overcome "a narrow secularist mindset."[191] Habermas has pronounced very strong statements in this regard. For example, he affirms in his "Religion in the Public Sphere":

> As long as secular citizens are convinced that religious traditions and religious communities are to a certain extent archaic relics of pre-modern societies that continue to exist in the present, they will understand freedom of religion as the cultural version of the conservation of a species in danger of becoming extinct. From their viewpoint, religion no longer has any intrinsic justification to exist. And the principle of the separation of state and church can for them only have the laicist meaning of sparing indifference. In the secularist reading, we can envisage that, in the long run, religious views will inevitably melt under the sun of scientific criticism and that religious communities will not be able to withstand the pressures of some unstoppable cultural and social modernization. Citizens who adopt such an epistemic stance toward religion can obviously no longer be expected to take religious contributions to contentious political issues seriously and even to help to assess them for a substance that can possibly be expressed in a secular language and justified by secular arguments.[192]

190. Cf. Habermas, *BNR*, 112.
191. Habermas, *BNR*, 140.
192. Habermas, RPS, 15.

Habermas insists that it is philosophy rather than religion that must shape up if genuine dialogue is to take place. He states that "when the secular side excludes religious fellow citizens from the circle of modern contemporaries and treats them as specimens to be protected like an endangered species, this corrodes the very substance of a membership based on equal rights in the universe of rational persons."[193]

The question, then, is how to incorporate the religious views of citizens in the public sphere, for certain groups of people will not have an alternative cognitive basis for their convictions. Habermas states: "The liberal state, which expressly protects such forms of existence as a basic right, cannot at the same time expect all citizens in addition to justify their political positions independently of their religious convictions or worldviews."[194] He also affirms:

> We cannot derive from the secular character of the state a direct obligation for all citizens personally to supplement their public statements of religious convictions by equivalents in a generally accessible language. And certainly the normative expectation that all religious citizens when casting their vote should ultimately let themselves be guided by secular considerations is to ignore the realities of a devout life, an existence guided by faith.[195]

Habermas is trying to do more than just calling for toleration of religious voices in the public square. He states:

> What is at stake is not a respectful sensibility for the possible existential significance of religion for some other person . . . but a self-reflexive overcoming of a rigid and exclusive secularist self-understanding of modernity. The admission of religious assertions into the political arena only makes sense if all citizens can be reasonably expected not to exclude the possibility that these contributions may have cognitive substance . . . Such an attitude presupposes a mentality on the part of secular citizens that is far from a matter of course in the secularized societies of the West. Instead, the insight by secular citizens that they live in a post-secular society that is epistemically adjusted to the continued existence of religious communities first requires a change in mentality that is no less cognitively exacting than the

---

193. Habermas, *Faith and Knowledge*, 1.33, quoted by Wolterstorff, "Engagement," 101–2.

194. Habermas, *BNR*, 128.

195. Habermas, *RPS*, 9.

adaptation of religious awareness to the challenges of an ever more secularized environment.[196]

In recent writings, such as his "Religion in the Public Sphere" (2006), Habermas has also attempted to redress the deficiency of Rawls's controversial "proviso," which states that policies advanced on the basis of religious reasons be admissible only insofar as they may be corroborated by properly political reasons.[197] According to Habermas, Rawls's "proviso" places an undue "cognitive burden" on those citizens who base their arguments on religious reasons or other worldviews, by forcing them to articulate their positions in terms that do not reflect their reasons for holding those positions in the first place. Habermas sees that there is a need to meet the liberal criterion of democratic legitimacy, on the one hand, and the need to secure the political inclusion of religious citizens that democratic legitimacy requires, on the other. Habermas agrees with the liberal position in defending the separation of Church and state, and on the institutional priority of non-religious reasons in politics. That means that Habermas accepts Rawls's "proviso" only with respect to political deliberation at the institutional level of the formal public sphere (parliaments, courts, ministries, and administrations). For that reason, Habermas proposes to eliminate the requirement of providing corroborating non-religious reasons in political deliberations in the informal public sphere whenever such reasons are not available. As Cristina Lafont comments, religious citizens who participate in political advocacy in the informal public sphere can offer exclusively religious reasons in support of the policies they favor in the hope that they may be successfully translated into non-religious reasons. Nevertheless, the obligation of translation should not fall exclusively on the shoulders of religious citizens, as Rawls's approach suggests. Instead, this obligation must be shared by all citizens involved in public deliberation, regardless of whether they consider themselves to be secular or religious citizens. Thus, Habermas's proposal is supposed to yield a more even distribution of cognitive burdens among citizens.[198]

In summary, what Habermas proposes, is that only "those who hold a public office or are candidates for such"[199] are required to do what ordinary citizens are not required to do. They "are subject to the obligation to remain neutral in the face of competing world views,"[200] he states. He also affirms: "Every citizen must know and accept that only secular reasons

---

196. Habermas, RPS, 15.
197. See Rawls, IPRR, 776, 83–84.
198. Cf. Lafont, "Religion and the Public Sphere," 233–34.
199. Habermas, RPS, 9.
200. Habermas, RPS, 9.

count beyond the institutional threshold separating the informal public sphere from parliaments, courts, ministries, and administration."[201] Thus, according to Habermas, "the truth content of religious contributions can only enter into the institutionalized practice of deliberation and decision-making if the necessary translation already occurs in the pre-parliamentarian domain, i.e., in the political public sphere itself."[202] Thus, in the informal public sphere, ordinary citizens are allowed to make use of any reasons they sincerely believe in, even if those reasons are exclusively religious. They are not obliged to come up with secular reasons; they are only obliged to do so if they want their reasons to count in the legislative process, since, according to Habermas's "institutional translation proviso," only secular reasons count beyond the institutional threshold.[203] Therefore, according to Habermas, religious reasoning should be avoided in the democratic political process only when it comes to the formal public sphere.

However, even though Habermas's proposal may seem less restrictive than Rawls's and thus more able to warrant the political inclusion of religious citizens, Cristina Lafont insists that Habermas's proposed "institutional translation proviso" does little to alleviate the burden, for it only shifts the exclusion of religious reasons from the informal public sphere to the realm of formal political institutions. Thus, severe restrictions on the types of reasons that may legitimately be used in political discussions in the public sphere seem to follow from this approach.[204] Even though Habermas's proviso only applies to the formal public sphere, it nevertheless shares the central constraint with Rawls's proviso, namely, "that only secular reasons count beyond the institutional threshold."[205] For Habermas, the reason for

---

201. Habermas, RPS, 9.

202. Habermas, RPS, 9.

203. Cf. Lafont, "Religion and the Public Sphere," 237–38.

204. Lafont notes, for example, that religious citizens should not appeal to religious reasons that deny the authority of science or the possible truth of other religions, and secular citizens should not appeal to secularist reasons that deny the possible truth of religious beliefs. Cf. Lafont, "Religion and the Public Sphere."

205. Habermas, RPS, 9. As Lafont notes: "To be sure, Habermas's proposal offers a solution to ordinary citizens confronted with a situation in which they cannot find any public reasons in support of the policies they favor, while Rawls's proviso may seem to ignore that possibility. However, once we contemplate a situation of genuine conflict between religious and public reasons, the requirements of Habermas's 'institutional translation proviso,' though certainly less demanding than Rawls's, would be equally impossible to meet. Translation presupposes that it is possible to come to the same results by different epistemic means. Thus, in cases of genuine conflict between secular and religious reasons, officials would not be able to fulfill their translation obligation simply by virtue of the proviso." See Lafont, "Religion and the Public Sphere," 237.

such constraint is that the liberal state is not only secular, but above all neutral when it comes to competing worldviews.

Some Comments Regarding Habermas's Position

To conclude this section on Habermas's view on religion and the public square in what he calls a "postsecular" age, there are a few points worth highlighting.

In the first place, there is Habermas's views religion as a category, synonymous to a worldview or comprehensive doctrine. The problem with this notion is that it does not seem to convey a proper idea of what religion really is. Religion is taken by Habermas to mean a dogma, when a close observation of the many phenomena that are considered religious show that it appears to be more than just that. It perhaps may be something different, though connected, to faith or dogmas. Why should we limit the notion of religion to just religious discourse?

In the second place, since religion is seen as a doctrine or worldview, it becomes a source of (religious) arguments which competes with its secular counterpart. According to Habermas, it is licit to employ these religious arguments in the informal public sphere without the need to translate them into secular terms when debating issues that affect us all as a society. However, when it comes to the formal public sphere, only secular reasons count, and therefore one should avoid any references to one's own religious worldview. Due to the pluralism present in contemporary societies, and in order to protect religious freedom, Habermas sees it necessary that the state remains secular, and, above all, that it be neutral with respect to competing worldviews. It is for this reason that one should only employ secular reasons when it comes to the formal political public sphere. It is not clear, however, whether Habermas proposes this solution as a prudent way of dealing with pluralism, and for the sake of unity and peace, or, as J. M. Bernstein argues, in order to keep things within a secular agenda.[206] If the state is to remain neutral, would not it make sense to exclude secularism as well? And what is meant by secularism in this particular instance? Is it just the separation of "religion" from the formal public sphere? From a secular perspective, then, the pluralism of doctrines is viewed as creating problems that can be overcome only by appealing to a neutral secular state. Habermas, in fact, states:

---

206. J. M. Bernstein argues that there is in Habermas's writings an explicit secularist orientation. Cf. Bernstein, "Forgetting Isaac," 158.

Only the ideologically neutral exercise of secular governmental authority within the framework of the constitutional state can ensure different communities of belief can coexist on a basis of equal rights and mutual tolerance, while nevertheless remaining unreconciled at the level of their substantive worldviews or doctrines.[207]

While it is true that different religious communities may remain unreconciled at the doctrinal level, it does not follow that they will coexist as equal and mutually tolerant communities only on the condition of there being an ideologically neutral exercise of secular governmental authority. Habermas faces the problem that was raised regarding Rawls's theory. From a prudential point of view, and in order to avoid the imposition of religious views on the rest of the population, it makes sense that one be aware of other people's views and employ appropriate arguments when it comes to framing coercive laws. Yet, what would this require? For Habermas, a postmetaphysical philosophy requires that one only produce public reasons, that is, those that can be accepted by all. Yet, we cannot place the requirement on just acceptance. There has to be a deeper and more meaningful element when dealing with the types of reasons allowed on the public sphere. Any reason, if it is based on rational premises, is public by nature, and always belongs to the public sphere, be it formal or informal.

Charles Taylor's Analysis of Secularism

Charles Taylor (1931) is one of the most important thinkers Canada has produced, and one of the world's leading political theorists.[208] He has produced a major and highly original contribution to the debates on secularization and pluralism in contemporary society. We cannot ignore his important contributions, then, when dealing with issues related to religious freedom and the place of religion in the public sphere. In this section, I will present Taylor's analysis on the meaning of the secular and secularism, and the place he grants to religion in the public sphere.

---

207. Habermas, *BNR*, 2–3.

208. A pupil of Isaiah Berlin at Oxford, Taylor taught at McGill from 1961 to 1997, and is now a professor emeritus. His teaching and research areas include philosophy of action, philosophy of social science, political theory, Greek political thought, moral philosophy, the culture of Western modernity, philosophy of language, theories of meaning, language and politics, German idealism, and the political culture of modernity.

The Meaning of the Secular and Secularism

In his *A Secular Age* (2007), Taylor assigns three meanings to the term "secular."[209]

The first meaning of the secular denotes a decline in the public role of religion. Thus, a nation is secular when religion is not visibly present in the public sphere.

The second meaning of the secular posits a "falling off" in religious adherence. In this sense, a nation becomes more secular as its citizens become less religious.

The third meaning of the secular refers to the conditions of belief whereby belief in God moves from being a given to becoming "one option among others."[210] European mediaeval societies, for example, were characterized for their unity in one faith. Nowadays, believing in God or adhering to a given religious group is just one option among many. For Taylor, this third development was itself a partially religious development rather than an inevitable outcome of processes of modernization. Thus, Taylor sees that our secular age is characterized neither by a necessary decline in religious belief nor by an incompatibility between religion and modernity, but by a plurality of forms of belief and unbelief which are themselves constantly interacting and changing.

In his "The Meaning of Secularism" (2010), Taylor gives a positive picture of secularism. He notes that it is generally agreed that modern democracies have to be "secular."[211] In fact, models of what constitutes a secular regime involve some kind of separation of church and state, for "the pluralism of society requires that there be some kind of neutrality,"[212] what he terms as "principled distance."[213] However, he laments that there is a tendency to define secularism or *laïcité* in terms of some institutional arrangement: people invoke the "Wall of Separation" as the ultimate criterion in the United States, or *laïcité* as the final word in France. Instead, Taylor proposes to define secularism taking into account its goals.[214]

According to Taylor, secularism involves a complex requirement, for it seeks diverse goods that can be classified in the categories of the French

---

209. Taylor, SA, 2–3.

210. Taylor, SA, 3.

211. See also Taylor, RRS, 34.

212. Taylor, MS, 23. He notes that in cases where the state is officially linked to some religious confession, as in England or Scandinavia, it is in a vestigial and largely symbolic sense.

213. Taylor, RRS, 34.

214. See, for example, his Taylor, MS; Taylor, RRS.

Revolution: liberty, equality, fraternity. Liberty, for no one must be forced in the domain of religion or basic belief; in terms of the First Amendment to the United States Constitution, this is described as the "free exercise" of religion: religious liberty, including the freedom not to believe. Equality is sought between people of different faiths; that means that no religious viewpoint or religious or areligious worldview can enjoy a privileged status, let alone be adopted as the official view of the state. Finally, fraternity is seen in that all spiritual families must be heard in the ongoing process of determining what the society is about, that is, its political identity, and how it is going to realize these goals, for example, in which regime of rights and privileges.[215] He also mentions a fourth goal, that we try as much as possible to maintain relations of harmony and comity between the supporters of different religions and worldviews, which may also be considered under the good of fraternity.[216] It is to be noted, however, that the three categories of the French Revolution that Taylor employs to define the place of religion were not about religion at all at the time of their inception. While this pedagogical presentation is enlightening in regard to the way religion should be taken into account, it may also be partially misleading to a certain point given the origin of these notions.[217]

Religion and the Secular Public Square

According to Taylor, one of the problems that follow from secularism and the establishment of these principles by pure reason alone, is that in reality,

> . . . there is no such set of timeless principles that can be determined, at least in the detail they must be for a given political system, by pure reason alone, and situations differ very much and require different kinds of concrete realization of agreed general principles, so that some degree of working out is necessary in each situation.[218]

---

215. Cf. Taylor, MS, 23; Taylor, RRS, 34–35.

216. Cf. Taylor, RRS, 35.

217. The French Revolution, in fact, was marked by a laicist agenda to free consciences and reason from the control of "religion," especially the Roman Catholic Church. For more on this, see Bourdin, 108–49. Thus, Taylor's evocation of the French Revolution may also be misleading as it might signal a favoring of the French model of secularism, when in fact Taylor is highly critical of its strict exclusion of religion from the public sphere. Cf. Spohn, "Jürgen Habermas and Charles Taylor on Postsecularism," 125.

218. Taylor, MS, 24.

Now, dictating the principles from some supposedly higher authority violates the good of fraternity, that is, the idea that all spiritual families must be heard. The consequence is that "this leaves us very often with difficult conflicts and dilemmas between our basic goals."[219]

A solution proposed by Taylor is that there is a need to alter the way in which we proceed when the range of religions or basic philosophies expands. Thus, religious groups must be seen as much as interlocutors and as little as menace as the situation allows. At the same time, Taylor sees that religious groups must get involved in a process of redefinition in a democratic, liberal context.

The problem behind all the conflicts regarding the place of religion in the public sphere, according to Taylor, is that the wrong secular model has taken hold of our minds. He states: "We think that secularism (or *laïcité*) has to do with the relation of the state and religion, whereas in fact it has to do with the (correct) response of the democratic state to diversity."[220] The answer lies in the response to the fact of pluralism. If the state is to remain neutral, it is "precisely to avoid favoring or disfavoring not just religious positions, but any basic position, religious or nonreligious. . . . We can't favor religion over against nonbelief in religion, or vice versa."[221] This meaning of the secular is new, and it is understood by Taylor as neutrality rather than as a rejection of religion, especialy taking into account the pluralism present in contemporary societies.

Taylor claims that we should move beyond the originating contexts of secularism, and instead look at the kinds of societies in which we are now living in the West. The first feature that strikes us, according to him, is the wide diversity, not only of religious views, but also of those which involve no religion, and of those which are unclassifiable in this dichotomy. Thus, according to Taylor, "the goals of liberty, equality, and fraternity require that we treat all of these even-handedly."[222] And in order to do so, one has to move beyond institutional arrangements, and instead start from the goals and derive the concrete arrangements from these.[223] This plurality of principles will help overcome "the illusion that there is only one principle here, say, *laïcité* and its corollary of the neutrality of public institutions or spaces." Thus, the "modern moral order" enshrines three principles:

219. Taylor, MS, 24.
220. Taylor, MS, 25. In the same line, Franklin Gamwell argues that the function of politics is to properly legitimate the plurality of religions. See Gamwell, *Meaning of Religious Freedom*, 6.
221. Taylor, MS, 25.
222. Taylor, MS, 27.
223. Cf. Taylor, MS, 28.

1) The rights and liberties of the members, 2) the equality among them (which has of course been variously interpreted, and has mutated towards more radical conceptions over time), and 3) the principle that rule is based on consent (which has also been defended in more and less radical forms).[224]

Taylor's response to pluralism is borrowed from Rawls. The secular state cleaves very strongly to certain political principles that represent the very basis of the state: human rights, equality, the rule of law, democracy. The state must support these principles. Now, this political ethics is shared by people of very different "comprehensive views of the good." While they concur on the principles, people also differ on the deeper reasons for holding to this political ethics. Thus, "the state must uphold the ethic, but must refrain from favoring any of the deeper reasons."[225]

Taylor also follows Rawls in noting that everyone should use a language which they could reasonably expect their fellow citizens to agree with. Secular reason seems to be a language that everyone speaks and can argue and be convinced in. Religious languages, on the other hand, operate outside this discourse by introducing extraneous premises that only believers can accept. Therefore, Taylor proposes that we should all talk the common language.[226] It is in this sense that, according to him, religious reason needs to be sidelined: "Religious reason either comes to the same conclusions as secular reason, but then it is superfluous, or it comes to contrary conclusions, and then it is dangerous and disruptive."[227] According to him, "secular reason suffices to arrive at the conclusions we need, such as establishing the legitimacy of the democratic state and defining our political ethic."[228] Together with Rawls and Habermas, Taylor also agrees that there are zones of a secular state in which the language to be employed has to be neutral. However,

> These do not include citizen deliberation, as Rawls at first thought, or even deliberation in the legislature, as Habermas seems to think. . . . This zone can be described as the official language of the state: the language in which legislation, administrative decrees, and court judgments must be couched.[229]

---

224. Taylor, MS, 32.

225. Taylor, MS, 25. See also Taylor, RRS, 36. For Rawls's position, especially see Rawls, "Overlapping Consensus"; Rawls, *PL*; Rawls, IPRR.

226. Taylor, RRS, 49.

227. Taylor, RRS, 49.

228. Taylor, RRS, 50.

229. Taylor, RRS, 50.

And Taylor stresses further: "The state can be neither Christian nor Muslim nor Jewish, but, by the same token, it should also be neither Marxist, nor Kantian, nor utilitarian."[230]

One can notice a major difference in Taylor's view of secularism over Rawls and Habermas. Habermas had already challenged Rawls's "proviso" by making room for religious discourse in the public informal sphere. Taylor goes even further by not accepting Habermas's restriction to just the informal level. Formal political deliberation may well include religious reasoning. The conclusions, however, what he terms as the "official language of the state," are to remain neutral. This is the common language that should avoid religious references for the sake of a healthy pluralism. Taylor's position, then, opens the door to a more fruitful deliberation between those that hold different worldviews.

Conclusion

The aim of this chapter was to present the work of some relatively recent and contemporary influential philosophers from various parts of the world that have dealt with the problems that have arisen regarding pluralism, secularism, and the place of religion in public life. The work of these authors has triggered a revision of theories about secularization, and it also shows how the proper relation between religion and politics has had, and continues to have, a significant place in contemporary political theory. For that reason, one must acknowledge their work in an investigation on religious freedom.

There is in our present world an increasing presence of a plurality of views, both religious and nonreligious. This motivated Rawls to affirm the principles of neutrality and equality, so that no religious reasoning may be used in the public political sphere, as it may be coercive to other worldviews. As a solution to the problem of pluralism, Rawls offers a freestanding political doctrine, one that is not tied to any one comprehensive doctrine. Yet, affirmation of his political liberalism offers room to religious views insofar as those who hold them are "reasonable," as they will find a path to affirmation from their own moral sources. Public reason belongs to the public political forum (which includes the discourse of a Supreme Court justice, a legislator, or a candidate for public office), distinct from the background culture (which includes the culture of churches and associations of all kinds, and institutions of learning at all levels, especially universities and professional schools, scientific and other societies, as well as voters and activists). Thus, religiously motivated actors must "translate" their reasons for advocating

---

230. Taylor, RRS, 50.

a particular policy. Rawls also insists that no comprehensive doctrine of whatever kind, including religious, can form the basis for political decisions regarding the use of coercive public power.

The last version of Rawls's theory, that of his "The Idea of Public Reason Revisited" (1997), presents a "wide view" of public reason, according to which citizens may introduce reasons from reasonable comprehensive doctrines, both religious and non-religious, without "translation," at any time into public discourse about constitutional essentials, provided that at some point in the future these reasons are translated into generally accessible public arguments. However, when citizens are making coercive decisions on constitutional essentials and matters of basic justice, they will still be bound by a duty to support only those policies that can in fact be justified by public reason only.

One of the innovations that Neuhaus, Casanova, Taylor, and Habermas proposed, was that the notion of secularism understood as progress that excludes religion does not work anymore. Habermas even suggested that we do not live in a secular age anymore. One of the problematic consequences of the "secularization thesis" is that, in order to progress, religion must be left aside. If societies become less religious as they become more modern, it means that religion is a stumbling block to progress and modernization. Sociologically, however, this thesis has been proven to be wrong, and has been put into serious question. This has led Habermas to state that we live in a postsecular world.

There is a problem, then, in how secularism is understood as opposed and against religion. This also means, then, that the notion of religion as opposed to secularism should be challenged as well. In fact, the notion of "religion" is sometimes employed as meaning a transhistorical and transcultural feature of human life, essentially distinct from "secular" features such as politics and economics, and which even has a peculiarly dangerous inclination to promote violence, as postulated by Rawls.[231] As a consequence, it has been argued that religion must be tamed by restricting its access to public power, or that in the name of neutrality and equality, no religious reasoning may be used in the political sphere, as it may be coercive to other worldviews. This secular stance instigated a reaction from those defending "religion" and its presence in the public sphere. Thus, secularism is seen as posing a threat to the exercise of religion in public life. It is in this context that Richard John Neuhaus denounced the separation of religion from politics.

---

231. See, for example, Rawls's "Introduction" to his *PL*.

According to Neuhaus, there has been an effort in contemporary secular societies to isolate and exclude the religious dimension of culture. Thus, Neuhaus was very much against secular liberalism's denial that America's political tradition is founded on freedoms and obligations that ultimately come from God. However, one of the tenets of secular liberalism is the affirmation that our common life can and should be ordered without appeal to a transcendent point of reference. It translates into the doctrine that the advance of liberal democracy requires the public retreat and perhaps private weakening of traditional religious faith. Neuhaus associated this view with philosophers like John Rawls, who asserted that a liberal order must exclude "comprehensive doctrines" from public debate. According to Neuhaus, this is hostile to the open spirit of true liberalism. No democracy can exclude from public debate any convictions, "whether drawn from the Torah, Chinese *Analects*, Cicero, the New Testament, or the *Baghavad Ghita*."[232]

Neuhaus also denounced how secularism eroded the First Amendment's protections of religious freedom. He attacked as spurious the legal reasoning by which the obligation to render free worship to God was turned into a private freedom of conscience, an interpretation that he believed endangers religious freedom by restricting its full exercise. In the end, secularism seems to be neither neutral nor hospitable with diversity. One of the problems with Neuhaus's exposition, however, is that he uses the term "religion" in different ways, and in some cases even as almost comprehending any human activity, to the point that it is not clear what does or does not count as religion. At the same time, he is not systematic in explaining what he means by the "public square." He just limits his exposition to examples in which religion is not allowed in different public spaces, such as prayer within the school system.

The publication of his book, then, sounded like a needed alarm. Yet, Neuhaus did not believe the American public square was stripped entirely naked. That is the reason why *The Naked Public Square* generated a serious debate about democratic discourse and the role of religion in that discourse. And the discussion became so vigorous that Rawls himself would later partially revise his view on where religion might fit in American political debate, and the notions of secularism was revised so as to give room to religious discourse and religious diversity. Yet, there is in Neuhaus's and Rawls's accounts of "public reason" more than a passing resemblance.[233] In fact, Neuhaus is critical of the religious new right for "making public claims on

---

232. Neuhaus, "Moral Progress," 21.
233. Cf. Galston, "Religious Pluralism," 152.

the basis of private truths."[234] Public decisions, according to Neuhaus, must be made through arguments that are "public in character." That is the reason why he argued for a need to translate religiously based values into terms that are accessible to those who do not share the same religious grounding.[235] Rawls also holds a similar concept of "translation" as Neuhaus's, for both affirm that religious reasons should be included in public debates as long as they could be translated into secular terms.

Neuhaus's challenge to the secular thesis had a positive effect. Rawls introduced the idea of the "proviso," so that religion is not totally excluded from public discussion. Later, the work by Casanova, Taylor, and Habermas helped debunk the "secularization thesis." We should also point out that Neuhaus's opposition is directed to ideological secularism, rather than to political secularism.[236] For that reason, Neuhaus's attack on ideological secularism does not apply to Taylor and Habermas's views of secularism and the role they assign to religion in the public square.

José Casanova's analytical distinction is of great value to understand the process of secularization, and the possible outcomes when secularization is transcended, and religion emerges, or survives, within this new setting. This might be an indication of a false dichotomy between religion and secularism, and which lead us to challenge these two categories that developed out of modernity. This is something that will be developed further in chapter 3.

Jürgen Habermas, on his part, introduced the term "postsecular" in order to indicate the renewed visibility of religion in contemporary culture, and the need for a model of law and politics in which religious arguments are not excluded.

According to Habermas, Rawls underestimates the existential force of religious belief. For some believers, their belief may provide the only sufficient basis for their political views. This may be the case even when public reasons might also be available to support the views in question. Thus, the demand that believers "translate" their comprehensive religious views into secular justifications imposes undue burdens on believers of this sort. Instead, Habermas proposes that the demand for translation pertains only to politicians and public officials with institutional power to make, apply, and execute the law.

234. Neuhaus, *NPS*, 36.

235. Cf. Neuhaus, *NPS*, 125.

236. Cf. Reno, "Neuhaus," 7. Especially note: "He was convinced that an ideological secularism (as opposed to a political secularism) undermines liberalism and over the long haul cannot sustain a free society."

For Habermas, constitutional religious freedom is the answer to the growing pluralism of contemporary secular societies. Now, he also states that in order to guarantee equal religious freedom for everybody, there are two conditions for this to take place: the secular character of the state, and neutrality of the state towards competing worldviews. Of these two conditions, Habermas considers neutrality to be the most important, for without restrains on religious reasons there would not be a true democratic procedure, and governmental authority would run the risk of becoming the agent of a religious majority. Thus, he states that "all enforceable political decisions *must be formulated* in a language that is equally accessible to all citizens, and it *must be possible to justify them* in this language as well."[237]

The restrain on religious reasons is expressed in terms of a "translation" into secular arguments. This translation, however, is to be employed only in what he calls the "formal political public sphere," that is, the realm of parliaments, courts, ministries, administration, and other political institutions At the same time, this "translation" does not mean that citizens must leave their religious views behind, or confine them to their private lives. Citizens should be allowed to express and justify their convictions in a religious language if they cannot find secular "translations" for them, so that other citizens may express these views in secular terms. In this we see that Habermas's theory allows for the inclusion of religious discourse in public debate, something which Rawls did not grant. Habermas also contends that one should take religious contributions to contentious political issues seriously. Thus, both believers and non-believers are involved in a complementary and cooperative learning process in which each side can learn from the other. In this way, translation makes demands on both sides, for the believer must seek publicly accessible arguments, whereas the non-believer must approach religion as a potential source of meaning and expressing truths about human existence that are relevant for all.

Charles Taylor argues that one of the problems that follow from secularism is that in reality the establishment of principles by pure reason alone does not suffice in order to work out solutions that emerge from a pluralist society. Thus, all spiritual families must be heard, for religious groups should be taken as interlocutors in political debate, especially in process of redefinition in a democratic, liberal context. For that reason, Taylor proposes that secularism should be understood not as a restriction of religion, but rather as the response of the democratic state to the fact of pluralism.

Taylor's view of secularism also grants more room to religious argument than the solutions proposed by Rawls and Habermas. According to

---

237. Habermas, RPS, 12.

Taylor, formal political deliberation may well include religious reasoning. It is the conclusions, however, what he terms as the "official language of the state," that are to remain neutral for the sake of a healthy pluralism. Taylor's position, then, opens the door to a more fruitful deliberation between those that hold different worldviews. Yet, Taylor does not offer a definition of what he means by religion. This is a problematic aspect, as one would expect that he be clear on that point, especially since he is in favor of the presence of religious argument in the public square. He limits his exposition to offering a description of religion, which is so vague that it cannot be taken as a point of departure for debates on religion in the public square.[238]

Having presented a summary of these author's theories, I will offer a few more remarks intended to make a final evaluation of their achievements, what is lacking in their theories, and what it is that should be done in order to move forward with regard to issues relating to religious freedom.

In the first place, "religion" is taken by Rawls, Neuhaus, Casanova, Habermas and Taylor to refer to a "dogma," the source of religious arguments and reasoning. While it is true that many communities have developed a religious dogma, creed, or central teaching, not all religious groups do so, and for that reason, defining religion as a dogma seems to be the wrong way to tackle a notion of religion. Taylor seems to include other aspects as well, but still his understanding of religion is centered on religion as a belief. Defining religion as a dogma leaves aside so many other aspects that are considered to be "religious" acts, such a popular religiosity and devotions (one may think of traditional processions, stations of the cross, pilgrimages, etc.), oaths, public prayer, worship, monetary offerings, the construction of religious sites and symbols in public places, etc. All of these acts, and many others that are guided by this spirit of religiosity, have had and still do have an undeniable impact on the public sphere and politics. It is therefore necessary to rediscover the true meaning of "religion," as this will assist us in order to have a correct understanding of the meaning of religious freedom, what it implies, and the guidelines that should be followed in order to protect it. The problem with a notion of religion as an overt system (whether of dogmas, beliefs, values, etc.) is that it will affect and restrict the meaning of religion freedom to just the ability to voice out one's religious views in the public sphere. But this does not seem right as religious freedom implies much more.

---

238. For example, Taylor affirms: "What is religion? If one identifies this with the great historic faiths, or even with explicit belief in supernatural beings, then it seems to have declined. But if you include a wide range of spiritual and semi-spiritual beliefs; or if you cast your net even wider and think of someone's religion as the shape of their ultimate concern, then indeed, one can make a case that religion is as present as ever." Taylor, *SA*, 427.

The consequence of taking religion as a dogma, is that when talking about the place of religion in the public square, these authors tend to express it as a matter of voicing out one's beliefs, or of translating these religious arguments into terms that are accessible to those who do not share that faith. As mentioned above, even though many communities have developed a religious dogma, creed, or central teaching, not all religious groups do so. That is the reason why defining religion as a dogma seems to be the wrong way to approach a notion of religion. Such an understanding will leave aside many other aspects that are considered to be "religious" acts.

In the second place, and in regard to the view which states that because of the fact of pluralism and the plurality of religious and nonreligious worldviews it is necessary to uphold neutrality of the state in order to avoid coercion of one group over another, we can point out a few things. While it is true that, because people who hold different worldviews, it would be easier to communicate among one another if there was one common language available for debate, such as a form of public reason or secular reasoning, that, of itself, would not prevent disagreements, as these will always persist. At the same time, one can also point out that arguments based on religious reasoning have not been adequately shown to be so seriously divisive in a liberal democratic order so as to justify restrictions. Yet, as Rawls has argued, it does not seem fair that coercive laws be imposed on all citizens based on a group's faith or worldview. Thus, freedom and the value of persons seem to be best protected when citizens, legislators, and judges abstract from their substantive conceptions of the good, and strive for neutral considerations that can justify state coercion to all. These appropriate considerations justifying coercion must be available to all citizens, and all must be reasonably expected to agree with those considerations if they are to serve up appropriate grounds for state coercion. What Rawls seemed to have missed, however, is that one day the state, judges, or legislators, employing purely secular reasoning, may impose coercive laws on religious citizens or institutions, against which these citizens or institution may only have religious arguments to offer in their defense. I will address this issue in the Conclusion of the book.

In the third place, it is necessary to move beyond the distinction between public reason and religious reasons. This distinction has not been able to solve the dilemma of the place of religion in the public sphere. As long as this distinction is upheld, the debate does not seem to move forward. Authors that distinguish between secular and religious reasons, confining the religious to the private sphere, or the informal public sphere, run the risk of restricting the religious freedom of citizens as well. One should then question whether religion is really a private affair. Reasons, if they are reasons, will always be public. Therefore, the question on religious arguments is not a question of religion being a private or public affair. Religious discourse is by nature political whenever it is exercised within the polis, within the public realm, and is intended to shape ways of thinking, acting, and policy making. As Neuhaus affirms, religion is not synonymous with conscience; it is not a private affair.[239] If religion was a private affair, on the other hand, the problem of pluralism would not even exist. Why would it be a political problem unless the religious is a public reality, which by its own nature interferes with public business? It is necessary, then, to move beyond this private/public categorization, and instead search for a more accommodating meaning of religion. Perhaps the dichotomy between religion and a plural secular society is not based on realistic premises. But in order to dismiss this dichotomy son, it is necessary to rediscover the true meaning of "religion" in order to have a correct understanding of religious freedom, what it implies, and the guidelines that should be followed in order to protect it.

In the fourth place, any kind of overlapping consensus seems dangerous to religious institutions, for those trying to achieve the consensus, like the courts through the imposition of laws, will eventually replace the role of these religious institutions in society and in culture. This, as Iain Benson notes, has to be prevented.[240] Religious groups, in their rightful places in public debate, will not be arbitrary arbiters of values, but rather advocates for the values each hopes will foster human flourishing. Maybe it is time to turn away from the idea that society will eventually agree on the matters that most deeply divide individuals, and this may be an important step towards genuine freedom, especially religious freedom. Citizens can share the civic space and respect one another without having to agree with each other's beliefs, so that the focus should not be on convergence or creating consensus but, as Benson affirms, "on finding a *modus vivendi* or means of living together alongside those with whom there is disagreement."[241] At the same time, if citizens are willing and able to be in conversation with each other about the conditions in which they are to live, work, and raise their children, there has to be a setting where such exchanges can take place. Thus, the public square has to be a space where humans can instill the habits and virtues required for the survival and flourishing of free, democratic institutions

239. Cf. Neuhaus, *NPS*, 80.

240. Cf. Benson, "Freedom of Conscience and Religion," 163. He also notes that "the ideology of liberal pluralism has supplanted traditional religion in defining public purpose for political and legal institutions, *while the courts, in many ways, have replaced the church* as the conscience of the nation" (118).

241. Benson, "Freedom of Conscience and Religion," 162.

in a pluralistic society. Instead of a "public reason" aimed at attaining an "overlapping consensus," we might want an alternative public ethos, one of "robust democratic contestation" among different explicitly expressed worldviews.[242] This may result in producing acceptable overlapping agreement on public issues without improper exclusions.

In the fifth place, even though public discourse is essential to politics, it will be properly public discourse when each person is able to participate and express not what just happens to occur to him at the moment, but what he considers as true, as Hannah Arendt states.[243] This will make it possible to create a public realm that is vibrant, engaging, and meaningful, one that allows one to speak truthfully, expressing the truth as fully as possible. The reason is that what one deems as true matters to politics, and it needs to be spoken out publicly.

In the sixth place, a word should be said with respect to the notion of "postsecularism." While it is true that the contemporary context may be described as a postsecularist space as far as the state and certain elite groups are concerned, it is perhaps better understood overall as a period in which, for the first time, as Bretherton affirms, "*multiple modernities, each with their respective relationship to religious belief and practice, are overlapping and interacting within the same shared, predominantly urban spaces.*"[244] This is of extreme importance for our discussion. This means that, within such interactions in a pluralist society, any existing binary oppositions that tend to frame political relationships, be that "secular" and "religious," "tolerant" and "intolerant," "public" and "private," break down, and become useless when trying to understand what is really going on in our pluralistic democratic and liberal societies. At the same time, there is also a need to redefine the notion of public space, for it is not a monolithic reality in terms of languages and topics of discussion.

It is clear by now, then, that a philosophical approach to religious freedom cannot ignore the contemporary debate on the place of religion in public life. Yet, the debate seems to really have to do with the place of religious reasoning in the public political sphere. All these approaches employ a use of religion that refers to a dogma. Thus, it is necessary to clarify the meaning of religion. At the same time, even if restricting religious argument in public was the solution to the problems raised by a secular and pluralistic society, will a restriction on religious reasoning necessarily mean a restriction on religious

---

242. On this, see Smith, "Democratic Responsibilities," 128–29; Smith, *Stories of Peoplehood*.

243. Cf. Arendt, *Men in Dark Times*, 25.

244. Bretherton, *Contemporary Politics*, 15.

freedom or imply the denial of one's religious convictions? The fact that religious citizens have to translate their religious arguments to make them available to those citizens that do not share their worldview does not seem to be a direct violation of their religious freedom. There is an exception, however, and that is in cases where one is dealing with coercive laws that threaten religious citizens or institutions. This would mean a violation of their religious freedom if they were not allowed to provide religious arguments in order to defend their case. Taylor's position is the only one sympathetic to this kind of possible scenarios. For example, a coercive law that prohibits the use of alcohol will limit the ability of Catholic priests to consecrate wine in their ceremonies. While priests may argue from the point of view of history and tradition, ultimately it will be theological reasons that mandate it be fermented grapes they use for their ceremonies. Were they to appear before the Supreme Court, should their reasoning be limited to secular arguments? This poses a serious challenge to the theories proposed by Rawls and Habermas.

There is a need to clarify a few points, then. What is the meaning of religious freedom? Even more specifically, of what kind of freedom are we talking about, and what is meant by religion? Is religious freedom merely tolerance? All of these notions and elements should be first established in order to be able to offer an appropriate view on issues related to religious freedom, the foundations of religious freedom, the criteria that act as guiding principles in political deliberations regarding religion and religious freedom, and the place of religion as a public reality.

CHAPTER 2

History, Definitions, and Foundations of the Right to Religious Freedom

THE AIM OF THE previous chapter was to present the debate on the place of religion in the pluralistic secular liberal state. This chapter will present another important contemporary debate in which the term "religion" appears once again: the debate on religious freedom. I will explore the ways in which the notions of freedom and religion are employed.

In the first place, I will start with a brief presentation on the history of religious freedom. In the second place, since historically there has been some confusion in relating religious freedom to tolerance, or the justification against religious intolerance, I will proceed to present Rainer Forst's work on tolerance, which will help us determine that tolerance is not the same thing as religious freedom. In the third place, I will analyze contemporary definitions of, and legal documents on religious freedom in order to explore the ways in which the notion of religion is employed in these instances, as well as its relationship to the public sphere. In the fourth place, I will present two contemporary foundations of religious freedom: David Schlinder's interpretation of *Dignitatis Humanae,* and the work of John Courtney Murray. The analysis of these justifications will aim at revealing the use these authors make of the notions of religion, freedom, and the relationship of religious freedom to the public square. Finally, in light of the definitions and justifications of religious freedom and taking into account the notion of "religion" employed, I will ask whether it is necessary to establish a right to religious freedom.

Brief History of Religious Freedom

A historical account of religious freedom, and the arguments that were developed in its defense are beyond the scope of this work. Here I will only mention in a brief way the historical development of what later came to be known as the human right to religious freedom.

Tolerance during the Time of the Roman Empire

The history of religious freedom is a history that can be traced back to antiquity, even though the terminology was formed much later. In its beginnings, religious freedom was understood as intimately connected to the concept of tolerance. As tolerance, religious freedom meant the practice of the state allowing certain religious practices. It is a negative view, for tolerance has to do with something one has to endure. Cicero and Seneca are in fact the first one to mention "tolerance," and it is in the context of an evil to be endured, that is, tolerated.[1]

From a political perspective, and as Garnsey notes, toleration was in the Roman Empire chiefly a function of insight into the limits of imperial power, and at the same time into the strategic possibility of maintaining it.[2] Toleration could be revoked at any time by the one in power. Tolerance was also granted to different religious groups according to different degrees, depending on whether they were classified as dangerous, or there was a prospect of useful alliances.[3]

Christian religious practices, in contrast to the religious practices of other cults, were not tolerated in the Roman Empire during the first three centuries of its existence. The reason was that the exclusive character of the Christian faith and its refusal to worship the emperor as godlike were incompatible with the Roman order.[4] The Church Fathers demanded for toleration to the Roman emperor, and it is here that the phrase "religious

---

1. "Tolerantia" is found for the first time at around 46 BC Cicero employs it in his work *Paradoxa stoicorum* to designate the virtue characteristic of the wise man, the man of "enduring fate, and contempt for human affairs," be it pain, misfortune or injustice. Cicero talks about "tolerantia fortunae, rerum humanarum contemptione." See Cicero, *Paradoxa stoicorum*, in Cicero, *Oratore*, vol. IV, 278. AND in his *De Finibus Bonorum et Malorum*, Cicero places particular emphasis on the dignified endurance of pain. See Cicero, *On Moral Ends*, bk. 2, §94. Seneca, on his part, talks about the "brave endurance" ("fortis tolerantia") under the pain of torture, and as a "branch of bravery," one of the cardinal virtues. See Seneca, *Letters*, 5 and 10. Cf. Forst, *TC*, 36.

2. Garnsey, "Religious Toleration," 9.

3. Forst notes that "Such constellations reveal, on the one hand, that granting liberties in accordance with the permission conception generally rests on strategic considerations, but also, on the other, that in such contexts the essential arguments for more extensive toleration are developed by the victims of persecution and oppression who oppose the existing social order." See Forst, *TC*, 36–37.

4. Cf. Garnsey, "Religious Toleration," 9–10.

freedom" appears for the first time ("libertas religionis"). Tertullian, for example, elaborates an argument from fairness which he addresses to the emperor and in which he denounces the unequal treatment of the Christians in comparison to the other forms of worship and cults tolerated by the Roman Empire. Tertullian argues that Christians should be allowed to perform their own "religion," which here means a form of worship, not religion as a category in the modern sense of the term. He states: "Every province even, and every city, has its god. . . we alone are prevented having a religion of our own."[5] And in a letter to the African proconsul Scapula (212 AD) he explains:

> It is a fundamental human right, a privilege of nature, that every man should worship according to his own convictions: one man's religion neither harms nor helps another man. It is assuredly no part of religion to compel religion—to which free-will and not force should lead us—the sacrificial victims being required of a willing mind. You will render no real service to your gods by compelling us to sacrifice.[6]

The future discussion of toleration developed out of this debate generated by the persecution of Christians under the Roman Empire. Here, toleration on the part of the state was understood as a permission in order to be able to worship according to one's own conscience, and in this sense it was a "vertical toleration" on the part of the state.[7] At the same time, there developed a horizontal, intersubjective toleration between people of different faiths.[8]

---

5. Tertullian, *Apologeticus*, §24. Tertullian offers fundamental reasons: "For see that you do not give a further ground for the charge of irreligion, by taking away religious liberty, and forbidding free choice of deity, so that I may no longer worship according to my inclination, but am compelled to worship against it. Not even a human being would care to have unwilling homage rendered him."

6. Tertullian, *Scapulam*, §2.

7. Forst summarizes in four points the central arguments of the debate advanced by the Christian apologists and Church Fathers in defense of their faith and their church against persecution and discrimination in the Roman Empire. In the first place, the two-kingdoms doctrine means that temporal power does not have any authority in religious matters. In the second place, coercion is illegitimate in religious affairs because it leads to a merely enforced and hypocritical faith which cannot be pleasing to God. In the third place, compulsion is useless in religious matters because belief cannot be coerced but must come about and be adhered to voluntarily. In the fourth place, universal toleration is possible because religions which confine themselves to inner convictions and to forms of worship cannot harm one another. Cf. Forst, *TC*, 43–44.

8. For more on this, see Forst, *TC*, 44–46.

The Christian arguments for religious freedom were realized when the emperors Constantine and Licinius granted the Christian and the pagan cults extensive freedom of religion in the famous Edict of Milan of 313.[9] It was after this time that Augustine developed important arguments for toleration: toleration from love; the doctrine of the two kingdoms; the preservation of unity through toleration; and finally, the argument from freedom and the non-coercibility of conscience.[10]

Tolerance during the Middle Ages

During the Middle Ages, the arguments for toleration did not go beyond what was already proposed by Augustine. One would also have to keep in mind that the temporal and spiritual power were regarded as hierarchically ordered parts of the "body of Christ." This is seen especially in the empire of Charlemagne. This constellation, then, exerted a pervasive influence over the political and social order of medieval society. This explains why the expansion of the Christian faith and the interests of the Church were also interests of the state, and why heresy became a public crime ("crimen publicum"). The reason is that the stability of the faith determined the stability of the state.[11] The situation of the Jews in medieval society is an example of how tolerance was applied at the time. Jewish communities were tolerated exclusively through the granting of safety guarantees by the Church and by princes, and this probably for pragmatic reasons, as a useful evil. Thus, they were only permitted to engage in certain activities, especially trade and finance, which were advantageous for the institutions which granted the permissions.[12]

---

9. See "Edict of Milan," in Ehler and Morrall, *Church and State*, 5. The Edict of Milan was annulled in the Edicts of Thessalonica (380) and Constantinople (392), when Christianity was elevated to the state religion and pagan cults were prohibited even in private. See Lecler, *Toleration and the Reformation*, 44–45.

10. For more on this arguments, see Forst, *TC*, 48–55. Forst also argues that these arguments from Augustine were inverted so as to justify intolerance.

11. As stated in a thirteenth century German document: "Church and Empire being one and the same" ("Ecclesiam et Imperium esse unum et idem.") Cf. Lecler, *Toleration and the Reformation*, 70.

12. On this, see Stow, *Alienated Minority*, Ch. 10.

Humanist and Protestant arguments for Tolerance

During the time of the Reformation, the medieval spiritual-political order gradually dissolved.[13] This new cultural upheaval fundamentally transformed the cultural conditions of the discourse over toleration. Both humanism and Protestantism led to an advance in individualization in the religious domain. Humanism made this possible through a new consciousness of human freedom and dignity, while in Protestantism it was the emphasis on religious immediacy and inwardness. Thus, the fifteenth and sixteenth centuries are marked by a multiplication of forms of religious life and by a heightening of religious conflicts over the contents and institutions of the true faith. It is for these reasons, coupled with the so-called wars of religion, that Forst argues that the issue of toleration became one of the central questions of this period.[14]

The essential humanist justification of toleration was not primarily that toleration is required for the sake of religious unity, but that toleration is enjoined as an expression of an already existing unity among human beings through God's will. Thus, one finds the attempt to single out a universal religious faith which includes all human beings and which makes possible an agreement on essential articles of faith.[15] Erasmus, for example, developed a doctrine on tolerance based on the notion that all Christians share a central religious doctrine, and are now arguing about inessential matters; that the pursuit of heretics is absurd and dangerous; love and peace help overcome the differences between human beings and lead them to unity in God's truth; and finally, freedom of conscience.[16]

The limit of Erasmus's and other humanists' arguments for toleration, however, is that they do not work regarding the interpersonal relations between Christians and members of other religious groups.[17]

Protestantism, on the other hand, through the Reformation, marked a decisive turning point in the modern development towards the autonomy

13. This period saw the dissolution of the two main components of this medieval spiritual-political order: the subsumption of the human being into religious-ecclesiastical structures of thought and action, and the subordination of secular to spiritual power. Cf. Forst, *TC*, 96.

14. Cf. Forst, *TC*, 97.

15. This can be found among important representatives of Italian humanism, for instance in Ficino and Pico, but most of all in Erasmus of Rotterdam and, with a specifically political twist, in Thomas More. Cf. Forst, *TC*, 98.

16. Cf. Erasmus, *Christian Knight*, 206–10. Erasmus defended a thoroughgoing reform of the Church; however, he rejected the Reformation because it was incompatible with his ideal of the concord of Christians and a unified Church

17. Cf. Forst, *TC*, 107.

of religious individuality regarding ecclesiastical-doctrinal authority and towards the formation of a secular conception of the state. This eventually led to the separation between secular and spiritual or ecclesiastical authority.

Instead of emphasizing human dignity and freedom, as in humanism, Luther emphasized the worthlessness of human beings before God, their sinfulness, fallen condition, and contingency on God's mercy. Thus, Luther's conception of the state was closer to Machiavelli's, for whom secular power was grounded in the need to suppress human wickedness.[18] Luther regarded the impossibility to be saved through one's actions as the necessary condition of the true faith. Forst states:

> Insofar as the Reformation can be seen as a move towards the increasing independence of religious subjectivity and the emergence of freedom of conscience, therefore, it can be so only indirectly by dint of an almost paradoxical dialectic in which the radical, anti-humanist problematisation of the subjective will and its autonomy places human beings directly before God, and thus makes them independent of the traditional mediating role of the Church and its authority.[19]

Luther views freedom of conscience not as the freedom to follow one's subjective ethical convictions, but rather as the freedom from false doctrines and authorities, such as the sale of indulgences, which, according to Luther, establish false hierarchies among equal believers and give the false impression of a justification through external works.[20] Therefore, only the rejection of these doctrines of the Roman Church makes it possible for man to enjoy the true freedom of conscience in its reliance upon, and utter subjection to God.[21] Thus, the basis for Luther's central argument for toleration is found in his understanding of conscience not as an expression of religious subjectivism, but rather as the work of God.[22] The consequence is that conscience cannot and should not be coerced.[23] Later, Luther understands freedom of

---

18. Cf. Forst, *TC*, 116–17.
19. Forst, *TC*, 117.
20. Cf. Luther, *Captivitate*.
21. Cf. Forst, *TC*, 117–18.
22. Cf. Luther, "Before the Diet."
23. Luther, however, contradicted his view on conscience when opposed with increasing severity the Anabaptist revolts lead by Thomas Müntzer, when the uprising itself was legitimated using Protestant-Christian arguments. Thus, in 1531 he sided with Melanchthon, who demanded the death penalty not only for rebellious Anabaptists but also for those who, even though they remained peaceful, nevertheless disrupted the ecclesiastical order. See Skinner, *Foundations*, 73–80; Forst, *TC*, 121–22; Kamen, *Toleration*, 30–42; Münkler, "Politisches Denken," 648–55.

conscience as freedom from direct compulsion to believe. This is important to note, because according to this conception, it no longer includes freedom of worship. This will also have an important impact in the way that religion is understood: it will have to do more with faith, rather than with acts of worship. Accordingly, religious differences can be tolerated, if at all, inwardly and in private. This, according to Forst, anticipated the principle of the Religious Peace of Augsburg of 1555, the so-called *cuius regio, eius religio*, which also played a leading role in the foundation of the Lutheran national churches, which were subordinated to the sovereign prince.[24]

"Tolerance," then, was employed by Luther in a negative way, that is, as a rejection of "perpetual tolerance" regarding the stable coexistence of the reformed and the Catholic teaching. Luther also defended the expulsion of members of other Protestant movements and Jews, towards whom, in view of their insistence on their faith, Luther adopted an increasingly hostile stance.[25]

This becomes clearer when considering that, during the period of the Reformation, Luther, Zwingli, and Calvin used secular power as an instrument for the purposes of institutionalizing the Church and promulgating of the truth.

Other reformers did not follow suit, such as the "spiritualists" Hans Denck, Sebastian Franck, and Caspar Schwenckfeld. They took as their starting point the Lutheran liberation of conscience from its bondage by the Church and its dogmas, and interpreted the Christian faith in an undogmatic, spiritual-individualist, and almost mystical way. Their justifications of toleration and freedom of conscience, in contrast to Luther's, emphasized the idea of doctrinal toleration.[26] This gave rise to the development of a vertical state toleration, which, according to Forst, implied that no human authority can legitimately prescribe or promulgate a positive form of faith, for God's people are free, and God wishes neither a faith pressed into rules nor a coerced, hypocritical faith. Since faith is God's work, then it follows that the temporal power has no authority in this domain.[27]

---

24. Cf. Forst, *TC*, 122–23. In this way, a system of state churches was erected which blurred the boundary between secular and spiritual power, so that the highest office of the prince was to promote God's honor and to avert blasphemy and idolatry.

25. In fact, Luther called for the suppression of the Jewish faith and the expulsion of the Jews. See Bienert, *Luther und die Juden*.

26. Cf. Troeltsch, *Social Teaching*, vol. 2, 691–799.

27. Cf. Forst, *TC*, 124–25.

The European Civil Wars and the International Protection of Religious Freedom

As a result of the Protestant Revolution initiated by Luther, Western Europe was torn apart by religious strife during the civil wars of the sixteenth and seventeenth century, which disrupted the medieval unity of the "*Corpus Christianum*". These civil wars raging in France, England, the Netherlands, and the German Empire had an enormous impact, for they destroyed the religious and political unity of Europe, and caused the deaths of thousands, as the new nations states fought in order to find a new configuration. It is in this context that freedom of religion was the first human right that found legal basis in constitutions and treaties in Western Europe.

Malcom Evans notes how the international protection of religious freedom has passed through different historical stages.[28]

The first protection of the right to religious freedom in this period was the *cuius regio, eius religio* model. This originated in the Religious Peace of Augsburg (1555).[29] The main justification for this model was the sake of peace in view of the division in religious belief.[30] According to this model, however, it was only the prince Electors that enjoyed freedom of conscience, not their subjects. Thus, the religious-political unity lost by the empire was restored at the level of the individual territories, and thus strengthened the position of the sovereign princes.

International peace treaties provided for territorial separation of people of different religious denominations, keeping Catholics and Lutherans apart in different countries, and providing for toleration of dissidents and their right to emigration should a new faith be imposed in the territory of the prince.[31] Subjects who did not want to follow the profession of faith of their sovereign prince had to emigrate, except in the imperial cities with populations of mixed denominations. For them, the "modus vivendi," which entailed separation at the level of the empire, was interpreted as prescribing peaceful

---

28. See Evans, "Historical Analysis"; Evans, *Religious Liberty*, chs. 2–9. However, as John Witte has noted, many argue that, while religious rights were among the first to be recognized, they were historically among the last to be widely accepted at law. Cf. Van der Vyver and Witte, *Religious human rights in global perspective*, xxxiii.

29. Even though it was inspired by this treaty that a German jurist gave origin to the famous principle *cuius region, eius religio*, it did not take place till a century later.

30. Cf. "Religious Peace of Augsburg" (1555), in Ehler and Morrall, *Church and State*, 164–72.

31. The Peace of Augsburg applied only to the adherents of the Catholic faith and those of the Lutheran Augsburg Confession. Other denominations or groups were expressly excluded and could continue to be treated and punished as heretics.

coexistence inside the city walls. According to this model, then, toleration was a "modus vivendi" and an instrument of social discipline.[32]

Among the early codifications of freedom of religion and protection against religious intolerance was the founding document of the Republic of the United Netherlands, the *Union of Utrecht* of 1579. The document stipulated that no one was to be persecuted because of his faith. Shortly thereafter, the *Edict of Nantes*, signed by King Henry IV of France in 1598, granted the Calvinists Protestants (Huguenots) substantial rights, mainly with the intention to promote civil unity. The *Treaty of Westphalia* of 1648, in Germany, signified a new stage in the history of religious freedom.[33] The Treaty is in fact usually taken as the commencement of the modern era and an important point in the evolution of religious freedom within Europe.[34] Even though it built upon the Religious Peace of Augsburg, it improved the legal status of tolerated members of different faiths, granted the reformed (Calvinist) confession equal status with the Augsburg Confession, and guaranteed the right to freedom of religion in private, and equal rights in all other fields of public life, regardless of the individual's religious faith.

In France, meanwhile, the Edict of Nantes led political thought and action to became increasingly independent of religious authorities. This context provided the backdrop for the decisive further development in the discourse of toleration, which was triggered by fierce religious wars leading to a secular understanding of the state, which counterpart was the increasing autonomy of individuals. It was during this period that, once the traditional constellation of church and state had collapsed, the political question of how to uphold the unity of the state and to preserve peace became central. Thus, there developed a discourse of sovereignty and toleration as the only rational option for securing peace, where the sovereign was understood as an increasingly neutral authority situated above the religious denominations.[35]

---

32. Cf. Forst, *TC*, 131–32. He states: "Hence, toleration in the sense of a strategically and pragmatically motivated coexistence conception reigned between the principalities, whereas within the political units only a toleration in accordance with the permission conception was possible (a toleration of difference as long as it remained silent: *haereticus quietus*); here the principle of one faith in one country officially held sway."

33. Cf. Vermeulen, "Freedom of Religion," 9–10.

34. Cf. Evans, "Historical Analysis," 4.

35. Cf. Böckenförde, "Rise of the State," 33–38.

The Enlightenment and Religious Freedom

The religious and political conflicts from the seventeenth century led to an amplification of the modern discourse concerning toleration which reached its political-philosophical culmination in the works of Spinoza, Locke and Bayle.[36] It was at this time that a new and revolutionary concept of politics was introduced: an individual natural right to freedom of religion which precedes the state and, as a personal possession or birthright, cannot be alienated. In fact, it was argued that the state was created by individuals in order to protect their rights.[37]

From this philosophical perspective, tolerance is not seen as "permission" on the part of the state. Individual rights are understood to be natural and conferred by God, while the state is artificial, and therefore the practice of religion or one's beliefs are above what the state commands. Locke, for example, considers that tolerance is a public policy that obliges governments to grant individuals and groups within their domains the liberty to practice and profess their religion as they see fit, so long as by doing so they do not infringe upon the liberty of others, jeopardize the social welfare, or presume to exercise civil power.[38] This understanding of the concept of tolerance

---

36. Due to the length of this work, and the main topic, it would be beyond the scope of this book to present and analyze the thought of these authors regarding their idea of tolerance.

37. Spinoza, for example, like Hobbes, aims at undermining the foundations of religious intolerance, and regards sovereign power as the guarantor of this goal. At the same time, he stresses that the purpose of the state is to assure the citizens' freedom of thought and speech or, to be more precise, their freedom to philosophize. Cf. Forst, *TC*, 423–24; Smith, "Spinoza's Tractatus." Strauss, *Spinoza's Critique of Religion*. Rik Torfs presents the situation in a slightly different way. He agrees in that the ideas of the Enlightenment and of liberalism were characterized by the idea of state sovereignty combined with a respect for the freedom of the individual. But this required balance, for on the one hand, the sovereign was entitled to govern the state, while on the other hand, the individual might seem to have been left alone in the hands of the government. Therefore, human rights became a defensive mechanism in favor of the individual against the state. Cf. Torfs, "Contractual Religious Freedom," 141–42.

38. Cf. Locke, *Letter*. This work counts as the most important modern text on toleration, as it raises the arguments for toleration to a new philosophical level. Its originality lies primarily in that it liberates the familiar arguments for tolerance more fully than previously from their religious garb and lends them systematic form. However, Locke's understanding of tolerance is still narrow, as it does not leave room for atheists and Roman Catholics. That atheists should not be tolerated follows from Locke's understanding that the doctrines that God exists and that God ought to be worshipped are rationally demonstrable, and from these may follow that there is a true "religion," not merely a natural religion, but one consisting of positive doctrines revealed by God. Locke also excluded Catholics from toleration, perhaps because of the political situation at the time in England, for in a Papal Bull of 1570, Pope Pius V excommunicated

signaled the birth of a doctrine (liberalism), according to which individual rights exist prior to the state and political authority is established through a contract subject to conditions.[39]

Thinkers writing during the Enlightenment relied on existing justifications, and thus did not bring forth fundamentally new arguments for toleration. However, due to the social revolutions, these arguments were so radicalized in important respects that they acquired a new form. Voltaire's approach, for example, represents the clearest attempt to resolve dogmatic religious conflicts and the associated intolerance in the spirit of the ideas of the Enlightenment. He attempted to replace the "positive religions" with a deistic rational religion of inclusive unity. This rational religion would then incorporate the rational elements of all other religious groups.[40]

Forst identifies three main aspects present within the toleration arguments of the Enlightenment.[41]

In the first place, criticism of religious intolerance was increasingly levelled not only against the Church with its social privileges, which was seen as despotic, but also against what the Enlightenment authors called "positive religion" as such.[42]

In the second place, although the idea of a religiously impartial state acquired increased prominence, criticism is levelled primarily against the Church as an institution and its privileges and only secondarily against the

---

Elizabeth, declaring her to be deposed and freeing her subjects from the duty of allegiance to the heretic. That meant, in turn, that observant Catholics in England were from now on regarded as traitors and were persecuted. Even more, following the execution of Mary Stuart in 1587, Spain attempted unsuccessfully to conquer England and various conspiracies to murder the queen came to light. Catholics were then suspected of being in league with foreign powers. For more on this, see Lecler, *Toleration and the Reformation*, vol. 2, 365–75.

39. The name "liberalism" was attached later to this doctrine. It is important to note that liberalism, however, is not the creator of the notion of tolerance, as it is many times presented. What liberal authors did was to incorporate in an ingenious way a series of prior, especially Protestant, arguments for toleration, such as the two-kingdoms doctrine and the idea of freedom of conscience as bound to God alone. This mistaken view can be seen, for example, in Mendus, *Toleration*, 622–28; Macedo, "Toleration and Fundamentalism."

40. See Voltaire, *Treatise on Tolerance*.

41. Cf. Forst, *TC*, 266–68.

42. A "positive religion" is contrasted with "natural religion." Hegel, for example, in his *Positivity of the Christian Religion* (1795), describes positive religion as being contranatural or supernatural. It contains concepts and information transcending understanding and reason and requiring feelings and actions which would not come naturally to men. He argues that the feelings are forcibly and mechanically stimulated, and that the actions are done from obedience without any spontaneous interest. See Hegel, *Positivität*.

inadequate political legitimation of the authority of a monarch, provided only that he guarantees religious freedom and abolishes censorship.[43]

In the third place, the discourse concerning toleration in the Enlightenment is marked by an increasing awareness of the historical and cultural distinctiveness of the different nations. This involves, on the one hand, accepting the differences among moral conceptions, as well as among diferent religions and confessions. This allows for a form of criticism of one's own society in comparison to others and even from the perspective of others, which leads to a relativisation of one's own conceptions. On the other hand, this is also taken as a sign of the deeper unity of all positive religions at the core of a universal religion and an inclusive moral identity. Yet, there is also a growing criticism of tolerance as something merely granted by the political ruler. It is in this sense that Kant speaks of the "arrogant name of tolerance."[44] There is, then, as Forst argues, a move towards a different concept of tolerance, one in which citizens will be required to tolerate their religious differences.[45]

Religious Freedom in the United States and France

In the United States, the American Revolution emphasized a religious component in the justification of human rights. Among the rights that were put forward we find freedom of conscience or religion.[46]

The declaration of independence proclaimed by the Second Continental Congress meeting in Philadelphia on 4 July 1776, is considered to be on of the strongest expressions of a declaration of human rights: "We hold these truths to be self-evident, that all men are created equal, that they are endowed by their Creator with certain unalienable Rights, that among these are Life, Liberty and the pursuit of Happiness."[47] The state of Virginia had already published a constitution in 1776 which became the model for analogous declarations by individual states, for the amendments to the new constitution of the United States (1791), and for the French declaration of

---

43. On this, see Kant, "Enlightenment."

44. Kant, "Enlightenment," 21. Even though Kant did not devote any single writing to toleration, the problematic runs through his whole work.

45. Cf. Forst, *TC*, 269.

46. The context here was to fight for the independence of the individual states, and then, in a second step, to consolidate the political unity among the states and to secure the independence of the new federal state against foreign threats, without allowing social transformations. Note the contrast, then, with the context of the French Revolution.

47. United States, *Declaration of Independence*.

human and civil rights.[48] The Constitution of the State of Virginia states regarding freedom of religion:

> That religion, or the duty which we owe to our Creator, and the manner of discharging it, can be directed only by reason and conviction, not by force or violence; and therefore all men are equally entitled to the free exercise of religion, according to the dictates of conscience; and that it is the mutual duty of all to practice Christian forbearance, love, and charity towards each other.[49]

This declaration, however, reveals the precarious character of a religious justification of religious freedom, for it assumes that anyone who claims freedom of conscience also possesses a religious conscience.[50]

It was the American declaration of rights which served as the draft for the French "Declaration of the Rights of Man," proclaimed on 26 August 1798.[51] This Declaration had to fulfil a twofold task. On the one hand, it was supposed to set forth the "natural, unalienable, and sacred rights of man in order that this declaration, [be] constantly before all the members of the Social body."[52] On the other, it had to form an inherent part of the founding document of the sovereign nation of all citizens, whose common will now constituted the basis of all rights. Thus, the document included the natural rights of individuals as human rights prior to the state,[53] while at the same time these rights could have validity only as rights of citizens as members of the sovereign nation which governs itself through the common will.[54] Article 10 states: "No one may be disturbed on account of his

---

48. This influence is stressed by Jellinek, *Declaration*.

49. Quoted in Sheldon and Dreisbach, *Religion and Political Culture*, 138.

50. On this, see Forst, *TC*, 337-38; Berman, "Religious Freedom," 40-53.

51. See Rials, *Déclaration*. The context here, however, was totally different that in the United States. The actors of the French Revolution were faced with the task of mastering a more profound social and political transformation, which included the abolition of feudal rule, the privileges of the clergy, and the question of what role a king could continue to play in the new social order. See Colliard, *Déclaration*; Habermas, "Natural Law and Revolution."

52. Rials, *Déclaration*.

53. In Article 1 it states: "Men are born and remain free and equal in rights"; and in Article 2: "The aim of all political association is the preservation of the natural and imprescriptible rights of man."

54. Article 3 states: "The principle of all sovereignty resides essentially in the nation." Gauchet notes the dilemma that this position entails. This twofold perspective on the person as a human being and as a citizen, or on their rights as "natural" and "political" rights, involves a paradox, which at the same time contains the possibility of a new understanding of the political as well as the danger that this will lead to the well-known

opinions, even religious ones, provided their manifestation does not disturb the public order established by law."[55] Religious freedom, however, was interpreted as what Forst calls "permission toleration." According to this conception, the right to religious freedom is already fulfilled when minorities are tolerated, even though they may be far from enjoying equal status.[56] Nevertheless, there appears with a system of equal rights a form of toleration which calls for respect among citizens.[57]

In the nineteenth century, several treaties protecting religious freedom in the European states followed.[58] The task of the state was not to defend and guarantee a transcendent religious truth, but only to realize secular goals, such as the maintenance of peace and order, and the advancement of prosperity.[59]

Religious Freedom in the Twentieth Century

The twentieth century was dominated by profound political-ideological conflicts which led to two world wars and ended with a multitude of struggles and wars involving complex political and religious antagonisms that have perdured till our day.

The call for the protection of human rights was as urgent as in earlier times. After the horrors of World War II, and with the founding of the United Nations, protection against religious intolerance found its way into modern international standard setting. The international community made a valuable effort to protect human rights through international treaties and supranational bodies monitoring the observance of these treaties. Thus, freedom of religion was incorporated in the middle of the twentieth century onwards as part of international law, imposing on states a legal and political obligation for the protection of all people within their jurisdiction.[60] Of

---

aporia of liberty rights and popular sovereignty. The failure of the revolution, according to Gauchet, goes back to Rousseau's conversion of the freedom of each into the authority of all. Cf. Gauchet, *Révolution*, 200. See also Habermas, "Popular Sovereignty.»

55. Rials, *Déclaration*.

56. Cf. Forst, Forst, *TC*, 345–46.

57. Forst states that "it is now the mutual tolerance of the citizens as lawmakers which requires that they observe the criteria of reciprocity and generality in justifying laws and not bypass them by imposing the ethical values of a majority." Forst, Forst, *TC*, 346.

58. However, legal protection of religious freedom was still combined with legally stipulated privileges for certain Christian confessions.

59. Cf. Vermeulen, *Freedom of Religion*, 11.

60. Cf. Lindholm, "Religious Justifications," 28.

particular relevance are the *United Nations Charter* (1945), the *Universal Declaration of Human Rights* (1948), the *European Convention for the Protection of Human Rights and Fundamental Freedoms* (1950), the *International Covenant on Civil and Political Rights* (1966), the *Helsinki Accords*, and the *Declaration on the Elimination of All Forms of Intolerance and Discrimination Based on Religion or Belief* (1981).[61]

In its current historical form, then, freedom of religion is a universally applicable human right codified in international human rights instruments. And at the normative level, it is considered to be a fundamental right, for religious freedom protections are nonderogable. Human rights are not limited any more to the vertical relationship between individuals and the state. A new horizontal dimension of fundamental rights was introduced, and it became an important issue as well, as for example in the case of anti-discrimination norms applicable in private relationships.[62]

Rainer Forst on Tolerance, and Religious Freedom

The idea that religious freedom was conceived with the occasion of the wars that disrupted Europe in the sixteenth and early seventeenth centuries, as it was an effective solution to the problem, is a generalized misconception.[63] As we have seen above, the Enlightenment philosophers adapted existing justifications for toleration. Yet, even though the arguments were not new, they acquired a new form in the context of the social revolution that took place. A prime example is John Locke and his *Letter Concerning Toleration* (1689), which sought to develop a principled argument for religious tolerance and freedom in the West. Thus, since religious freedom has been many times understood as equivalent to tolerance, it is important to consider the notion of tolerance in a critical way. This will aid us to later question the notion of public realm and religion at work in contemporary debates.[64] In order to do so, I will present some considerations by the German philosopher Rainer Forst on tolerance,[65] and then will compare the notions of tolerance and religious freedom

---

61. For a summary of the steps taken in international law to guarantee freedom of religion, see Lerner, "Nature and Minimum Standards"; Tahzib, *Freedom of Religion*; Evans, *Religious Liberty*, 6–171.

62. See Torfs, *Religious Freedom*, 142.

63. See, for example, Zagorin, *Idea of Religious Toleration*.

64. See, for example, Leiter, *Why Tolerate Religion?*

65. Rainer Forst is professor of political theory and philosophy at the Goethe University in Frankfurt am Main, Germany.

Rainer Forst's Theory of Tolerance

It seems that the concept of tolerance has played a central role in pluralistic societies. Tolerance is commonly perceived as being based on reasons for coexistence in conflict. The truth, however, is that one of the distinctive features of tolerance is that it does not resolve, but merely contains and defuses, the dispute in which it is invoked.[66] At the same time, a critical examination of the concept of tolerance makes it clear that its content, or better its conception, is a contested matter, as there are different conceptions of tolerance and ways it was applied throughout processes of conflict. That is the reason why Forst argues that the concept of tolerance itself stands in conflict: "The meaning of toleration is not only unclear but also profoundly controversial, both in the history of the concept and in the present day."[67] In order to bring clarity, Forst presented a thorough reconstruction of the history of toleration and offered a novel understanding of the concept in his *Toleration in Conflict* (2003).[68] Forst states:

> 'Toleration in conflict' means that the parties to the conflict adopt an attitude of tolerance because they recognize that the reasons for mutual objection are counterbalanced by reasons for mutual acceptance which do not annul the former but nevertheless speak for toleration, or even require it. The promise of toleration is that coexistence in disagreement is possible.[69]

According to Forst, tolerance has three components: objection, acceptance, and rejection.[70] He states, in a debate he engaged with the American philosopher Wendy Brown, that if one tolerates something, it is because one must think it is wrong, otherwise one is indifferent about it. Tolerance presupposes an objection component. Yet, for tolerance to come up, there has to be a second component, that of acceptance. Forst states that "you have to find reasons why the things you believe are wrong or bad ought to be tolerated." And finally, there is a third component, that of rejection: "these beliefs or practices are bad to an extent that they cannot be tolerated.

---

66. Cf. Forst, *TC*, 1.

67. Forst, *TC*, 2.

68. His *Toleranz im Konflict* (2003) contains what may perhaps be the most complete account of the history of the notion of tolerance. On his work on tolerance, especially note Forst, *Toleranz im Konflikt*; Forst, *TC*; Forst, *JC*; Brown and Forst, *Power of Tolerance*. For a comprehensive overview of tolerance and the history of the concept, see Forst, *TC*, chs. 1–8.

69. Forst, *TC*, 1.

70. Cf. Forst, *JC*, 127.

So that is where the famous limits of toleration lie."[71] And in his *Justification and Critique*, Forst affirms:

> First, a tolerated belief or practice has to be judged as false or bad in order to be a candidate for toleration; second, apart from these reasons for objection, there have to be reasons why it would still be wrong not to tolerate these false or bad beliefs or practices—that is, reasons of acceptance. Such reasons do not eliminate the reasons of objection; rather, they trump them in a given context. And third, there have to be reasons for rejection that mark the limits of toleration. These limits lie where reasons of acceptance run out, so to speak. All three of those reasons can be of the same kind—religious, for example—yet they can also be of different kinds (moral, religious, pragmatic, to mention a few possibilities).[72]

Forst also argues that in respect to certain issues one should not employ the concept of tolerance, as for example with the case of "race." If I were to be tolerant of those that take a racist stance, that "would mean that you accept in a certain way the objections that a racist has against other people and just ask him to have additional reasons to be tolerant, that is, not to act on his racist impulses."[73] The right reaction, instead, is not to ask a racist to be tolerant, but rather to fight his racism.

Tolerance, as a skill in democratic citizens, is a way of reflecting on whether one's reasons for objecting to a practice that one thinks is wrong are sufficient to reject that practice if one were a law-making citizen. If it seems right to object to something, that is, that the practice is indeed wrong and that one's objection to it is not just because of one's own religious or ethical view or some traditional belief that cannot be generally justified in a pluralist society, then one needs to give an additional reason as to why the rejection component can be filled out by what one believes.[74] This is a similar approach to what Rawls and others demand about offering public reasons, that is, reasons that would be accepted by all. Forst states:

> The art of toleration is an art of finding proper reasons that can be presented to others when you think that they should conform to a norm that they don't agree with in their practices and

---

71. Brown and Forst, *Power of Tolerance*, 23–24.
72. Forst, *JC*, 127–28.
73. Brown and Forst, *Power of Tolerance*, 24. See also Forst, *TC*, 19–20; 402.
74. Cf. Brown and Forst, *Power of Tolerance*, 31.

beliefs. It consists in distinguishing your reasons for objection from mutually justifiable reasons for rejection.[75]

Forst insists in distinguishing between reasons for objection and reasons for rejection. These are two of the elements of tolerance, together with acceptance. Tolerance, then, for Forst, is related to the proper justification one can offer when objecting or rejecting something:

> My positive understanding of toleration is not . . . one of happily coexisting with each other and respecting each other as private individuals. It is also not one that is focused on rights. It is focused on the proper justifications that can be given for subjecting people to political and legal norms.[76]

The ideal within society, however, is not tolerance, but questioning and freeing oneself of the objection component found in tolerance.[77] The reason is that, even though tolerance is equated with recognition or respect, it may result in an attitude of domination. Forst affirms:

> Toleration can be based on mutual *recognition* and respect, and it can also be an expression of disrespect and *domination*, which, however, also figures as a kind of "recognition" of minorities. *Emancipation*, to mention the third concept in my title, can then at the same time mean to fight for and to fight against toleration, that is, to fight for and against certain forms of recognition.[78]

That is the reason why, during the Enlightenmnet, there was a growing criticism of tolerance as something merely granted by the political ruler, which led Kant to speak of the "arrogant name of tolerance."[79] For that reason, Forst introduces the idea of a limitation to tolerance in society:

> Toleration always implies, as I said, components of objection and of rejection. That is, there is an important normative negative judgment in place, and there is a limit to toleration. Toleration thus can never be a "complete" form of the positive recognition of the other's identity. And compared with such an ideal of recognition, toleration indeed implies an insult.[80]

---

75. Brown and Forst, *Power of Tolerance*, 31.
76. Brown and Forst, *Power of Tolerance*, 32.
77. Cf. Brown and Forst, *Power of Tolerance*, 38.
78. Forst, *JC*, 127.
79. Kant, "Enlightenment," 21. Even though Kant did not devote any single writing to toleration, the problematic runs through his whole work.
80. Forst, *JC*, 144.

Forst presents two meanings of tolerance: the "permission conception" and the "respect conception" of tolerance.

According to the "permission conception," toleration is a relation between an authority and a dissenting minority or minorities. Toleration understood as permission means that the authority gives qualified permission to the members of the minority to live according to their beliefs on the condition that the minority accepts the dominant position of the authority. Forst explains that as long as the expression of their differences remains within limits and "private," and as long as these groups do not claim equal public and political status with the majority, they can be tolerated on both pragmatic and normative grounds according to the permission conception. Forst states that a group can be tolerated:

> On pragmatic-strategic grounds because this form of toleration is regarded as the least costly of all possible alternatives and does not disturb civil peace and order as the dominant party defines it (but rather contributes to it), and on normative grounds because the authority may find it wrong (and in any case fruitless) to force people to give up their deep-seated beliefs or practices.[81]

According to this conception, then, toleration as permission means that the authority that has the power to interfere with the practices of the minority nevertheless tolerates it, while the minority accepts its dependent position. If one speaks in terms of the three components of toleration (objection, acceptance, and rejection), all three of them are being defined by the authority alone.[82] Forms of the "permission conception" of tolerance, for example, are the recognition of minorities by a majority, or those cases where the authority protects the minorities' basic security and liberty. Yet, Forst argues that his form of tolerance is still a complex form of power in a repressive and a productive mode.[83]

This notion of tolerance as permission is not only problematic, but also dangerous for individuals and associations that are the subject of toleration on the part of the state. At any time the state may revoke its permissons, with grave consequences for those affected. Forst affirms:

> The exercise of toleration on the part of 'the state' presupposes a dismissive judgement concerning the practices and convictions of certain individuals or groups who as a result are seen from

---

81. Forst, *JC*, 130.

82. Cf. Forst, *JC*, 130.

83. Cf. Forst, *JC*, 145. See also Forst, *TC*, 27–28. See also Beaman, "Tolerance and Accommodation."

the outset as 'politically different'; even if they are tolerated, on whatever grounds, they are not counted among the 'normal' citizens or they do not conform to the official norms, but are merely 'tolerated' citizens. Hence, the state functions as the supreme authority and simultaneously as an actor who, when it comes to a conflict of toleration, abandons its higher-level, neutral status by adopting the position of one side and merely tolerating the other side. In this way, however, it not only sacrifices its neutrality but also in a certain sense is intolerant because it takes sides and lays down particular norms that privilege one side.[84]

As a consequence, Forst rejects the idea of the "tolerant state." It is the citizens, Forst argues, that are the agents of tolerance, not the state. This view of tolerance has to do with interpersonal respect, what Forst terms the "respect conception" of toleration.

The "respect conception" of toleration, according to Forst, has a number of historical and normative roots. He states that:

> Its most plausible justification is the one that has recourse to a basic right to justification in combination with a theory of the difference between general knowledge, on the one hand, and ethical belief or religious faith, on the other, the latter being subject to reasonable disagreement.[85]

Thus, since one considers the others to be one's moral equals and fellow citizens, one knows that you owe them a fundamental form of respect, and that you owe them certain reasons for norms and institutions to which they are subject. The complexity here resides in the fact that one has to be able to hold onto one's ethical beliefs and yet partially relativize them in situations of an ethical disagreement about the good—and be tolerant, Forst affirms. And what this means in practice will naturally be heavily contested.[86]

Thus, according to the respect conception, people and communities or associations will see themselves as ethically autonomous authors of their own lives, while being legally equal. That means, according to Forst, that the basic structure of social and political life should be governed by norms which can be accepted by all citizens alike without privileging any single group or community. At the same time, the respect conception does not require that the tolerating parties must regard and value the others' conceptions of the

---

84. Forst, *TC*, 519. Forst notes the danger in taking sides. However, even more dangerous seems the fact that the state may take its own side, as for example if the secular liberal state tries to impose its own secular agenda on all citizens.

85. Forst, *JC*, 145.

86. Cf. Forst, *JC*, 145.

good as equally true and ethically good. It only requires that they should be able to view other people's conceptions as the result of independent choices or as not immoral. Thus, Forst argues that while the person of the other is respected, it is his convictions and actions that are tolerated.[87]

Tolerance and Religious Freedom

Forst considers religious freedom as a human right. He states that it is a right which "no human being can deny to others with good reasons," and thus, the principle of reciprocal and general justification underlies religious freedom "not just in a theoretical, but also in a practical sense."[88] Religious freedom, as any other human right, rests on the right to justification and expresses all of those rights that human beings can claim on this basis, not just in the procedural sense, according to Forst. It can be "traced back to respect for others as free and equal, but express this also in a political-legal, practical manner."[89] No human being could justifiably deny to others the right to religious freedom, and this standard of treatment protected by this right should be secured in a legitimate social order.

Forst makes an important contribution on religious freedom as based on the person's inner freedom, which should be always respected and legally protected. According to Forst's insight, any objection against religious freedom would never be properly justified, and for that reason religious freedom is not the object of tolerance. Yet, this does not seem to be that simple, as there are actions that are claimed to be religious, but which are nevertheless heavily contested, and should be rightly so. This is the case, for example, of actions deemed religious which denigrate the human person, such as genital mutilation, use of drugs in rituals, or different forms of abuse. There are also actions that directly attempt against human life, such as Satanit rituals that include human sacrifices. One can properly justify objections against these practices, so that they be banned and legally prosecuted. For that reason, if one were to uphold Forst's views on tolerance as respect among citizens, we should, in the first place, define what is meant by religious freedom and its proper sphere for action. Certain actions should never be tolerated, and Forst would certainly agree with that. Yet, what if the perpetrator of certain immoral actions claims he is acting prompted by his religion, and therefore argues that those actions should be protected instead? Should we offer some

---

87. Cf. Forst, *TC*, 30.
88. Forst, *JC*, 12.
89. Forst, *JC*, 12.

kind of respect tolerance? This is another reason why religious freedom and the meaning of religion must be clearly defined.

Nevertheless, even though we have not established the meaning of religious freedom, we may adopt Forst's distinction between tolerance as permission and tolerance as respect. We can state that religious freedom must never be taken as meaning any kind of permission on the part of the state. To do so would run the risk of endangering or restricting the freedom of citizens in regard to religious acts. Thus, if religious freedom is understood as religious tolerance, it then implies that religious exercise is a mere favour or privilege granted by the state. In this sense, one's religious acts are merely tolerated, but no more. As Paul Kauper explains:

> [R]eligious freedom is deemed to be not a concession or grant by the state but an indefeasible *right* of the person, which the government must recognize, respect and protect. *Religious liberty is not to be confused with religious tolerance.* Tolerance as a legal concept is premised on the assumption that the state has ultimate control over religion and the churches, and that whether and to what extent religious freedom will be granted and protected is a matter of state policy. Tolerance of minority religious groups and of nonconformists was *an important halfway step* in the struggle for religious liberty . . . But our constitutional system embodies the full-blown concept of religious freedom as a natural right which limits the government, rather than a *privilege* dispensed by governmental authority in pursuing a policy of benevolent toleration.[90]

There is room, however, for a "respect" conception of toleration among fellow citizens living in a pluralistic society. We should note, nevertheless, that the effort by individuals and communities to live out their freedom in a virtuous way, and to manifest their religiosity in a way that is in accordance with reason, should never be the object of toleration. A virtuous way of life should never be the object of tolerance, as there is no objectionable element in such a lifestyle. A respect tolerance refers to the fact that one may not agree with one's neighbor's faith, and the ways in which he performs religious acts, for example. It is only aspects like these which might be the object of tolerance as respect on behalf of fellow citizens.

Thus, even though tolerance as a virtue is obviously important in pluralistic contemporary societies, it is a concept that should not be understood

---

90. Kauper, "Legal Aspects," 25. Gamwell is also of the opinion that toleration is not a coherent resolution to the modern political problematic of a plurality of religions. See Gamwell, *Meaning of Religious Freedom*, 39.

as "permission" when it comes to the exercise of religion by virtuous citizens. In the following chapters, it will become clearer later that religious freedom and tolerance should not be considered as the same category. Even more, we will explore the meaning of religious freedom and see that it is not a matter of accommodation or toleration on behalf of the state.

Definitions of Religious Freedom

One of the first obstacles one faces in an investigation of religious freedom, and which perhaps is at the root of all the debates and disagreements that have followed, is that there are different opinions on what religious freedom means and entails. A sound definition should at least qualify what is meant by "religion," and which are the essential rights and liberties of persons in relation to "religion." At the same time, in elaborating the meaning and definition of religious freedom, the result should be independent from any historically given political community or political system, for religious freedom in itself is not dependent on the constitution of any political system, even though in practice, religious freedom should enjoy constitutional protection in order to ensure it is respected by all.[91]

I will especially stress in this section the way in which the notion of religion is taken, for it will greatly influence one's conception of religious freedom. Thus, in the first place, I will first present various definitions of religious freedom offered by authors such as John Courtney Murray, Christoph Engel, Rex Ahdar and Ian Leigh. In the second place, I will present the mentions of religious freedom found in various international and legal documents. Finally, I will offer an evaluation of these definitions.

Contemporary Definitions of Religious Freedom

The American theologian and philosopher John Courtney Murray (d. 1967), tackled most of the problems that preoccupied Americans since 1945. Of these problems, Murray gave great attention to the difficulties of intercredal cooperation in religiously pluralistic America. For that reason, he devoted himself to the study and defense of religious freedom as a civil right. Murray is considered to have developed a complex, coherent, and historically sophisticated defense of religious freedom, which will be presented in the next section.

---

91. Gamwell notes, for example, that one should avoid presenting religious freedom as coherent by reason of its being coherent within the constitution of a political community. See Gamwell, *Meaning of Religious Freedom*, 13.

In his *The Problem of Religious Freedom* (1965), Murray defines religious freedom in terms of freedom of conscience, and as immunity from all external coercion. He states:

> In its juridical sense, freedom of conscience is the human and civil right of the human person to immunity from all external coercion in his search for God, in the investigation of religious truth, in the acceptance or rejection of religious faith, in the living of his interior religious or nonreligius life. In a word, it is the freedom of personal religious decision. This freedom is essentially social.[92]

Murray claims that the state acts as a corporate person, which then demands the noninterference in the practice of religion of one's choice. For that reason, Murray insists on a negative notion of religious freedom, that is, as immunity from all external coercion. Murray even highlights this aspect as the essential element of religious freedom, for according to him, the very question of religious freedom concerns the limits of public power in religious matters.[93]

Murray also distinguishes the social aspect of the free exercise of religion as "ecclesial or corporate religious freedom." This is the right of religious communities within society to corporate internal autonomy.[94] This freedom, he states, is the corporate counterpart of personal freedom of conscience.[95] Thus, religious freedom is properly, for Murray, the right of a religious community, which in the person is described as freedom of conscience.

There are a few issues we should note regarding Murray's definition of religious freedom.

The reason why, according to Murray, people and religious groups enjoy religious freedom is because the state acts as a corporate person which demands the noninterference in the practice of religion of one's choice. However, Murray's meaning of nonintervention is very broad and vaguely defined. He does not identify the proper sphere or spheres that belong to the

---

92. Murray, *Problem of Religious Freedom*, 24.

93. Cf. Murray, "Arguments," 238–41.

94. Murray distinguishes two general areas of religious freedom as a corporate right. The first aspect includes the internal affairs of a community: its organization, manner of government, worship, the erection of churches, possession of property, and the selection, training, appointment, and transferal of ministers. The second area is that of the external action of the community: the public witness to its own faith as such, and its further witness to the values of its faith in their relation of the affairs of the temporal order. Cf. Murray, "Church and State," 590.

95. Cf. Murray, *Problem of Religious Freedom*, 25.

religious freedom of individuals and the sphere of the state. Therefore, he fails to clarify to which sphere he is referring to when affirming that the state has no jurisdiction upon religious practices. According to Murray, the state acts as a corporate person; however, one may question whether it is in relation to other persons, or other "corporate persons," such as religious institutions recognized as such. Another consequence is that if religious freedom means "ecclesial or corporate religious freedom," he is presupposing that these groups have been recognized by the state as "corporate persons." What about groups and religious communities which have not been granted this status, or individuals acting on their own according to their conscience?

Another problem with Murray's definition is that the religious freedom of the person is understood as freedom of conscience. The reason why he identifies these two rights, perhaps, is because Murray understands religion as a system of beliefs that needs to be protected. If what is in need of protection is one's belief or faith, then he is right in assigning it to freedom of conscience. However, this would leave no room for freedom of religion for the human person as such. Religious freedom would only belong to recognized religious corporations. This, then, would lead to innumerable problems, for a group would not claim a religious legal status unless its members would unite themselves in order to practice and perform the acts that they considered to be religious, and which they perhaps already practice and perform in the privacy of their lives. These citizens may decide to unite with others in order to find encouragement and support within the setting of a community.

Christoph Engel, in his article "Law as a Precondition for Religious Freedom" (2012), provides two definitions of religious freedom: as a social reality, and as a constitutional guarantee. In the first place, as a social reality religious freedom characterizes a society in which everyone is in principle free to hold the religious beliefs of their choosing, and to live their lives in line with the commands of their religions. The second meaning is doctrinal, and it refers to the protection of religious freedom by the Constitution. Thus, the Constitution obliges government to act in a way that makes peaceful coexistence practical. To that end the Constitution guarantees freedom of religion as a fundamental right.[96]

We may point out a few issues with Engel's understanding of religious freedom. In the first place, Engel's definition of religious freedom is both vague and problematic. He identifies two stages or spheres were religious freedom is played out: in society and in constitutional law. Engels description of religious freedom as a social reality is not just too vague, but also seems to identify it with freedom of conscience. What is the need for religious

---

96. Cf. Engel, "Religious Freedom," 395.

freedom, then? In the second place, Engel does not clarify which one is the proper sphere of religious freedom within society. In the third place, there is also a problem with his understanding of religion as well, for it is taken to mean a belief. If religion is the same as belief, and one is to hold the religious beliefs of one's choosing, and to live one's life in line with its commands, then we should instead speak about problems of conscience and its protection. And this is where the problem just begins because, according to Engel's second definition of religious freedom as a doctrine, the government, in order to make religious freedom possible, has to, through the law, create a space for the practical peaceful coexistence of "religions."[97] Yet, in reality, the commands and beliefs of some religious groups are incompatible with the commands and beliefs of other groups at different social and political levels. Thus, when religion is seen as meaning a belief or dogma, the state and governments get tangled in very complicated issues, such as having to potentially judge between "religions" as being more or less plausible, more or less legitimate, based on the substance of what they teach.

Similar problems can be noted in Rex Ahdar and Ian Leigh's consideration on the particular facets of the concept of religious freedom. In their article "Is Establishment Consistent with Religious Freedom?" (2003), they distinguish between the internal and external dimensions of religious freedom:

> Internal religious freedom, as a purely internal freedom to believe, has sometimes been described as an "absolute" religious freedom. The external dimension can be divided into positive religious liberty and negative religious liberty. Positive religious liberty is the freedom to actively manifest one's religion or belief in various spheres (public, private, etc.) and in a variety of ways (worship, teaching, and so on). . . . Negative religious liberty is the freedom from coercion or discrimination on the ground of religious (or nonreligious) belief.[98]

There are a few issues with their definition of religious freedom. In the first place, internal religious freedom is understood as freedom to believe, which means that religion is understood as a system of belief. We should rather speak of freedom of conscience. In the second place, and as a consequence of their understanding of internal religious freedom, positive religious freedom is understood as the protection of a belief that should be

---

97. Engel talks about the protection of religious freedom by the constitution of a country, which however is not the case in every nation. It would be more precise to talk about legal protection instead.

98. Ahdar and Leigh, "Religious Freedom?," 650–51.

manifested in various spheres and ways. At the same time, there is no clarification in what is meant by the private and public spheres in which belief should be manifested. This could lead to the unsolvable problem of how to deal in a practical way with plurality of beliefs. If this is what religious freedom means, then religious freedom entails a problem for the peaceful coexistence of religious groups, as instead it will just lead to controversy and dissent. In the third place, if religious freedom is understood as freedom from coercion, as Murray does, it will rather belong to freedom of conscience to protect what one believes to be the truth, so that there seems to be no need to establish a human right protecting freedom of religion. In the fourth place, Ahdar and Leigh acknowledge that positive religious freedom, being a social freedom, is subject to certain limitations to preserve social order and the rights of other citizens. Yet this contradicts their claim that, as a negative right, religious freedom is the freedom from coercion or discrimination on the ground of religious (or nonreligious) belief. Thus, to understand religious freedom as protection of belief is problematic, and it leads to unnecessary dilemmas.

David Novak, in his book *In Defense of Religious Liberty* (2009), also takes "religion" to mean a belief system, which leads to the aforementioned problems found in the previous definitions of religious freedom. He is of the opinion that negative religious freedom, or the noninterference by the state, protects not just those who want to practice their own religion (freedom *for* religion), but also the freedom from the imposition of any religion either by the state or any private person or group (freedom *from* religion).[99] If this is the meaning of religious freedom, then it seems to be unnecessary, for the protections mentioned by Novak are already covered by freedom of conscience. One can argue that religious freedom is a special case, for it refers to a "religious belief." However, that would open the door to innumerable problems, for then the state, in the constitutional or legal protection of religious freedom, would have to be the one deciding what is to be considered as a religious belief.

Frederick Gamwell, in his book *The Meaning of Religious Freedom* (1995), understands religious freedom as the solution to pluralism in contemporary liberal societies, for it insists on the plurality of religions, and it proscribes certain state activities. According to him, religious freedom is a political principle by which "a plurality of legitimate religions internal to a political community is consistent with its unity."[100] Gamwell argues that society faces a multitude of comprehensive questions, and every "religion"

---

99. Cf. Novak, *In Defense of Religious Liberty*, 9.
100. Gamwell, *Meaning of Religious Freedom*, 10.

will provide an answer. For Gamwell, in fact, religion is defined as the answer to a comprehensive question, so that religious freedom means "the political expression of the comprehensive question."[101] A society in which there is a plurality of religions will thus be politically unified in principle through a full and free debate. Since the political community cannot give one answer, for it would mean the establishment of a single religion, religious freedom will solve the problem by allowing a free political discourse, that is, "a free discussion and debate that includes differing religious convictions."[102] This, according to Gamwell, will provide an answer to what he considers Rawls's failed attempt. The problem, once again, is that religion here is taken to mean a system of belief. Since there are many systems of belief, a plurality of "religions," it is necessary to open the space to debate so that, by giving everyone a voice, unity will be manifested in the freedom to express one's own faith, religion, or comprehensive answer, all of which seem to be the same for Gamwell.

Thomas Reese, in his article "Religious Freedom is a Fundamental Human Right" (2014), identifies religion with a belief system. However, he states that freedom of religion protects not only one's choice to believe, but even the choice not to believe in anything. This seems an evident contradiction, for religion is not only understood as a belief, but also as the denial of a belief. He states:

> What is religious freedom? The first point to be made is that religious freedom is not just for believers. It also includes nonbelievers. Properly speaking, it is "freedom of religion or belief." It protects a person's right to hold or not hold any religion or belief. So religious freedom must also protect the atheist.[103]

The atheist would be surprised, and probably shocked, to hear that his intellectual position is a belief or religion to be protected. The problem, once again, is found in what is understood by "religion," which directly influences what is meant by religious freedom.

---

101. Gamwell, *Meaning of Religious Freedom*, 38.

102. Gamwell, *Meaning of Religious Freedom*, 35. Gamwell also affirms: "Religious freedom means a free political discussion and debate among answers to the comprehensive question" (p. 161).

103. Reese, "Religious Freedom".

Definitions of Religious Freedom in International and Legal Documents

I will present in this section the definitions of religious freedom provided by some of the most important international and legal documents on the subject: The *Universal Declaration of Human Rights* (1948); "Article 9" of the *European Convention for the Protection of Human Rights and Fundamental Freedoms* (1950); The Vatican Council II's *Declaration on Religious Freedom Dignitatis Humanae* (1965); the *International Covenant on Economic, Social and Cultural Rights* and the *International Covenant on Civil and Political Rights* (1966); the *Declaration on the Elimination of All Forms of Intolerance and Discrimination Based on Religion or Belief* (1981). Given the impact it has had on the understanding of religious freedom, I will mention the notion of freedom of religion as found in the First Amendment of the United States *Constitution* (1791).

The aim of this section is to see whether these documents provide a clear meaning of religion in their definitions of religious freedom, and whether they identify a space or sphere where religious freedom belongs to, especially in connection to the due limits that governments may impose on religious freedom as a human right.

Universal Declaration of Human Rights (1948)

After the traumas of the Second World War, the United Nation's *Universal Declaration of Human Rights* (1948) was the first global expression of rights to which all human beings are inherently entitled. The *Declaration* has been taken as a model for subsequent declarations, and the model of many Bills of Rights entrenched in the Constitutions of countries that have become independent since then. In fact, this declaration is considered to be one of the most authoritatively legal articulation of religious freedom as a right.[104] "Article 18" states:

> Everyone has the right to freedom of thought, conscience and religion; this right includes freedom to change his religion or belief, and freedom, either alone or in community with others and in public or private, to manifest his religion or belief in teaching, practice, worship and observance.[105]

---

104. See Durham et al., *Freedom of Religion*, xxxvii.
105. United Nations, *Human Rights*, 4.

"Article 18" consists of three parts. Firstly, it guarantees what is generally described as the *forum internum*, that is, it protects the right to freedom of thought, conscience and religion. Secondly, it addresses conversion and religious proselyting. Thirdly, it addresses the *external forum*, that is, the manifestation of religious freedom. The exercise of this right and freedom, however, is subject to certain limitations. "Article 29.2" reads:

> In the exercise of his rights and freedoms, everyone shall be subject only to such limitations as are determined by law solely for the purpose of securing due recognition and respect for the rights and freedoms of others and of meeting the just requirements of morality, public order and the general welfare in a democratic society.[106]

There are a few remarks to be said about the notion of religious freedom found in the *Universal Declaration*.

In the first place, the enunciation of the right in "Article 18" opens the door to confusion and misunderstandings, as it seems to say that freedom of thought, conscience, and religion are all protected under the same right. Are thought, conscience and religion species of a more general category, or different ways to express the same human reality, or three different human rights? From the description of what the right includes, it seems that thought, conscience and religion are all aspects of one and same reality.

In the second place, we should note that religion is understood as belief. In fact, the *Declaration* talks about freedom to change or manifest one's own "religion" or "belief." Why not just declare a protection of freedom of conscience, then? It seems that this would suffice, especially since religion is understood as belief, which has to do with matters of knowledge. The framers of this *Declaration* were certainly right in acknowledging the religious aspect of man, and the necessity to protect its manifestations. However, by stating that religion is a belief, it seems that they are leaving out a host of other actions considered to be religious in themselves. There are many religious people that, even when their religious group adheres to a certain faith or belief, do not know well their faith or content of teachings. This definition would not accommodate those that are religious but adhere to no faith content whatsoever either. At the same time, such definitions of religious freedom as freedom to believe or profess one's faith may be one of the main reasons why the debate on the place of religion in the public square is understood as the public political manifestation of one's own faith or belief. If

---

106. United Nations, *Human Rights*, 6. That means, as Finnis interprets it, that even though these rights are inalienable, are nevertheless subject in their exercise to various limitations. Cf. Finnis, *Natural Law*, 213.

religion is a belief, as the *Declaration* affirms, then there are so many beliefs people can profess, that it will be impossible to reach an understanding on the ordering of society and the political sphere based on everyone's views or faith. What we all humans have in common is reason, not faith, and it is based on reason that one should debate issues of public political concern. However, if religion is faith, then "religion" will be inevitably left aside, which does not seem right either. The problem, then, is found in that the notion of "religion" that is being employed leads to contradictions in the public political forum: one the one hand, religion as faith must be protected; on the other hand, the ordering of political life cannot be based on one's faith or religion in detriment of other groups. This leads to the problem of pluralism and the search for a common consensus. For that reason, it is argued that religion must be left aside when it comes to the public political forum and the decisions that should be made, especially those of a coercive nature, such as laws. Unless the terms are clarified, then, the debate will continue to revolve around this vicious circle.

In the third place, in "Article 29.2," which concerns the limitations of rights, the *Declaration* fails to identify the proper space or sphere that belongs to the right identified as freedom of thought, conscience, and religion. At the same time, even though it states that the law can only limit the right to religious freedom in order to secure due recognition and respect for the rights and freedoms of others and to meet the just requirements of morality, public order and the general welfare in a democratic society, the *Declaration* does not offer any guidelines in order to identify what those just requirements are. This is a serious deficiency.

European Convention for the Protection of Human Rights and Fundamental Freedoms (1950)

Meeting in Rome in November 4, 1950, the ministers, representing member states of the Council of Europe, signed a *Convention for the Protection of Human Rights and Fundamental Freedoms*, which went into effect on September 3, 1953. "Article 9" of the *European Convention for the Protection of Human Rights and Fundamental Freedoms* (1950) mentions freedom of thought, conscience and religion. It states:

> 1. Everyone has the right to freedom of thought, conscience and religion; this right includes freedom to change his religion or belief and freedom, either alone or in community with others

and in public or private, to manifest his religion or belief, in worship, teaching, practice and observance.

2. Freedom to manifest one's religion or beliefs shall be subject only to such limitations as are prescribed by law and are necessary in a democratic society in the interests of public safety, for the protection of public order, health or morals, or for the protection of the rights and freedoms of others.[107]

The first part of section 1, guarantees the inviolability of the "forum internum," that is, inner freedom: freedom of thought, conscience, and religion, and freedom to change one's religion or belief. The second part protects freedom to manifest one's religion "in foro externo." There is also a restriction on actions, which seems to presuppose a traditional understanding of what counts as religion and religious manifestations: "worship, teaching, practice and observance." Section 2, on the other hand, opens the possibility to restrictions, but only with respect to the external expressions of thought, conscience, and religion.[108]

One can identify in this "Article 9" the same problems found in the *Universal Declaration*'s definition. Religion is understood as a belief, and that the notions of public and private sphere, where this right is being exercised, are not identified.

Vatican Council II's *Declaration on Religious Freedom Dignitatis Humanae* (1965)

The Vatican Council II's *Declaration on Religious Freedom Dignitatis Humanae* (1965), even though not an international and legally binding document, has had a lasting impact on the subject, especially within the context of Catholic theologians' discussions on the subject. In this *Declaration*, the non-coercion aspect of religious freedom is stressed out in the first place. It states:

> This freedom means that all men are to be immune from coercion on the part of individuals or of social groups and of any human power, in such wise that no one is to be forced to act in a manner contrary to his own beliefs, whether privately or publicly, whether alone or in association with others, within due limits.[109]

---

107. Council of Europe, *Convention*, 10–11.
108. Cf. Vermeulen, "Freedom of Religion," 12–13.
109. Vatican Council II, *DH*, n. 2.

This element of non-coercion is founded on the fact that man is impelled by nature to seek religious truth, according to which man orders his whole life. Thus, the *Declaration* adds a new aspect to the definition of religious freedom: the search for the truth, especially religious truth. It states:

> It is in accordance with their dignity as persons—that is, beings endowed with reason and free will and therefore privileged to bear personal responsibility—that all men should be at once impelled by nature and also bound by a moral obligation to seek the truth, especially religious truth. They are also bound to adhere to the truth, once it is known, and to order their whole lives in accord with the demands of truth.[110]

The *Declaration* makes the argument that man is able to do so only if he enjoys immunity from external coercion as well as psychological freedom. Thus, the right to religious freedom has its foundation in the very nature of the human person. In conclusion, it states that "the right to this immunity . . . and the exercise of this right is not to be impeded, provided that just public order be observed."[111]

From *Dignitatis Humanae*'s definition, we can point out that "religion" is once again understood as a belief, with all the problems that follow from this understanding. Religious freedom is therefore understood as the search for religious truth. On the other hand, it is interesting that the Declaration does not affirm that it is a duty of the state to uphold. It only states that all men are to be immune from coercion within due limits. These due limits, however, are not identified, and no guiding principles are offered as to establish the proper sphere of religious freedom.

International Covenant on Civil and Political Rights (1966)

The United Nations took another step in identifying and protecting religious rights when it promulgated the 1966 *International Covenant on Economic, Social and Cultural Rights*, and the 1966 *International Covenant on Civil and Political Rights*. The latter document is one of the most important universal treaties on human rights, and it is in fact the only binding treaty specifically containing a more articulated explanation of what religious freedom entails. "Article 18" reads:

> 1. Everyone shall have the right to freedom of thought, conscience and religion. This right shall include freedom to have

---

110. Vatican Council II, *DH*, n. 2.
111. Vatican Council II, *DH*, n. 2.

or to adopt a religion or belief of his choice, and freedom, either individually or in community with others and in public or private, to manifest his religion or belief in worship, observance, practice and teaching.

2. No one shall be subject to coercion which would impair his freedom to have or to adopt a religion or belief of his choice.

3. Freedom to manifest one's religion or beliefs may be subject only to such limitations as are prescribed by law and are necessary to protect public safety, order, health, or morals or the fundamental rights and freedoms of others.[112]

One should note that, once again, we find under the same heading the right to freedom of thought, conscience and religion. Religion is also understood to mean a system of beliefs. This religion or belief can be manifested in worship, observance, practice and teaching. What is problematic with this exposition, besides employing a confusing and unclear notion of "religion" as a belief, is that the sphere where this right can be exercised is not specified either. The Convenant talks about ways in which religious freedom may be manifested, such as in worship, observance, practice and teaching. Nevertheless, one finds in paragraph 3 that this freedom is subject to limitations in order to "protect public safety, order, health, or morals or the fundamental rights and freedoms of others." The problem here is rooted in a confusing notion of "religion," and in not assigning the proper stage that belongs to each of the different ways in which what is understood as religion may be manifested. There is a need to establish a clearer understanding of religion and its proper sphere of action, for it would make it easier for the law to prescribe the proper limits to the ways in which freedom of religion may be manifested, while distinguishing it from freedom of thought and conscience.

Declaration on the Elimination of All Forms of Intolerance and Discrimination Based on Religion or Belief (1981)

On November 25th, 1981, the General Assembly of the United Nations proclaimed the 1981 *Declaration on the Elimination of All Forms of Intolerance and Discrimination Based on Religion or Belief*, which although not binding, is presently the most important global instrument regarding religious rights, and therefore implies an expectation of observance. "Article 1" reads:

112. United Nations, "Covenant," 178.

1. Everyone shall have the right to freedom of thought, conscience and religion. This right shall include freedom to have a religion or whatever belief of his choice, and freedom, either individually or in community with others and in public or private, to manifest his religion or belief in worship, observance, practice and teaching.

2. No one shall be subject to coercion which would impair his freedom to have a religion or belief of his choice.

3. Freedom to manifest one's religion or beliefs may be subject only to such limitations as are prescribed by law and are necessary to protect public safety, order, health or morals or the fundamental rights and freedoms of others.[113]

As with the previous declarations, the understanding of religion here is equated to belief. The title itself talks about "religion or belief," as if the two were one and the same reality. The Declaration also lacks a specification on the proper sphere of action of what is understood as religion or belief. Thus, the Declaration does not offer any guidance with respect to the limitations this right may be subject to.

The First Amendment of the U.S. Constitution (1791)

In the First Amendment of the U.S. Constitution (1791) there are two mentions of "religion": "Congress shall make no law respecting an establishment of religion or prohibiting the free exercise thereof."[114] In the first participial phrase, the Constitution prohibits the government from establishing a "religion," that is, giving a "religion" or belief system a special official recognition or protection. In the second participial phrase, the Constitution prohibits the government from infringing the "free exercise" of "religion." American constitutional lawyers are aware that there is a conflict between these two "clauses," for the first of these clauses often conflicts with the second.[115] What they seem not to be aware of, is that the meaning of "religion" is different in both uses of the word. In the first case, "religion" is employed as meaning a belief system, so that government will not recognize any of the many belief systems present in the country as the official "religion" of the State. In the second use, "religion" is employed in order to signify the acts that are considered to be religious, so that the government will never infringe the

---

113. United Nations, *Human Rights*, 151.
114. United States, *Constitution*.
115. See, for example, Jeffries Jr. and Ryan, "Establishment Clause."

exercise of religion. There is here a serious contradiction that once again makes it clear that there is a need to redefine the terms of what is meant by religion and religious freedom.

Evaluation

It is a shortcoming in all these definitions of religious freedom that the notions employed are not clearly defined, and therefore open the way to confusion and misunderstandings on what religious freedom truly is.

In the first place, the notion of religion as belief is very problematic, for what one claims as a faith may differ immensely from what someone else considers the truth to be. "Religion" is being employed to designate so many different things, such as different beliefs, that if one equates religion to a belief, then the notion of religion is not useful anymore in order to find the proper meaning of religious freedom. Besides, in dealing with religious freedom, the state will have to necessarily mingle with questions of faith, then, for it will have to adopt a concrete understanding of religion as belief, and there are so many beliefs that in a pluralistic society this debate will never end. One can argue that religion is used as a category to refer to all belief systems. However, religion is also employed to refer to a number of different religious acts that are distinct from belief, even if these actions are motivated by one's own faith. It will be necessary, then, to better define what is meant by "religion." If religion is not the same as one's faith or belief, then it will have an impact on the way religious freedom is seen to be connected to personal freedom of conscience and to live according to the commands of one's own faith.

In the second place, definitions of religious freedom fail to assign the proper space or stage, in the public or private sphere, for the exercise of religious freedom. Thus, when it is affirmed that religious freedom entails immunity from external coercion, that is, the noninterference by the state either in prohibiting or enforcing the practice of religion, except in what respect social order, morals, and respect for the freedom of others, one may encounter contradictions in its concrete application. This problem is a consequence of not employing a clear notion of religion, for doing so will be helpful in establishing the stage that properly belongs to acts that are considered to be religious. Once the acts that belong to religion and their proper space of action are identified, it will be easier to see whether what a group or individual claims as "religion" should be respected, or if respected, whether it is the proper space for performing it.

Contemporary Justifications of Religious Freedom

I will now proceed to present some recent and contemporary foundations and arguments that support a human right for religious freedom. We will see whether these arguments clarify what is meant by religious freedom and its place in the public square.

The literature on the right to religious freedom is truly immense, as the debate has increased within the last thirty years. In the following pages, I will present the interpretation of one of the most important documents regarding the civil right to religious freedom: the Vatican Council II's *Declaration on Religious Freedom* (1965), as interpreted by David Schlinder and John Courtney Murray. Their work represents an important contribution to the scholarship on religious freedom. I will pay particular attention to the meaning these authors confer to religious freedom, and whether their approach is helpful in clarifying what is meant by religion, freedom, and the proper space allotted to religious freedom.

David Schlinder's Interpretation of Vatican Council II's *Declaration on Religious Freedom Dignitatis Humanae* (1965)

The Declaration *Dignitatis Humanae*, a magisterial document from the Catholic Church, is an important document to analyze, for it implies that there has to be a philosophical foundation of religious freedom.[116] The Declaration, in fact, has given rise to numerous theological and philosophical commentaries and debates. Here I will only discuss the philosophical foundations of religious freedom in the Declaration, as interpreted by David Schlinder, and the ways in which the notions of religion and freedom are employed, as well as its proper setting or stage.[117]

The Declaration on Religious Freedom from Vatican Council II, *Dignitatis Humanae*, was approved by the end of 1965. The important aspects it declares are: (1) that the Church ought to be free to be about its business, which includes the obligation of the laity to sacralize culture, (2) that everyone has the duty and therefore the right to freely fulfill their obligation to worship God, and (3) that this right ought to be given constitutional expression. Thus, all persons have a right, as individuals and as groups, not to be coerced by

---

116. See Meinvielle, "Libertad Religiosa," 215.

117. The document divides the consideration of the right to religious freedom into two parts. The first section defines, explicates, and justifies the right by reference to natural reason alone. The second part shows how it is rooted in Christian revelation and doctrine.

government either to perform or not to perform religious acts. This right is limited only by the needs of public order (the need to protect the right of others and uphold public peace and public morality).[118]

Granted that this right is founded in the dignity of the human person, on what does the dignity of the human person itself finally rest, and how does one's conception of these foundations affect the nature of the right? Herminio Rico questions whether, according to the Declaration, human dignity stems from the freedom that is inherent in every person, a freedom which can be used well or not, or rather stems from "the person's relationship with transcendent truth."[119] The first view is understood to be the "juridical" approach of the Council bishops from America, and the theologian John Courtney Murray. The second view is understood to be the "ontological" approach, characteristic of the French bishops and of Karol Wojtyła, the future John Paul II.[120]

Schlinder argues that, according to the Declaration, the notion of human dignity stems from an originally given, intrinsic relation between freedom and truth. Thus, the Declaration arrives at an adequate notion of a positive right to religious freedom, in contrast to a merely negative conception of freedom.[121] In the first place, I will present in this section the dignity of the human person as the foundation of religious freedom; in the second place, the notion of freedom employed as having an intrinsic relation to truth; in the third place, the acknowledgment of this right in the constitutional order; in the fourth place, religious freedom as a negative right; and finally, I will make an evaluation of the Declaration's foundation of religious freedom as a human right.

---

118. Cf. Hittinger, "Dignitatis Humanae," 1044. It is important to note that the Council put the issue of corporate obligations to confess the truth to one side. Instead, the bishops investigated the narrower issue of the civil freedom of human persons in matters religious, and subsequently addressed the question of the liberty and mission of the Church.

119. Rico, *John Paul II*, 142. Prevalent readings of *Dignitatis Humanae* today fail for the most part to take note of the profound ways in which the issue of truth emerges as centered in the person.

120. As Schlinder notes, Wojtyła/John Paul II made several important interventions during the redactions of the document, supported the changes that were introduced in the fifth schema and retained in the final document, and placed the problem of religious freedom and its relation to truth in the forefront of his concerns as pontiff. See Schlinder, FTHD, 212.

121. See Schlinder, FTHD; Schlinder and Healy, *Freedom, Truth, and Human Dignity*.

The Dignity of the Human Person

The Declaration proclaims religious freedom as a human right and holds that human dignity is its philosophical foundation. Right at the beginning, the Declaration states that the principle and philosophical foundation of religious freedom is the dignity of the human person, which demands respect and certain inalienable rights that belong to man by nature, for he has a duty to make a responsible use of his freedom, but this should never be by means of coercion.[122] This is a truth that does not depend on international declarations or agreements, and for that reason, the declaration appeals to the "consciousness of contemporary man." There is a right to be free, and therefore, to enjoy religious freedom, within a responsible use of freedom, that is, as long as there is no harm of the common good of society:

> It is in accordance with their dignity as persons-that is, beings endowed with reason and free will and therefore privileged to bear personal responsibility—that all men should be at once impelled by nature and also bound by a moral obligation to seek the truth, especially religious truth. . . . The exercise of this right cannot be interfered with as long as the just requirements of public order are observed.[123]

The references to human dignity as the foundation of religious freedom are numerous throughout the Declaration. It states, for example, that "the right of man to religious freedom has its foundation in the dignity of the person,"[124] a dignity which is "known through the revealed word of God and by reason itself. This right of the human person to religious freedom is to be recognized in the constitutional law whereby society is governed and thus it is to become a civil right."[125] The main question is, on what does the dignity of the human person itself finally rest, and how does one's conception of these foundations affect the nature of the right?

---

122. Cf. Vatican Council II, *DH*, n. 1. See: "A sense of the dignity of the human person has been impressing itself more and more deeply on the consciousness of contemporary man, and the demand is increasingly made that men should act on their own judgment, enjoying and making use of a responsible freedom, not driven by coercion but motivated by a sense of duty."

123. Vatican Council II, *DH*, n. 2.

124. Vatican Council II, *DH*, n. 9. It also states that: "Truth, however, is to be sought after in a manner proper to the dignity of the human person and his social nature." Vatican Council II, *DH*, n. 3.

125. Vatican Council II, *DH*, n. 2.

The Intrinsic Relation between Freedom and Truth

The Declaration centered the Church's understanding of religious freedom and rights on the human person and developed more fully and explicitly the Catholic doctrine on, and commitment to, the right to religious freedom. At the same time, the Declaration did so by way of affirming the person within a new unity of freedom and truth before God. Even though the Declaration may not have developed a fully integrated theory in defense of this ontological unity of freedom and truth characteristic of the person in relation to God, David Schlinder thinks that we find key elements for such an integrated theory in the text itself.[126]

The main argument of the fifth and final text of the Declaration is grounded on the human right to search after the truth and to embrace the truth once found. The Council bishops who supported the changes in the final Declaration recognized that only an adequate view of the truth about man and his freedom in relation to God alone can sustain rights for every human being with objective moral consistency. The Declaration states:

> It is in accordance with their dignity that all men, because they are persons, that is, beings endowed with reason and free will and therefore bearing personal responsibility, are both impelled by their nature and bound by a moral obligation to seek the truth, especially religious truth. They are also bound to adhere to the truth once they come to know it and direct their whole lives in accordance with the demands of truth. But men cannot satisfy this obligation in a way that is in keeping with their own nature unless they enjoy both psychological freedom and immunity from external coercion. Therefore the right to religious freedom has its foundation not in the subjective attitude of the individual but in his very nature. For this reason the right to this immunity continues to exist even in those who do not live up to their obligation of seeking the truth and adhering to it.[127]

As Schlinder notes, the crux of the argument is that the right to immunity from coercion in matters of religious truth resides in every person because it is rooted in the "very nature" of the person. Human persons are naturally endowed with reason and free will even as they are naturally

---

126. As Schlinder argues, the text bears a unity of meaning, one that consists in its affirmation of an intrinsic relation between freedom and truth, and thus of the positive relation of truth to freedom as the internal context for the negative meaning of the right to religious freedom. See Schlinder, FTHD, 296.

127. Vatican Council II, *DH*, n. 2.

moved by, and morally bound to seek, the truth, especially with respect to religious matters.[128] The Declaration continues:

> Everybody has the duty and consequently the right to seek the truth in religious matters so that, through the use of appropriate means, he may prudently form judgments of conscience which are sincere (recta) and true. The search for truth, however, must be carried out in a manner that is appropriate to the dignity of the human person and his social nature, namely, by free enquiry with the help of teaching or instruction, communication and dialogue. . . .[129]

The claim of a right, then, is tied to human dignity, and this dignity is tied to a view of the human person who, properly conceived as free and intelligent, is naturally inclined, and hence morally obliged, to seek the truth. The right to religious freedom is thus rooted in the person's natural inclination to seek the truth. However, this inclination is rightly realized only via the freedom and intelligence that define his human nature.[130] At the same time, that religious freedom is rooted in a natural inclination also means that this right is founded on the very nature of man. For that reason, the right is objective and not merely subjective: it is retained by every person regardless of whether he lives up to the obligation to search the truth, and "as long as the just requirements of public order are observed."[131]

According to the doctrine of the Declaration, this right must be founded on a human dignity intrinsically linked with a transcendent relation and obligation to truth, especially religious truth. This truth is understood to be reasonable and therefore accessible in principle to all.[132] At the same time, man "must not be forced to act contrary to," nor "prevented from acting according to," his conscience, "because the practice of religion of its very nature consists primarily of those voluntary and free internal acts by which a man directs himself to God."[133]

---

128. Cf. Schlinder, FTHD, 262.
129. Vatican Council II, *DH*, n. 3.
130. Cf. Schlinder, FTHD, 263. See also Meinvielle, *Declaración Conciliar*, 219.
131. Vatican Council II, *DH*, n. 2.
132. However, this truth is nevertheless also understood by the Document to find its full and proper meaning only in the light of the revelation of Jesus Christ as carried in the sacramental tradition of the Catholic and Apostolic Church. Cf. Schlinder, FTHD, 239.
133. Vatican Council II, *DH*, n. 3.

Article 3 states further that the free exercise of religion in society can be denied only "when the just requirements of public order are violated." To deny this free exercise when these just requirements are observed is:

> ... to do an injustice to the human person and to the very order established by God for men. Furthermore, the ... acts of religion by which men direct themselves to God ... transcend of their very nature the earthly and temporal order of things. Therefore the civil authority, the purpose of which is the care of the common good in the temporal order, must recognize and look with favor on the religious life of the citizens.[134]

The reason is that: "All men are bound to seek the truth, especially in what concerns God and his Church, and to embrace it and hold on to it as they come to know it."[135]

Every human being is endowed with reason and free will and bearing personal responsibility, are therefore everyone is impelled by nature and also bound by a moral obligation to seek the truth, especially religious truth. Thus, the Declaration claims that because every person is positively impelled by nature to seek the truth, every person has a right to seek the truth. The Declaration states that there actually exists no freedom outside of its naturally given movement toward truth and toward God. Such a recognition of the movement toward God and of a moral obligation to seek the truth, especially religious truth, is rooted "not in the subjective disposition of the person but in his very nature." That is the reason why "the right to ... immunity continues to exist even in those who do not live up to their obligation of seeking the truth and adhering to it."[136]

These elements call attention to how frequently and emphatically the Declaration refers to truth, especially concerning God, as the foundation of human dignity, thereby indicating the ground of the right to religious freedom.

Religious Freedom and the Liberal Constitutional Order

According to the Declaration, it is in principle legitimate for a government to privilege a specific religious community in its civil order, provided that the government at the same time protects the right to freedom in religious matters of all citizens and of other religious communities. It states: "If because

---

134. Vatican Council II, *DH*, n. 3.
135. Vatican Council II, *DH*, n. 1.
136. Vatican Council II, *DH*, n. 2.

of the circumstances of a particular people special civil recognition is given to one religious community in the constitutional organization of a State, the right of all citizens and religious communities to religious freedom must be recognized and respected as well."[137]

The intrinsic relation between freedom and truth implies an intrinsic relation between man as subject of a moral right to religious freedom and man as subject of a distinct civil right to religious freedom. *Dignitatis humanae* states that "the right to religious freedom ... based on the very dignity of the human person ... must be given such recognition in the constitutional order of society as will make it a civil right."[138] It is precisely the naturally or ontologically rooted moral right to religious freedom proper to the human person as such that is to be recognized as a civil right.[139] The following two texts show how the right to religious freedom is something that pertains to man in his intrinsic reality as man, and how it is operative within the civil right to religious freedom. The Declaration states: "This right of the human person to religious freedom must be given such recognition in the constitutional order as will make it a civil right;"[140] "for this reason everybody has the duty and consequently the right to seek the truth in religious matters so that, through the use of appropriate means, he may prudently form judgments of conscience which are right and true."[141]

Thus, the right to religious freedom is something that pertains to man in his intrinsic reality as man. The right to religious freedom is to be recognized in the constitutional order so that this natural right will become a civilly recognized right. The natural, ontological, and moral right to religious freedom is understood to be operative within the civil right to religious freedom precisely as the inner ground for affirming this right in its distinctly civil or juridical sense.[142] The Declaration states that the social nature of man requires that he should give external expression to his internal acts of religion. Thus, "injury is done to the human person and to the very order established by God for human life, if the free exercise of religion is denied in society, provided just public order is observed."[143] For that reason, "the protection and promotion of the inviolable rights of man ranks among the essential duties of government," especially "the safeguard

137. Vatican Council II, *DH*, n. 6.
138. Vatican Council II, *DH*, n. 2.
139. Cf. Schlinder, FTHD, 305.
140. Vatican Council II, *DH*, n. 1.
141. Vatican Council II, *DH*, n. 3.
142. Cf. Schlinder, FTHD, 286.
143. Vatican Council II, *DH*, n. 3.

of the religious freedom of all its citizens, in an effective manner, by just laws and by other appropriate means."[144]

Religious Freedom as a Negative Right

We read in the Declaration something that approaches a negative conception of religious freedom, that is, as immunity from external coercion "on the part of individuals or of social groups and of any human power, in such wise that no one is to be forced to act in a manner contrary to his own beliefs, whether privately or publicly, whether alone or in association with others, within due limits."[145] It should be noted, however, that the Declaration ties the meaning of a right to a human subjectivity understood to be originally ordered to truth, found in the world and, implicitly and more profoundly, in one's relation to the Creator. It states:

> Man perceives and acknowledges the imperatives of the divine law through the mediation of conscience. In all his activity a man is bound to follow his conscience in order that he may come to God, the end and purpose of life. It follows that he is not to be forced to act in a manner contrary to his conscience. Nor, on the other hand, is he to be restrained from acting in accordance with his conscience, especially in matters religious.[146]

The right to religious freedom is an immunity from coercion only inside, and by virtue of, this naturally given positive relation to God and others. On the Declaration's view, what is primary in the self's relation to the other is a positive letting be. On the juridical view, by contrast, what is primary is a (negative) avoidance of constraint or intrusiveness with respect to the other. The negative sense of the right as conceived by the Declaration is essential to the right's proper meaning. Yet, this negative sense is understood to take its inner dynamic from within the human being's original true and positive relation to God and to other human creatures.

A purely "negative" concept of religious freedom as an "immunity from coercion" lacks an adequate sense of the right to religious freedom as an intrinsically positive good owed to all persons. Emphasizing religious freedom only in the negative terms of immunity leaves this right logically vulnerable to indifference in the matter of truth. As Avery Dulles affirms, "the merely negative definition could easily be exploited to promote

---

144. Vatican Council II, *DH*, n. 3.
145. Vatican Council II, *DH*, n. 2.
146. Vatican Council II, *DH*, n. 3.

unacceptable forms of liberalism or indifferentism."¹⁴⁷ The "negative" concept abstracts the roots of human dignity from man's positive relationship to God. Thus, Dulles continues, "It was imperative . . . to work with a positive conception of religious freedom, rooted in a theological understanding of the dignity of the person in relationship with God."¹⁴⁸

As Schlinder notes, the "freedom from" intrusive activity by others characteristic of a right already presupposes and is ordered in terms of "freedom for" the truth, especially about God. One has a right to be free from coercion because one is made for truth and God, for the purpose of seeking the truth and God.¹⁴⁹ Thus, to remove the act of freedom from this original "for" is, according to the Declaration, to remove from the person the very dignity that warrants this claim to the right of freedom from coercion in the first place. Freedom from is essential to the meaning of a right; however, this essential negative meaning has its integrity as negative only as founded in and initially informed by the human act's positive movement toward, as well as obligation to seek, the truth, especially about God.

Evaluation

The Declaration on Religious Freedom by the Vatican Council II seems to be more careful than other international declarations when talking about "religion" in reference to religious freedom. The Declaration makes reference to "religious matters," "the practice of religion . . . by which man directs himself to God,"¹⁵⁰ and "the acts of religion by which men direct themselves to God."¹⁵¹ Yet, it does not specify in what these acts and religious matters consist. The Declaration states that there is a moral obligation to search the truth, especially "religious truth," which in turn gives origin to religious freedom as a right. Thus, the Declaration implies that "religion" is understood as something related to knowledge, since to search for the truth is a function of the intellect. We should object to this view. One can certainly argue that, given man's natural tendencies, there is an obligation to search for the truth. One can also argue that searching for and knowing the truth belongs to man as such, and that in order to do so one ought to be free. Yet, if religious freedom is understood as this obligation to search for "religious truth," one would be leaving aside a number of actions that religious people

---

147. Dulles, "Religious Freedom," 165.
148. Dulles, "Religious Freedom," 165.
149. Cf. Schlinder, FTHD, 287.
150. Vatican Council II, *DH*, n. 3.
151. Vatican Council II, *DH*, n. 3.

perform, and which are considered to be essentially "religious." Thus, even though these religious actions may be related to or motivated by a certain knowledge, belief, or faith, these acts (such as prayer, worship, offerings, etc.) are not the same reality as faith or belief, or searching for the truth. The argument based on the obligation to search for the truth, especially religious truth, and the freedom that it implies may certainly be employed as a foundation for human rights. However, this obligation seems to be related to intellectual freedom and freedom of conscience instead, rather than to religious freedom as such. The Declaration, in fact, states:

> In all his activity a man is bound to follow his conscience in order that he may come to God, the end and purpose of life. It follows that he is not to be forced to act in a manner contrary to his conscience. Nor, on the other hand, is he to be restrained from acting in accordance with his conscience, especially in matters religious.[152]

My objection, then, is that the Declaration does provides a good argument for human rights based on the human person, but which nevertheless does not properly apply to religious freedom. One can argue, instead, that it provides a stronger foundation for a freedom of conscience right, which then may be applied in a subsequent step to religious freedom in the sense that once man recognizes the truth about himself and his freedom in relation to God, this knowledge, faith, belief, will be the source and motivation for religious acts. But the source of these actions, such as faith or knowledge about God, are not the same reality as the religious actions it may motivate, such as praying to and offering God the honor that is his due.

At the same time, by connecting the search for religious truth to religious freedom, the Document employs a notion of "religion" that is in itself unclear and confusing, as it seems to refer to the content of faith. This understanding of "religion" contradicts the understanding of "religion" found in other places throughout the Document when referring to "religious matters," "the practice of religion," and "the acts of religion." This internal contradiction regarding the notion of "religion" is evidence that the meaning of religion has to yet be established, and which the Declaration fails to do.[153]

Another shortcoming of this Declaration, is that there is no specific mention of the proper stage or sphere for the acts that belong to religious

---

152. Vatican Council II, *DH*, n. 3.

153. This shortcoming is also evident throughout Schlinder's interpretation of the Declaration. He talks about the "nature of religion," for example, without ever clarifying what he means by that. See Schlinder and Healy, *Freedom, Truth, and Human Dignity*, 123.

freedom. It only mentions that "public order" should be respected, and that man may perform acts of religion "privately or publicly." Thus, the Declaration states that the use of freedom should be done responsibly, so as not to harm the common good of society: "The exercise of this right cannot be interfered with as long as the just requirements of public order are observed."[154] And "no one is to be forced to act in a manner contrary to his own beliefs, whether privately or publicly, whether alone or in association with others, within due limits."[155] One should note that in this context, "actions" are distinguished from one's own "belief," so that one may act according to, or against, one's own belief. This confirms the point I made above: within the internal context of the Declaration, a "belief" and the "actions" it motivates are two different things. This is an internal contradiction within the document. The Declaration, then, is really offering a foundation to protect one's own search for the truth, which is a protection of conscience and intellectual freedom, so that one may freely act according to it.

Now, these actions that are being motivated by faith may not all be necessarily religious actions. Motivated by faith one can pray, and perform many other religious acts as such, or one may also volunteer to serve soup at a homeless shelter, or tutor a friend's child out of charity or good will. All of these attitudes may certainly be motivated by one's own belief or faith, but the outcomes are completely different. It seems that when it comes to beliefs in a human rights' context, one should be talking about protection of conscience instead.

Thus, the meaning of religious freedom, and of the notion of religion itself should be established, in order to then be able to identify its proper actions and its sphere of action. Only then the conditions for the exercise of religion may at the same time be encouraged and protected from any negative intervention by the state or by any other individual or group that may threaten its rightful exercise.

John Courtney Murray's Juridical Approach to Religious Freedom

When analyzing Murray's notion of religious freedom, I criticized his juridical approach, for he views religious freedom as a negative right, limited to immunity from external coercion, and religion as a belief. Still, it is important to consider in this section Murray's contribution regarding the defense and foundation of religious freedom. I will present the different

154. Vatican Council II, *DH*, n. 2.
155. Vatican Council II, *DH*, n. 2.

arguments he offered throughout the years, especially with the occasion of the Vatican Council II.

The Problem of Religious Freedom (1965)

With the occasion of his participation in Vatican Council II, Murray presented an argument on religious freedom that was distributed to all participants. This document was an earlier version of the argument found in *The Problem of Religious Freedom* (1965), where he states:

> Religious freedom is a human freedom in the external forum of society. It is a personal and corporate right to immunity from coercion by any legal or extralegal forces in the profession and practice of religion. This right is grounded in the law of nature—or, if you will, in the exigence of reason—which manifests itself, in today's social historical context, both through the mature personal consciousness which claims the right and also through the mature political consciousness which forbids the state to deny or diminish it.[156]

According to Murray, the right to religious freedom as defined by the Declaration on Religious Freedom, *Dignitatis humanae*, is "an immunity; its content is negative," that is, a "formally juridical concept."[157] For Murray, the content of religion exceeds the juridical order. For that reason, religious freedom is seen just as immunity from coercion on the part of the state. Any other argument, according to him, does not sufficiently settle the question of the justification of religious freedom as a human right.[158] The reason is that only juridical formulas are concerned with interpersonal relationships, setting outside limits to a sphere of human activity, and guaranteeing this sphere against forcible intrusion from without.[159]

One should note that the "negative" content of the Declaration is not understood by Murray to imply a rejection of man's positive relationship to truth and to God, but only an abstraction from this relationship for purposes of the exercise of civil authority. Murray interprets the Declaration according to the juridical formula of the First Amendment of the United States Constitution regarding the free exercise of religion. According to Murray, it is empty of any "ideology," and this ideological emptiness is

---

156. Murray, *Problem of Religious Freedom*, 80.
157. Murray, *End and Beginning*, 27.
158. Cf. Murray, "Arguments," 237–40.
159. Cf. Murray, *End and Beginning*, 28–29.

common to both the Declaration and the United States Constitution, for in none of the documents the juridical formula contains a "positive evaluation of the religious phenomenon in any of its manifestations."[160] Thus, the notion of the right to religious freedom as a negative immunity implies "the constitutional concept of government as limited in its powers."[161] According to Murray, that means that the "government denies to itself the competence to be a judge of religious belief and action."[162] This denial, however, is not an assertion of indifference to the values of religion to man and to society, nor an affirmation that religion is a purely private matter. For Murray, "it is simply a recognition of the limited functions of the juridical order of society as the legal armature of human rights."[163]

According to Murray's conception, Schlinder notes, the function of government is limited to the securing of public order, so that it becomes more properly "coercive" than "pedagogical" in nature. The function of the state, then, is to essentially insure that citizens do not interfere with each other in an intrusive manner.[164]

Once the Council issued the Document on religious freedom in December of 1965, Murray wrote three articles in 1966 in response to the Council, and which I will present in the following sections.[165]

"The Issue of Church and State at Vatican II" (1966)

In this article, Murray notes a development in the Church's understanding of the constitutional order of society, especially in its acceptance of religious freedom as a fundamental right of the human person. To protect and promote religious freedom is a secular function, for freedom in general, and religious freedom in particular, is a secular value "rooted in the truth about the human person, which is the truth upon which the whole social and political order rests."[166] Murray also notes that the autonomy of the secular order requires

---

160. Murray, "Declaration," 568. Yet, this lack of a positive evalutation of what religion is has led to an unending debate and confusion regarding the place of religion in the public sphere.

161. Murray, *End and Beginning*, 36.

162. Murray, *End and Beginning*, 36–37.

163. Murray, *End and Beginning*, 36–37.

164. Cf. Schlinder, FTHD, 220.

165. The reason why Murray developed his own line of argumentation while commenting the *DH*, is because he did not believe the argument provided in the Declaration is "the best one that can be made." Cf. Murray, "Declaration," 570.

166. Murray, "Church and State," 587. However, Murray also notes that the text of Declaration is inadequate in its treatment of the essentially juridical function of government.

that, within this order and in the face of its constituted organs of government, the Church should present her claim to freedom on these secular grounds, that is, "in the name of the human person, who is the foundation, the end, and the bearer of the whole social process."[167]

According to Murray, given his juridical approach, the function of the state with regard to religion is limited to creating free conditions wherein religion might be fostered, as distinct from fostering religion itself. He states:

> It would seem to be in the sense of the Declaration to say that governmental favor of religion means favor of the freedom of religion. Similarly, conditions favorable to religious life should be understood to mean conditions favorable to the free profession and practice of religion. Government does not stand in the service of religious truth, as an instrument for its defense or propagation. Government, however, must somehow stand in the service of religion, as an indispensable element of the common temporal good. This duty of service is discharged by service rendered to the freedom of religion in society.[168]

"Arguments for the Human Right to Religious Freedom" (1966)

In this article, Murray establishes that in the sphere of religion no one is to be compelled to act against his conscience. As a consequence, he argues that the discussion of the human right to religious freedom calls for further inquiry into the foundations of the juridical relationship among human beings in civil society. A juridical relationship includes the notion of a correspondence between right and duties. That means that if a person has a right to something, there is a corresponding duty incumbent on others to do or give or omit something. In the case of religious freedom, "the human person demands by right the omission of all coercive action impeding a person or a community from acting according to its conscience in religious matters."[169] According to Murray, the whole matter hinges on this argument for the juridical actuality of the immunity. Now, the only power in human society that would possess the right to prohibit religious practice is the state. Therefore, in order to establish that the human person enjoys a right to full religious freedom, one must first establish that the

---

167. Murray, "Church and State," 591.
168. Murray, "Church and State," 598.
169. Murray, "Arguments," 231.

public power has no right to restrict religious freedom. Rather, the state has the duty to acknowledge and protect it.[170]

The state of the question, then, is: On what justifying argument does this denial rest? Why may the limitation placed on the public power in matters of religion be considered just and legitimate? Murray proceeds to evaluate in his article the various arguments put forward by the Declaration that aim to confirm the person's right to religious freedom. What he is trying to establish is whether any or all of these arguments provide a strong foundation for limiting public power when it comes to religious freedom. Murray classifies these arguments according to different categories: arguments from conscience, from the obligation to search after the truth, from the person's social nature, and finally, arguments from the limits of public power.[171]

1. Argument from Conscience

The basis of this argument is the moral principle that in religious matters man is held bound to follow his conscience even if erroneous. From this moral principle, the Declaration deduces the moral-juridical principle that to man is due the right to be free in society in order to follow his conscience. Yet, according to Murray, this is not a universal principle. He states that no difficulty arises if the conscience in question is right and true. The moral principle is then valid that a man is duty-bound always to follow his conscience. From this follows the moral-juridical principle that man has the right to fulfill his duty. However, Murray argues that "if the conscience in question is right but erroneous, it cannot give rise to a juridical relationship between persons. From one human being's erroneous conscience no duty follows for others to act or perform or omit anything"[172] Therefore, since the state may act and intervene in matters of erroneous conscience, as for example when a sect or religious group performs acts that are against the public order or the lives of citizens, the argument fails to demonstrate why the public power lacks this right to restrict religious freedom.

---

170. Cf. Murray, "Arguments," 231–32.
171. Cf. Murray, "Arguments," 233–40.
172. Murray, "Arguments," 233.

2. Argument from the Obligation to Search after the Truth

The conciliar Declaration on religious freedom attempts to ontologically ground religious freedom on a "moral obligation to seek the truth."[173] The argument deduces, from this moral obligation, a human right to immunity from external coercion that every man enjoys in order to fulfill his obligations, as long as just public order is observed.[174]

According to Murray, the argument is valid and on target. The demand for religious freedom has its basis in man's intellectual nature, in one's capacity to seek, to embrace, and to manifest by one's way of life the truth to which one is ordered. One cannot perform this duty toward truth except by a personal assent and free deliberation. No one is to be forced to act against his conscience or against the demands of the truth that one has found, for it would be to act against one's intellectual nature. However, according to Murray, this demand for freedom does not have enough power to establish a true right from a juridical perspective. It does not establish that no one is to be impeded from acting according to his conscience in religious matters. He states:

> Are man's natural and moral links to truth powerful enough to engender a political relationship between the human person and the public power so that the latter is duty-bound not to prevent the person from acting according to his conscience—whether the person acts alone or in association with others? It seems not.[175]

The reason adduced by Murray is that civil power might still repress false forms of worship or religious error, which still would be compatible with man's moral obligation to seek the truth in order to act according to it. Public activities that proceed from a basis in error should in fact be prevented if they cause harm to the public good. Thus, Murray doubts that it is correct to place the ontological ground for religious freedom in man's natural and moral relationship to truth.[176]

---

173. Vatican Council II, *DH*, n. 2.
174. Cf. Vatican Council II, *DH*, n. 2.
175. Murray, "Arguments," 234.
176. Cf. Murray, "Arguments," 235–36.

3. Argument from the Person's Social Nature

The Declaration argues that every human being is subject to the divine law, and that we participate in this eternal law through the natural law, that is, from within our nature and natural inclinations. Thus, there is a moral obligation to investigate what those precepts of the divine law might be. Then, according to Murray, the Declaration's argument validly shows that no one is to be forced to act against his conscience, for by so acting a person would be doing wrong. The Declaration also states that this investigation ought to be conducted in a social manner, according to man's social nature. Murray grants this. However, he objects the fact that there is a question that recurs in this argument as well: "Does it follow from this argument that no one is to be prevented from acting in public according to his conscience?" The argument appeals to the necessary connection between internal acts of religion and those outward acts by which, in keeping with his social nature, a human being displays his religious convictions in a public way. This is how, according to the argument, immunity from external coercion is established. Thus, the argument concludes that a purely human power cannot forbid external acts. Yet, Murray disagrees with this manner of arguing, for it must be first established that no power exists in society that may legitimately forbid public acts of religion, even acts that transgress objective truth or divine law or even the common good. According to Murray, this is the very heart of the matter under discussion.[177]

4. Argument from the Limits of Public Power

Murray considers the political argument of primary importance, for, according to him, the previous arguments do not sufficiently settle the question of the justification of religious freedom as a human right. The reason is that, for Murray, the very question of religious freedom concerns the limits of public power in religious matters.

This argument from the limits of public power is constituted by five coherent principles which constitute the relationship between the human person and the public juridical order. The first two principles are the dignity of the human person and the social principle. These two principles taken together give rise to the principle of the free society and the principle of juridical equality in society of all citizens. Finally, there is the political principle. Taken together, it is these five principles that establish religious freedom.[178]

---

177. Cf. Murray, "Arguments," 237.
178. Cf. Murray, "Arguments," 239.

The first principle of the argument is the dignity of every human being. This, according to Murray, is an ontological principle. Thus, every human person is endowed with a dignity that surpasses the rest of creatures because the human person is independent. Human dignity demands, then, that man act responsibly "by his own council and purpose, using and enjoying his freedom, moved, not by external coercion, but internally by the risk of his whole existence."[179]

Murray emphasizes that the dignity and freedom of the human person should receive primary attention, since they pertain to the goods that are proper to the human spirit: "The foundation of human society lies in the truth about the human person, or in its dignity, that is, in its demand for responsible freedom."[180] When it comes to making a fundamental religious option, human dignity demands that "a person should act by his own deliberation and purpose, enjoying immunity from all external coercion so that in the presence of God he takes responsibility on himself alone for his religious decisions and acts."[181] This is the ontological ground of religious freedom and of any other human freedom.

The second principle in the argument is a social principle, which states that "the human person is the subject, foundation, and end of the entire social life."[182] The force of this principle, according to Murray, lies in the fact that it establishes an indissoluble connection between the moral and the juridical orders. The connection of both orders is the human person itself, for in association with others, "it transcends by reason of its end both society and the whole world."[183] Thus, the human is a moral-juridical subject furnished with rights that flow directly from human nature. For that reason, the juridical order cannot be sundered from the moral order.[184]

According to Murray, the arguments for religious freedom that underscore the natural human impulse to seek truth and the person's moral obligation to live according to the truth once found, ought to be situated within the ontological and social principles.[185] These first two principles will give rise to the third and fourth principles.

The third principle is that of a free society. According to Murray, "man in society must be accorded as much freedom as possible, and that freedom

---

179. Murray, "Arguments," 238.
180. Murray, "Arguments," 241.
181. Murray, "Arguments," 240.
182. Murray, "Arguments," 238.
183. Murray, "Arguments," 238.
184. Cf. Murray, "Arguments," 238.
185. Murray, "Arguments," 238–39.

is not to be restricted unless and insofar as is necessary . . . for preserving the public order in its juridical, political, and moral aspects."[186]

The fourth principle is the juridical principle. According to Murray, it "maintains that all citizens enjoy juridical equality in society."[187] It is founded on the first two principles because all persons enjoy human dignity, and every human being is equally the subject, foundation, and end of human society.

Finally, the fifth principle is the political principle. The duty of every public power is to protect the inviolable rights proper to human beings and their dignity. Thus, the first four principles define the function of the public power.[188] Human freedom is based on the objective truth of the person in society. For that reason, Murray argues that the demand for freedom engenders the juridical relationship between the person and the public power. As a consequence, "the public power is duty-bound to acknowledge the truth about the person, to protect and advance the person, and to render the justice owed the person."[189]

All five principles make up the juridical argument related to the limit of power. It is this argument that properly, for Murray, justifies the right to religious freedom, for these principles "are sufficient to constitute that relationship between the human person and the public juridical power."[190]

Thus, Murray presents the demand for religious freedom as grounded in the objective truth about the human person. Yet, religious freedom has to be considered from a juridical perspective, for only then it can impose upon the public power the duty to refrain from keeping the human person from acting in religious matters according to his dignity. Therefore, the public power is bound to acknowledge and to fulfill this duty by reason of its principal function, which is the protection of the dignity of the person. Human dignity demands, then, immunity from coercion in religious matters, so that once this duty is demonstrated and acknowledged, it becomes the object of a right. As Murray states, the juridical actuality of a right is established wherever a corresponding duty is established and is acknowledged, and once the validity of the ground for a right is assured and recognized.[191] Murray concludes the argument put forward in the article by stating that no one is to be prevented in the matter of religion from acting according to

---

186. Murray, "Arguments," 239.
187. Murray, "Arguments," 239.
188. Cf. Murray, "Arguments," 239.
189. Murray, "Arguments," 241.
190. Cf. Murray, "Arguments," 239.
191. Cf. Murray, "Arguments," 240.

the demands of his dignity or according to his inmost religious convictions. This immunity does not cease, except where just demands of public order are proven to have the urgency of a higher force.[192]

"The Declaration on Religious Freedom" (1966)[193]

In this article, Murray states that "it is not necessary to believe that the Conciliar argument is the best one that can be made."[194] In fact, Murray is very critical of the Declaration's linking of freedom with truth. For him, this connection weakens rather than strengthens the right to religious freedom. His criticism is centered on the fact that a government claiming to know the truth about the human being will be logically inclined to short-circuit the freedom of its citizens.[195] Instead, he proposes what he believes is "a more cogent argument," one that "can be constructed from the principles of the Declaration itself, assembled into an organic structure."[196]

Murray argues that the marks of man as a person are his personal autonomy and his personal responsibility. That man is responsible means that the imperatives of his conscience should conform to the transcendent order of truth, manifested in his actions. Yet, on the horizontal plane of intersubjective relationships, and within the social order, this responsibility is juridically irrelevant. The reason, for Murray, is that no authority exists within the juridical order that is capable or empowered to judge in this regard. Instead, what is juridically relevant and relevant, is the personal autonomy which is constituent of man's dignity. There is an exigence in man to act on his own initiative and on his own responsibility. And for Murray, "this exigence is the basic ontological foundation, not only of the right to religious freedom, but of all man's fundamental rights."[197]

---

192. Cf. Murray, "Arguments," 241.
193. See Murray, "Declaration," 565–76.
194. Murray, "Declaration," 570.
195. Cf. Murray, "Declaration," 571–72; Murray, *Religious Liberty, an End and a Beginning*, 36–37. Schlinder is critical of Murray's position, for Murray assumes that linking freedom with truth, bringing them into intrinsic relation with each other, constitutes a principled threat to the integrity of freedom as well as to the right that is a function of this freedom. Such a claim, however, presupposes that freedom and truth have their original integrity as extrinsic to each other, as not interiorly open to one another such that each would have its integrity only as already given "form" by the other. Cf. Schlinder, FTHD, 276.
196. Murray, "Declaration," 571–72.
197. Murray, "Declaration," 571–72.

Even though in his argument Murray clearly affirms man's responsibilities as a moral subject in his "vertical relationship to the transcendent order of truth," he also emphasizes that civil rights essentially concern rather the "horizontal plane of intersubjective relationships." Since man's responsibility to truth is important, the burden of a right is seen as having negative content in order to create the free conditions necessary to enable the person's search for truth.[198] Therefore, religious freedom is seen as a negative right, one by which man is immune from state coercion. Murray proceeds in this way on order to safeguard a universal civil right to religious freedom in a pluralistic society, a right not tied intrinsically to any particular claim of truth or belief.

Evaluation of Murray's Justification of Religious Freedom

We already noted above that there are a few problems with Murray's juridical understanding of religious freedom. I will add here a few more comments based on what he argues in his articles on the justification of religious freedom.

According to Murray, religious freedom is a juridical formula which, by setting outside limits to a sphere of human activity, it guarantees the religious sphere against external coercion. Yet, he fails to establish what the proper sphere of religious freedom is, and in what this religious freedom consists. We should note that the "profession and practice of religion" may entail things that are not ordered according to reason and which may be harmful to individuals or society. Murray acknowledges this fact when stating that an erroneous conscience cannot give rise to a juridical relationship between persons,[199] for in these cases the state may intervene, especialy with respect to acts that are against the public order or harmful to the lives of citizens. Thus, one cannot just guarantee protection against external coercion to anything that may be labeled under the catefory of "religion." For that

---

198. The operative principle here is Murray's distinction between state and society. Cf. Murray, *We Hold These Truths*, 27–43. According to Murray, man's natural relation and obligation to a transcendent order of truth, and ultimately to God, are the proper concern of the institutions of society such as the family and the Church, not of government. Natural law is operative in man, binding and obligating him, within this realm of society. Even though this obligation is irrelevant from the juridical point of view, it does not mean that it is irrelevant to man and society as such. What is important for the juridical order, according to Murray, is "man's nature qua exigent to act on his own initiative and responsibility, *not* qua obligated to transcendent truth," as Schlinder notes. See Schlinder, FTHD, 223.

199. Cf. Murray, "Arguments," 233.

reason, the meaning of the notion of "religion" needs to be established in the first place, as well as the proper place where its actions belongs to. Only then will one be able to identify the "conditions favorable to the free profession and practice of religion."[200] Murray proceeds in this way in order to avoid the state the task of a "positive evaluation of the religious phenomenon in any of its manifestations."[201] Yet, by proceeding this way, it is clear that Murray understands "religion" as a belief system, and it is for that reason he considers the juridical argument to be the best argument, for it is not the task of the state to mess with religion, or evaluate their legitimacy or plausibility on the basis of what they teach. As a consequence, there seems to be an incoherence within such exposition of religious freedom. Murray is trapped within the vicious circle of trying to make a juridical case for immunity of coercion for religion, while arguing at the same time that the argument of conscience is not the best argument because the state, in certain cases, may in fact intervene if certain actions cause harm to the public good. This way of proceeding highlights an internal contradiction within the argument. There is a problem, then, by not clarifying the meaning of the notion of religion employed and by not establishing its proper sphere of action. At the same time, this understanding of "religion" as a belief system is in contradiction with other expressions he uses throughout his argument, such as "religious decisions and acts," or "religious action," which do not have the same meaning as belief.

Murray also understands religious freedom as freedom of conscience. This is probably a logical consequence from the fact that he understands "religion" as a system of beliefs which enjoys immunity from external coercion, for it is outside the jurisdiction of the state. In the conclusion to this chapter, I will elaborate more on why it is necessary to define the meaning of religion in order not to mistakenly understand religious freedom as freedom of conscience.

Is There a Need for a Right to Religious Freedom?

From our analysis of the various definitions and justifications of religious freedom, it seems that what is at stake is a defense of freedom of conscience. The reason why I say this is because the notion of "religion" employed has to do with beliefs and the freedom to act accordingly, which points out to matters of conscience. Yet, the problem that follows from this perspective is that one can then argue that there seems to be no need for

---

200. Murray, "Church and State," 598.
201. Murray, "Declaration," 568.

religious freedom. Why would religion be granted a special consideration when it comes to issues of conscience? What does it make it different from any other issue of conscience?

If "religion" is nothing else than a system of beliefs, then the protection granted by freedom of conscience seems to suffice. Thus, it seems that religious freedom is under serious threat regarding its purpose. Unless we establish that "religion" is not the same as belief, and therefore not a matter of conscience solely.

The understanding of religion as belief may be the root of the problem in debates and disagreements on issues of religious freedom. Perhaps those arguing for a protection of their right to religious freedom employ the wrong argument. Why would one argue for the protection of religious freedom when freedom of conscience would suffice? This is an issue I will especially address in the last chapter.

In this section, I will explore the difficulty that arises from considering religious freedom as a protection of one's beliefs. For now we can say that, if "religion" is understood as a belief, one of the consequences that follow is that there is no justification for offering "religion" a right to special protection that is exclusive to theistic religions. This is the argument Ronald Dworkin makes in his *Religion without God* (2013).[202] He states:

> We must expand that right's scope to reflect a better justification. How? The answer might seem obvious: we must just declare that people have a right in principle to the free exercise of their profound convictions about life and its responsibilities, whether derived from a belief in god or not, and that government must stand neutral in policy and expenditure toward all such convictions.[203]

Dworkin's notion of religion includes life's intrinsic meaning and nature's intrinsic beauty, which are the paradigms of a fully religious attitude to life.[204] "Religion," for Dworkin, has to do mainly with the interests one may have, and which regulate one's own life, regardless of what those interests might be. For that reason, he states that "we need to identify some particularly important interest people have, an interest so important that it deserves special protection against official or other injury."[205] Religious freedom, from this perspective, would mean the protection of that which one holds dear, one's highest interest. Yet, what would justify for a special

---

202. Cf. Dworkin, *Religion without God*, 117.
203. Dworkin, *Religion without God*, 117.
204. Cf. Dworkin, *Religion without God*, 11.
205. Dworkin, *Religion without God*, 111.

right regarding these special interests if they could well be considered under freedom of conscience? Dworkin sees that it is necessary to redefine religion in order to make it inclusive of nonreligious interests, yet, by doing so, he undermines even more the need for religious freedom.

Dworkin also states: "Each person has an intrinsic and inescapable ethical responsibility to make a success of his life. That responsibility is part of the religious attitude that both believers and atheists can share."[206] This opens the door to including within religious freedom any decision one may make regarding one's own life.[207] Dworkin is aware of the difficulty that his notion of religion implies, and agrees that "If we decided that all religious attitudes are entitled to special protection, we would need a more restrictive definition of a religious attitude than I have so far provided."[208] Thus, he distinguishes between a functional and a substantive definition of religion. A functional definition fixes on the role of the putative conviction in a person's overall personality, while a substantive definition designates only certain convictions about how to live as deserving constitutional protection.[209]

Dworkin rejects a functional definition of religion, for then any conviction a person might hold which functions as a "religion" within his life would qualify for religious freedom protection. Instead, Dworkin advocates for a substantive definition of "religion," for it restricts the range of passionate convictions that a right to religious freedom should protect. This, according to him, "identifies religious convictions that qualify for protection through their subject matter, not the fervor with which they are held."[210] Thus, for Dworkin, the definition of "religion" that should be employed in understanding religious freedom has to do with the answer to the deeper existential questions by connecting individual human lives to a transcendent objective value.[211] From this perspective, then, "religion," for Dworkin, has to do with a belief regarding what is best for one's own life, whatever the content of that belief might be,[212] so that even a woman's right to an early abortion might qualify

---

206. Dworkin, *Religion without God*, 114.

207. He states: "It includes a responsibility of each person to decide for himself ethical questions about which kinds of lives are appropriate and which would be degrading for him. A state violates that right whenever it prohibits or burdens homosexual practice, for instance." Dworkin, *Religion without God*, 114.

208. Dworkin, *Religion without God*, 118.

209. Cf. Dworkin, *Religion without God*, 118.

210. Dworkin, *Religion without God*, 120.

211. Cf. Dworkin, *Freedom's Law*, 101.

212. He states: "I can think of no plausible account of the content a belief must have, in order to be religious in character." Dworkin, *Freedom's Law*, 108.

for religious freedom protection.[213] However, he acknowledges that, "once we break the connection between a religious conviction and orthodox theism, we seem to have no firm way of excluding even the wildest ethical eccentricity from the category of protected faith."[214]

There is a serious problem with Dworkin's approach. "Religion" is being understood as an intellectual conviction, and religious freedom as protecting not just a faith or belief system, but any conviction regarding what is best for one's own life, regardless of the objective content of that belief. What is the need for a religious freedom protection, then? Freedom of conscience would suffice, besides the fact that an atheist or anyone argueing there shouldn't be any religions at all would be surprised that their conviction might be a religious right after all.[215]

The notion of religion offered by Dworkin is so vague, that its definition contradicts what it is trying to establish, that there is something called "religion." This has direct implications on religious freedom, for, if the notion of religion is so vague as to imperil its existence, then religious freedom itself is at risk. Aware of the problems that arise, and in order to solve this dilemma, Dworkin proposes to do away with freedom of religion, and instead adopt a right that protects "ethical independence."[216]

Dworkin is consistent with the logical step that follows if one holds a vague and loose definition of religion. If the notion of "religion" is in itself troublesome, then religious freedom is in itself a "troublesome special right."[217] The conclusion is that it should be abandoned. Yet, there is the religious protection granted by international declarations and by many constitutions from around the world. Dworkin's solution, then, is a "right to ethical independence," aimed at regulating and fixing the relation between government and citizens. This right, for Dworkin, would limit the reasons government may offer for any constraint on a citizen's freedom at all. Thus, the right includes and goes beyond religious exercise.[218]

The advantage of this new approach, according to Dworkin, is that it will be more helpful when dealing with dilemmas that arise between religious practices that attempt the good of society. Thus, in cases where religious freedom is usually advocated in order to advance practices that are harmful, such

---

213. Cf. Dworkin, *Religion without God*, 121.

214. Dworkin, *Religion without God*, 124.

215. In the same line, for example, the U.S. Supreme Court, in the *Torcaso* decision, listed among religions meeting the test it had in mind humanist societies that are explicitly atheistic. See *Torcaso v. Watkins*, 367 U.S. 488 (1961).

216. Cf. Dworkin, *Religion without God*, 132.

217. Cf. Dworkin, *Religion without God*, 133.

218. Cf. Dworkin, *Religion without God*, 133.

as religious rituals involving drug use, the free exercise of religious practice will be denied a special right. In these cases, one will only rely on the general right to ethical independence, so that then "religions may be forced to restrict their practices so as to obey rational, nondiscriminatory laws that do not display less than equal concern for them."[219]

The problem with Dworkin's proposal is that, if there is a problem with the notion of "religion," the first step towards achieving a solution should be to determine the correct meaning of the notion of religion, not a rejection of the right to religious freedom in favor of a new one. One should try to first first establish the terms, especially what is meant by "religion," in order to then be able if there is any feasible solution to the problems that arise from an unclear concept of religion. Dworkin does not question the confusing meaning of the notion of religion. He just accepts an unclear and vague notion of "religion," confusing as it is, and shows how it does not help to solve complicated cases where the exercise of religion contradicts the law. Dworkin avoids confronting the issue found within the notion of "religion" itself. He offers a different approach, that is, the rejection of religious freedom in favor of a "right to ethical independence." I believe that Dworking should have pointed out instead that the notion of religion is problematic, and that it is such an unclear notion of religion that causes so much confusion and dilemmas. Thus, Dworkin's solution seems to be superficial, as it does not get to the heart of the question in the debates on the place of religion in the public square and the exercise of religious freedom. Nevertheless, those who advocate for a right to religious freedom and for a place of religion in the public square should be aware of the problems found within an unclear notion of religion, for there is a risk that the right to religious freedom may disappear if the term is not clarified. This is what I found of value within Dworkin's approach, for he logically concludes that, if such is the notion of "religion," then we should not be talking about religious freedom, but about something else instead.

If, on the other hand, "religion" is taken to mean a belief system, the status and nature of religious freedom is also at risk. If such is the understanding of "religion" employed, then we may not need religious freedom at all, for freedom of conscience, as already argued, would well do the job. If "religion" may just mean so many things as to include belief in God, or nonbelief in God, one's values, the meaning of life, appreciation of nature's intrinsic beauty, etc., then religious freedom just disappears and gives way to the protection of what one in conscience holds to be the truth or the best for one's life.

---

219. Dworkin, *Religion without God*, 136.

Conclusion

In this chapter, we have seen how the right to religious freedom has historically been taken in two ways: as (religious) tolerance, and as freedom of conscience. The problem we face now is that none of these two understandings offers a secure notion of religious freedom.

The first section of this chapter, which aimed at presenting a very brief history of religious freedom, showed that the development in the understanding of the right to religious freedom revolves around the notions of religious tolerance and intolerance. Tolerance is a concept that has made its appearance at various times in the history of ideas since ancient Rome. Yet, following the strife of the Protestant reformation, tolerance has become a more relevant notion.[220] Thus, one can talk of a history of toleration which would take the form of a history of the codification of basic liberties, especially regarding freedom of religion, and other basic liberties such as freedom of conscience, freedom of speech, and freedom of the press. A notion of tolerance implies in its understanding that one is to be immune from external coercion in matters of conscience or belief. However, both tolerance as immunity from coercion and human conscience do not offer a proper foundation for religious freedom as a special human right.

Rainer Forst has argued that tolerance is a notion that acquired new meanings depending on the context and the specific conditions of political and cultural conflict in which different authors were developing arguments in favor or against religious tolerance. The content of these ideas, however, has transcended their own context and has continued to shape contemporary discourse on religious freedom understood as tolerance. Nevertheless, Forst argues that by reason of the variety of meanings and arguments in favor of tolerance, it is in itself a conflictive notion. Tolerance has been firstly understood as "permission toleration." This is the case when, for example, the state that grants qualified permission to the members of a religious group to live according to their beliefs on the condition that they accept the dominant position of the authority. Secondly, tolerance has been understood as a "respect conception," that is, when citizens see each other as legally equal participants in the building of society and aware of the right of others, which should always be respected.

I concluded that religious freedom must never be taken as meaning any kind of permission on the part of the state. It is in regard to this conception, then, that it is imperative to explore the meaning of religious freedom

---

220. It is in this particular respect that Forst argues that "it can be described as an inherently 'modern' concept, perhaps even as the modern concept par excellence." Forst, *TC*, 359.

in order to be able to justify the political and legal protection of this human right, for a notion of tolerance as permission is in itself destructive of what the notion of religious freedom is intended to signify. On the other hand, one can argue in favor of a "respect" conception of toleration among fellow citizens living in a pluralistic society. This understanding will aid in the mutual comprehension and building of society. However, the notion of tolerance as respect is not sufficient in order to establish a political right. There is still a need to redefine religious freedom, for tolerance as respect refers more to the attitude citizens should have, rather than to the religious freedom they should enjoy.

In the second section, we concluded that all the definitions and arguments in favor of religious freedom presented in this chapter, regardless of the point of view and way of proceeding in its justification, seem to fail in presenting a coherent notion of what is meant by "religion." A confused and unclear notion of "religion" has inevitable consequences on the understanding of religious freedom and its proper space in both private and public life. In most cases, religious freedom is understood as synonymous with freedom of conscience. This shows us how precarious is the character of such a justification of religious freedom, for it assumes that anyone who claims freedom of conscience also possesses a religious conscience. It is obvious that one does not follow from the other, for one can act in conscience without having been instructed in, or being guided by, a religious belief. And even if one were trying to argue in favor of religious freedom as protection of one's conscience, this leads to a serious misunderstanding of religious freedom. Freedom of conscience protects a judgment or decision made by a person regarding a particular action, which may onot be religious at all. A doctor can claim an argument based on his conscience in order not to perform an abortion, for example, which is something totally different from what is considered to be a religious act, such as praying, worshipping, etc. A person who follows his own conscience, which may not necessarily have been informed by faith, but instead by secular values, or knowledge gathered from experience, may consider that to perform certain acts may not be conducive to the good of the human person. Acting upon a judgment about a particular action, whether it may have been informed by faith or by reason alone or by both, is in itself a human act which may not necessarily have any religious implications. If the government were to force a person to act against his own conscience to perform an act that in itself is not religious, this would constitute a violation of his freedom of conscience, but not of his religious freedom, even if the conscientious judgment has been informed by faith. It would be different if the object of the government's coercive intervention has to do with a religious act in itself, such as praying, worshipping, sacrificing to a god, or regarding acts that are ordered to religious acts, such as the prohibition to build a church. And in those cases that seem to properly belong to religious freedom, such as praying, one would still have to establish the proper sphere of that religious acts in order to be able to discern the limits of this right, and the cases where it is necessary some sort of protection or intervention for the sake of the common good and public order.

Different contemporary approaches to justify religious freedom have signified an important and invaluable contribution to the understanding and defense of religious freedom, regardless of the strength or weakness of their arguments. However, there is a lack of clarification in these justification on what is meant by "freedom" and "religion," from which guidelines can be established on the practice of religion in society. The notion of religion, for example, is employed as a category, and in some cases even as meaning a dogma. If "religion" is understood as a category which designates a system of beliefs, practices, or values, then one can argue that it is not necessary to posit such a special right, for "freedom of conscience" suffices in protecting these acts. Thus, there is a problem with the meaning of "religion" as employed by the defenders of "freedom of religion." Such a notion of religion only leads to more confusion. Unless such a meaning of religion is question, there seems to be no clear solution to the contemporary debate on religious freedom and the place of religion in the public square. We need to employ a notion that is clear, one which will aid us in establishing the guidelines for state action regarding issues of freedom of religion and the "due limits" of this right.

Therefore, it is still necessary to build these foundations and arguments in favor of religious freedom on a clearer understanding of both freedom and religion, and the proper sphere of agency. This will help solve the dilemmas that arise when "religion" enters the public square, or instances when religious freedom is used to advance practices that seem dangerous for individuals and society. We will now move on to establish what is meant by both religion (chapter 3) and freedom (chapter 4) in order to argue for a right to religious freedom.

CHAPTER 3

Religion: History and Meaning of an Uncertain Concept

THE DEFINITION OF RELIGION has direct implications for any working through of the notion of religious freedom. Yet, "religion" has meant different things throughout history. For that reason, it is imperative that, in order to address the problems around religious freedom, one possess a correct understanding of "religion," especially in order to stand afloat current debates that employ different meanings of religion. Thus, in this chapter I will proceed to do a verbal inquiry into the notion of religion. The aim will be to see whether it is possible to find an appropriate notion of religion, one that will help us aid us in a proper definition of religious freedom and in dealing better with the difficulties found in contemporary debates on religion in the public square.

In the previous chapters, we have seen that the notion of "religion" employed in contemporary debates and definitions of religious freedom tends to be vague. Religion is sometimes employed to refer to a variety of things, such as a belief system or dogma, a kind of argumentation (religious reasoning), or a group, church, or institution. Other times it is employed to refer to "religious phenomena." Yet, if we were to consider the phenomena called religious, these are so varied in human life, that it seems impossible to offer a coherent notion of religion that distinguishes itself from other aspects of one's life. At the same time, the concept of religion is employed as a notion that retains the same essence over time and across space, and is at least theoretically separable from secular realities, such as political institutions, education, etc. Yet, historically, religion has had different connotation depending on diferent historical settings. For that reason, it is important that I leave aside any number of assumptions about what does and does not count as religion, in order to do a historical investigation into the meaning of religion.

It is essential to do an investigation into the meaning of religion, for otherwise the meaning of religious freedom stands uncertain and vague. What are we referring to when we talk about "religion" in general, or "freedom of religion" in particular? This is especially true when it comes to religious traditions that are not Christian or Western. There is, in fact, a growing body of scholarly work that explores how the category "religion" has been invented in the modern West and in colonial contexts according to specific configurations of political power.[1] It is important, then, to explore the meaning and origin of "religion," in order to properly define the meaing of religious freedom. This entails a philosophical critique of "religion," putting into question the meanings offered in recent debates, at a time when all European languages seem to speak in vain, for words are being redefined in order to fit a new order of things.[2]

The verbal inquiry I offer in this chapter will attempt to offer a genealogy of the concept of religion in the West, that is, how the concept has been formed and employed in different times and places. This will be done in order to see whether it is possible to find an appropriate meaning of religion. In itself, this is a task that goes beyond the scope of this book. For that reason, I will briefly refer to different uses of the term "religion" in Greek and Roman thought, in the work of Thomas Aquinas in the Middle Ages, the use of "religion" in Modernity, the use of religion outside the Western context, and finally, I will analyze some contemporary definitions of religion. This will also allow us to understand how the authors treated in chapters 1 and 2 arrived at the notion of religion they employ in their argumentations, and why a problematic understanding of religion has grave consequences to the understanding and meaning of religious freedom.

Firstly, then, I will present the meaning and use of "religion" in Greek and Roman thought, for it is in this historical context that the term appears for the first time. In connection with the origin of religion, I will also introduce here the work done by Giorgio Agamben on the oath as a juridical and religious institution in Greek and Roman thought that gave origin to the religious and the law.

Secondly, I will present Thomas Aquinas's notion of religion as a moral virtue, which gathers a constellation of acts, such as devotion, prayer, oaths,

---

1. Cf. Cavanaugh, *Myth*, 3.

2. One can recall here how the Little Sisters of the Poor have argued that the government, in the HHS mandate, is redefining the notion of "religion" and what it means to be "religious" in order to make room for their agenda without violating the right to religious freedom. There is also the United States Supreme Court decision in 2015 to redefine the meaning of marriage. For more on the redefinition of terms such as religion and marriage, see Anderson, *Truth Overruled*.

vows, and tithing. I will also investigate within Aquinas's notion of religion the connection between the acts of this virtue and the public square.

Thirdly, I will make a historical presentation on the invention of "religion" as a category in modernity. It was at this time that for the first time ever the notion of religion was employed to mean an interior disposition reducible to a belief.

Fourthly, I will make an inquiry into the ways in which the concept of religion as a category has been employed in colonial contexts outside the West. This perspective will offer an important insight, for it will show us that, since religion as a category is an invention of modernity, there is no notion outside the West that resembles what is meant by "religion" as a political and theological category.

Finally, I will present contemporary uses and definitions of religion. This analysis will make it clear that the term "religion" as a category should be dropped entirely in contemporary debates if one is willing to overcome the impasse present in contemporary discussions.

The Oath as a Juridical and Religious Institution in Ancient Greece and Rome

This first section will present the origins of the term "religion" in Western civilization. As it will be seen, its origins are tied to the institution of the "oath." For that reason, it will also be necessary to analyze the origins of the concept of the oath in ancient Greece and Rome.

Paolo Prodi, in his *Il sacramento del potere* (1992), argued that there is in Western Christian culture a dual belonging between religion and politics, which is testified by the role of the oath.[3] According to him, the oath is foundational for Western politics, for, as a "sacrament of power," it is the most sacred form of language, for its words are meant to become reality. Thus, in our Western tradition, the oath has had a special and powerful kind of performative speech act. Through the oath, humans have invoked or called upon the divinity as a witness in order to attest either to the truth of an assertion or to the sincerity of a promise.[4]

Giorgio Agamben, in his *Il sacramento del linguaggio: archeologia del giuramento* (2008), argues that the oath points toward a particular response to the experience of language, a response that gave birth to both religion and the law.[5] Stefania Tutino, in fact, states: "In the Western tradition the oath has

---

3. Cf. Prodi, *Sacramento del Potere*, 522.
4. Cf. Tutino, *Shadows of Doubt*, 149.
5. Cf. Agamben, *SL*. English trans.: Agamben, *Sacrament of Language*. On the

been generally understood as both a powerful way to connect humans with the divinity (in this respect oaths are intrinsically linked to the sphere of the sacred) and an equally powerful way to connect humans with one another (in this respect oaths are intrinsically linked to the sphere of law)."[6]

For Agamben, rather than the "sacrament of power" (as in Prodi), the oath is more properly the "sacrament of language," for, aside from and before binding men to either God or to each other, the oath binds men to their own word.[7] Thus, the oath represents the "verification of words in facts," that is, the "precise correspondence between words and reality."[8] Agamben's work is very useful in this respect, for he undertakes "a philosophical archeology of the oath."[9] He starts his analysis with the notion of the oath in ancient Greece, for it is in this epoch in which we find the earliest written documents on the oath.[10]

The Function of the Oath

In his *Against Leocrates*, Lycurgus (800–730 BC), the legendary lawgiver of Sparta, states that "the power that holds together our democracy is the oath."[11] This, according to Agambern, expresses the essential function of the oath in the political constitution.[12] The Neoplatonic philosopher Hierodes (fifth century AD) seems to confirm this centrality of the oath by making it the principle that completes the law. Hierodes states:

> We have previously shown that the law is the always uniform operation by means of which God eternally and immutably leads everything to existence. Now we call oath that which, following this law, conserves all things in the same state and renders them stable in such a way that, as they are held in the guarantee of the

---

dispute on the ways in which the oath connects the sphere of the sacred and that of the law, see Agamben, *SL*, 1–19.

6. Tutino, *Shadows of Doubt*, 150.
7. Cf. Agamben, *SL*, 71.
8. Agamben, *SL*, 21.
9. Agamben, *SL*, 4. Agamben's hypothesis is that the enigmatic institution, both juridical and religious, that is designated with the term "oath" can only be made intelligible if it is situated within a perspective in which it calls into question the very nature of man as a speaking being and a political animal. Hence the contemporary interest of doing an archaeology of the oath. Cf. Agamben, *SL*, 16.
10. Cf. Agamben, *SL*, 25.
11. *Against Leocrates* in Lycurgus, *Minor Attic Orators*, 79.
12. Cf. Agamben, *SL*, 5.

oath and maintain the order of the law, the immutable stability of the order of creation is the completion of the creating law.[13]

Agamben notes that it is necessary to pay attention to the words that express the function of the oath in these two passages from Lycurgus and Hierocles. In none of these passages the oath creates anything, nor does it bring anything into being, but rather keeps united and conserves what something or someone else (in Hierocles, the law; in Lycurgus, the citizens or the legislator) has brought into being.[14]

Prodi, instead, offers as a fundamental text concerning the institution of the oath a passage from Roman juridical culture, taken from Cicero's *De officiis*, in which he defines the oath as follows:

> But in taking an oath it is our duty to consider not what one may have to fear but wherein its obligation lies: an oath is a religious affirmation; because that which is affirmed should be taken as promised before God as one's witness. For the question concerns not the wrath of the gods (for there is no such thing) but what belongs to justice and good faith.[15]

It is the "religious affirmation" (*affirmatio religiosa*) what confirms and guarantees the oath. The oath has a function of stability and guarantee, and for that reason, Cicero draws attention to it by stating that, "in the sacrament it is important to consider not so much the danger that it generates, but its own efficacy."[16] That means that what is of importance in the oath is not so much the curse it generates for the one that may break it, but rather the efficacy or power it has in in motivating one to fulfill one's word. Thus, the *vis* or power of the oath is not a matter of the anger of the gods, for they do not exist (*quae nulla est*), but of trust (*fides*). For that reason, Cicero states that, "whoever, therefore, violates his oath violates trust."[17] Faithfulness is

---

13. Cited by Hirzel, *Eid*, 74.

14. Cf. Agamben, *SL*, 6.

15. Cicero, *Officiis*, III, 29, 10. The context of this definition is the behavior of Attilio Regolo, who, sent to Rome by the enemies of whom he had been a prisoner with the oath that he would return, decides to return knowing that he will be put to death. Thus, the question that Cicero asks concerns the origin of the binding power of the oath. "What significance, then, someone will say, do we attach to an oath? It is not that we fear the wrath of Jove, is it?" (Cicero, *Officiis*, III, 102.). And yet, Cicero answers, all the philosophers affirm that the gods do not become angry at or harm men. Cf. Agamben, *SL*, 31–32.

16. Cicero, *Officiis*, I, 23.

17. Cicero, *Officiis*, III, 104.

the correspondence between language and actions, notes Agamben.[18] This faithfulness, or *fides*, performed an important function not just in regulating personal relationships, but also in international public law, in the special relationships that were established by means of *fides* between cities and peoples. Thus, there is a connection between faith and oath; for example, the cities and people who mutually bound themselves in the *deditio in fidem* exchanged solemn oaths to sanction this relationship.[19]

Émile Benveniste, at the beginning of his 1948 article on the oath ("L'expression du serment dans la Grèce ancienne"), defined the function of the oath as such:

> [The oath] is a particular modality of assertion, which supports, guarantees, and demonstrates, but does not found anything. Individual or collective, the oath exists only by virtue of that which it reinforces and renders solemn: a pact, an agreement, a declaration. It prepares for or concludes a speech act which alone possesses meaningful content, but it expresses nothing by itself. It is in truth an oral rite, often completed by a manual rite whose form is variable. Its function consists not in the affirmation that it produces, but in the relation that it institutes between the word pronounced and the potency invoked.[20]

The oath, then, has to do with the assurance of its truthfulness and its actualization, that is, with the guarantee of its efficacy. For that reason, Agamben states that the oath seems to be a linguistic act intended to confirm a meaningful proposition (a *dictum*), whose truth or effectiveness it guarantees.[21]

There are two texts by the Hellenistic Jewish philosopher Philo of Alexandria (25 BC—50 AD) that confirm this central function of the oath. The first text is a passage from Philo's *Legum allegoriae*. In discussing the oath that God makes to Abraham in Genesis 22:16-17, Philo places the oath in a constitutive relationship with the language of God. The main implication of this brief treatise on the oath is that the oath is defined by the verification of words in facts, that is, by the precise correspondence between words and reality. Philo states that "God's words are oaths receiving confirmation by

---

18. Cf. Agamben, *SL*, 32.

19. Cf. Agamben, *SL*, 36-37. Agamben also states: "The *fides* is, then, a verbal act, as a rule accompanied by an oath, with which one abandons oneself completely to the 'trust' of someone else and obtains, in exchange, that one's protection. The object of the *fides* is, in every case, as in the oath, conformity between the parties' words and actions" (p. 37).

20. Benveniste, "L'expression du Serment dans la Grèce Ancienne," 81-82.

21. Cf. Agamben, *SL*, 9.

accomplishment in act."[22] Philo also states that "the very words of God are oaths,"[23] and that the oath is the *logos* of God, and only God swears truly:

> He alone shall affirm anything regarding Himself since he alone has unerringly exact knowledge of His own nature. God alone therefore is the strongest security first for Himself, and in the next place for his deeds also, so that He naturally swore by Himself when giving assurance as to himself, a thing impossible for anyone but God.[24]

A consequence of this is that men do not swear by God but by the name of God, for "naturally no one swears by Him, since he is unable to possess knowledge regarding His nature."[25] Since we know nothing of God, the only certain definition that we can give of him is that God is the being whose *logoi* are *horkoi*, that is, whose word testifies with absolute certainty for itself.

We see here how the oath, defined by the correspondence between words and actions, performs an absolutely central function. What is of great interest, as Agamben notes, is that this happens not only on the theological level, in that it defines God and his *logos*, but also on the anthropological level, since it relates human language to the paradigm of divine language.[26]

The second text is from Philo's *De sacrificiis*. Here, Philo presents the oath as the language that is always realized in facts, and this is the *logos* of God. Philo states that "God spoke and it was done, with no interval between the two."[27] In God, speaking and the result of what is being stated are one and the same thing. Thus, the oath of men is an attempt to conform the human model to the divine model by bringing into action what one has promised, thus making one's own word as credible as possible. This function of the oath is confirmed again when Philo writes:

> Now men have recourse to oaths to win belief, when others deem them untrustworthy; but God is trustworthy in his speech as elsewhere, so that his words in certitude and assurance are no different from oaths. And so it is that while with us the oath gives warrant for our sincerity, it is itself guaranteed by God. For God is not trustworthy because of the oath; but it is God that assures the oath.[28]

22. Philo of Alexandria, *Genesis*, 204–8.
23. Philo of Alexandria, *Genesis*, 204–8.
24. Philo of Alexandria, *Genesis*, 204–8.
25. Philo of Alexandria, *Genesis*, 204–8.
26. Cf. Agamben, *SL*, 29–30.
27. Philo of Alexandria, *Sacrificiis*, 65.
28. Philo of Alexandria, *Sacrificiis*, 93.

As in the Greek tradition, in which even the gods are subject in some way to the oath, in Philo not only human language but even God himself is irresistibly drawn into the sphere of the oath.[29]

The Oath as a Juridical and Religious Institution

The oath appears in the earlies documents as a juridical institution which includes elements associated with the religious sphere. Dumézil, for example, quotes an inscription on the vase of Dvenos (dated to the end of the sixth century BC) from the Roman tradition, and which was probably buried by a priest of Proserpina. The vase depicts a marital image and a promissory formula of an undoubtedly juridical and religious character: "He who sends me, implores the gods Jove, Vejove, and Saturn . . . ." The oath consists in the guarantee given by the woman's guardian to her future husband at the moment of the marriage or engagement.[30] What is of extreme interest, is that the first documents that testify to the oath include both the juridical and the religious. For that reason, Agamben argues that it would be arbitrary to distinguish in the oath a more archaic phase, consisting only in a religious rite, from a more modern phase, in which the oath belongs entirely to law.[31] He states:

> In the most ancient sources that the Latin tradition permits us to reach, the oath is a verbal act intended to guarantee the truth of a promise or an assertion, which presents the same characteristics attested by the later sources and that we have no reason to define as more or less religious, more or less juridical.[32]

The same holds for the Greek tradition. The most ancient Greek sources present the oath as entailing the testimony of the gods, which always has a juridical nature. This is seen, for example, in the pacts between federated cities, where the oath is defined as "legal."[33] According to Hesiod, even the gods swear invoking the waters of the Styx, and they are also subject to the authority of the oath. That means that if a god committed perjury, even

---

29. For the Greek tradition, see the chapter by Isabelle C. Torrance entitled "The Oaths of the Gods," in Sommersteine t al., *Oaths and Swearing*, 195–212. See also Agamben, *SL*, 31.

30. The formula, written in an archaic Latin, reads: "iovest deiuos quoi me mitat." Cf. Dumézil, *Idées Romaines*, 14–15. For an analysis of the text, see Claflin, "Inscription of Dvenos," 418–20.

31. Cf. Agamben, *SL*, 25.

32. Agamben, *SL*, 26.

33. See Glotz, "Iusirandum," 749.

he would be punished by the curse.³⁴ And Aristotle, in his *Metaphysics*, informs us that the oath is the most ancient thing, no less ancient than the gods, who are in fact subject to it in some way. He states:

> The ancients who lived long before the present generation, and first framed the accounts of the gods ... made Ocean and Tethys the parents of creation, and described the oath of the gods as being by water, which they themselves call Styx; for what is oldest is most honorable, and the most honorable thing is that by which one swears.³⁵

Agamben argues that the context of the passage, which is that of the reconstruction of the thought of Thales within the brief history of philosophy that opens the *Metaphysics*, leads one to situate the oath among the "first principles" of the pre-Socratic philosophers, as if the origin of the cosmos and of the thought that understands it implied the oath in some way.³⁶ This highlights the point that, in the oath, there is no distinction between the juridical and the religious. Agamben states:

> Not only do we have no reason for postulating a prejuridical phase in which the oath belonged solely to the religious sphere, but perhaps our entire habitual way of representing to ourselves the chronological and conceptual relationship between law and religion must be revised. Perhaps the oath presents to us a phenomenon that is not, in itself, either (solely) juridical or (solely) religious but that, precisely for this reason, can permit us to rethink from the beginning what law is and what religion is.³⁷

A similar consideration can be drawn from the concept of the *fides*. In its original Roman sense, *fides* meant "reliablilty," that is, the trust between two parties if a relationship between them was to exist.³⁸ The *fides* had also both le-

---

34. Styx was the goddess of the underworld River Styx and the eldest of the Oceanids. She was also the spirit personification of hatred (stygos). Horkos was the personified spirit of oaths who punished perjurers. He was a punitive companion of the goddess Dike (justice). In his *Theogony* Hesiod affirms: "So deathless Styx came first to Olympus with her children through the wit of her dear father. And Zeus honored her, and gave her very great gifts, for he appointed her to be the great oath of the gods, and her children to live with him always" (lines 399–400). "Such an oath, then, did the gods appoint the eternal and primeval water of Styx to be: and it spouts through a rugged place" (line 805). See Hesiod, *Theogony*. See also Sommerstein et al., *Oaths and Swearing*, 195–212.

35. Aristotle, *Metaphysics*, bk. I, 983b32–35.

36. Cf. Agamben, *SL*, 27.

37. Agamben, *SL*, 27.

38. According to Cicero the essential meaning of fides is truth and reliability in

gal and religious consequences. Thus, Agamben argues that we find ourselves in a sphere in which the problem of the genetic relationship between religion and law has to be taken up again on new foundations.

The institutions of the oath and *fides* are indeed very complex, for they seem to be at once moral, religious, social, and juridical, which obliges us to reconsider our definitions of what is juridical and what is religious.[39] The reason, Agamben argues, is that "the oath presents us, rather, in a still undivided unity, what we are accustomed to call magic, religion, and law, which result from the oath as its fragments.[40] Religion and the law, then, are born as the attempt to secure trust, by separating in specific institutions blessing and *sacratio*, oath and perjury, for the one who speaks in the oath is co-originarily exposed to both truth and lying, to both bene-diction and male-diction. Thus, the curse becomes at this point something that is added to the oath to guarantee what at the beginning was entrusted entirely to *fides* in speech, so that the oath can be presented as that which was invented to punish perjury. Agamben states: "The oath is not a conditional curse: on the contrary, the curse and its symmetrical *pendant*, the blessing, are born as specific institutions from the division of the experience of speech that was in question in the oath."[41]

The need for the profession of oaths was caused by the fallibility of human speech. The fact that words may not coincide with reality, requires one to formulate a verdict as an assertion, an oath as a denotative expression, and a profession of faith as a dogma. However, it is then that the experience of speech splits, and perjury and lie irreducibly spring up. It is in the attempt to check this split in the experience of language, then, that law and religion are born, both of which seek to tie speech to things and to bind, by means of courses and anathemas, speaking subjects to the veritable power of their speech, to their "oath," and to their declaration of faith.[42] For that reason, Agamben holds that: "Religion and law do not preexist the performative

---

words and actions. Cf. Cicero, *Officiis*, I, 23.

Christian writers employed *fides* as meaning the theological virtue of "faith," which is not totally disconnected to the legal and religious meaning it was granted by the Romans. In fact, to profess the faith is an oath in which one testifies what God has said to be true.

39. Cf. Agamben, *SL*, 37–38.
40. Cf. Agamben, *SL*, 59.
41. Agamben, *SL*, 59–60.
42. Cf. Agamben, *SL*, 79–80. Agamben also states: "The oath seems, then, to result from the conjunction of three elements: an affirmation, the invocation of the gods as witnesses, and a curse directed at perjury" (43).

experience of language that is in question in the oath, but rather they were invented to guarantee the truth and trustworthiness of the *logos*."⁴³

Religion and the Oath

Ancient Greek and Latin languages have no word whose meaning approximates what modern English speakers mean by "religion."⁴⁴ The word is etymologically derived from the ancient Latin word *religio*. For the Romans, however, *religio* was only one of a constellation of terms surrounding social obligations in ancient Rome, and when employed, the word signified something quite different from religion in the modern sense. In Rome, there was no neat division between religion and politics. The notion of Roman *religio* was inextricable from duty to the emperor and to the gods of Roman civic life. Thus, when law and religion are placed in opposition to each other, Agamben argues that it is necessary to remember that the Romans considered the sphere of the sacred as an integral part of law.⁴⁵ *The Digest*, for example, opens with the distinction between *ius publicum* (public law), which concerns the *status rei publicae* (status of public things), and *ius privatum* (private law), which concerns the *singulorum utilitatem* (utility of individuals). Yet, immediately after, the *ius publicum* is defined as that law "which consists in sacred things and rites, in priests and in magistrates."⁴⁶ It is in the same sense that Gaius, in his *Institutiones*, offers a *summa divisio* [chief division] of things internal to law. He distinguishes things according to whether they belong to the *ius divinum* [divine law] or to the *ius humanum* [human law], specifying that of the class *divini juris* are things sacred or religious.⁴⁷

One of the most probable derivations of *religio* is from *re-ligare*, to rebind or relink, that is, to reestablish a bond that has been severed. For the Romans, the saying "*religio mihi est*," that is, that something is "*religio* for me," meant that it was something that carried a serious obligation for a person. This obligation included not only cultic observances, which were themselves sometimes referred to as *religiones*, such that there was a different *religio* or set

---

43. Agamben, *SL*, 80.

44. Wilfred Cantwell Smith cites the scholarly consensus that neither the Greeks nor the Egyptians had any equivalent term for "religion," and he adds that a similar negative conclusion is found for the Aztecs and the ancient civilizations of India, China, and Japan. Cf. Smith, *Meaning and End of Religion*, 54–55.

45. Cf. Agamben, *SL*, 27–28.

46. Ulpian, *Commentaries and Rules*, D. 1, 1, 1, 2.

47. Gaius, *Institutiones*, II, §2, p. 122.

of observances at each shrine, but also civic oaths and family rituals, things that modern Westerners normally consider to be secular.[48] Thus, *religio* referred to a powerful requirement to perform some action. In fact, Adolf Berger, in his *Encyclopedic Dictionary of Roman Law*, affirms that *religio*, when used with reference to public officials, judges, etc., meant "conscientiousness, scrupulousness in the fulfillment of official duties."[49]

In the passage already cited from Cicero's *De officiis*, he states that it is the "religious affirmation" (*affirmatio religiosa*) what confirms and guarantees the oath.[50] In *The Institutes of Gaius*, *res religiosae* were the things "dedicated to the gods of lower regions," the infernal gods, such as tombs or burial grounds, in contraposition to the sacred things, which are "those which are consecrated to the gods above."[51] In this sense, the *religiosus* is the grave, the place in which a *corpus* (corpse) has been buried.[52] Berger notes that a piece of land being in private ownership became *locus religiosus* when the owner or another person acting with his permission, buried a human body in it. A burial by an unauthorized person, on the contrary, did not render the soil *religiosus*. *Res religiosae* could not be the object of a legal transaction, and thus were removed from profane use and commerce.[53] The owner who legally made a *res religiosa* of his land, especially when the funeral of the deceased person was his duty, had no ownership on the place, but he acquired a special right on the grave (*ius sepullcri*), which implied various duties, such as taking care of the tomb, observing sepulchral cult, sacrifices, and the right to bury other dead there (*ius mnortuum inferendi*).[54] More generally, the religious thing is subject to a series of ritual prescriptions, which render it inviolable and which must be scrupulously observed.

Having noted this, one can then understand in what sense Cicero speaks of the oath as a "religious affirmation." As Agamben notes:

> The "religious affirmation" is a word guaranteed and sustained by a *religio*, which removes it from common use and, consecrating it to the gods, makes it the object of a series of ritual prescriptions (the formula and gesture of the oath, calling of the

---

48. Smith, *Meaning and End of Religion*, 19–21.
49. Berger, *Dictionary of Roman Law*, 673.
50. Cf. Cicero, *Officiis*, III, 29, 10.
51. Gaius, II, §4, p. 122.
52. The Roman distinguished the corpse from a cadaver. For them, the *corpus* designates a dead body in a grave, while the *cadaver* designates a dead body deprived of a grave.
53. See Thomas, "Corpus."
54. Berger, *Dictionary of Roman Law*, 679.

gods as witness, the curse in case of perjury, etc.). The double sense of the term *religio*, which according to the lexicons means both "sacrilege, curse" and "scrupulous observation of formulas and ritual norms," can be explained in this context without difficulty.[55]

It is in this sense that Cicero can speak of a "religion of the oath" (*religio iusiurandi*), for here one finds the two meanings of the term.

When *religio* did refer to temple sacrifices, it was possible in ancient Rome to practice *religio*, and not necessarily believe in the existence of gods. This was common among certain intellectuals, as for example Cicero, who affirms in his definition of the oath that "there is no such a thing" as gods.[56] As S. N. Balagangadhara points out, this was possible because *religio* was largely indifferent to theological doctrine, and was primarily about the customs and traditions that provided the glue for the Roman social order.[57] Thus, as Agamben notes, it is anachronistic to project the modern concept of "religion" onto the past, as when one speaks of a "Roman religion."[58] According to the definition of *religio* that Cicero puts in the mouth of the pontifex maximus Cotta, religion was nothing but the sum of the ritual formulas and practices to be observed in the *ius divinum*. Cicero states: "The Religion of the Roman people comprises ritual [and] auspices,"[59] that is, in consecrations and the auspices to be consulted before every important public act. For Cicero, the origin of the word *religio* is found in the verb *relegere*, to observe scrupulously: "Those on the other hand who carefully reviewed and so to speak retraced all the lore of ritual were called 'religious,' from *relegere*."[60] Yet, one can argue that the sense of binding (*religare*) is still present here, for public officials bound themselves to carefully fulfill their duties, which include the careful reading and reviewing of the law and customs.

---

55. Agamben, *SL*, 33. In a passage of the *De Natura Deorum*, for example, the two senses are at the same time distinct and juxtaposed. The consul Tiberius Gracchus, who bad forgotten to take the auspices at the moment of the designation of his successors, prefers to admit his error and annul the election that has taken place contrary to *religio* rather than allow a "sacrilege" (*religio*) to contaminate the State. Cicero, *Natura Deorum*, II, 11.

56. Cicero, *Officiis*, III, 29, 10.
57. Balagangadhara, *Blindness*, 37–43.
58. Cf. Agamben, *SL*, 34.
59. Cicero, *Natura Deorum*, III, 5.
60. Cicero, *Natura Deorum*, II, 72.

Conclusion

In order to conclude this section on the oath as a juridical and religious institution in ancient Greece and Rome, and its relationship to *religio*, I will present a series of ideas that summarize our presentation of Agamben's investigation.

In the first place, it is the oath, as the original performative experience of the word, that can explain religion and law as appearing in a public setting. This is the reason why, in the classical world, Horkos, the personified god of the curse that would befall upon any person that broke an oath they had taken, was the most ancient being, the sole potency to which the gods are submitted for punishment. Later, in monotheism, God is identified with the oath, as for example in Philo. Thus, God is the being whose word is an oath, for it is efficiently fulfilled in creating through his word "in the beginning."

In the second place, the proper context of the oath is among those institutions whose function is to performatively affirm the truth and trustworthiness of speech. This is the reason why oaths are present in both religion and the law. Oaths are par excellence reliable, and for that reason, in ancient Rome and Greece, the gods were summoned in the oath in order to testify to this reliability. Later, monotheistic religious traditions, especially the Christian tradition, inherited from the oath the centrality of faith in the word as the essential content of religious experience: because God revealed it, it is true. Thus, it was through creeds that religious groups created a codified system of truths, and their task became the attempt to reconcile faith as the performative experience of truth with belief in a series of dogmas. It is in this sense that philosophy may also be a true religion, for it testifies in every event of language the experience of being, of the real.

In the third place, the religious and the juridical are both present in the oath. The religious element testifies to the truthfulness of one's word, while the juridical, the law, testifies to the curse that will befall on the perjurer.

In the fourth place, man, through human language, found himself co-originarily exposed to the possibility of both truth and lie. It was only then that he committed himself to respond with his life for his words, to testify in the first person for them. Thus, Agambens asserts, "the oath express the demand, decisive in every sense for the speaking animal, to put its nature at stake in language and to bind together in an ethical and political connection words, things, and actions."[61]

---

61. Agamben, *SL*, 95.

Finally, there is in Western Christian culture a dual belonging between religion and politics, which is testified by the role of the oath.[62] The oath is foundational for all of the political institutions in our Western civilization. However, that also means that a decline on the power of the oath cannot but entail a transformation in the forms of political association. Can we say that, perhaps, this decline on the power of the oath is the result of how "religion" is understood to mean? At the same time, if there is a belonging between law and religion, testified by the oath, would not the public square, then, be the proper place not only for politics but also for religion? This may lead one to question contemporary understandings of notion of the public sphere. Can we affirm, then, that "the religious" is a purely separate sphere? In order to answer these questions, then, it is crucial to clarify of what is meant by the term "religion."

Thomas Aquinas's Notion of Religion

In the medieval period, the term "religion" became even less frequently used in Christian discourse. As John Bossy states: "With very few exceptions, the word was only used to describe different sorts of monastic or similar rule, and the way of life pursued under them."[63] In the early thirteenth century, for example, we find references to "religion" as indicating a particular monastic or religious order or rule,[64] such that by 1400 we find references to religions in the plural to refer to the different religious orders. Thomas Aquinas, for example, wrote two addresses in which declensions of the word *religio* appear in the title, and both are defenses of religious orders.[65]

Regarding the ancient meaning of "religion" as duty or reverence, Bossy argues that it "disappeared" in the medieval period.[66] However, Bossy cannot be taken literally, for Aquinas used the term religion in the older sense of "rites" and "piety," and in the sense of rendering that which is due.[67]

---

62. Cf. Prodi, *Sacramento del Potere*, 522.

63. Bossy, "Some Elementary Forms of Durkheim," 4.

64. Thus, the adjective "religious" was used to designate a member of one of the Orders, distinguished from lay Christians.

65. See Aquinas, *Contra Impugnantes*; Aquinas, *Contra Retrahentes*. Monasticism, guided by the Rule of St. Benedict, is for Aquinas the most refined form of *religio*, such that he identifies monastic life as religious life proper. Cf. Aquinas, *S. Th.*, II–II, q. 81, a. 1, ad 5.

66. Bossy, "Some Elementary Forms of Durkheim," 4.

67. See, for example, Aquinas, *S. Th.*, II–II, q. 80, a. 1.

Thomas states in the Prologue to his *Summa Theologiae* that his intention is to describe the Christian "religion" as a whole.[68] What is novel in Aquinas, is that he deals with religion as a virtue, as leading man to good acts.[69] This section is found in *S. Th.* II–II.

In this presentation of Aquinas's notion of the virtue of religion, I will treat in the first place the virtue of religion itself (q. 81). Then, in the second place, I will present the principal and secondary acts of religion, both interior and exterior (qq. 82–91). Finally, in the third place, I will present Aquinas's notion of religion as a virtue in relation to the proper place for the performance of its acts, namely, whether they belong to the private or the public sphere.

The Virtue of Religion

Thomas locates "religion" in *S. Th.* II–II as the most important of those virtues that are related to the virtue justice,[70] for its actions are directly and immediately ordered to the honor of God.[71] In fact, Aquinas argues that the virtue of religion is the closest we can come to justice when it is God, not man, to whom we are giving what is due,[72] for there is a "debitum," something owed to God, which man will never be able to cancel out by his own power.

The section so called "*de religione*" runs from *S. Th.* II–II, q. 81 to q. 91.[73] According to Thomas, "religion has certain interior acts that principally and essentially (*per se*) belong to religion, while its external acts are secondary, and ordained to the internal acts."[74] The principal activities of the religious person are devotion (q. 82), and prayer (q. 83). Aquinas then deals with the external acts of of religion, which are ordained to the aforementioned internal acts: adoration through bodily reverence (84), the offering of sacrifices (q. 85), oblations and first-fruits (q. 86), tithes (q. 87), the taking of vows (q. 88), and the taking of God's name by oath (q. 89),

68. Cf. Aquinas, *S. Th.*, "Prooemium".

69. Cf. Aquinas, *S. Th.*, II–II, q. 81, a. 4.

70. The whole section on justice is found in Aquinas, *S. Th.*, II–II, qq. 57–122.

71. Cf. Aquinas, *S. Th.*, II–II, q. 81, a. 1, ad 4. Aquinas also considers religion to be the most important of all moral virtues. Cf. Aquinas, *S. Th.*, II–II, q. 81, a. 6.

72. Cf. Aquinas, *S. Th.*, II–II, q. 80, a. 1.

73. Moreover, as Dewan notes, the treatise does not present itself as a complete treatment; thus, the prologue to question 89 says that it should include a discussion of sacraments, but that these will be discussed instead in the third part of the Summa. Cf. Dewan, "Philosophy of Religion," 352.

74. Aquinas, *S. Th.*, II–II, q. 81, a. 7.

adjuration (q. 90), and praise (q. 91). Thus, the virtue of religion is considered by Aquinas not only as an internal disposition of the person, but also in its external manifestations.

In considering Thomas's presentation of religion, there are three things we have to take into account: firstly, it is a virtue that makes reference to the relationship of man towards God; secondly, for Aquinas, religion is a virtue; and thirdly, the virtue of religion is a species of justice. Then, in the fourth place, I will mention a few considerations regarding religion as a virtue.

The Virtue of Religion and the Relationship of Man towards God

For Aquinas, the virtue of religion makes reference to the relationship of man towards God. Thus, in presenting the different etymologies of the term "religion," Aquinas affirms that whether religion take its name from frequent reading (*relegere*), or from a repeated choice (*religere*) of what has been lost through negligence, or from being a bond (*religare*), "religion denotes properly a relation to God."[75] For Aquinas, we ought to be bound to God as to our unfailing principle, directing our choices to him, as to our last end, and if we neglect him by sin, we should recover by believing in him and confessing our faith. Yet, even though this virtue makes reference to the relationship of men towards God, it is not of a supernatural sort, in the sense of being a supernaturally infused virtue. Thomas argues for the natural character of religion by distinguising between the object or matter of the virtue of religion (the worship that is offered), and that to whom worship is offered, that is, God.[76] Thus, he affirms states that "God is related to religion not as matter or object, but as end: and consequently religion is not a theological virtue whose object is the last end, but a moral virtue which is properly about things referred to the end."[77] And it is its order to the end, then, the reason why the virtue of religion excels among the moral virtues.[78]

---

75. Cf. Aquinas, *S. Th.*, II–II, q. 81, a. 1. On the etymology of religion as *religare*, *ligare*, and *obligare*, see also Aquinas, *SCG*, bk. III, ch. 119.

76. Cf. Aquinas, *S. Th.*, II–II, q. 81, a. 5.

77. Aquinas, *S. Th.*, II–II, q. 81, a. 5. See also Aquinas, *S. Th.*, II–II, q. 81, a. 5, ad 2.

78. Cf. Aquinas, *S. Th.*, II–II, q. 81, a. 6. In q. 93, a. 2, referring to divine worship, Thomas states in fact that the end of divine worship is that man may give glory to God, and submit to Him in mind and body.

Religion as a Virtue

Aquinas treats religion under the heading of virtue. In defining virtue in *S. Th.* I–II, q. 55, a. 3, Aquinas affirms: "Human virtue which is an operative habit, is a good habit, productive of good works."[79] Thus, following Aristotle's definition, Thomas affirms that: "A human virtue is one 'which renders a human act and man himself good.'"[80] Therefore, all good acts belong to a certain virtue. In the case of religion, Aquinas argues in II–II, q. 81, a. 2 that its proper act is to pay due honor to God, which is in itself a good act.[81] Religion, then, is the virtue that inclines man to manifest to God the honor and submission that is due to him as man's creator. As a consequence, Aquinas states that since the human person is ordered to God as end, it belongs to religion to commands all other virtues. Thomas states in q. 81, a. 1, ad 1:

> Religion has two kinds of acts. Some are its proper and immediate acts, which it elicits, and by which man is directed to God alone, for instance, sacrifice, adoration and the like. But it has other acts, which it produces through the medium of the virtues which it commands, directing them to the honor of God, because the virtue which is concerned with the end, commands the virtues which are concerned with the means.[82]

This is a very important aspect to consider, especially in trying to discern the space of religion in the public square. Religion not only commands its proper (religious) acts, but also the acts of other virtues, including those that belong by nature to the public political square, such as justice and political prudence.

For Aquinas, the self-development of each human being depends on both the acquisition of virtue, and acting in an informed way by this principle of action.[83] In this respect, virtues come to the aid of natural inclinations. That means that it is natural for human being to be virtuous; yet, there is a complement needed, and that is acting in a virtuous way. Thus, Thomas states that "virtues perfect us so that we follow in due manner our natural

---

79. Aquinas, *S. Th.*, I–II, q. 55, a. 3.

80. Aquinas, *S. Th.*, II–II, q. 58, a. 3. The definition is borrowed from Aristotle, *Nicomachean Ethics*, II, vi.2, p. 88.

81. Cf. Aquinas, *S. Th.*, II–II, q. 81, a. 2.

82. Aquinas, *S. Th.*, II–II, q. 81, a. 1, ad 1. In a. 4, obj. 1, it is argued that since every virtuous deed belongs to religion, consequently religion is not a special virtue. Aquinas replies that it shows how religion commands all other virtues. See Aquinas, *S. Th.*, II–II, q. 81, a. 4, ad 1.

83. Cf. Dewan, "Philosophy and Spirituality," 360.

inclinations, which belong to the natural right."[84] The virtue of religion, then, like in all other virtues, is acquired and developed through the repetition of religiously virtuous acts. Thus, the virtue of religion presupposes and orders man's natural inclination to God. Thomas states that it belongs to the dictate of natural reason that man should do something through reverence for God; yet, what it is that should be done is established by divine or human law.[85] Thus, religion as a virtue helps man achieve that which by his natural reason he perceives as the right thing to do.

The Virtue of Religion as a Species of Justice

Finally, religion as a virtue, for Aquinas, is a potential part of justice.[86] Even though religion has something in common with justice, in some respect it falls short of the perfection of justice.[87] The reason is that, according to Aquinas, the essential character of justice consists in rendering to another his due according to equality.[88] However, as Thomas affirms in S. Th. II–II, q. 80: "In two ways may a virtue directed to another person fall short of the perfection of justice: first, by falling short of the aspect of equality; secondly, by falling short of the aspect of due." Thus, in man's relationship to God, religion falls short of the aspect of equality. The reason is that "whatever man renders to God is due, yet it cannot be equal, as though man rendered to God as much as he owes him."[89] Therefore, religion is subordinate to justice, for through the virtue of religion man pays to God his debts of worship and honor, a debt which is owing in justice but which man will never be able to fulfill. Thus, Aquinas discusses the virtue of religion in terms of principles of justice. He affirms regarding religion's belonging to justice:

---

84. Cf. Aquinas, S. Th., II–II, q. 108, a. 2.

85. Cf. Aquinas, S. Th., II–II, q. 81, a. 2, ad 3.

86. Albert the Great introduced a triple distinction within the notion of the virtue of fortitude: essential, integral, and potential virtue. Aquinas would later apply it to all four cardinal virtues. Potential virtues are those virtues that are related to and placed under the umbrella of a cardinal virtue, but which nevertheless are ordained to other actions or secondary objects and do not possess the capacity of the main virtue. Besides religion, Aquinas classifies as potential parts of justice the virtues of piety (q. 101), observance (qq. 102–5, which comprises dulia and obedience), gratitude (q. 106), vengeance (q. 108), truth (q. 109), friendliness (q. 114), liberality (q. 117), and prodigality (q. 119).

87. Cf. Aquinas, S. Th., II–II, q. 80, a. 1.

88. Cf. Aquinas, S. Th., II–II, q. 58, a. 11.

89. Aquinas, S. Th., II–II, q. 80, a. 1.

> Religion . . . is a part of justice, and observes a mean, not in the passions, but in operations directed to God, by establishing a kind of equality in them. I say equality not in an absolute way, because it is not possible to pay God as much as we owe Him, but equality in consideration of man's ability and God's acceptance.[90]

There are two reasons offered in II–II, q. 81 on why man should offer God the honor that is due to him.

In the first place, because human beings, as created beings, owe a debt to the author of one's own being.[91] Aquinas assigns to the virtue of religion all of the acts that have as an aim to render due honor to God, for he is the first principle of the creation and government of things.[92]

In the second place, man should give God his due and honor by reason of his excellence, as God surpasses all things in this regard, and therefore, honor is a proper response of the created will to the supreme being. It is this special honor to God that constitutes religion as a special virtue, for "wherever there is a special aspect of good, there must be a special virtue."[93]

It is interesting to see that, in assigning to the virtue of religion this aspect of justice, Aquinas considers religion not to be a private reality, for, as it is the case with all matters related to justice, the virtue of religion is interrelational, and part of a complex understanding of sociability and social interactions. Acts of the virtue of religion are by their own nature directed to someone other than the agent. Religion, then, is shown by Aquinas to be something beyond the holding of beliefs or the practice of rites. It is a virtue that involves interactions with others in a social setting. This view of Aquinas on religion is an important aspect to consider in order to understand the true and proper meaning of religion. Religion, for Aquinas, is the most excellent of all moral virtues, for it aims at rectifying the will.[94] As such, the virtue of religion promotes the optimal moral flourishing of individuals, as well as the realization of justice within society.

---

90. Aquinas, *S. Th.*, II–II, q. 81, a. 5, ad 3.

91. For Thomas Aquinas, man can reach the truth that the world has been created by God by the sole use of reason. cf. Aquinas, *S. Th.*, I, q. 44.

92. Cf. Aquinas, *S. Th.*, II–II, q. 81, a. 3.

93. Aquinas, *S. Th.*, II–II, q. 81, a. 4.

94. Cf. Aquinas, *S. Th.*, II–II, q. 58, a. 4.

Some Considerations Regarding the Use of the Term "Religion"

For Aquinas, religion is a virtue, a type of habit, a disposition of the person toward moral excellence produced by highly specific disciplines of body and soul. As a virtue, religion is directed to doing good, leading man to good acts, and this good consists in ordering man to God through that which belongs to divine worship.[95]

In his *S. Th.*, Aquinas quotes different etymological origins of the term *religio*. He concludes that whether religion take its name from frequent reading (*relegere*), or from a repeated choice or re-election (*religere*) of what has been lost through negligence, or from being a bond (*religare*), religion denotes properly a relation to God, the bond that unites the soul with God.[96] In *S. Th.* II–II, q. 80, a. 1, ad 2, Aquinas refers to Macrobius's consideration on doing good as an integral part of justice. Among these good acts, Thomas mentions two good acts that have to do with one's relations toward superiors, namely, "piety" to parents, and "religion" to God.[97] And in his *Contra impugnantes*, Thomas explicitly follows Augustine in accepting the etymological derivation from *ligare*, to bind: "Hence every rational creature ought to be reunited to God. . . . Therefore, Augustine says in *De Vera Religione*: Religion reunites us to the one Almighty God."[98]

Aquinas also distinguishes between religion in itself as a moral virtue, and the proper and immediate acts that belong to, and are elicited by, this virtue.[99] Of these elicited acts, some are principal and interior, others are secondary and exterior. Therefore, religion is understood as something both interior and exterior, and therefore, as it will be seen below, it does not belongs just to the private sphere or monastic life, as it has public manifestations of worship. Thus, religion incorporates both the devotion and piety of the worshipper, and the external rites and disciplines of the worship. Religion as a virtue is a type of habit, and habits are caused by the repetition of acts.[100] Such acts necessarily involve the body, for soul and body are one psychosomatic unity, in which the soul is the "form" of the body.[101] Although, according to Aquinas, the internal acts of religion take precedence over the external rites, the external rites are not expendable or

---

95. Cf. Aquinas, *S. Th.*, II–II, q. 81, a. 4; q. 82, a. 2, ad 1.
96. Cf. Aquinas, *S. Th.*, II–II, q. 81, a. 1.
97. Cf. Aquinas, *S. Th.*, II–II, q. 80, a. 1, ad 2.
98. Aquinas, *Contra Impugnantes*, I.
99. Cf. Aquinas, *S. Th.*, II–II, q. 81, Prol.
100. Cf. Aquinas, *S. Th.*, I–II, q. 51, a. 2–3.
101. Cf. Aquinas, *S. Th.*, I, q. 76, a. 1.

superfluous, for "the human mind, in order to be united to God, needs to be guided by the sensible world."[102]

Thomas also states that the virtue of religion commands all other virtues directing them to the honor of God.[103] The reason is that religion, which is in the will, directs the acts of the other powers to the reverence of God.[104] This is of central importance when considering the place of religion in the public square. Since the virtue of religion commands all other virtues, it can be observed that, consequently, the virtue of religion will have implications not only for the life of moral reason, but also for the constitution of political society. Once religion is considered as a virtue in Aquinas's sense, then its role in the public square becomes more evident.

Aquinas also employs the term religion to refer to the inner motivation towards worshipping God, and to worship itself.[105] In his *Contra impugnantes*, Thomas states that "*latria*, which is the worship of God as the beginning of all things, is the duty of man in this life. Hence, religion, primarily and chiefly, signifies latria, which renders worship to God by the expression of true faith."[106]

Religion is also taken as an outward expression of faith. Thomas states that, "just as religion is not faith, but a confession of faith through outward signs, so superstition is a confession of unbelief through external worship."[107] In this way, true faith is connected with the practice of the virtue of religion. Thus, as a virtue, religion is more perfect the better knowledge one has of God; otherwise, one's actions may resemble acts of the vice of superstition rather than acts of the virtue of religion.[108]

Religion is not understood by Aquinas as a universal genus of which Christianity, Islam, or Judaism are particular species. Thus, religion is not taken to mean a system of propositions or beliefs about reality. He never, in fact, presents Christianity as a religion to be set aside or against other "religions," that is, other worldviews, doctrines, or systems of propositions about the nature of things and their attendant rites. Aquinas, for example, acknowledges that religion is found everywhere that proper worship is

102. Aquinas, *S. Th.*, II-II, q. 81, a. 7.
103. Cf. Aquinas, *S. Th.*, II-II, q. 81, a. 1, ad 1.
104. Cf. Aquinas, *S. Th.*, II-II, q. 83, a. 3, ad 1.
105. *S. Th.* II-II, q. 80, a. 1, ad 4: "*Eusebeia* [piety] means 'good worship' and consequently it is the same as religion." And in II-I, q. 88, a. 5, talking about vows as being acts of religion, Thomas equates *latria* to religion.
106. Aquinas, *Contra Impugnantes*, I.
107. Aquinas, *S. Th.*, II-II, q. 94, a. 1, ad 1.
108. For Aquinas treatment of superstition and irreligiosity, see Aquinas, *S. Th.*, II-II, q. 92–102.

offered to the true God. Aquinas even limits the meaning of religion to the explicit worship of God or gods. Aquinas cites Cicero's definition of religion in his *Rhetoric* as consisting "in offering service and ceremonial rites to a superior nature that men call divine."[109] Aquinas would also use the word religion to describe the pagans' worship of their gods, and would also acknowledge that pagan worship contains within an inchoate groping toward the one true God, if through the act of worship, or through discussion with the worshipper, it is manifest that it is a virtue (religion) that is structuring that act.[110] However, for Aquinas, when worship is not directed to the true God, as in paganism, then pagan worship is false religion, for it does not serve the only true God.[111] The one true religion worships God the Father, Son, and Holy Spirit, and for that reason Aquinas would not acknowledge a common essence of religion underlying the various manifestations of the world's religious traditions.

Acts of the Virtue of Religion

The virtue of religion manifests itself through different good acts that make man good. This is the purpose of all virtues.[112] Thus, in the questions following his treatment of the virtue of religion, Aquinas goes on to consider the various kinds of actions which are either commanded by the virtue of religion or appropriate to it. And among the acts that belong to religion there is an order. Thus, Thomas affirms that the interior acts principally and essentially (*per se*) belong to religion, while its external acts are secondary, and ordained to the internal acts.[113] In this section, then, I will present these interior and exterior acts of the virtue of religion in order to be able to identify in the following section the proper spheres or settings in which these acts take place.

I will first present the internal acts of the virtue of religion: devotion (q. 82), and prayer (q. 83). Then, I will present the external acts of religion,

109. Aquinas, *S. Th.*, II–II, q. 81, a. 1.

110. In the same way, Aquinas would certainly question certain acts of worship in Christians which may not be motivated by virtue. An example may be found in a Philipines's tradition in which Christians self-flagellate in a bloody Holy Week ritual.

111. Aquinas affirms that "it belongs to religion to show reverence to one God under one aspect, namely, as the first principle of the creation and government of things" (Aquinas, *S. Th.*, II–II, q. 81, a. 3.). And he adds: "The three Divine Persons are the one principle of the creation and government of things, wherefore they are served by one religion." Aquinas, *S. Th.*, II–II, q. 81, a. 3, ad 1.

112. Cf. Aquinas, *S. Th.*, I–II, q. 55, a. 4.

113. Cf. Aquinas, *S. Th.*, II–II, q. 81, a. 7.

which are ordained to the internal acts: adoration through bodily reverence (84); the things offered to God by the faithful, such as the offering of sacrifices (q. 85), oblations and first-fruits (q. 86), tithes (q. 87), and the taking of vows (q. 88); and the acts of religion which include the taking of God's name, such as oaths (q. 89).[114]

Internal Acts of the Virtue of Religion: Devotion and Prayer

The first internal act of religion presented by Aquinas is "devotion," in *S. Th.* II–II, q. 82. Devotion is defined by Thomas as the special act of "the will to give oneself readily to things concerning the service of God."[115] Given its direct orientation to God, Aquinas places devotion as first among the interior acts of religion, for it presides over all of our actions in this domain.[116] And since matters related to the worship of God belong to religion, it belongs to religion to have the will ready to do such things, for this is what it means to be devout for Aquinas.[117]

It is important to note here that it is through the act of devotion that the virtue of religion influences and directs the acts of other virtues. In this way, even though devotion is an internal act, it may have an impact on other spheres of human life, such as the public political space.

Regarding the cause of the act of devotion, Aquinas affirms that the extrinsic and main cause of devotion is God, but the intrinsic cause on our part must be meditation or contemplation. It is from some consideration on the nature of God, that man willingly surrenders himself readily to the service of God. Thus, Aquinas affirms:

> Indeed a twofold consideration leads him [to surrender himself to God's service]. The first one is the consideration of God's goodness and loving kindness . . ., which is the proximate cause of devotion. The other consideration is that of man's own shortcomings, on account of which he needs to lean on God . . .; and this consideration shuts out presumption whereby

---

114. I will leave aside the acts of adjuration (q. 90) and praise (q. 91), as they do not have an important connection to our topic.

115. Aquinas, *S. Th.*, II–II, q. 82, a. 1. As Dewan affirms: "It is an interior act that imbues everything we do with the character of 'giving the whole of oneself to God.'" Dewan, "Philosophy and Spirituality," 362.

116. Cf. Aquinas, *S. Th.*, II–II, q. 82, a. 1, ad 1. See also Aquinas, *S. Th.*, II–II, q. 83, a. 3, ad 3.

117. Cf. Aquinas, *S. Th.*, II–II, q. 82, a. 2.

man is hindered from submitting to God, because he leans on his strength.[118]

Thus, the schema Thomas presents us with begins in contemplation of the immensity of the Creator in his goodness and power, and our own createdness and fallibility (II–II, q. 82, a. 3), which lead to devotion. This helps us understand, then, that devotion is internally caused by the exercise of prayer.[119]

Prayer is located in *S. Th.* II–II, q. 83, and is made up of seventeen articles.[120] Since some of them treat purely theological issues, I will only mention some philosophical aspects of prayer present in the first three articles: that prayer is an act of the intellect; more specifically, that it belongs to practical reason; and finally, that prayer is an act of virtue.

In the first place, as devotion is presented as an act of the will, prayer is presented by Aquinas as an act of the intellect. This is, according to Aquinas, the essence of prayer. He states:

> Religion, which is in the will, directs the acts of the other powers to the reverence of God. Now among the other powers of the soul the intellect is the highest, and the nearest to the will; and consequently after devotion which belongs to the will, prayer which belongs to the intellective part is the chief of the acts of religion, since by it religion directs man's intellect to God.[121]

More specifically, prayer is presented by Thomas as an act of "practical reason." It is something that pertains to us as causes. Aquinas shows in II–II, q. 83, a. 1 that something is the cause of another in two ways: perfectly, as when the effect is wholly subject to the power of the cause; or imperfectly, by merely disposing to the effect, for the effect is not wholly subject to the power of the cause. Now, reason is the cause of something according to the first way when it imposes necessity by commanding the members of the body, or when directing human subjects. Regarding the second way, reason is the cause of something by leading up to the effect, and, in a way, disposing to it. In this second sense, reason asks for something to be done by someone not subject to it, whether they be its equals or its superiors. It is in this way that practical reason has a causative role through prayer. Thus,

---

118. Aquinas, *S. Th.*, II–II, q. 82, a. 3.

119. On devotion as the foundation of religious activities, see Dewan, "Philosophy and Spirituality," 362.

120. These articles correspond in a general way to those found in the *Commentary on the Book of Sentences*; nevertheless, here in *S. Th.* they have been thoroughly reordered. See Aquinas, *Sent.*, bk. 4, d. 15, q. 4.

121. Aquinas, *S. Th.*, II–II, q. 83, a. 3, ad 1.

"it is evident that prayer, as we speak of it now, is an act of reason."[122] For Aquinas, to pray is to act as a cause of the things prayed for, and therefore, the act of asking is an act of causing.[123]

Next, Thomas presents the utility of prayer, that is, prayer is an activity that makes sense, for it has its place in a universe presided over by an all-knowing, unchangeable God. We pray, then, not to change a divine disposition, but that we may obtain that which God arranged was to be accomplished through prayer.[124]

Finally, in II–II, q. 83, a. 3, Aquinas presents prayer as an act of the virtue of religion. The act of asking for something from God implies a manifestation of reverence, and accordingly it is an act of worship. And since worship or religion is a virtue, prayer is the act of a virtue.[125] Dewan also notes that Aquinas presents the act of prayer as a virtuous action for its performance implies right acting in a human mode, that is, in a rational way, as it is an act of practical reason.[126]

When it comes to praying, even though this act is in itself an interior act, it can also be said in a loud voice, within the context of community prayer, as when other faithful gather to pray. Thus, in II–II, q. 83, a. 12, while discussing whether prayer should be vocal, Aquinas notes that prayer is twofold: common and individual. He states:

> Common prayer is that which is offered to God by the ministers of the Church representing the body of the faithful: wherefore such like prayer should come to the knowledge of the whole people for whom it is offered: and this would not be possible unless it were vocal prayer. Therefore it is reasonably ordained that the ministers of the Church should say these prayers even in a loud voice, so that they may come to the knowledge of all.[127]

Common prayer, which by its own nature is vocal, takes place during the gathering of the faithful to offer worship to God. This requires a kind

---

122. Cf. Aquinas, *S. Th.*, II–II, q. 83, a. 1.

123. Dewan comments: "Yet what do we do in prayer? We ask God to make things happen. This is the primary practical thing to do, considering that he is the creator and universal provider and governor. We can be said to have a share in bringing about what our well-placed friend brings about at our asking." See Dewan, "Philosophy and Spirituality," 362–63.

124. According to Aquinas, prayer does not impose necessity on human affairs subject to divine providence, nor does it imply changeableness on the part of the divine disposition. Cf. Aquinas, *S. Th.*, II–II, q. 83, a. 2.

125. Cf. Aquinas, *S. Th.*, II–II, q. 83, a. 3.

126. Cf. Dewan, "Ontology of Prayer," 367.

127. Aquinas, *S. Th.*, II–II, q. 83, a. 12.

of public space within the church, so that the gathering and communal activity may take place.

Acts of Adoration through Bodily Reverence

Of the external acts of worship (*latria*) that belong to the virtue of religion, the first to be considered by Aquinas is adoration, "whereby one uses one's body to reverence God."[128] Since to reverence of God belongs to the virtue of religion, adoration is one of its acts.[129]

Adoration is presented as a manifestation of, and ordered to exciting, devotion.[130] Aquinas explains that, since the human nature is both intellectual and sensible, there is a twofold adoration one offers to God: "A spiritual adoration, consisting in the internal devotion of the mind; and a bodily adoration, which consists in an exterior humbling of the body."[131] Now, since in all acts of worship that which is external is referred to that which is internal and principal, it follows that "exterior adoration is offered on account of interior adoration."[132] Thus, adoration is not purely external, for it consists chiefly in an interior reverence of God, and secondarily in certain bodily signs of humility.[133] It presupposes internal acts, such as the intellectual recognition of the divine excellence, and the submission of one's own will; and it leads to an external act, which consists in a manifestation of the internal disposition, and which also leads to devotion as an act of virtue. Now, since secondarily adoration includes bodily signs, it follows that a definite place is required for adoration by reason of a certain fittingness, for bodily signs must of necessity be in some definite place and position.[134] This, Aquinas argues, is not on account of God who is adored, for he is not enclosed in a place, but on account of the adorers.[135] This is an important aspect of the virtue of religion to be considered when discussing issues of religious freedom, and the proper sphere of virtuous acts, that is, the place in which these acts take place. Another aspect one can also consider is the time allotted to divine worship. Yet, it is also important to note that, for Aquinas, the presence of a community is not essential to the act of religion.

128. Aquinas, *S. Th.*, II–II, q. 84, pr.
129. Cf. Aquinas, *S. Th.*, II–II, q. 84, a. 1.
130. See Aquinas, *S. Th.*, II–II, q. 84, a. 2, ad 1.
131. Aquinas, *S. Th.*, II–II, q. 84, a. 2.
132. Aquinas, *S. Th.*, II–II, q. 84, a. 2.
133. Cf. Aquinas, *S. Th.*, II–II, q. 84, a. 1, ad 2.
134. Cf. Aquinas, *S. Th.*, II–II, q. 84, a. 3.
135. Cf. Aquinas, *S. Th.*, II–II, q. 84, a. 3, ad 2.

The community has a pedagogical role, for within it men to learn how to worship in a virtuous way, and following certain traditions; yet, it is not absolutely necessary for the act of religion to take place.

"Things" offered to God by the Faithful

Following his consideration on acts of adoration, Aquinas directs our attention to those acts whereby external things are offered to God. These acts can be considered in a twofold manner: those in which things are given to God by the faithful, such as the offering of sacrifices (q. 85), oblations and first-fruits (q. 86), and tithes (q. 87); and those whereby something is promised to God, such as vows (q. 88).[136]

SACRIFICES

In his *S. Th.* II–II, q. 85, a. 1, Aquinas asks whether offering a sacrifice to God belongs to natural law. On the first step of his reply, Aquinas argues that God exists; however, he does not present a scientific demonstration for the existence of God. Instead, Thomas reports and attempts to describe what Dewan calls a "universal spontaneous natural inference."[137] Thomas affirms:

> Natural reason declares to man that he is subject to some higher being, because of the deficiencies that he experiences in himself, with respect to which he needs to be helped and directed by some higher being. And whatever that is, it is that which everywhere is called God.[138]

Aquinas appeals to our experience of our own imperfection. Man experiences himself as a being that cannot stand by itself, without aid, and who cannot survive without direction from some source of intelligent direction, moving things along for man's protection and welfare. Thus, the universal spontaneous natural inference is that we all need God.

Aquinas goes on to say that just as among natural things the lower are naturally subjected to the higher, in the same way natural reason decrees to man, in accordance with natural inclination, that he show submission and honor to that which is above man, and that he do so in a way that accords with human nature. This involves the manifesting of the human mind's

---

136. Cf. Aquinas, *S. Th.*, II–II, q. 85, pr.
137. Cf. Dewan, "Moral Order," 207–08.
138. Aquinas, *S. Th.*, II–II, q. 85, a. 1.

sentiments through the use of material things and gestures. Thus, Aquinas concludes that sacrifices and using sensible things as offerings to God is naturally right, that is, it belongs to the natural law.[139]

As Dewan notes, this is a remarkable article for many reasons.[140]

In the first place, the offering of sacrifices is presented as something extremely fundamental in the moral life. Aquinas is not asking whether one should offer sacrifices, but whether it pertains to natural law that one do so. By associating sacrifices with natural law, Aquinas seems to argue that it has the character of a principle.

In the second place, and as a consequence of its character of a principle, we should note the universality of such a precept. The "sed contra," while maintaining that it is something belonging to natural law, stresses the universality of the practice of sacrifices: "In every age, among all nations of men, there has always been some offering of sacrifices, and what is the same with everyone seems to be natural. Therefore the offering of sacrifices is of the natural law."[141]

Finally, Aquinas highlights the "natural" aspect of sacrifices, for offering sacrifices is a manifestation of our very nature and the natural order of things.[142] The offering of sacrifices is something that is done out of reverence for God;[143] yet, in order to be a virtuous act, it should be done freely, according to reason, and towards a good end, that is, towards the worship of God. This is what distinguishes sacrifice as a virtuous act from idolatry.[144]

Man's knowledge of a higher being, whih is called God, does not have to be perfect. Aquinas, in fact, indicates at least a confused knowledge of God, which opens the door to many possible errors regarding the superior being. Aquinas limits himself to mentioning "a higher being." According to

139. Cf. Aquinas, *S. Th.*, II–II, q. 85, a. 1.

140. See Dewan, "Moral Order," 207–08.

141. Aquinas, *S. Th.*, II–II, q. 85, a. 1, s. c. This is an anthropological argument in favor of religiosity. According to Pieper, the human being is by nature, and most profoundly, religious, that is, open to and interiorly oriented at the core of his being toward God. See Pieper, *Living the Truth*, 11–105. Cf. also André-Vincent, *Liberté Religieuse*, 191. He affirms that the act of religion is the fundamental act of man: "It embraces the whole of man and of the universe."

142. This natural inclination is not according to the dictate of reason, but all the way around. As Thomas affirms, the dictate of reason is according to the natural inclination. Cf. Aquinas, *S. Th.*, II–II, q. 85, a. 1.

143. Cf. Aquinas, *S. Th.*, II–II, q. 85, a. 3.

144. According to Aquinas, idolatry takes place when divine worship is given to whom it should not be given, that is, other than the most-high uncreated God. For Aquinas, it is superstition to give worship to any creature whatsoever. Cf. Aquinas, *S. Th.*, II–II, q. 94, a. 1.

Dewan, the very paucity of description is undoubtedly deliberate.[145] This knowledge of God is natural, it refers to a reasoning process that any human being may spontaneously carry through. It begins with one's grasp of being a deficient being, and thus depending on someone greater that oneself. And as Dewan states, "it is our ability to appreciate that one being can depend for its being on another that is crucial here."[146]

There is also an exclusive aspect of sacrifices, for they are offered to God alone.[147] The reason is that a sacrifice is a representation of something. In this way, outward sacrifices represent the inward spiritual sacrifice of the soul, for the outward acts of religion are directed to the inward acts.[148] Now, the soul should offer itself in sacrifice to God, for God is our soul's creator,[149] and the end of our beatification, for in God alone consists the beatitude of our soul.[150] Therefore, Aquinas argues that just as to God alone ought we to offer spiritual sacrifices, so too ought we to offer outward sacrifices to Him alone.[151]

Oblations and First-Fruits

Among those things offered to God by the faithful, Aquinas deals next with oblations and first-fruits (q. 86). Oblations are presented as having a broader status than sacrifices. All sacrifices are oblations, but not all oblations are sacrifices, since an oblation only implies the offering of something to God without doing anything to the thing offered.[152] Thus, Aquinas affirms in a. 1: "The term oblation is common to all things offered for the worship of God, so that if a thing be offered in worship of God as something sacred which fire should consume, it is both an oblation and a sacrifice."[153] Other aspects

---

145. Cf. Dewan, "Moral Order," 207.
146. Dewan, "Wisdom and Human Life," 13. See also Dewan, *Form and Being*, ch. 5.
147. Cf. Aquinas, *S. Th.*, II–II, q. 84, a. 1, ad 1.
148. Cf. Aquinas, *S. Th.*, II–II, q. 81, a. 7.
149. See Aquinas, *S. Th.*, I, q. 90, a. 3. See also a. 2, where Aquinas shows that the soul can only be produced by way of creation by reason of its mode of being, since it is a subsisting form which cannot be made out of pre-existent matter. Then, Aquinas concludes in a. 3 that it is created by God, for God alone can create. The reason is that the first agent alone can act without presupposing the existence of anything. And since the rational soul cannot be produced by a change in matter, it cannot be produced, save immediately by God.
150. See also Aquinas, *S. Th.*, I–II, q. 2, a. 8; q. 3, aa. 1, 7 & 8.
151. Cf. Aquinas, *S. Th.*, II–II, q. 85, a. 2.
152. Cf. Aquinas, *S. Th.*, II–II, q. 85, a. 3, ad 3.
153. Aquinas, *S. Th.*, II–II, q. 86, a. 1.

noted by Aquinas are that "an oblation must not be made of things unjustly acquired or possessed,"[154] and that they should be voluntary.[155]

TITHES

The last item to be treated by Aquinas among those things offered to God by the faithful, are tithes (q. 87). Aquinas considers the precept regarding the paying of tithes to be partly moral, and as such to belong to the natural law, and partly judicial, deriving its force from divine law.[156] Thomas argues for the natural law aspect of tithing by comparing the service of those who minister the divine worship for the welfare of the people to other services that come to aid the common good of society, such as taxes to support those that rule, men in service (police, army, etc), healthcare, education, etc.[157] Since to form a society belongs to the natural law, it also belongs to the natural law that the members of a political society administer the necessaries of life of public servants and ministers of worship.[158]

THE TAKING OF VOWS

In *S. Th.* II–II, q. 88, Thomas Aquinas deals with vows, whereby something is promised to God. Aquinas classifies the profession of vows within the acts that belong to the virtue of religion because vows are promises made to God, that is, a directing of the thing vowed to the worship or service of God. And since the worship of God is properly the act of religion, a vow is an act of religion.[159]

In the first article, Aquinas notes that a vow denotes a binding to do or omit some particular thing. This act properly belongs to reason, for it is the work of reason to direct one's own life. Now, through vows one binds himself to another by means of a promise, which is a way of directing oneself. Thus, by promising, Thomas argues that a man directs what he himself is to do for another.[160] At the same time, promises between men can only be

---

154. Aquinas, *S. Th.*, II–II, q. 86, a. 3.
155. Cf. Aquinas, *S. Th.*, II–II, q. 86, a. 1 & a. 4, ad 3.
156. Cf. Aquinas, *S. Th.*, II–II, q. 87, a. 1.
157. Cf. Aquinas, *S. Th.*, II–II, q. 87, a. 1.
158. The fixing of the proportion to be offered to the ministers of divine worship, however, does not belong to the natural law, but was determined by divine institution. Cf. Aquinas, *S. Th.*, II–II, q. 87, a. 1.
159. Cf. Aquinas, *S. Th.*, II–II, q. 88, a. 5.
160. Cf. Aquinas, *S. Th.*, II–II, q. 88, a. 1.

expressed in words and other outward signs, while promises to God can be made by the mere inward thought.[161] Now, a promise is the outcome from a purpose of doing something, and a purpose presupposes deliberation, since it is the act of a deliberate will.[162] Thus, according to Aquinas, there are three elements essential to the taking of a vow: "The first is deliberation. the second is a purpose of the will; and the third is a promise."[163]

Regarding that which one promises through a vow, its matter, Aquinas notes that it has to be voluntary, for a promise is about something that one does voluntarily for someone else, and it has to be something acceptable to the one to whom something is being promised.[164] Thus, the matter of a vow should be some act of virtue, for no work is acceptable to God unless it be virtuous.[165] It also includes that which is not necessary, neither absolutely, nor on the supposition of an end, for a vow denotes a voluntary promise, and necessary things fall outside the realm of freedom. However, one can promise something necessary on the supposition of an end in so far as it is done voluntarily.[166]

Man is bound by natural law to fulfil a vow. Aquinas affirms: "Honesty demands that a man should keep any promise he makes to another man, and this obligation is based on the natural law."[167] Now, regarding promises made to God, man ought to be faithful to God above all, both on account of God's sovereignty, and on account of the favors he has received from God. Thus, "man is obliged before all to fulfill the vows he has made to God, since this is part of the fidelity he owes to God. On the other hand, the breaking of a vow is a kind of infidelity."[168]

The Taking of God's Name: Oaths as Acts of Religion

For Aquinas, an oath is an act of religion for he that swears calls God to witness in confirmation of what he says. Now nothing is confirmed save by what is more certain and more powerful. Therefore, in the very fact that a

---

161. Cf. Aquinas, *S. Th.*, II–II, q. 88, a. 1.

162. Cf. Aquinas, *S. Th.*, II–II, q. 88, a. 1.

163. Cf. Aquinas, *S. Th.*, II–II, q. 88, a. 1. Aquinas later affirms that when deliberation of reason and purpose of the will are lacking, vows are invalid. See Aquinas, *S. Th.*, II–II, q. 88, a. 9.

164. Cf. Aquinas, *S. Th.*, II–II, q. 88, a. 2.

165. Cf. Aquinas, *S. Th.*, II–II, q. 88, a. 2.

166. Cf. Aquinas, *S. Th.*, II–II, q. 88, a. 2.

167. Aquinas, *S. Th.*, II–II, q. 88, a. 3, ad 1.

168. Aquinas, *S. Th.*, II–II, q. 88, a. 3.

man swears by God, he acknowledges God to be more powerful, by reason of his unfailing truth and his universal knowledge; and thus, in a way, he shows reverence to God. And since to show reverence to God belongs to religion, it is evident that an oath is an act of religion.[169]

Agamben, in his treatment of the oath, discusses the so-called "ontological arguments" for the existence of God. For Agamben, Anselm's definition of God as "that than which no greater can be thought" is the most fitting name of God, for it expresses "that experience of language in which it is impossible to separate name and being, speech and thing."[170] Leaving aside Aquinas's criticism of Anselm's argument, Thomas states that in God his being and essence are identical,[171] and for that reason the most fitting name of God is "he who is".[172] For Aquinas, it is impossible to separate in God his essence from his being. At the same time, the name of God names a being that is absolute and undetermined by anything added, and thus it signifies a sea of being that is infinite and as if indeterminate, so that there remains in our intellect the fact that God is, and nothing more.[173] Comenting on this, Agamben states that the meaning of the name of God suspends and puts in parenthesis every meaning in order to affirm through a pure experience of speech a pure and bare existence.[174] Talking about the function of the name of God within the oath, Agamben continues:

> We can therefore specify further the meaning and function of the name of God in the oath. Every oath swears on the name par excellence, that is on the name of God, because the oath is the experience of language that treats all of language as a proper name. Pure existence—the existence of the name—is not the result of a recognition, nor of a logical deduction: it is something that cannot be signified but only sworn, that is, affirmed as a name.[175]

For Aquinas, the oath does have a function of stability and guarantee, for one calls upon the name of God to witness in confirmation of what one affirms, that is, as a way of binding oneself to do what one has promisssed, so that one's words may become a reality. Now, one calls upon God as a witness for particular contingent facts on account of man's lack of truth and

---

169. Aquinas, *S. Th.*, II–II, q. 89, a. 4.
170. Agamben, *Sacrament of Language*, 52.
171. Cf. Aquinas, *S. Th.*, I, q. 3, a. 4.
172. Cf. Aquinas, *S. Th.*, I, q. 13, a. 11.
173. Cf. Aquinas, *Sent.*, I, d. 8, q. 1, a. 1, ad 4.
174. Cf. Agamben, *Sacrament of Language*, 53.
175. Agamben, *Sacrament of Language*, 53.

lack of knowledge.¹⁷⁶ For that reason, Thomas states that there is a need to have recourse to a divine witness, for neither can God lie, nor is anything hidden from him. Aquinas continues:

> To call God to witness is named *jurare* [to swear] because it is established as though it were a principle of law [*jure*] that what a man asserts under the invocation of God as his witness should be accepted as true. Now sometimes God is called to witness when we assert present or past events, and this is termed a declaratory oath; while sometimes God is called to witness in confirmation of something future, and this is termed a promissory oath.¹⁷⁷

This is the reason why, for Aquinas, "there is great danger in swearing, both on account of the greatness of God who is called upon to bear witness, and on account of the frailty of the human tongue, the words of which are confirmed by oath."¹⁷⁸ Thus, the virtue of religion plays a central role, for Aquinas, in the act of swearing. In contraposition to Cicero, for whom the gods did not exist,¹⁷⁹ the taking of the name of God as a witness is a manifestation of submission to someone greater than oneself, which pertains to the reverence and honor of God.¹⁸⁰ For Aquinas there is a God who watches over us, and who sees all men as equal. This is the foundation of justice, which takes into account the dignity inherent in every human being.

The oath, then, does fulfill a political function in both interpersonal relationships and between cities and peoples, a function that is not only religious, for God is the witness, but also legal, as the trust that is tied to the oath is the basis of justice.¹⁸¹ Thus, in Aquinas, the oath has to do with trust (*fides*) as well as with reverence and honor of God. And we see once again, in undivided unity, the acts of religion and the law.

Aquinas employs the notion of *fides* in various occasions as the basis, the origin, and the cause of justice.¹⁸² Here I will only consider an instance

---

176. Aquinas, *S. Th.*, II–II, q. 89, a. 1.
177. Aquinas, *S. Th.*, II–II, q. 89, a. 1.
178. Aquinas, *S. Th.*, II–II, q. 89, a. 3, ad 3.
179. Cf. Cicero, *Officiis*, III, 29, 10.
180. Cf. Aquinas, *S. Th.*, II–II, q. 89, a. 4, ad 2.
181. For a study on Aquinas's notion of *fides* as the basis of justice, see Brook, "Faith: The Basis of Justice."
182. However, one should note that in these various occasions, he means something different by faith and by justice. Sometimes *fides* is used in an ordinary sense, as when one person trusts in another; other times it is employed as meaning the infused theological virtue of faith. See, for example, Aquinas, *S. Th.*, II–II, q. 104, a. 6; Aquinas, *Trin.*, q. 3, a. 1. Justice is also employed in some cases in a human or natural sense, and in others as referring to the acquisition of internal justice (or justification) through God's

in which it is meant as trust, that is, *fides* in an ordinary and natural sense, in contraposition to a supernatural sense of *fides*.

In his Commentary on Boethius's *De Trinitate*, q. 3, a. 1, *s. c.*, Thomas follows Aristotle's *Nicomachean Ethics* to argue that faith (*fides*) as trust is a necessary condition for the conservation and preservation of society. Aquinas states that, "without faith human society cannot be preserved, since it is requisite that one man believe in the promises of another and in his testimony and the like, for this is necessary if they are to live together; therefore, faith is most necessary for mankind."[183] It is to this sense of trust or *fides* that the power of the oath is related. This is the kind of trust that is the basis of any genuinely human relation and interaction. It is in this sense, then, that trust (*fides*) is necessary and foundational for a community in pursuit of the common good. Thomas states:

> ... because in human society one person must make use of another just as he does himself in matters in which he is not self-sufficient, he must take his stand on what another knows and is unknown to himself, just as he does on what he himself knows. As a consequence, faith [*fides*] is necessary in human society, one person believing what another says. As Cicero remarks, this is the basis of justice.[184]

Trust is the basis of justice, a statement that Thomas borrows from Cicero, who states: "The foundation of justice, moreover, is good faith—that is, truth and fidelity to promises and agreements."[185] And in the religious man, this oath to be faithful to one's word, to make what one promises a reality, is backed by God's witness. It is this religious aspect of the act of swearing that for the one who believes in God has a powerful meaning. This faith is what will make him aware that he should be responsible and faithful regarding his public and civic duties, be honest, have integrity, and faithfully represent his constituents (in a representative democracy). Thus, we can see how trust or faith is the foundation of justice, that is, of the right relations between persons. At the same time, the relationship towards the divine will serve for the virtuous man as a model for the right relations between men within society.

To conclude this point, then, we see that the actions that involve taking the name of God, such as oaths, manifest an aspect of the virtue of religion that has an important impact on the public political life of a nation.

---

grace. See Aquinas, *S. Th.*, II–II, q. 58, a. 2.

183. Aquinas, *Trin.*, q. 3, a. 1, s.c.
184. Aquinas, *Trin.*, q. 3, a. 1.
185. Cicero, *Officiis*, bk. I, VII, 23.

One can think about the role that the oath played in the political pact of the West, and which gave origin to our political institutions, and which is reenacted in the swearing in office of government officials, or in the invocation of God's name to open city council meetings. At the same time, one often hears that there is little faith in the political system, that corruption has infested politics, and that personal interest override the common good of society. The virtue of religion is perhaps one of the ways to instill once again the trust between peoples, which will lead to a correct understanding of justice, one established on trust.

The Exercise of the Virtue of Religion and the Public Square in Aquinas

Aquinas employs the notions of private (*privatum*) and public (*publicum*) in numerous occasions in connection to the virtue of religion and its numerous acts. He talks about private and public persons, private and public acts, public sins, public profession of one's faith, public prayer, public vows, matrimonial consent given in public, the public good of the community, etc. Aquinas also talks about "public places," such as streets, and this resembles the modern notion of public space.[186] He argues that the faith should be defended in public, and that there should be public debates regarding theological matters (these would take place in universities).[187] He defends the preaching of the faith in public, such as streets (a public and common place to all),[188] and places where the preacher can be seen and heard by all.[189] Thomas states that Jesus, in fact, preached his doctrine in "public places,"[190] that is, in the temple and synagogues, and could be seen and heard by others.[191] Aquinas also talks about actions taking place in public within the church.[192] These actions enjoy a public character, first, because they are directed to the good of the community and the

---

186. See, for example, Aquinas, *In Psalmos*, 54, 11.
187. Cf. Super II Tim., cap. 2 l. 2.
188. Cf. Aquinas, *In Psalmos*, 24, 4.
189. Cf. Aquinas, *Trin.*, I, q. 2, a. 4, ad 3. And regarding the public activity of the apostle Paul, see Aquinas, *Corinthios*, ch. 3, lect. 1.
190. Cf. Aquinas, *Io.*, ch. 18, lect. 3.
191. Cf. Aquinas, *Io.*, ch. 7, lect. 1.
192. Thomas argues, for example, that Christian doctrine is preached publicly in the church. Cf. Aquinas, *Titum*, ch. 1, lect 3.

edification of its members, and second, because the acts themselves are seen and heard by the members of the community.[193]

Aquinas also talks about private or domestic communities, and public political communities, and their respective leaders. He states:

> A city possesses a political community whereas a household has a domestic one, and these differ in two respects. For those who belong to the domestic community share with one another in having private activities; but those belonging to the civil community have in common with one another public activities. Thus, those that belong to the domestic community are governed by the head of the family; while those in the civil community are ruled by a king. Hence: what the king is in the realm, the father is in the home.[194]

Thomas also employs the notions of interior and exterior acts, founding this distinction in those acts which by their own nature are, or should remain, hidden, and those acts that are seen by others in the community, and which as a consequence need a kind of public stage.

With respect to the virtue of religion, following the thought of Thomas Aquinas, we can identify four spheres or stages of action, that is, the proper places where the acts of religion take place.

In the first place, for Aquinas, the proper stage of religion is the interior life of the soul. It is on this stage that the interior acts of prayer and devotion take place, within what we may call, in a metaphorical way, the household of the soul. Aquinas is mindful of Jesus' teaching, who admonishes the faithful not to pray like the hypocrites, "for they love to pray standing in the synagogues and on the street corners to be seen by others." Instead, "when you pray, go into your room, close the door and pray to your Father, who is unseen. Then your Father, who sees what is done in secret, will reward you."[195]

For Aquinas, prayer is intimate, it belongs to the contemplative life of the soul[196] it is secret,[197] and therefore it should not be said in order that one

---

193. Cf. Aquinas, *Sent.*, bk. 4, d. 38, q. 1, a. 2, qc. 2, ad 1.
194. Aquinas, *Eph.*, ch. 2, lect. 6.
195. Matthew 6:5–6, in Nestle et al., *Novum Testamentum Graece*, 12–13.
196. Cf. Aquinas, *Sent.*, bk. 3, d. 1, q. 1, a. 3, qc. 3, s.c. 2.
197. Cf. Aquinas, *Eph.*, ch. 5, lect. 7.

be seen by others.[198] Prayer is essentially mental or interior, even though it can also be manifested in words as "vocal prayer."[199]

In the second place, the virtue of religion has secondary acts, some of which have to do with the liturgy, and which by nature are exterior, such as public prayer and the profession of vows.[200] For Aquinas, these external acts of religion are secondary in the sense of being ordered to support the inner realm, that of the primary acts of religion, such as the life of prayer and devotion. These acts are public for two reasons: principally, because they are directed to the good of the community and the edification of its members, and secondarily, because the acts themselves are seen and heard by the members of the community.[201] Thus, for example, believers get together to pray and worship, profess their faith, and some of the faithful also profess vows before the community. In order to perform these acts, religious communities need a physical space. Even though the faithful get together as a community, and their acts are considered to be "public prayer," "public vows," "public profession of faith," these acts are not "public" in the sense of having a public character in the modern sense of the term. These liturgical acts are not about a church manifesting its presence. It is within the community that these acts have a public character, for they are performed in a kind of public stage, because by being directed to the good of the community, and by being seen and heard by others, one is manifesting one's faith, is a witness to it, and at the same time encourages others to do the same.[202] These virtuous

---

198. Cf. Aquinas, *S. Th.*, II–II, q. 83, a. 12, ad 3. See also Aquinas, *S. Th.*, II–II, q. 187, a. 6, ad 3; Aquinas, *Io.*, ch. 4, lect. 2; ch. 7, lect. 1; ch. 20, lect. 4; Aquinas, *Phil.*, ch. 4, lect. 1.

199. Aquinas explains the seeming contradiction between Jesus' command to pray in secret, and the fact that prayer takes place in a public setting within the church, by distinguishing between the good act in itself, and the intention or reason for which it is done. Good works should be done in public by reason of the good example they offer, while the intention of the heart, which should be to seek God's glory, remains in secret. Cf. Aquinas, *Sent.*, bk. 4, d. 15, q. 4, a. 2, qc. 1, ad 1.

200. Cf. Aquinas, *Sent.*, bk. 4, d. 15, q. 4, a. 2, qc. 1, ad s.c. 2.

201. Cf. Aquinas, *Sent.*, bk. 4, d. 38, q. 1, a. 2, qc. 2, ad 1. "Public prayer," for example, is the prayer that is said for the community by the ministers of the church, which is distinct from "private prayer," which is that which the faithful may say by themselves for their own intentions or those of the community. Public prayer could be mental or vocal prayer, and the latter includes singing. Cf. Aquinas, *Contra impugnantes*, II, ch. 4, ad 11. See also Aquinas, *Sent.*, bk. 4, d. 15, q. 4, a. 2, qc. 1.

202. Aquinas argues that certain sacraments must be given in "public" by reason of what they entail. Confirmation, for example, entails strongly defending the dignity acquired. Cf. Aquinas, *Sent.*, bk. 4, d. 7, q. 3, a. 3, qc. 2, ad 1. Matrimony, instead, can take place either in private or in public. Cf. Aquinas, *Sent.*, bk. 4, d. 28, q. 1, a. 3, s.c. 1. The same holds for vows. Cf. Aquinas, *Sent.*, bk. 4, d. 38, q. 1, a. 2, qc. 2, ad 1. Aquinas also mentions that the exercise of certain acts of religion, which usually take place in public,

acts bring with their performance an aspect of mutual edification, which is the case with all virtuous action that is seen by others. These actions may also have public consequences, as in the case of those religious orders whose members perform works of charity, provide education, run hospitals, etc. For that reason, we may locate under this sphere the profession of vows, as in the case of religious life. These men and women devote their lives to serve God and others, and for that reason, their voluntary consecration to this way of life, marked by the virtue of religion, exercises in many cases a positive impact in society and in the lives of citizens.

It is within this public stage of the community that Aquinas also locates priests and bishops, that is, those who preside ceremonies on behalf of the community. Thus, priests and bishops are considered by Aquinas to be "public persons"[203] because they are the principal members of the community, have a special influence on all other members of the community,[204] protect the common good of the community,[205] and in the name of the community offer prayers and sacrifices before God.[206] And by reason of their duty to care for the common good of the community, they also enjoy public authority.[207] The laity or faithful, on the other hand, are "private persons" within the community.[208]

In the third place, Aquinas locates within this setting religious acts which are directed to secure a physical space, and to support the liturgical life, such as the offering of oblations, first-fruits, sacrifices, and tithing.[209] The goal of these acts of the virtue of religion is to support the works of the

---

before the community, sometimes should be done in a private way, as for example when someone's reputation has been hurt as a consequence of a scandal or public sin. Thus, in theses cases, the reception of the sacraments should be offered in private, not in public. Cf. Aquinas, *Sent.*, bk. 4, d. 9, q. 1, a. 5, qc. 2. On the other hand, when a faithful repents from public, sinful behavior, his acts of reparation and penance should be performed in public, that is, in a way that his actions may be seen by the community. Cf. Aquinas, *Sent.*, bk. 4, d. 14, q. 1, a. 5, qc. 1, s.c. 2. On the private and public character of sins, see Aquinas, *S. Th.*, II-II, q. 33, a. 7; Aquinas, "Quaestiones Disputatae de Virtutibus," q. 3, a. 2.

203. Cf. Aquinas, *Quodlibet (qq. 7–11)*, VIII, q. 4, a. 2. See also Aquinas, *Sent.*, bk. 3, d. 9, q. 2, a. 3, ad 3.

204. Cf. Aquinas, *Sent.*, bk. 4, d. 8, q. 1, a. 1, qc. 1, ad 1.

205. Cf. Aquinas, *Sent.*, bk. 4, d. 19, q. 2, a. 1, ad 6.

206. Cf. Aquinas, *Sent.*, bk. 4, d. 8, q. 2, a. 4, qc. 3.

207. Cf. Aquinas, *S. Th.*, II-II, q. 64, a. 3.

208. Cf. Aquinas, *Sent.*, bk. 4, d. 23, q. 2, a. 1, qc. 1, ad 1.

209. One of the reasons offered by Aquinas is on account of the need of the Church, for instance if her ministers were without means of support. See Aquinas, *S. Th.*, II-II, q. 86, a. 1.

liturgy primarily, but also to help the poor and those in need, educate children, care for the sick, etc. Some of these actions usually do have a direct impact on society and the public realm, for they are directed to activities which usually take place on streets and public places. Even though these actions take place in a public realm, Aquinas stresses that these acts, such as tithing, should never be done in order to be seen by others, or in order to seek human favors.[210]

In the fourth place, Aquinas locates within this stage the acts of the virtue of religion that take place on the political public forum. There are certain acts that help people towards the common good, such as oaths, swearing, and the invocation of God's name. These are public acts in the modern sense of the term, for they take place within the public political sphere and its public institutions, and are the basis of the political pact, such as the swearing in office by a president or prime minister, the oaths when testifying before the court, the invoking of God's name before starting sessions at Congress or Parliament, etc.[211] Aquinas also locates here certain acts by which the faithful may manifest in a public way the profession of the name of Christ, especially in times of persecution. During persecution, Thomas states, when most people believe in a secret way, some faithful, the martyrs, choose to manifest their faith in public before the courts or government officials.[212]

Within this public realm proper we may locate the acts of those virtues that are commanded by the virtue of religion, for it has an important impact in the life of the faithful. In fact, Thomas states: "Every deed, in so far as it is done in God's honor, belongs to religion, not as eliciting, but as commanding."[213] According to Aquinas, religion has two kinds of acts. Some are its proper and immediate acts, which it elicits, and by which man is directed to God alone, such as sacrifices, adoration and the like. Religion also commands other acts which it produces through the medium of other virtues, directing them to the honor of God. The reason why religion commands the acts of other virtues, some of which have a public character, is that the virtue which is concerned with the end commands the virtues which are concerned with the means.[214]

---

210. Cf. Aquinas, *Super Mt.*, ch. 12, lect. 3; Aquinas, *Thessalonicenses*, ch. 1, lect. 1. Aquinas reminds the reader of the words of Jesus: "Be careful not to perform your righteous acts before men to be seen by them.... So when you give to the needy, do not sound a trumpet before you, as the hypocrites do in the synagogues and on the streets, to be praised by men." Matthew 6:1–2, in Nestle et al., *Novum Testamentum Graece*, 12.

211. Cf. Prodi, *Sacramento del Potere*, 11.

212. Cf. Aquinas, *Sent.*, bk. 4, d. 7, q. 2, a. 1, qc. 1.

213. Aquinas, *S. Th.*, II–II, q. 81, a. 4, ad 2.

214. Cf. Aquinas, *S. Th.*, II–II, q. 81, a. 1, ad 1.

As explained above, devotion, since it is the special act of "the will to give oneself readily to things concerning the service of God,"[215] it "prescribes the mode to human acts, whether they be acts of the will itself about things directed to the end, or acts of the other powers that are moved by the will."[216] Thus, it is through devotion that the religious man tends to honor God through all of his virtuous acts.[217] For Aquinas, religion is a virtue that orders the whole life of a person, and in this sense it is the same as holiness. Holiness, for Aquinas, encompasses all of the good works that a person performs, either in private or in public. For that reason, holiness has an undeniable impact on the person's performance in the public stage, for there is no act that can be disconnected from sanctity.[218] People may lead a more or less holy or sinful way of life, which inevitably will have consequences on their actions performed in the privacy of their homes, and in the public stage of political life. One can think about acts of courage, generosity, political prudence, honesty, justice, faithfulness to one's oath in public office, etc., as well as acts of dishonesty, corruption, betrayal, theft, or injustice, all of which may have good or bad consequences in the public political realm. Thus, when devotion and prayer, and the other acts of religion, structure a person's own life, that person may bring all of his virtuous actions to bear on that, which as a consequence will be manifested in those virtuous actions performed in the public stage, those that belong to virtues which manifest themselves publicly, such as justice, temperance, honesty, fortitude, political prudence, etc. It is still about the individual, but in this case doing something good for the people, so that it is in this way that religion as a virtue has an impact on the public political life of a community.[219]

It is also true, at the same time, that the acts of public virtues exercised under the command of the virtue of religion may not be considered under the virtue of religion necessarily. The fact that these virtuous acts are commanded by the virtue of religion does not transform the nature of the acts themselves. An act of political prudence will be an act of prudence even

---

215. Aquinas, *S. Th.*, II–II, q. 82, a. 1. As Dewan affirms: "It is an interior act that imbues everything we do with the character of 'giving the whole of oneself to God.'" Dewan, "Philosophy and Spirituality," 362.

216. Aquinas, *S. Th.*, II–II, q. 82, a. 1, ad 1.

217. For Aquinas notion of the will as commanding acts, see Aquinas, *S. Th.*, I–II, q. 17.

218. Now, for Aquinas, religion does not differ essentially from sanctity, but differs only logically, in that religion refers to communal and individual rites that offer worship to God, while holiness refers to these and the works of all the other virtues as commanded by the virtue of religion. Cf. Aquinas, *S. Th.*, II–II, q. 81, a. 8.

219. Cavanaugh, in fact, affirms that in medieval Christendom religion was not a separate sphere of concern and activity, but permeated all institutions and activities. Cf. Cavanaugh, *Myth*, 68.

if commanded by religion. Yet, the point I want to make here is that, for the religious person, those acts that have an impact on the political life of society are in fact commanded by the virtue of religion, and for that reason one can start to see the place of religion in the public sphere and why it is necessary to protect religious freedom.

The virtue of religion, then, has implications not only for the life of moral reason but also for the constitution of political society. Aquinas defines law as an ordinance of reason, for the common good, made by those who have care for the community, and promulgated.[220] Now, since law is a work of practical reason, and right willing is required for the right unfolding of practical reason, so that practical reason may reach conclusions that are in accord with the objective demands of the natural law,[221] it means that the acts of the virtue of religion play an essential role in right willing.[222] The religious man will be motivated by religious virtue to promote laws that foster the common good. And it is here that is perhaps best expressed the connection between the virtues of justice and religion: through its acts and the acts of other virtues that it commands, religious virtue ensures an optimal degree of justice in society.[223]

Conclusion

Aquinas's most important work, his *Summa theologiae*, could be read as a study on the religious dimension of the human being.[224] It shows the ascendant itinerary of all beings to the Supreme Being, and the place of freedom in this search. His work is an attempt to know the mystery of God, implicit in all knowledge and every desire. For Aquinas, man, in his constitutive relation, is truly related to God, who is the beginning and end of man. In this theological context, Aquinas places religion as a moral virtue, annexed to justice. Justices gives to each his due, in the measure that that is possible. When it comes to God, this possibility almost disappears, as it is little that man can return to God for all one has received.

220. Cf. Aquinas, *S. Th.*, I–II, q. 90, a. 4.

221. For Aquinas, human laws are to be expressions of the natural law in order to be true laws. Cf. Aquinas, *S. Th.*, I–II, q. 95 a. 2.

222. In a similar fashion, Kevin O'Reilly argues that divine worship constitutes a necessary (albeit not sufficient condition) for the promulgation of laws that foster the common good. See O'Reilly, "Significance of Worship."

223. From a Thomistic perspective, one can argue that the virtue of religion directs man towards God, the true end of human existence, who is also the source of the natural law from which just laws are determined.

224. Cf. Lobato, "Lo Sacro y la Religión," 141–42.

Aquinas argues that religion is a virtue because it offers God the honor that is due to him as the principle and final end of creation. It is a moral virtue, because its object is the worship of God, not God in himself. Religion, in so far as it becomes holiness, is the most perfect among the moral virtues, for it orders human activity to God.

The principal acts of religion are the internal acts of devotion and prayer, and its external and secondary acts are ordained to these internal acts.[225] These external acts, even though secondary, are of great importance, as they usually take place before others and within different stages and contexts, such as within the community of the faithful, and within civil and political institutions. These acts are a sign of the honor that is due to God alone. Thus, the virtue of religion is not only considered by Aquinas as an internal disposition of the person, but also in its external manifestations which come to aid the faithful in order to perform the interior acts of religion. Thus, adoration presupposes an internal act in the intellectual recognition of the divine excellence, and the submission of one's own will; and it also presupposes an external act in the public manifestation of the internal disposition, which in turn leads one and others to internal acts of religion. This double aspect is seen in other acts of religion such as sacrifices, bodily reverence, the offering of oblations and first-fruits, tithes, and the taking of vows.

For Aquinas, man is naturally inclined to his own true good end. However, this inclination is not so strong as to guide man without error by reason of a fallen human nature and the effects of original sin. Theologically, man is in need of grace in order to find true and perfect fulfillment. From the natural point of view, it is through virtue (aided by grace), that man will fulfill his natural inclination to goodness. Thus, the virtue of religion plays the role of perfecting that natural inclination to God that man finds within himself.[226] In order to fulfill this inclination, man must devote himself to the worship of God by himself and in community with others, which implies the necessity of establishing spaces of worship.

Finally, once the proper stages for the acts of the virtue of religion have been identified, it can be seen how Aquinas's notion of religion as virtue is very hepful in order to discern the place of "religion" in the public political forum.

---

225. Cf. Aquinas, *S. Th.*, II–II, q. 81, a. 7.

226. For Aquinas, it will be grace that will elevate this inclination to the maximum of its possibilities. Man is by nature capable of God (cf. Aquinas, *S. Th.*, I, q. 12.), but needs of the assistance of grace in order to order his whole being and actions to God alone.

The Invention of Religion as a Category in the Modern West

This section will briefly address the history of the development of the idea of "religion" in the Renaissance and early modern periods.

In his landmark book *The Meaning and End of Religion* (1962), Wilfred Cantwell Smith showed that the notion of religion as a discrete category of human activity separable from culture, politics, and other areas of life is an invention of the modern West. He even went as far as stating that, outside of the modern West, there is no significant concept equivalent to what we think of as religion.[227] Thus, with the dawn of modernity, a new concept with a much wider and different significance came to operate under the term "religion."

The beginning of the transition to the modern category of religion has been identified in the thought of two Christian Platonist thinkers: Nicholas de Cusa (1401–1464), and Marsilio Ficino (1433–1499).[228]

Nicholas de Cusa, in his *De Pace Fidei*, uses *religio* to indicate the various ways in which God is worshipped. Thus, there are Jewish, Christian, and Arabic religions, that is, Jewish, Christian, and Arabic ways of worshipping God, though there are as yet no religions called Judaism, Christianity, or Islam.[229] As Cavanaugh notes, what is novel about Cusa's use of *religio* is that ritual practices are not essential to it; instead, *religio* is a universal, interior impulse that stands behind the multiplicity of rites.[230] Cusa identifies religion with an interior wisdom that underlies all rites: "All who use their reason have one religion and cult which is at the bottom of all the diversity of rites."[231] Thus, "man would have to walk according to his interior rather than his exterior nature."[232] It is in Cusa, then, that we find the beginnings of religion as an interior impulse, universal to human beings, and which stands behind the multiplicity of exterior rites that express it.

The other major contributor to the creation of the modern notion of religion was Marsilio Ficino. He made one of the first uses of Christianity as a religion in his work *De Christiana Religione* (1474).[233] However, Ficino did not mean "Christian religion" in the sense of a system of doctrines and

---

227. Smith, *Meaning and End of Religion*, 18–19.

228. Cf. Cavanaugh, *Myth*, 70.

229. Cf. Cusa, "Pace Fidei," 219.

230. Cf. Cavanaugh, *Myth*, 70.

231. Cusa, "Pace Fidei," 203.

232. Cusa, "Pace Fidei," 198–99.

233. In the "Prologue" to his *S. Th.*, Thomas Aquinas also employs *religio* in a similar sense.

practices. Religion, for Ficino, meant something like piety, a piety that is both interiorized and universalized. This is what distinguishes his usage of the term religion from the ancient and medieval usages. Religion is located as a natural, innate impulse of the human heart, the fundamental human characteristic common to all men. Ficino treats religion, then, as an unchanging and constant essence across time and space in all human societies: "all opinions of men, all their responses, all their customs, change—except religion."[234] Religion is also distinguished from the multiple external actions or rites. For Ficino, this variety of rites is ordained by God to give beauty to the world. Thus, each external form of worship is a more or less true approximation of the Platonic ideal. For Ficino, therefore, there is but only one universal "religion" implanted in the human heart, while there are different degrees of genuineness in living it out, the highest of which is exemplified by Christ.[235] Any faith, for Ficino, can be "Christian" religion, even if there is no connection to the historical Christian revelation or church.[236]

This move toward religion as an interior and universal impulse present in Cusa and Ficino would be complemented later in the sixteenth and seventeenth centuries by an emphasis on belief over practice.[237] It is during this period during and following the Reformation that religion would come to mean a system of doctrines and intellectual propositions that could be either true or false. The Reformation, in fact, brought in its wake numerous attempts to encapsulate the Christian faith in a set of beliefs to be confessed.

The French humanist Guillaume Postel, for example, tried to reconcile the pluralism of beliefs around certain essential propositions which according to him were central to all of the world's religions. Postel listed sixty-seven such propositions in his *De orbis terrae Concordia* (1544). According to him, these were common to all religions, and around which the people of the world could unite, if only they would shed the superfluous externalities of rite and practice. People had only to agree on these first principles, and then agreement on the final truths would just follow. The end result of such agreement would be that people would not be Catholics, Lutherans,

---

234. Marsilio Ficino, *Christiana Religione*, quoted in Smith, *Meaning and End of Religion*, 33.

235. Ficino did not regard Christ as the true content of the universal religion. For Ficino, the "Christian" in "the Christian religion" meant "pertaining to Christ." That means that those who come the closest to the ideal worship of God are those who worship as Christ did. This is, then, the practice of Christian religion: Christ's way of worshipping God.

236. Smith, *Meaning and End of Religion*, 33–34; Cavanaugh, *Myth*, 71. See also Harrison, *Religion*, 13.

237. Cf. Cavanaugh, *Myth*, 72.

or adherents of any particular religion, but would simply invoke the name of Jesus.[238] Postel talks about religions in the plural to refer to "the diversity of customs, languages, opinions, and religions"[239] of the world's people, and religion in the singular to refer to the concord underlying all of the various religions. Even though he comes close to introducing the idea that Christianity and Islam are species of the genus religion, he persists in identifying the true religion with Christianity.[240]

Richard C. McCoy notes how the internal-external and belief-practice binaries were crucial to the continued formation of the religion-secular binary in the sixteenth century,[241] to which we could also add the modern natural-supernatural divide. Graham Ward also points out how God's presence was presented as only available through the eyes of faith, and faith was understood as a set of doctrinal principles and interpretive keys to be taught and passed down for one's experience in the world.[242] Peter Harrison, on his part, sees the transition to religion as a state of mind as especially clearly present among Calvinists.[243] John Calvin retained the medieval meaning of religion as a worshipful disposition of the person. Yet, in Calvinist circles, there was an emphasis on religion as saving knowledge understood in the context of election and predestination. Thus, Jacobus Arminius (1560–1609) proposed a conditional predestination which sought to allow human agents to play a role in their salvation without giving the impression of earning it. Human freedom was manifested in the act of intellectual assent, as a mere "I believe" in certain central Christian doctrines. No moral acts or works were required of the human agent, thus avoiding the charge of Pelagianism that Calvin wanted to avoid. The result, however, was a tendency to identify religion with assent to doctrine.

In the seventeenth century, following the Reformation, competing Christian confessions stated their differences between them clearly and succinctly, which resulted in an "explosion of books and pamphlets attempting to present 'the Christian Religion,' 'the Protestant Religion,' 'the true Catholic Religion,' or simply 'Religion' in propositional form."[244] As a

238. Cf. Guillaume Postel, Πανθενωσια, quoted by Bouwsma, *Concordia Mundi*, 194, n. 70.

239. Bouwsma, *Concordia Mundi*, 130.

240. Cf. Cavanaugh, *Myth*, 72.

241. Cf. McCoy, *Alterations of State*, 2. This can be seen, for example, in sixteenth-century England, where reformers such as Thomas Becon (1512–1567) were intent on purifying religion of dependence on the external physical world.

242. Cf. Ward, *True Religion*, 22.

243. Cf. Harrison, *Religion*, 23–24.

244. Cavanaugh, *Myth*, 74.

consequence, the use of "religions" in the plural became normal.[245] It also became possible to see Christianity as one species of the genus religion,[246] which in turn introduced the term "Christianism," or body of beliefs, and pushed aside the meaning of Christianity as a body of people.[247] Religion is employed to name a system in general, though it increasingly includes the system of ideas in which men of faith were involved or with which men of potential faith were confronted.[248]

Hugo Grotius (1583–1645), in his *De Veritate Religionis Christianae* (1627), intended to show that the Christian religion was the true religion, meaning that Christian doctrines were statements of fact. Thus, religion had by this time acquired a new meaning, which enabled Grotius to state that the Christian religion is a dogma, rather than simply the correct worship of God.[249]

Locke, in his proposal for toleration, defines religion as a state of mind. He states: "All the life and power of true religion consist in the inward and full persuasion of the mind."[250] This is the reason why Locke denies to the magistrate any power to enforce religion, because the magistrate cannot penetrate the inner reaches of the personal conscience where true religion resides. Locke also draws a distinction between the "outward force" used by the civil magistrate and the "inward persuasion" of religion, and he argues that "such is the nature of the understanding that it cannot be compelled to the belief of anything by outward force."[251] According to Locke, there is only one true way to eternal happiness, and religion is essentially about discovering the saving truths that reveal this way.[252] As a consequence, true religion is essentially a private matter of uncovering saving knowledge.[253] Thus, Locke is equating religion to faith, and the content of religion to a dogma.

In the context in which Locke developed his theory of toleration, the state church was engaged in public acts of worship, and he assumed that condition. For that reason, Locke's theory of toleration does not result in

---

245. Bossy notes that the earliest form of pluralization in the modern sense is found after 1590 in Richard Hooker, from the Anglican side, and Robert Parsons, from the Catholic side. They both wrote about their "religions" as objective and opposing sets of doctrines. Cf. Bossy, "Some Elementary Forms of Durkheim," 5–6.

246. Cf. Bossy, "Some Elementary Forms of Durkheim," 7–8.

247. Cf. Bossy, *Christianity in the West*, 171.

248. Cf. Smith, *Meaning and End of Religion*, 38.

249. Cf. Smith, *Meaning and End of Religion*, 39.

250. Locke, *Letter*, 18.

251. Locke, *Letter*, 18.

252. Locke, *Letter*, 25–26, 31.

253. Cf. Locke, *Letter*, 31. See also Locke, *Human Understanding*, I.ii.15–21.

a strict privatization of Christian worship and practice. However, Locke sought to promote civil peace by establishing a strict division between the state, whose interests are public in origin, and the church, whose interests are private in origin. This resulted in the notion of a secular public space, in which the concerns of the state were purely secular.[254] In Locke, then, we find already a modern version of the religious-secular binary, where the secular refers to some spatial area of interest autonomous from the church's concern.[255] Thus, the opposition of religious clergy to secular clergy present in the Middle Ages was transferred to the new conception of religion and secularism in the early modern era. Religion became synonymous with a private concern and dogma, while the secular retained its oppositional character and became that which is not religious in the modern sense. It was at this time, as Cavanaugh notes, that Christianity was seen as "a species of the genus religion, a universal, interior human impulse, reducible to propositions or beliefs, essentially distinct from secular pursuits such as politics and economics."[256]

Jean-Jacques Rousseau, in his *The Social Contract* (1762), introduced the term "civil religion." Rousseau proposes an explicit civil religion as a cure for the divisive influence of Christianity, which had divided people's loyalties between church and state, potentially fueling conflicts and social tensions. Rousseau wishes to reduce Christianity to a "religion of man" that "has to do with the purely inward worship of Almighty God and the eternal obligations of morality, and nothing more."[257] Civil religion will be the fully public cult of the nation-state. Rousseau states: "The sovereign is entitled to fix the tenets of a purely civil creed, or profession of faith. These would not be, strictly speaking, dogmas of a religious character, but rather sentiments deemed indispensable for participation in society." The civil religion proposed by Rousseau had its dogmas, and the consequences of disobedience were severe.[258]

---

254. Cf. Locke, *Letter*, 17.

255. In the medieval period, the *saeculum* had both a temporal and spatial dimension; it referred to this world and age, encompassing all of creation, written into the providential plan of God. Thus, the root notion of the secular is a contrast not to religion but to eternity. Cf. Cavanaugh, *Myth*, 80; Calhoun, "Rethinking Secularism," 38.

256. Cavanaugh, *Myth*, 81.

257. Rousseau, *Social Contract*, 154.

258. Rousseau states: "As for that man who, having committed himself publicly to the state's articles of faith, acts on any occasion as if he does not believe them, let his punishment be death. He has committed the greatest of all crimes: he has lied in the presence of the laws." Rousseau, *Social Contract*, 160.

We can see now how the Enlightenment narrative invented a dichotomy between the religious and the secular. The religious was seen as an irrational and dangerous impulse that must give way in public to rational, secular forms of power. This is the origin of the contemporary debates on the place of religion in the public square. And by this time, the notion of religion as a virtue was lost. As Cavanaugh states, "there is no reason to suppose that medieval *religio* simply morphed into modern religion and that, underneath the changes, it has the same essential qualities."[259]

The Enlightenment, in its comprehensive world outlook which stressed an intellectualist and impersonal schematization of things, drove home the notion that "religion is something that one believes or does not believe, something whose propositions are true or are not true, something whose *locus* is in the realm of the intelligible."[260]

Then came the notion of "natural religion," which signified beliefs about God, man and the world that are supposedly common to mankind or attainable by the use of reason alone. In contraposition, the eighteenth century saw the novel and revolutionary concept of "revealed religion." The concept of revelation as such was standard in Christian thinking from its beginnings. However, no one before the eighteenth century had ever supposed that what was revealed was a religion. The reason is that God did not reveal a religion, but himself.[261] The view of religion as revealed, then, will have consequences later on, leading to much trouble and confusion.[262]

A development that there followed was the birth of the notion of "religions" in the plural, and the concept of "religion" in a generic way. This generic concept of religion designates as an external entity the total system or sum of all systems or beliefs.[263] Friedrich Schleiermacher was perhaps the first to write on religion itself as a generic something in 1799.[264] He also pleaded his readers to think of religion in terms of the heart rather than of belief or practice. The result, paradoxically, was not a shift of the meaning of the term back to the inward and nonintellectual part of religious life, but

---

259. Cavanaugh, *Myth*, 81.

260. Smith, *Meaning and End of Religion*, 40.

261. Cf. Smith, *Meaning and End of Religion*, 40–41, 128.

262. It is common to see in contemporary debates on the place of "religion" in the public square to find this notion of "religion" as revealed, or supposedly revealed, which leads to different "religions" competing against one another in the shaping of contemporary society. Thus, religion must be left outside the debate, in order to reach conclusions that are agreeable to everyone, including those from different religious traditions or no "religion" at all.

263. Cf. Smith, *Meaning and End of Religion*, 43.

264. See Schleiermacher, Über die Religion.

an expansion of the concept "religion," so that since then, as an intellectual concept, it has included within its content both the nonintellectual and the intellectual elements.[265]

Then there came Hegel, who wrestled with the problem of conceptualizing religion in the flux of history. He not only coined the phrase "philosophy of religion," but also posited "religion" as a *Begriff*, a self-subsisting transcendent idea or concept that unfolds itself in dynamic expression in the course of the ever-evolving history. Religion, then, unfolds itself as "positive religion," and as a series of positive historical religions.[266]

Ludwig Feuerbach, in 1851, published a book on the essence of religion, suggesting that religion, and a religion, have an essence.[267] This idea of religion as something with a definite and fixed form was then widely accepted. This is what gave origin to the problem and attempt of defining religion.

Agamben notes how, at the end of the nineteenth century, religion in Europe had for all appearances become, at least for those who wanted to gather the history and build the science of religion, something so strange and indecipherable that they had to seek the key to it among primitive peoples rather than in their own tradition. Yet, the primitive peoples could only return as in a mirror the same extravagant and contradictory image that these scholars had projected onto them.[268]

Thus, it can be seen that the modern concept of religion indicates a universal genus of which the various religions are species. Each religion is demarcated by a dogma or system of propositions. Religion became an essentially interior disposition and reducible to belief. Religion comes to be seen as essentially distinct from secular pursuits such as politics, economics, and the like. In the Modern West, the rise of the concept of religion established Christianity's proper sphere as the interior life, without direct access to the political. The rise of the new concept of religion is accompanied by the rise of its twin, the secular realm, a pairing which will gradually remove the practice of Christian religion from a central place in the social order of the West. At the same time, there was no secular sphere until it was invented in modernity. As Smith remarks, "the rise of the concept of 'religion' is in

---

265. Smith notes that the impact of the Enlightenment of Europe was too powerful and deep for its rationalism to be swept aside. Cf. Smith, *Meaning and End of Religion*, 46.

266. See Hegel, *Vorlesungen*. It is from this time on, Smith notes, that religion in the singular is a concept not of the humanities but of the social sciences. Cf. Smith, *Meaning and End of Religion*, 47.

267. See Feuerbach, *Wesen der Religion*.

268. Cf. Agamben, *SL*, 22.

some ways correlated with a decline in the practice of religion itself."[269] That means that the invention of the modern concept of religion accompanies the decline of the church as the public, communal practice of the virtue of religion.[270] This is what has caused the contemporary debate on the place of religion in the public square.

Should we not abandon, then, the concept of religion as a theological and political category in favor of a notion that is faithful to its original meaning? What will the fate of religious freedom be if one undertakes the task to overcome a notion of "religion" that is in itself unclear? Would not the notion of religious freedom be strengthened if it is seen under a new light, one that may help overcome the difficulties that the contemporary debate faces?

Genealogy of the Concept of Religion in Colonial Contexts outside the West

"Religion" as a political and theological category was invented in Early Modernity. The notion itself and the attempts to define it were already problematic. On top of that, there was a shift to also include within this category other non-Western groups and manifestations. Thus, it will be useful to see the use of "religion" when applied to contexts outside the West, in order to question its meaning and its use in contemporary debates.

The work by David Chidester, S. N. Balagangadhara, Timothy Fitzgerald, Tomoko Masuzawa, and Wilfred C. Smith, has shown that the notion of "religion" was borrowed from or imposed by Westerners in much of the rest of the world during the process of European colonization.[271] Smith states: "One is tempted, indeed, to ask whether there is a closely equivalent concept in any culture that has not been influenced by the modern West. I think that the answer to this is 'no.'"[272] In fact, there are relatively few languages into which one can translate the word "religion," and especially its plural "religions," outside Western civilization.

The concept of religions, as contraposed ideological communities and belief systems, is a modern invention which the West has exported to the rest

---

269. Smith, *Meaning and End of Religion*, 19.

270. Cf. Cavanaugh, *Myth*, 69–70.

271. See Balagangadhara, *Blindness*; Chidester, "Colonialism"; Chidester, *Empire of Religion*; Fitzgerald, *Ideology*; Masuzawa, *Invention of World Religions*.

272. Smith, *Meaning and End of Religion*, 18–19. Smith goes on to say that the case of Islam might be a partial exception to his "no," but only because of a link with Judeo-Christian developments in the origin of Islam.

of the world, leading people everywhere to think of themselves as members of one exclusive salvation-offering society against others. Smith has shown that the notion of a religion as a particular system of belief embodied in a bounded community was unknown prior to the modern period. He notes that neither the classical Sanskrit of the Hindu, nor the Mahayana Buddhist scriptures, nor the Pali of the Theravada Buddhist writings, nor ancient Egyptian, nor classical Chinese, nor the Hebrew of the Jewish scriptures, nor the Greek of the New Testament, has a word for the modern concept of religion or religions. Instead, these literatures speak of such living matters as doctrine, faith, obedience and disobedience, piety, worship, the truth, and the way, but not of "religions" as communally embodied systems of belief.[273]

As Jacques Derrida and Russell McCutcheon have observed, religion is a manufactured universal, whose boundaries and definition emerge from a very specific Christian-inspired academic discourse. In fact, as a modern category, religion owes many of its contours to the specific structure of Christianity.[274]

From all the examples one can cite, then, I will make a brief presentation on the cases of what is called Hinduism and Buddhism in India, Japan, and China. I have chosen these examples because these cultures remained uninfluenced for centuries by the West, and therefore offer us an insight into the meaning of the notion of "religion" as a category once it was introduced and imposed in a foreign context.

Of all the religious groups present in India, we can identify Hinduism and Buddhism as being of Indian origin. Most people in the West would agree that these are "religions" in the modern sense of the term. However, the concept of religion has been imposed over both Hinduism and Buddhism. There was a time when no one in India thought there was a religion named Hinduism, or that they were professing belief in a set of Hindu doctrines. The term "Hindu" as a religious designation was developed after the Islamic invasion of India in the second millennium AD. For the conquerors, it served to designate the aliens whom they conquered. The term also retained a geographical reference, that is, Indian.[275] A change major occurred, however, only after more than a century of British rule. Frits Staal came to the conclusion that: "Hinduism does not merely fail to be a religion; it is not even a meaningful unit of discourse."[276] He is not the only scholar to acknowledge the problems. R. N. Dandekar writes, for example,

---

273. Cf. Smith, *Meaning and End of Religion*, xi.
274. See Derrida and Vattimo, *Religion*; McCutcheon, *Manufacturing Religion*.
275. Cf. Smith, *Meaning and End of Religion*, 64.
276. Staal, *Rules without Meaning*, 397. See also Balagangadhara, *Blindness*, 315.

that: "Hinduism can hardly be called a religion in the properly understood sense of the term."[277] On his part, Simon Weightman concludes in his article on "Hinduism," that it displays few of the characteristics that are generally expected of a religion.[278] Weightman lists a few elements present in other "religions" that Hinduism lacks: it has no founder, no prophets, no creed, no dogma, no system of theology, no single moral code, no uniquely authoritative scripture, no ecclesiastical organization, and the concept of a god or gods is not centrally important.[279] Even more, he found that it is possible to find groups of Hindus whose respective beliefs have almost nothing in common with one another, and it is also impossible to identify any universal belief or practice that is common to all Hindus.[280] Weightman's list of what is generally expected of a "religion" would only fully apply to Christianity, which shows that religion is originally a Western concept.[281]

S. N. Balagangadhara describes Hinduism as "an imaginary entity."[282] The fact is that there are Hindus, but there is no Hinduism.[283] However, Hinduism as a religion was a useful concept to the colonizers, because Hinduism originally included all that it means to be Indian, that is, religion, politics, economics, etc. Thus, once the Modern concept of religion was introduced, a concept that is opposed to the secular, then its content could be essentially removed from the realm of worldly power.[284]

Something similar may be said of the phenomena we call Buddhism. Even though the figure of the founder, his teachings, and the institutions dedicated to them are ancient, it was not clear that there was a separate religion called Buddhism until the nineteenth century. It was at that time that Sanskrit texts were discovered, and thus different kinds of rites were traced back to the figure of Gautama. The invention of Buddhism as a distinct religion

277. Dandekar, "Hinduism," 237. This recognition, however, does not stop him from treating Hinduism under the rubric of religion. See Balagangadhara, *Blindness*, 15.

278. Cf. Weightman, "Hinduism." See also Balagangadhara, *Blindness*, 15.

279. One can note how all of these characteristics that Weightman are protestant in origin.

280. Cf. Weightman, "Hinduism."

281. Cf. Cavanaugh, *Myth*, 89.

282. Balagangadhara, *Blindness*, 116.

283. Cf. Smith, *Meaning and End of Religion*, 65.

284. As Richard Cohen points out, contemporary advocates of Hindutva (Hindu nationalism) reject the confinement of Hinduism to religion. Cohen states: "The proponents of Hindutva refuse to call Hinduism a religion precisely because they want to emphasize that Hinduism is more than mere internalized beliefs. It is social, political, economic, and familial in nature. Only thus can India the secular state become interchangeable with India the Hindu homeland." Cohen, "Indian Buddhism," 27.

was based on this discovery. Buddhism was understood by Western scholars to be originally a textual religion. Thus, the actual living manifestations of Buddhist rites were understood by these scholars as corruptions from the original spirit of the texts. On top of that, one of the greatest difficulties with the construction of Buddhism as a religion is that many Buddhist traditions explicitly deny belief in a god or gods.[285]

The notion of Buddhism as a religion, however, was not merely a European creation. In the late nineteenth century, monastic elites in Sri Lanka, China, and Japan began to posit Buddhism as a world religion, fully equal with Christianity, with its own founder, scriptures, and established set of doctrines. Jason Josephson, in his "When Buddhism became a Religion," and referring to Meiji Japan (1868–1912), states:

> As part of the climate of modernization, foreigners, government officials, and the press increasingly identified Buddhism as superstitious and backward. In response, Buddhist leaders divided traditional Buddhist cosmology and practices into the newly constructed categories "superstition" and "religion." Superstition was deemed "not really Buddhism" and purged, while the remainder of Buddhism was made to accord with Westernized ideas of religion. . . . Not only did Buddhism became a religion in Meiji Japan but also in order to do so it had to eliminate superstitions, which included numerous practices and beliefs that had previously been central.[286]

Josephson also recounts how, when Japanese translators first encountered the English word "religion" in the international trade treatises of the late 1850s, they were perplexed and had difficulty finding the proper corresponding term in Japanese, for there was no indigenous word that referred to something as broad as "religion," nor a systematic way to distinguish between "religions" as members of a larger generic category.[287] According to Josephson, "In the pre-Meiji period Buddhism was largely understood as something one did, not something one believed. It was only under the influence of the Western concept of religion that Buddhism

---

285. Cf. Cohen, *Beyond Enlightenment*; Pyysiäinen, "Buddhism." See also Cavanaugh, *Myth*, 92–93.

286. Josephson, "Buddhism," 143. He notes that both demons and this-worldly magic were fundamental to Buddhism in canonical texts and in daily practices (p. 153). One of the consequences of these changes is that there has been "an increasing dissonance between Buddhism as a 'philosophical religion' and Buddhism as a lived practice" (p. 164).

287. Cf. Josephson, "Buddhism," 144.

became a commitment to a series of propositions rather than rituals."[288] And later he adds: "By becoming a religion, Buddhism has been reduced to a specific sort of personal belief based on faith in the absolute with perhaps a smattering of ethics."[289]

In China there happened something similar to Japan. Modernizing elites in the late nineteenth century adopted the term "religion," but refused to identify those traditions most closely identified with the national character as religion. Peter Beyer is of the opinion that Chinese elites rejected "religion" for two reasons: in the first place, because it was highly individualistic, and therefore inimical to national unity; and in the second place, because it was nonprogressive, and therefore inimical to the modernization of China. Chinese elites therefore championed "Confucianism" as indigenous, unitive, and progressive, but also as definitely not religious.[290] In China, Buddhism would then join a category that included Protestantism, Catholicism, Islam, and Daoism, but not Confucianism.[291] Wilfred Cantwell Smith even points out that a single Chinese can be a Confucianist, a Buddhist, and a Daoist at the same time.[292]

It is obvious by now, then, that the notion of religion as a political and theological category is a product of modernity and of the West. The notion of "religion" suffers from a definitional problem, as it is an uncertain concept. This problem is strained even more when the category is used to include other non-Western groups and manifestations.

Contemporary Uses and Definitions of Religion

In order to see the usefulness or lack thereof of a concept of "religion" for a correct understanding of freedom of religion, it is important to consider contemporary uses and definitions of religion in the West.

The main question now is to ask whether the notion of "religion" as a category can be used as an objective tool of analysis in order to establish a correct understanding of religious freedom, and in order to bring light into the debates regarding the place of religion in the public square.

The definitions presented in this section hinge on the Early Modern invention of religion as a theological and political category, a shift that

---

288. Josephson, "Buddhism," 160. See also Isomae, "Deconstructing Japanese Religion."
289. Josephson, "Buddhism," 162.
290. Beyer, "Defining Religion," 174–75.
291. Cf. Josephson, "Buddhism," 144.
292. Cf. Smith, *Meaning and End of Religion*, 69.

went as far as including other non-Western groups and manifestations, and which has strained even more the already tensed definitional situation. The problem, then, is how can a notion of "religion" that is already problematic be employed in defining religious freedom and the place of religion in the public square?

Even within the modern West, the notion of religion remains a widely contested notion, as there are a variety of opinions on what is understood by religion.[293] It is a term notoriously difficult to define, for there is no such a thing as an essence of religion. Jonathan Z. Smith, for example, points out that it has been defined in more than fifty different ways,[294] and no definition has commanded wide acceptance. One can think of the great historic faiths, with or without explicit belief in supernatural beings, or with a wide range of spiritual and semi-spiritual beliefs, or even think of someone's religion as the shape of their ultimate concern. And this is the heart of the problem. Smith states that: "It is the richness, the radical diversity, the unceasing shift and change, the ramification and complex involvement, of the historical phenomena of 'religion' or of any one 'religion' that create the difficulty."[295] He even goes as far as recommending that the term religion be dropped entirely, concluding that the term is "confusing, unnecessary, and distorting."[296] The reason is that the noun religion is an unhelpful reification of what does not as such exist.

Another problem one faces in trying to find a definition of religion, is that definitions of religion are usually unjustifiably clear about what counts as religion and what does not.[297] Definitions encounter the difficulty of having to identify the many phenomena that are understood as "religious" or "religion." As Taylor states: "But what is 'religion'? This famously defies definition, largely because the phenomena we are tempted to call religious are so tremendously varied in human life.... We are facing a hard, perhaps insuperable task."[298]

293. Ronald Dworking, for example, states: "People who use the concept do not agree about precisely what it means: when they use it, they are taking a stand about what it should mean." See Dworkin, *Religion without God*, 7.

294. Smith, "Religion, Religions, Religious," 281.

295. Smith, *Meaning and End of Religion*, 144–45.

296. Smith, *Meaning and End of Religion*, 19, 50.

297. Cavanaugh argues, for example, that things like Christianity and Buddhism and Shinto are considered to be self-evidently religions, while things like nationalism and Marxism are considered to be secular phenomena. Yet, as he argues, these definitions are not clear in why some things count as religion while others don't. Cf. Cavanaugh, *Myth*, 102.

298. Taylor, *SA*, 15. Thus, as Gamwell notes, the definition of religion cannot be dependent on the particular convictions of a historically given religion or set of religions.

There is the attempt to identify religion with belief, a comprehensive view, or as the answer to a comprehensive question.[299] This has to do with the nature of reality. However, when faced with the question of God or gods, it is regarded as too restrictive as a single criterion, because it would exclude some "belief systems" such as Buddhism, Confucianism, and Daoism. In order to avoid this problem, the category of the "transcendent" is sometimes offered in place of God or gods. In this way, transcendence is meant to be an inclusive concept that would cover both gods and other phenomena. However, one runs with the problem that the inclusiveness of transcendence depends on how it is defined. Daniel Dubuisson, for example, notes that many scholars deny that Confucianism has any concept of transcendence;[300] and Jan Bremmer states that "the gods of the Greeks were not transcendent but directly involved in natural and social processes."[301] Another problem, as Timothy Fitzgerald points out, is that transcendent notions can include ideas such as "The 'Nation,' the land, the principles of humanism, the ancestors, Communism, atman-brahman, the goddess of democracy and human rights, Cold Speech, Enlightenment, the right to private property, witchcraft, destiny . . . ."[302]

Another problem with transcendence is that, in order to be inclusive enough, it must be vague. At the same time, the meaning of transcendence is modeled on Judeo-Christian theological definitions based on the relationship of a Creator God to the created world. Therefore, if emptied of its true meaning, transcendence ends up meaning whatever one may like it to mean. The same holds if one were to employ the notions of the sacred, or the supernatural, or the supraempirical. Thus, a consequence that follows from defining religion in terms of the "transcendent," or the sacred, or the supernatural, or the supraempirical, is that it begs the question as to what those terms mean. The definition of religion would then require that the terms employed in the definition be defined as well. If these terms are made vague enough as to be transcultural, then the inevitable consequence is that

---

At the same time, the phenomena called religious are so varied and complex as to preclude the possibility of any fully general definition. See Gamwell, *Meaning of Religious Freedom*, 13.

299. Rawls, for example, views religion as a comprehensive doctrine. Especially see Rawls, *PL*; Rawls, *IPRR*. Gamwell views religion as a primary form of culture "in terms of which the comprehensive question is explicitly asked and answered and, further, so answered that human authenticity is derived from the character of reality as such." See Gamwell, *Meaning of Religious Freedom*, 30.

300. Dubuisson, *Construction of Religion*, 42.
301. Bremmer, *Greek Religion*, 5.
302. Fitzgerald, "Response," 114.

they become so inclusive as to shatter the exclusivity of the category religion. Thus, either religion applies only to just one religious movement, such as Christianity, or it becomes so vague, in order to include other groups, that the notion of religion makes no sense any more.

When definitions of religion attempt to be inclusive, they fall into internal contradictions, as they are not clear in justifying the reasons why certain phenomena or behaviors are considered to be religious while others are not. Matt Rossano, for example, tries to find an "inclusive" definition of religion that will apply to both religious people and skeptics. According to him, devout religionists and scientific skeptics hold certain religious ideas in common. In order to find a definition of religion that is acceptable to, and inclusive of both parties, Rossano proposes that they must make compromises if a synthesis is to be successful. Thus, he claims that those that are religious should remove belief in the supernatural and place behavior above belief, while skeptics must abandon explanatory exclusivity, acknowledge the authority of moral experts, and recognize the necessity of community in achieving moral excellence.[303]

There are also definitions that focus on the way that a given "religion" functions in people's lives.[304] Yet, these definitions expand the category of religion so broadly that the notion loses meaning. According to a functional definition, almost every ideological system or set of practices can be considered a religion. Therefore, calling something a "religion" or "religious" does not help to distinguish it from anything else. For example, Fitzgerald notes that totems, the principle of hierarchy, Christmas cakes, witchcraft, unconditioned reality, the rights of man, the national essence, Marxism, Freudianism, the tea ceremony, nature, and ethics can all be found treated under the rubric of religion in the published works of religious studies scholars.[305] Cole Durham and Elizabeth Sewell also cite examples of sports, free market ideology, mathematics, belief in the possibility of cold fusion, radical psychotherapy, the consumption of healthy food, and nothingness itself as being discussed under the category "religion."[306]

One of the origins of this broad notion of religion can be found in Émile Durkheim's *Les Formes élémentaires de la vie religieuse* (1912). Durkheim stated that "a religion is a unified system of beliefs and practices

---

303. Cf. Rossano, "Religion."

304. See, for example, Durkheim, *Elementary Forms of Religious Life*, 46 & 174; Durham and Sewell, "Definition of Religion," 3–5; Sölle, "Jeans," 159; Loy, "Religion of the Market," 275.

305. Cf. Fitzgerald, *Ideology*, 17.

306. Cf. Durham and Sewell, "Definition of Religion," 3–5.

relative to sacred things, that is to say, things set apart and surrounded by prohibitions."[307] Durkheim's definition of religion depends on the distinction of sacred and profane; however, he does not define sacred and profane based on their content. For Durkheim, anything can be considered sacred by a given society.[308] No wonder, then, why so many disparate and different things have ended up being labeled under the category "religion."

There are also the uses of politics as a religion.[309] Most authors that use the term "political religion" see religion as a basic element of any social order. Emilio Gentile, in his *Politics as Religion*, states that a "religion of politics" is religious insofar as it is "a system of beliefs, myths, rituals, and symbols that interpret and define the meaning and end of human existence by subordinating the destiny of individuals and the collectivity to a supreme entity."[310] It is also a secular religion, because it creates "an aura of sacredness around an entity belonging to this world."[311] For Gentile, it is the distinction between "this world" and "other world" that defines the divide between secular and traditional religions.[312]

Gentile distinguishes between two different types of religion of politics: "political religion," and "civil religion."[313] "Political religion," according to Gentile, applies primarily to totalitarian regimes, such as Marxism/communism, German Nazism, and Italian fascism.[314] Gentile defines political religion as "the sacralization of a political system founded on an unchallengeable monopoly of power, ideological monism, and the obligatory and unconditional subordination of the individual and the collectivity to its code of commandments."[315] The Italian Marxist philosopher Antonio Gramsci, for example, stated that Marxism is "the religion that has to kill off Christianity," and that "it is a religion in the sense that it is also a faith with its own

---

307. Durkheim, *Elementary Forms of Religious Life*, 46.

308. Durkheim writes, "Religious force is the feeling the collectivity inspires in its members, but projected outside and objectified by the minds that feel it. It becomes objectified by being anchored in an object which then becomes sacred, but any object can play this role." Durkheim, *Elementary Forms of Religious Life*, 174.

309. Gentile states that Condorcet, Abraham Lincoln, Reinhold Niebuhr, and Karl Polanyi have used the term "political religion." However, it became popular by the work of Erich Vogelin, *Politischen Religionen*.

310. Gentile, *Politics as Religion*, xiv.

311. Gentile, *Politics as Religion*, 1.

312. Cf. Gentile, *Politics as Religion*, 3–9.

313. See also Cristi, *Political Religion*.

314. Wiker also includes liberalism as a political religion. See Wiker, *Worshipping the State*.

315. Gentile, *Politics as Religion*, xv.

mysteries and practices, and because in our consciences it has replaced the transcendental God of Catholicism with faith in Man and his best energies as the only spiritual reality."[316] Benito Mussolini also called for "a *religious concept of socialism*."[317] And critics of the fascist and Nazi regimes have noted the intensely ritualistic and all-absorbing nature of ideology, to the point of calling them "religions."[318]

On the other hand, "civil religion," according to Gentile, applies primarily to democratic regimes. He states:

> Civil religion is the conceptual category that contains the forms of sacralization of a political system that guarantee a plurality of ideas, free competition in the exercise of power, and the ability of the governed to dismiss their governments through peaceful and constitutional methods.[319]

Yet, Gentile warns that the distinction between political and civil religion is not always a sharp one. Thus, governing regimes may be located in a position between the two types when, for example, a democratic civil religion becomes intolerant of dissent and invasive regarding citizens' rights.

Gentile and several other scholars have argued that many liberal democracies rely on a strong civil religion to provide a common meaning and purpose for liberal nation-states.[320] According to Gentile's definition, civil religion is not a type of "politicization of religion," in which traditional religion merges with the state. Civil religion is a new creation that confers sacred status on democratic institutions and symbols, though it may occasionally borrow elements from traditional religion.[321] In the United States, for example, there is a widespread belief in the righteousness of the nation and its solemn duty to impose liberal democracy on the rest of the world. This phenomenon has all of the ultimate concern, community, myth, ritual, and required behavior of any so-called religion, as Marty implies.[322] Already

---

316. Antonio Gramsci, quoted in Gentile, *Politics as Religion*, 31.

317. Benito Mussolini, quoted in Gentile, *Politics as Religion*, 31.

318. See, for example, Gentile, *Sacralization of Politics*; Maier, *Totalitarianism and Political Religions*; Tal, *Third Reich*. There is also the journal *Totalitarian Movements and Political Religions* dedicated to the study of fascism and communism. For Gentile on Italian fascism and German Nazism as religions, see also Gentile, *Politics as Religion*, 33–38, 45–109.

319. Gentile, *Politics as Religion*, xv.

320. See also Lewin, *Civil Religion*; Beiner, *Civil Religion*; Weed and Heyking, *Civil Religion*; Hvithamar et al., *Holy Nations*; Parsons, *Perspectives*.

321. Gentile, *Politics as Religion*, xvi; Cavanaugh, *Myth*, 113.

322. See Marty and Moore, *Common Good*.

in 1749, Benjamin Franklin had argued for "the Necessity of a Public Religion," that is, a cult of the nation and the duties of the citizen.[323] Robert Bellah, in his famous 1967 article "Civil Religion in America," noted that there is "an elaborate and well-institutionalized civil religion in America," which "has its own seriousness and integrity and requires the same care in understanding that any other religion does."[324] However, references to Christ and the church are kept to a private, voluntary sphere of worship.[325] Thus, it is not religion, but traditional religion that is privatized, while the civic religion of politics occupies the public realm.[326]

To conclude this section, it is obvious by now that we, in the twenty-first century, are heirs to a chaotic development of the notion of religion in its many and varied senses.

In the first place, there is the notion of religion as something interior, personal, in the sense of personal piety. According to this sense, religion has no place in the public square.

In the second place, there is the notion of religion as a system, whether of beliefs, practices, values, etc. Religion as a system has an extension in time, some relation to an area, and is related to a particular community, such as Christianism, Islam, Judaism, etc. In this sense, there is the notion of "religions" of the world.

In the third place, there is also the notion of a religion of politics, as when the state proposes a system of beliefs, myths, rituals, and symbols that interpret and define the meaning and end of human existence.

Finally, there is the notion of "religion" as a generic summation, that is, "religion in general." The meaning of this loose term of religion will be derived by the one employing it from any of the other senses of the term. It is used commonly to discriminate religion from other aspects of human life, so that, for example, religion should not mingle with politics, the economy, etc.

This summary of contemporary different uses and definitions of religion should suffice to show that the notions of religion offered are not helpful when trying to establish the meaning of religious freedom. Since what is understood by religion is so varied, vague, and loose, it seems impossible that with such a notion one will be able to overcome the difficulties raised by the contemporary problematic on religious freedom and the place of

---

323. Cf. Gentile, *Politics as Religion*, 17–18. Franklin, in fact, was typical of Enlightenment figures who looked to the model of republican Rome, and saw how religion provided a unified sense of civic duty and loyalty. Cf. Cavanaugh, *Myth*, 115.

324. Bellah, "Civil Religion in America," 21.

325. Cf. Bellah, "Civil Religion in America," 28–30.

326. Cf. Cavanaugh, *Myth*, 116.

religion in the public square. The fact that there is a repeated failure to agree, to reach any satisfying answer, or even to make any discernible progress towards the question on the nature and definition of religion, may be a sign that we have been asking the wrong question. As Smith affirms:

> In this instance one might argue that the sustained inability to clarify what the word 'religion' signifies", in itself suggests that the term ought to be dropped; that it is a distorted concept not really corresponding to anything definite or distinctive in the objective world. The phenomena that we call religious undoubtedly exist. Yet perhaps the notion that they constitute in themselves some distinctive entity is an unwarranted analysis.[327]

Unless we find a new tool to guide us in this process, and abandon entirely the notion of religion as a category, the reigning confusion will just continue to be perpetuated.

Conclusion

The term "religion" has been used in different times and places by different people according to different interests. As an invented category, religion is tied up with the history of Western modernity and is inseparable from the notion of secularism.[328] It is a mistake and a deeply problematic assumption to treat religion as a constant in human culture across time and space, as the history of the term religion shows. It wasn't until after the Reformation, when the thought of the reformers and contra-reformers was shaped into the abstract theological disputes of the seventeenth century, that the notion of a religion as a system of doctrines was effectively formed. This notion was joined soon thereafter by the idea of a human population which professes and preserves these doctrines, so that by the eighteenth century we have an understanding of "religions" as alternative belief systems embodied in mutually exclusive ideological communities. The historical dimension of these "religions" was added in the nineteenth century, perceiving the phenomena now called Christianism, Judaism, Islam, Hinduism, Buddhism, Sikhism, Confucianism, Taoism, etc., as complex organisms, each with its own long history, which nineteenth and twentieth century scholarship traced and studied in great particularity. Thus, the history of the uncertain concept of religion shows how something adjectival,

---

327. Smith, *Meaning and End of Religion*, 17.

328. Talal Asad, in fact, has called religion the "Siamese twin" of secularism. Cf. Asad, "Reading a Modern Classic," 221.

the qualities of man's response and relationship to the divine, became congealed in Western thought and language into something substantival, the supposedly rival entities known as the world's "religions."

There is a problem with the use of "religion" as a category, and it bears consequences on the idea of religious freedom. Religion is not a neutral descriptor of a reality that is simply out there in the world. Reality is definable; however, since there is not actually anything out there such as religion, for it is not a real entity, we can at best state its meaning. Yet, there is no entity in the objective world to which religion corresponds, and therefore it is impossible to offer a definition of "what "religion is.""[329] "Religion," then, is a "constructed category," as Cavanaugh notes.[330] Even further, we can well affirm that there is no such thing as religion. It may only exist in certain cultures as a product of human construction. As a consequence, we should discard the use of freedom of religion that takes the religious life of men as divided into a number of theological and historical complexes called Christianity, Judaism, Islam, Hinduism, Buddhism, Sikhism, Confucianism, Taoism, and so on, and instead focus on protecting the acts elicited by religious virtue.

Thus, in our investigation on the meaning of religion in debates on religious freedom and the place of religion in the public square, the very question "What is the nature of religion" is itself very problematic, and must be set aside as inapt, or dropped entirely, if one is to succeed in moving forward in understanding the varied and evolving religious situation of mankind. The reason is that neither "religion" in general, nor any of the "religions," are in themselves intelligible entities, valid objects of inquiry or of concern.[331] The notion of "religion" as a category is imprecise and liable to distort what it is supposed to represent.

The aim of this chapter has been, then, not to show that "religion," just like that, is meaningless, but rather that, for the reasons mentioned above, the notion of "religion" as a category should be abandoned in favor of a

---

329. See Aristotle's remarks in his *Posterior Analytics* of a mythical animal, a goat-stag, to which one may give the meaning of a word that names it, but to which it is not possible to give a definition of, since there is actually not such animal. One can use the term "goat-stag," or "unicorn," and may state its meaning, but since there is no entity in the objective world to which it corresponds, it is not possible, therefore, to state and define what a "goat-stag," or a "unicorn," really is. Cf. Aristotle, *Posterior Analytics*, bk. 2, ch. 7.

330. Cf. Cavanaugh, *Myth*, 58.

331. Smith states: "On the verbal plane, I seriously suggest that terms such as Christianity, Buddhism, and the like must be dropped, as clearly untenable once challenged. The word 'religion' has had many meanings; it too would be better dropped. This is partly because of its distracting ambiguity, partly because most of its traditional meanings are, on scrutiny, illegitimate." See Smith, *Meaning and End of Religion*, 194.

notion of "religion" as virtue, such as the one presented by Thomas Aquinas. The reason is that, fundamentally, one has to do not with "religions," but rather with religious persons who manifest their movement towards the divine through acts of virtue.

This proposal to move aside from a notion of religion as a category to a notion of religion as virtue is not as disruptive as it may appear. I believe that this way of looking at religious acts and phenomena, which does not attempt to locate an essence of religion, is of great service for the questions that have arisen in contemporary debates. This understanding of religion as virtue in debates regarding religious freedom and the place of religion in the public square is meant not to subvert a fixed position, but rather, it is offered as carrying forward new developments that will allow us overcome the impasse into which contemporary discussions have been sidetracked.

CHAPTER 4

Hanna Arendt's Notions of Freedom and the Public Sphere

IN THE PREVIOUS CHAPTER, we concluded that there is a need to elucidate the meaning of religion in order to provide a better understanding of what is meant by religious freedom as pertaining to the presence of "religion" in the contemporary public square. In the same way, it is also necessary to clarify what is meant by freedom, for as seen on chapter 2, the meaning of freedom is a contested issue in political philosophy, so much so that it is common to refer to two concepts (or conceptions) of freedom in relation to religious freedom: a negative concept focusing on the feature of absence of interference (notion employed by Murray), and a positive concept focusing on the realization of freedom in practice (Schlinder).

In this chapter, I will first focus on Hanna Arendt's notion of political freedom, that is, freedom as a phenomenon of virtuosity that takes place in a public stage or space as a politically guaranteed public field of activity.[1] She claims that this was the original experience of freedom in ancient Greece and Rome. Only when the view of freedom as a phenomenon of virtuosity had in practice disappeared in the late Roman Empire, was then freedom understood in connection with the will. However, she acknowledges that freedom as a phenomenon of virtuosity continued to exist in a hidden form in all human activities. I will borrow from Arendt's presentation, in order to enrich the notion of religious freedom understood as the practice of religion as virtue.

---

1. Cf. Arendt, "Freedom and Politics," 192. Hannah Arendt (1906–1975) was one of the most influential political philosophers of the twentieth century. She was born into a German-Jewish family, and for that reason, she was forced to leave Germany in 1933. She lived in Paris for the next eight years, and in 1941 she immigrated to the United States, where soon became part of New York's intellectual circle. Arendt held a number of academic positions at various American universities until her death in 1975.

In the second place, I will explore the meaning of "public stage" for Arendt. In order to do so, one should explore what Arend meant by the public sphere, the notion of the private realm, and the rise of society in modernity. I will also come back to her notions of the *polis* and the public, in order to see how Arendt's notion of the public differs from notions of the public square presented in chapter 1.

Freedom

In the first place, we will face what Hanna Arendt characterized in her "What is Freedom?" (1961) as the seemingly hopeless enterprise of defining freedom, the last of the time-honored great metaphysical questions to become the subject of philosophical debate. In her article, Arendt bases her treatment of freedom not on philosophical and metaphysical arguments, but on evidence of the experience of freedom as a living, worldly, political reality.[2]

Arendt notes that the first appearances of freedom in the Western philosophical tradition had to do with experiences of religious conversion which gave rise to freedom: that of Paul, and then Augustine. There took place a discovery of the will when the will was seen not so much as powerful but as impotent. Only when this kind of inner freedom was discovered, a kind of freedom which had no relation to politics, did the concept of freedom enter the history of philosophy. Thus, historically, freedom became one of the chief problems of philosophy when it was experienced as an internal reality, outside the relations between men. In this way, free will and freedom became synonymous notions.[3]

In ancient Greece, however, freedom was a purely political concept, at the core of the city-state and citizenship. Yet, this idea of freedom as the center of politics, as the Greeks understood it, was an idea which did not enter the framework of Greek philosophy.[4] It is to this notion of freedom as related to politics that Arendt wishes to return to, and in order to do so, Arendt makes a strong case for a revival of this kind of "political freedom." I

---

2. Arendt, "What Is Freedom?," 143. See also Arendt, "Freedom and Politics."

3. Cf. Arendt, "What Is Freedom?," 145–46. Historically, however, the presence of freedom in philosophy was much more complex.

4. The way of life chosen by the philosophers was understood by many philosophical schools as in opposition to the political way of life. The philosophers' abstention from politics was seen as a prerequisite for the contemplative life, the highest and freest way of life. This Greek understanding of philosophy is found in Habermas, for example, who distinguishes between the philosopher and the politician, to the point that intellectuals cease to be intellectuals once they assume public office. See Habermas, *Zwischen Naturalismus und Religion*, 26.

will argue in this section that this notion of political freedom is very helpful in order to overcome the conflict generated by the contemporary discussions on the place of religion in the public square.

Political Freedom in Hanna Arendt

Arendt distinguishes between inner freedom, and external or political freedom. Inner freedom is the inward space into which men may escape from external coercion and feel free. It is in this sense that the philosophical tradition has addressed the question of freedom. The freedom of political theory, on the other hand, is the very opposite of "inner freedom." However important inner and nonpolitical freedom may seem to be, Arendt argues that:

> Man would know nothing of inner freedom if he had not first experienced a condition of being free as a worldly tangible reality. We first become aware of freedom or its opposite in our intercourse with others, not in the intercourse with ourselves. Before it became an attribute of thought or a quality of the will, freedom was understood to be the free man's status, which enabled him to move, to get away from home, to go out into the world and meet other people in deed and word.[5]

For that reason, Arendt claims that the original field of freedom is the realm of politics and human affairs in general.[6] In order to see this point, Arendt reminds the reader that, in ancient Greece, the political realm was distinguished from the household, which belonged to the private realm. She states:

> What all Greek philosophers, no matter how opposed to *polis* life, took for granted is that freedom is exclusively located in the political realm, that necessity is primarily a prepolitical phenomenon, characteristic of the private household organization, and that force and violence are justified in this sphere because they are the only means to master necessity . . . and to become free.[7]

In the household, on the other hand, one did not experience freedom, for the household had to deal with the necessities of life (such as food), and its members were either in command (the head of the household), or under

---

5. Arendt, "What Is Freedom?," 148.
6. Cf. Arendt, "What Is Freedom?," 146.
7. Arendt, *HC*, 31.

the command of another.⁸ Arendt notes that to be free "meant neither to rule nor to be ruled."⁹

When it comes to political matters, it seems a self-evident truth that man is free by nature, and therefore it is impossible not to at least assume that man is free, that freedom exists. It is for this reason that men are held responsible for their actions. When it comes to human agency and politics, Arendt states: "In all practical and especially in political matters we hold human freedom to be a self-evident truth, and it is upon this axiomatic assumption that laws are laid down in human communities, that decisions are taken, that judgments are passed."¹⁰ At the same time, it is almost impossible not to touch political issues without touching upon issues of man's political freedom. Political life is meaningless without freedom. As Arendt affirms: "The *raison d'être* of politics is freedom, and its field of experience is action."¹¹

Therefore, before freedom became an attribute of thought or a quality of the will, it was understood to be the status of the free man. This freedom, or status, is what allowed man to liberate himself from the necessities of life and go out into the world and act in deed and word. As mentioned above, political freedom is located within the sphere of the *polis*, in opposition to the sphere of the household and family, which dealt with the necessities of life. Man had to liberate himself from want and need, that is, from the necessities of life, the realm of the household, in order to neither rule nor be ruled. It was only then that he could enter the public realm, that of the *polis*. This liberation was understood in terms of violence, as the pre-political act of liberating oneself from the necessity of life for the freedom of the world.¹² Liberation, for Arendt, refers then to the lifting of the biological and legal barriers to entering the public realm in order to act politically. To be liberated is to have a status for political participation, and to be free is to make use of that status. Political participation, at the same time, means to be able to take part in deliberations, to be able to hold a public office, and be responsible for the actions taken while holding it, the ability to vote, etc.¹³

8. Cf. Arendt, *HC*, 32.

9. Arendt, *HC*, 32.

10. Arendt, "What Is Freedom?," 143. Thomas Aquinas affirms that this self-evidence of freedom is manifested in the fact that if it were otherwise, then counsels, exhortations, commands, prohibitions, rewards, and punishments would be in vain. See Aquinas, *S. Th.*, I, q. 83, a. 1.

11. Arendt, "What Is Freedom?," 146.

12. Cf. Arendt, *HC*, 31.

13. Yet, one should keep in mind, when arguing for a place for "religion" in the political public square, that none of these acts that Arendt mentions have to do with the religious freedom of citizens.

Arendt introduces an interesting element in her discussion on political freedom, that of sociability and of a public space: "Freedom needed, in addition to liberation, the company of other men who were in the same state, and it needed a common public space to meet them–a politically organized world, in other words, into which each of the free men could insert himself by word and deed."[14] However, freedom can make its appearance only if there is "a politically guaranteed public realm." Thus, "freedom as a demonstrable fact and politics coincide and are related to each other like two sides of the same matter."[15] The problem is that, and this is the case of religious freedom in many areas of the world, one cannot take for granted the coincidence of politics and freedom. Arendt's words regarding the totalitarian state are clear:

> The rise of totalitarianism, its claim to having subordinated all spheres of life to the demands of politics and its consistent non-recognition of civil rights, above all the rights of privacy and the right to freedom from politics, makes us doubt not only the coincidence of politics and freedom, but their very compatibility.[16]

Arendt also accuses liberalism of having had its share in banishing freedom from the political realm by creating a gigantic sphere of social and economic life the liberal state must administer in order to take care of all of man's necessities.[17] It is in this sense of politics that Arendt speaks of "freedom from politics." One has to remember here once again the distinction between the realm of the *polis* and that of the household found in ancient Greece. In the modern nation-state, however, the dividing line was entirely blurred "because we see the body of peoples and political communities in the image of a family whose everyday affairs have to be taken care of by a gigantic, nation-wide administration of housekeeping."[18] Thus, Arendt states, "the collective of families economically organized into the facsimile of one super-human family is what we call 'society,' and its political form of organization is called 'nation.'"[19] The fact that there is a "political economy,"

---

14. Arendt, "What Is Freedom?," 148.
15. Arendt, "What Is Freedom?," 149.
16. Arendt, "What Is Freedom?," 149. It is interesting to note that the decline of freedom in the late Roman Empire led to the attempt to divorce the notion of freedom from politics, so that one may be a slave in this world and still be free. Such is the case, for example, of Epictetus's formulation of freedom, according to which man is free if he does not reach into a realm where he can be hindered.
17. Cf. Arendt, "What Is Freedom?," 155.
18. Arendt, *HC*, 28.
19. Arendt, *HC*, 29.

which in ancient Greece belonged to the household and would have meant a contradiction in terms, shows that there is a necessity, and therefore the room for freedom is denied. In ancient Greece, "whatever was 'economic,' related to the life of the individual and the survival of the species, was a non-political, household affair by definition."[20]

How many people in today's world in fact do think that freedom begins where politics ends? That is the result when politics overrules every aspect of society. Arendt states:

> Indeed, do we not rightly measure the extent of freedom in any given community by the free scope it grants to apparently nonpolitical activities, free economic enterprise or freedom of teaching, of religion, of cultural and intellectual activities? Is it not true, as we all somehow believe, that politics is compatible with freedom only because and insofar as it guarantees a possible freedom from politics?[21]

Freedom as Virtuous Action

The separation of politics from freedom is in fact a fruit of the modern age. However, as mentioned above, political life is meaningless without freedom. Which kind of freedom does Arendt refer to when she relates it to political life? She is not speaking of inner freedom, freedom as a phenomenon of the will.[22] Instead, she refers to freedom as related to action: "Men *are* free—as distinguished from their possessing the gift for freedom—as long as they act, neither before nor after; for to *be* free and to act are the same."[23] Freedom, for Arendt, happens through action, which is essentially public. She states: "Because of its inherent tendency to disclose the agent together with the act, action needs for its full appearance the shining brightness we once called glory, and which is possible only in the public realm."[24]

This kind of freedom, which is inherent in action, is, according to Arendt, best illustrated by the concept of "virtue," and its meaning best rendered by "virtuosity," that is, the "excellence we attribute to the performing arts (as

20. Arendt, HC, 29.
21. Arendt, "What Is Freedom?," 149.
22. She affirms: "We deal here not with the *liberum arbitrium*, a freedom of choice that arbitrates and decides between two given things, one good and one evil, and whose choice is predetermined by motive which has only to be argued to start its operation." Arendt, "What Is Freedom?," 151.
23. Arendt, "What Is Freedom?," 153.
24. Arendt, HC, 160.

distinguished from the creative arts of making), where the accomplishment lies in the performance itself and not in an end product which outlasts the activity that brought it into existence and becomes independent of it."[25] In politics, in fact, virtuosity of performance is decisive.

The metaphor based on the distinction between the performing arts and the creative arts of making that Arendt employs in order to explain political freedom is just perfect, as it clearly shows what is at play in political activity. Without acting men, men that perform in the public square, there is no politics. While the work of art as a product of making enjoys independent existence from its maker, performing artists need an audience to show their virtuosity, and a publicly organized space for their work. It is in this virtuous work or performance that political freedom is manifested. The Greek polis, in fact, was the form of government which provided men with a space of appearances where they could act, and it was in this theater that freedom could appear. It was in the polis, in fact, that the essence and the realm of the political was first discovered. These ancient political communities were set up with the express intention of serving those that were free. This is what expresses best the relation of freedom to politics. Arendt states: "If, then, we understand the political in the sense of the polis, its end or *reason d'être* would be to establish and keep in existence a space where freedom as virtuosity can appear."[26] It is through these virtuous actions that freedom becomes a reality, "tangible in words which can be heard, in deeds which can be seen, and in events which are talked about, remembered, and turned into stories before they are finally incorporated into the great storybook of human history."[27]

For that reason, Arendt calls for a shift in one's conception of freedom. She denounces that here is a dominant notion that freedom is an attribute of will and thought rather than of action. That is the reason why "every attempt to derive the concept of freedom from experiences in the political realm sounds strange and startling."[28] And she laments:

> Because of the philosophic shift from action to will power, from freedom as a state of being manifest in action to the *liberum arbitrium*, the ideal of freedom ceased to be virtuosity ... and became sovereignty, the ideal of a free will, independent from others and eventually prevailing against them.[29]

25. Arendt, "What Is Freedom?," 153.
26. Arendt, "What Is Freedom?," 154.
27. Arendt, "What Is Freedom?," 154–55.
28. Arendt, "What Is Freedom?," 155.
29. Arendt, "What Is Freedom?," 163. Thus, for example, Rousseau derived his

Thus, she claims that it is necessary to go back to antiquity, to its political and pre-philosophical traditions "because a freedom experienced in the process of acting and nothing else ... has never been again articulated with the same classical clarity."[30] There is a need to revive a freedom understood as doing and acting.

Since the faculty of freedom, the capacity to begin all human activities, the source of production of all things human, remains always intact, even when political life disappears, one might be tempted to think that freedom is not political, that is, a tangible reality. Yet, Arendt affirms that:

> Because the source of freedom remains present even when political life has become petrified and political action impotent to interrupt automatic processes, freedom can so easily be mistaken for an essentially nonpolitical phenomenon; in such circumstances, freedom is not experienced as a mode of being with its own kind of "virtue" and virtuosity, but as a supreme gift which only man, of all earthly creatures, seems to have received, of which we can find traces and signs in almost all his activities, but which, nevertheless, develops fully only when action has created its own worldly space where it can come out of hiding, as it were, and makes its appearance.[31]

The proper place for freedom to appear is in the *polis*, in the public sphere, and it is done through virtuous action. Thus, the excellence of action is constituted by virtue. Now, from among the virtues that belong to the public realm, Arendt emphasizes courage, readiness to forgive, and commitment to promises, that is, the oath, which for Aquinas is an act of the virtue of religion.[32] Courage is necessary in order to appear in public at all, and face the unpredictable outcome of one's acts, independently of any danger or hostility one may thus encounter.[33] Forgiving tempers the

---

theory of sovereignty directly from the will, conceiving of political power in the image of individual will-power.

30. Arendt, "What Is Freedom?," 165.
31. Arendt, "What Is Freedom?," 169.
32. Cf. Aquinas, *S. Th.*, II–II, q. 89.
33. Cf. Arendt, *HC*, 166; Arendt, "What Is Freedom?," 156. Arendt also affirms: "To leave the household, originally in order to embark upon some adventure and glorious enterprise and later simply to devote one's life to the affairs of the city, demanded courage because only in the household was one primarily concerned with one's own life and survival. Whoever entered the political realm had first to be ready to risk his life, and too great a love for life obstructed freedom, was a sure sign of slavishness. Courage therefore became the political virtue par excellence, and only those men who possessed it could be admitted to a fellowship that was political in content and purpose and thereby transcended the mere togetherness imposed on all—slaves, barbarians, and Greeks alike—through the urgencies of life." Arendt, *HC*, 36.

irreversibility of one's actions, for "without being forgiven, released from the consequences of what we have done, our capacity to act would, as it were, be confined to one single deed from which we could never recover; we would remain the victims of its consequences forever."[34] Promising tempers the unpredictability of one's actions.[35] And as a remedy for this unpredictability, we have the oath, the commitment to make reality that which one has verbally promised.

There are, however, some objections to Arendt's notion of freedom.

Arendt's notion of political freedom has been criticized as inherently individualistic, and her ideal of virtue as excessively egotistic, for it is expressed in terms of self-distinction, fame and immortality.[36] Arendt connects her notion of political freedom to the Greek notion of αρήτή, the "excellence" that the Romans named *virtus*. This human excellence in acting, according to Arendt:

> ... has always been assigned to the public realm where one could excel, could distinguish oneself from all others. Every activity performed in public can attain an excellence never matched in privacy; for excellence, by definition, the presence of others is always required, and this presence needs the formality of the public, constituted by one's peers, it cannot be the casual, familiar presence of one's equals or inferiors.[37]

Thus, against the challenge of individualism and egotism, we see that, according to Arendt, what action realizes is neither a purely subjective nor a purely particular value, since it is interpreted by others and emerges in the act rather than just in the intention of the actor. Even more importantly, its internal goods are not a purely individual benefit, but a social good, with benefits to others, and realizing principles beyond the actor. Arendt is not implying that virtuous actions simply need spectators, but rather that the exercise of virtue communicates and exemplifies to others regarding excellence itself, and motivates others to acts of courage, honor, justice, religion, etc. Virtuous action is more than just displaying individual virtuosity, for those virtues that belong to the public sphere by nature transcend any narrow interests and self-awareness. Thus, examples of virtue expand our understanding of human possibilities in general, including the actor's own. It is for that reason that Arendt argues that virtuous individual development is only possible as part of a social endeavor.

34. Arendt, *HC*, 237.
35. Cf. Arendt, *HC*, 243–437.
36. See, for example, Pitkin, "Justice," 337.
37. Arendt, *HC*, 49.

That is the reason why, in Ancient Greece and Rome, the idea of the hero occupied a central place in the education and transmission of values. The works of Homer and Virgil testify to this. Thus, in continuity with this tradition, Arendt borrows this idea of the hero not as someone who stands out against everyone else, but rather as someone who represents to everyone the extension of their capabilities through good acting. Thus, the actions of the hero, or in our case, the virtuous citizen, have "exemplary validity," as Arendt puts it.[38] Throughout history, in fact, people have become aware of, and open to moral principles and virtues through the example of others. Arendt states: "Whenever we try to perform a deed of courage or of goodness, it is as though we imitated someone else."[39] And this is true not just of action in relation to virtue, but of speech as well. Public speech and argument seek the agreement of others, that is, their intellectual consent. A good and true argument always enlightens the mind. Thus, it is more than merely the opportunity to issue a statement of position, or to express oneself in public.[40]

George Kateb raises another objection to Arendt's concept of action and freedom. He holds that if for Arendt action is a self-justifying activity to which no external criteria can be applied, then it seems to be a radically voluntaristic concept, incompatible with any concept of practical reason, which then seems to admit evil. Thus, Arendt's notion of freedom may admit, Kateb suggests, the deeds of totalitarian leaders.[41]

In order to reply to this objection, we should note again that Arendt's concept of freedom is not radically individualistic, for it brings about social good through works of virtue, which are communicable and encouraging to observers. Arendt does acknowledge that the actions freely performed on the public stage may be bad ones, as she speaks of good and bad deeds performed in the *polis*.[42] However, it is only the good and virtuous actions that truly manifest political freedom. Thus, the Greek poet accomplished a political function by disclosing the story of a hero whose courage and boldness (in disclosing and exposing himself in a willingness to speak and to act) are to be remembered and emulated, for these are acts of virtue, in contraposition to vicious acts, which are to be rejected and avoided. Good

---

38. Cf. Arendt, "Truth and Politics," 247–48; Arendt and Beiner, *Lectures on Kant's Political Philosophy*, 76–77; Arendt, *Life of the Mind*, 272.

39. Arendt, "Truth and Politics," 248.

40. Arendt states: "To be political, to live in a *polis*, meant that everything was decided through words and persuasion and not through force and violence." Arendt, *HC*, 26.

41. Kateb, *Arendt*, 39.

42. Cf. Arendt, *HC*, 197.

deeds will be lauded in an everlasting remembrance to inspire admiration in the present and in future ages. Thus, good deeds deserving fame would not be forgotten, and would actual become immortal.[43] As a consequence, Arendt's notion of freedom does not admit, as Kateb suggests it may, the deeds of totalitarian leaders, however radical, public, and rhetorically good they may be.

Finally, I will make a reference, before closing this section, to Murray's notion of negative freedom.[44] In Murray's view, religious freedom is a negative right, one by which man is immune from external coercion. For Murray, negative liberty places central value on the freedom of the individual to choose for himself what is good for him, and for that reason he considered it better attuned to deal with issues related to religious pluralism in contemporary societies. Arendt, on the contrary, does not share a negative view of freedom. For her, the political freedom to act is a more fulfilling ideal than a negative view of freedom because it is only in political action that man's potentiality is actualized, his unique identity manifested, and his being-in-the-world-with-others reaffirmed. For Arendt, human potentiality can be fully realized only in political life, and for that reason one must choose to speak and act in the public realm if one is to live a genuinely good life. Thus, it is through these freely performed works of virtue that man is to be fully human.

The Public Sphere

Hannah Arendt has employed different expressions to refer to the public square, such as "public sphere," "political space," "public space," "public stage," "public field of activity," "public realm," etc. This public space, for Arendt, is a condition for freedom to take place; she states: "If there existed no politically guaranteed public field of activity, freedom would find no place in the world."[45] In her *The Human Condition* (1958), she states: "Before men began to act, a definite space had to be secured and a structure built where all subsequent actions could take place, the space being the public realm of the *polis* and its structure the law."[46] And in *On Revolution* (1963), Arendt describes

---

43. This is the reason, Arendt notes, Homer has been called the "educator of all Hellas." See Arendt, *HC*, 197.

44. For Murray, religious freedom is a personal and corporate right to immunity from coercion, and its content is negative. See Murray, *Problem of Religious Freedom*, 80.

45. Arendt, "Freedom and Politics," 192.

46. Arendt, *HC*, 194–95.

revolutions as the political events that attempt to found a new political space, a space where freedom can appear as a worldly reality.[47]

In this second section, I will present Arendt's understanding of the public and private realms, society, and her notions of the *polis* and the public.

The Public and the Private Realm

In a chapter entitled "The Public and the Private Realm," in her book *The Human Condition* (1958), Hannah Arendt presents her understanding of the distinction between the public and the private realm, and how the social emerged in modernity from the private to the public sphere.[48]

Arendt, in her explanation of the public and the private realms, relies once again on Greek thought. For the ancient Greeks, the human capacity for political organization is not only different from, but stands in direct opposition to that natural association whose center is the home (*oikia*) and the family.[49] She also notes that:

> Of all the activities necessary and present in human communities, only two were deemed to be political and to constitute what Aristotle called the *bios politikos*, namely action (*praxis*) and speech (*lexis*), out of which rises the realm of human affairs from which everything merely necessary or useful is strictly excluded.[50]

The public realm is the stage of freedom, and for that reason, that which is merely necessary is strictly excluded, for it belongs to the realm of the household, the private realm. Thus, Arendt insists on a strict separation between the private and the public, and between the social and the political:

---

47. Cf. Arendt, *On Revolution*, 21. In a revolution, Arendt states, courageous individuals interrupt their routine activities, and step forward from their private lives in order to create a public space where freedom could appear. Arendt cites as examples the American Revolution, when the act of foundation took the form of a constitution of liberty, the revolutionary clubs of the French Revolution, the Paris Commune of 1871, the creation of Soviets during the Russian Revolution, the French Resistance to Hitler in the Second World War, and the Hungarian revolt of 1956. She states that these "spaces of freedom" appear as islands in a sea or as oasis in a desert (p. 275).

48. See Arendt, *HC*, Ch. 2, 22–78.

49. Cf. Arendt, *HC*, 24. Werner Jaeger, in fact, states that the rise of the city-state meant that man received "besides his private life a sort of second life, his *bios politikos*. Now every citizen belongs to two orders of existence; and there is a distinction in his life between what is his own (*idion*) and what is communal (*koinon*)." See Jaeger, *Paideia*, III, 111.

50. Arendt, *HC*, 24–25.

> The distinction between a private and a public sphere of life corresponds to the household and the political realms, which have existed as distinct, separate entities at least since the rise of the ancient city-state; but the emergence of the social realm, which is neither private nor public, strictly speaking, is a relatively new phenomenon whose origin coincided with the emergence of the modern age and which found its political form in the nation-state.[51]

The consequence of this development of the social into public life in the modern world, according to Arendt, is that in this context it is extraordinary difficult to understand the division between the public and private realms, and thus identify what belongs to the sphere of the polis and to the the sphere of household and family. It is upon this division that all ancient political thought rested as self-evident and axiomatic.[52]

The Public Realm

The public realm, for Arendt, is not a space in a topographical or institutional sense. Public space is the space where freedom can appear through virtuous acts. Without this "politically guaranteed public field of activity, freedom would find no place in the world."[53] Thus, any place that is the object and location of an action in concert can become a public space, as Benhabib notes.[54]

The life of the citizen in the public realm, once he had transcended the necessities which belong to the household, was called by Aristotle the "good life," a life which was not merely better, more carefree or nobler than ordinary life, but of an altogether different quality, Arendt states, because "by having mastered the necessities of sheer life, by being freed from labor and work, and overcoming the innate urge of all living creatures for their own survival, it was no longer bound to the biological life process."[55] For that reason, Plato and Aristotle never doubted the distinction between the spheres of household and political life. At the same time, Arendt points out how the life within the household "exists for the sake of the 'good life' in the *polis*."[56] There is an order between both spheres, so that, even though they are

51. Arendt, *HC*, 28.
52. Cf. Arendt, *HC*, 28.
53. Arendt, "Freedom and Politics," 192.
54. Cf. Benhabib, "Models of Public Space," 78.
55. Arendt, *HC*, 37.
56. Arendt, *HC*, 37.

distinct, they are also connected, the private for the sake of the public. This is seen in education, which for Arendt belongs to the private sphere, and is ordered to political life, as it prepares students for this stage. Classrooms, she argues, should be spaces where the authority of adults is used to prepare children for entry into the public realm, but they should not be public spaces themselves. Thus, schools should be institutions that are interposed between the private domain of home and the world in order to make the transition from the family to the world possible at all.[57]

In order to understand Arendt's notion of the public sphere, one has to consider three features or interrelated dimensions: the public space or stage of appearance, the artificial quality of public life, and the spatial quality of public life as a common public space.

In the first place, public realm, for Arendt, is distinct from the "space of appearance." In this sense, "public" signifies "that everything that appears in public can be seen and heard by everybody and has the widest possible publicity."[58] The space of appearance is the result of men gathering together in speech and action. It becomes the public realm only when it is formally constituted. She states:

> The space of appearance comes into being wherever men are together in the manner of speech and action, and therefore predates and precedes all formal constitution of the public realm and the various forms of government, that is, the various forms in which the public realm can be organized.[59]

Thus, the space of appearance is the space of political freedom and equality which comes into being whenever citizens act in concert through the medium of speech and persuasion. The *polis*, in this sense, is the space of appearance *"in the widest sense of the word, namely, the space where I appear to others as others appear to me, where men exist not merely like other living or inanimate things, but to make their appearance explicitly."*[60] Since the space of appearance is a creation of action, it is highly fragile and exists only when actualized through the performance of deeds or the utterance of words.[61]

The space of appearance, then, must be continually recreated by action, for its existence is secured only when actors gather together for the

57. Cf. Arendt, *Between Past and Future*, 88–89.
58. Arendt, *HC*, 50.
59. Arendt, *HC*, 199.
60. Arendt, *HC*, 198–99.
61. Cf. Arendt, *HC*, 199.

purpose of discussing and deliberating about matters of public concern, and it disappears the moment these activities cease. It is always a potential space that finds its actualization in the virtuous acts and speeches of individuals who have come together to undertake some common project.

In the second place, Arendt stressed the artificiality of public life and of political activities in general for, according to her, they are man-made and constructed rather than natural. Politics for her was not the result of some natural predisposition, or the realization of the inherent qualities of human nature. Rather, it was a cultural achievement of the first order, enabling individuals to transcend and liberate themselves from the necessities of life in order to fashion a world within which free political and virtuous action and speech could flourish. Political participation is of essential importance for Arendt because it allows the establishment of relations of civility and solidarity among citizens.[62]

In the third place, Arendt stressed the spatial quality of public life, that is, the fact that political activities are located in a public space where citizens are able to meet one another, exchange their opinions and debate their differences, and search for some collective solution to their problems. In that sense, "the term 'public' signifies the world itself, in so far as it is common to all of us and distinguished from our privately owned place in it."[63] Politics, for Arendt, is a matter of people sharing a common world and a common space of appearance so that public concerns can emerge and be articulated from different perspectives.[64] Arendt does not agree in just having a multitude of individuals voting separately and anonymously according to their personal opinions. Rather, individuals must be able to meet and talk to one another in a public-political space, so that their differences as well as their commonalities can emerge and become the subject of democratic debate. The "common public world," then, is the shared and public world of human artifacts, institutions and settings which separates us from nature and which provides a relatively permanent and durable context for our activities.

According to Arendt, the space of appearance and the common world are essential to the practice of citizenship. The space of appearance provides the spaces where human beings can flourish, while the common world

---

62. See Campillo, "Aristóteles, Arendt y Nosotros," 174–76.

63. Arendt, *HC*, 52. This world, she explains, "is related, rather, to the human artifact, the fabrication of human hands, as well as to affairs which go on among those who inhabit the man-made world together."

64. For Arendt, to be engaged in politics means to actively participate in the various public forums where the decisions affecting one's community are taken. Since politics is something that needs a worldly location and can only happen in a public space, one must be present in such a space in order to be engaged in politics.

provides the stable background from which public spaces of action and deliberation can arise. For Arendt, then, the reactivation of citizenship in the modern world depends upon both the recovery of a common, shared world and the creation of numerous spaces of appearance in which individuals can disclose their identities through virtuous acts and establish relations of reciprocity and solidarity.

Arendt's notion of a common public space as a feature of the public sphere shows that, according to her, it is possible to form political opinions which are reducible neither to private preferences or worldviews, nor to a unanimous collective opinion or "overlapping consensus." Arendt also distrusted the term "public opinion," since it suggested the mindless unanimity of mass society. One can only have representative opinions when citizens actually confronted one another in a public space, so that they could examine an issue from a number of different perspectives, modify their views, and enlarge their standpoint to incorporate that of others. For that reason, political opinions can never be formed in private. Instead, they are formed, tested, and enlarged only within a public context of argumentation and debate. Arendt's view, then, is superior to that of Rawls, who relegates to the realm of the "nonpublic" the arguments and debates that are developed and offered by churches, universities and of many other associations in civil society.[65] Arendt notes, instead, that citizens actually confront one another in a public space, within a public context of argumentation and debate, where political opinions are formed, and does not deny that the sources of argumentation and debate may have originated somewhere else.

Arendt's notion of a common public space has also implications on the formation of a political community in the midst of pluralism present in contemporary societies. For Arendt, the unity of individuals that hold different views is not achieved through a sort of overlapping consensus, but rather by sharing a public space and a set of political institutions, and engaging in the practices and activities which are characteristic of that space and those institutions. In this way, Arendt avoids the problems that follow from a pluralism of views and comprehensive doctrines envisioned by Rawls. It is not about reaching an "overlapping consensus," but rather sharing a public space in a way that freedom as virtue can make its appearance. Only then, citizens will be able to truly engage in the practices and activities which are characteristic of public space and political institutions.

65. Cf. Rawls, *PL*, 213.

The Private Realm

According to Arendt, "the private realm of the household was the sphere where the necessities of life, of individual survival as well as of continuity of the species, were taken care of and guaranteed."[66] These were very relevant matters which, however, could only survive in the realm of the private. On the public realm, on the other hand, only what was considered to be relevant, worthy of being seen or heard, could be tolerated, so that the irrelevant became automatically a private matter.[67]

Arendt notes that the natural community in the household was born of necessity, and necessity ruled over all activities performed in it.[68] The private realm dealt with the mastering of the necessities of life in the household, and this mastering was what allowed one to enter the *polis* and enjoy freedom through virtuous acts. Arendt holds that "within the realm of the household, freedom did not exist, for the household head, its ruler, was considered to be free only in so far as he had the power to leave the household and enter the political realm, where all were equals."[69]

In modernity, however, the private is taken as the opposite not of the political sphere but of the social. In antiquity, on the contrary, the social was more closely and authentically related to the private. The private realm, in its etymology, was related to the privative trait of privacy, a state of being deprived of something, such as entering the public realm. The term "private," in its original privative sense, has meaning with respect to this multiple significance of the public realm. Arendt states:

> To live an entirely private life means above all to be deprived of things essential to a truly human life: to be deprived of the reality that comes from being seen and heard by others, to be deprived of an "objective" relationship with them that comes from being related to and separated from them through the intermediary of a common world of things, to be deprived of the possibility of achieving something more permanent than life itself.[70]

At the same time, property, which was connected to the private realm, offered a location that was properly one's own, and this allowed citizens to participate in the affairs of the world, those of the public realm.[71] This is

---

66. Arendt, *HC*, 45.
67. Cf. Arendt, *HC*, 51.
68. Cf. Arendt, *HC*, 30.
69. Arendt, *HC*, 32.
70. Arendt, *HC*, 58.

71. Thus, private property legitimates the participation of the individual in the political life. See Morariu, "Public and Private," 148.

what "prevented the *polis* from violating the private lives of its citizens and made it hold sacred the boundaries surrounding each property."[72] There was an ordered connection, then, between the private and the public realms, the private for the sake of the public.

Another outstanding non-privative characteristic of privacy, according to Arendt, is that:

> The four walls of one's private property offer the only reliable hiding place from the common public world, not only from everything that goes on in it but also from its very publicity, from being seen and being heard. A life spent entirely in public, in the presence of others, becomes, as we would say, shallow. . . . The only efficient way to guarantee the darkness of what needs to be hidden against the light of publicity is private property, a privately owned place to hide in.[73]

For that reason, Arendt affirms that the distinction between the private and the public realms, seen from the viewpoint of privacy rather than of the body politic, equals the distinction between things that should be shown and things that should be hidden. This is an aspect that allows us to discern, then, the place and role of virtue in both the public and the private realms. There are virtues that by their own nature belong to the household and the intimacy of one's life, such as the exercise of religion through acts of prayer and devotion, and there are virtues that enjoy a more public character, such as courage and political prudence. In reference to the hidden character of certain human acts, Arendt states: "The most elementary meaning of the two realms indicates that there are things that need to be hidden and others that need to be displayed publicly if they are to exist at all."[74] Among these, Arendt refers to "goodness": "The one activity taught by Jesus in word and deed is the activity of goodness, and goodness obviously harbors a tendency to hide from being seen or heard."[75] The reason, Arendt states, is that the moment a good work becomes known and public, it loses its specific character of goodness, of being done for nothing but goodness' sake: "When goodness appears openly, it is no longer goodness, though it may still be useful as organized charity or an act of solidarity."[76]

72. Arendt, *HC*, 29–30.
73. Arendt, *HC*, 71.
74. Arendt, *HC*, 73.
75. Arendt, *HC*, 74.
76. Arendt, *HC*, 74.

The *Polis* and the Notion of "Public"

Arendt borrows from Aristotle the definition of man as a political animal. By "political animal," Arendt understands the ideal of man who comes to the *polis*, or public realm, out of concern for its welfare, and deliberates and exchanges opinions with his fellow citizens on the common good, on what the community should strive for, and on how to achieve the ends agreed upon with others. In engaging in this kind of activity, man as a political animal is rewarded with perfection, self-development, and the disclosure of identity, as he is supposed to perform in this public stage through virtuous acts that manifest his freedom.

The "region" of the public, that of free action, was called the polis, and for that reason Arendt talks about "the public realm of the *polis*."[77] This is "the space of appearance in the widest sense of the word, namely, the space where I appear to others as others appear to me, where men exist not merely like other living or inanimate things but make their appearance explicitly."[78] The *polis*, for Arendt, is political; however, the *polis* arose prior to the state.

Arendt brought to light once again the Greek concept of the *polis*, a concept that was not used much in contemporary political philosophy. In employing this term, she is not simply referring to the political institutions of the Greek city-states (bounded as they were to their time and circumstance), but to all those instances in history where a public realm of action and speech was set up among a community of free and equal citizens. Arendt states: "The *polis*, properly speaking, is not the city-state in its physical location; it is the organization of the people as it arises out of acting and speaking together, and its true space lies between people living together for this purpose, no matter where they happen to be."[79]

Contemporary authors, usually employ the term "public" instead. We can say that Arendt employed the term *polis* in order to recover a notion of the public that had been lost. For that reason, one has to note that there are differences in how the two concepts, *polis* and public, are used, and in understanding these differences, one will have a clearer understanding of how freedom takes place in a secure and definite place.

There is little or no agreement on the meaning and nature of the public.[80] However, we can say that there are perhaps two elements that are common to almost all present-day understandings of the public sphere. In

---

77. Arendt, *HC*, 194–95.
78. Arendt, *HC*, 198–99.
79. Arendt, *HC*, 198.
80. On this debate, see also Geuss, *Public Goods, Private Goods*.

the first place, political philosophers talk about public reason, and modes of arguing in public. Thus, freedom in the public is manifested as speech. In the second place, political philosophers usually agree that the public is a "place" where humans engage in debate and discussion on political matters related to the state. This speech and debate centered on political issues is supposed to bring about more freedom for the individual, or to be more conducive for political conditions.[81] We can point out four major differences between Arendt's understanding of the *polis*, and some notions and aspects of the "public" seen in chapter 1.

In the first place, for Arendt, the *polis* is not tied to the state, for it arose prior to the formation of the state in Western history. At the same time, the rise of the state led to the erosion of the *polis*, and the social came to replace the *polis*. However, this does not mean that the *polis* has disappeared; it only means that it has been eroded for humans.[82]

The second difference is that theories such as that of Rawls's do not fully account for freedom or action, or even virtue, in their considerations of the public sphere. The focus, instead, is on speech and modes of argument (secular vs religious arguments) that have a political import. According to Arendt, however, in the *polis* there was no conception that speech would lead to action, for speech and action were intimately connected. Thus, for Arendt, the *polis* is a place where a certain type of rhetorical argumentation takes place freely, and argument and mode of speech about justice that is already part for the act of justice itself. In contemporary theories, on the contrary, speech does not necessarily lead to action, especially in the political arena of the state.

The third difference is that the *polis* does not mediate the relation between the state and the population, which seems to be the case in contemporary notions of the public. The *polis*, Arendt argues, was about freedom of the participants, not about justice or protection of inhabitants, which are all issues involving relations between the state and the population. What mattered in the *polis* were those matters that gained the participants recognition by others involved in the *polis*. The polis was about self-expression through free virtuous acts. Performing virtuous deeds, because they were free, revealed the nature of the person doing them. Immortality was achieved through the production of good works, deeds, and words, all actions that excelled as judged by the spectators. Rawls, on the other hand, in respecting "the fact of pluralism" characteristic of modern democratic societies, seeks to realize a thinly "political" conception of justice on which citizens, in spite

81. See, for example, Habermas, *Structural Transformation*.
82. Cf. Arendt, *HC*, 33.

of their numerous differences as individuals, can agree through "overlapping consensus," while holding their own conception of the good. Thus, opinions are formed in the "background political culture," according to Rawls, that is, prior to the public political realm, and public reason comes into play as a particular mode of "secular" discourse which safely regulates the exchange of these pre-established points of view. This project, from Arendt's perspective, seems to fail to see that the purpose of political participation is not only to exercise some control over collective decision-making but also to acquire a sense of what a person can achieve as an actor in the public square through works of virtue. At the same time, Arendt argues that one's own opinions and thoughts are formed and depend upon conditions of critical publicity, that is, the scrutiny of others. The testing of one's position arises from the critical interaction with other people's forms of thinking, something that is prevented in Rawls's model.[83]

The fourth difference with some of the approaches from chapter 1, finally, is that, for Arendt, the notion of public space is not a fixed notion.[84] There is a historical and institutional variability of the standard of publicity, and therefore it is essential to politics to keep that standard open to a variety of concerns and voices, including questions of religious faith. She states:

> Life changes constantly, and things are constantly there that want to be talked about. At all times people living together will have affairs that belong in the realm of the public—"are worthy to be talked about in public." What these matters are at any historical moment is probably utterly different. For instance, the great cathedrals were the public spaces of the Middle Ages. The town halls came later. And there perhaps they had to talk about a matter which is not without any interest either: the question of God. So what becomes public at every given period seems to me utterly different.[85]

Thus, for Arendt, the status of the "public" is an open field, a constitutive feature of a free political life in common with others.[86]

---

83. Cf. Arendt, "Truth and Politics," 234–35.

84. Habermas would agree with Arendt on this point. See Habermas, *Structural Transformation*.

85. Arendt, "On Hannah Arendt," 316. See also Button, "Arendt, Rawls, and Public Reason," 268.

86. Cf. Arendt, "What Is Existential Philosophy?," 186–87.

Conclusion

This chapter, which focused on the political thought of Hanna Arendt, has attempted to find a new insight into the notion of freedom and the public sphere in order to avoid many of the dilemmas that current debates encounter.

Arendt developed a conception of freedom that is peculiar to her thought.[87] She strove to articulate a philosophical concept of freedom that is distinct from independence or mastery; one that would be true to the elementary political experience of freedom, and which corresponds to the inherently social or plural nature of human life, that is, freedom is experienced in our dealings with others, not with ourselves. Freedom, for Arendt, appears as a phenomenon of virtuosity, rather than a phenomenon of the will; and is not the end purpose of politics but its very *raison d'être* or substance.

Arendt argues that man is free by nature, and this is made evident in human agency and politics. True freedom is not related to the actions performed due to the necessities of life. True freedom is manifested mainly in virtuous action, in company with others, within the context of a common public space. In this sense, she talks about political freedom as the original meaning of the freedom. It is the political sphere that provides men with a space of appearances where they could act, and it is in this theater that freedom as virtuous action can appear.

Arendt also makes a stern distinction between the public and the private spheres. She is firm in stating that certain activities must be kept private for they belong to the realm of necessity, as opposed to the public sphere or *polis*, which is the realm of freedom. At the same time, Arendt attempts to demonstrate throughout her work that an existence worth living must be rooted in the public as well as in the private realm. Even if one were not to accept such strict division, Arendt's insight and demarcation between the private and the public seems to be more valuable than the secular-religious distinction that is one of the most prominent features surrounding contemporary political debate.[88] I argued in chapter 1 that it is necessary to abandon this secular-religious distinction if one is to move forward in contemporary debates regarding the place of religion in the public sphere. For that reason, Arendt's political thought can provide an important insight into the contemporary controversy on religious freedom and the place of religion in the public sphere.

87. Cf. Winham, "Rereading Hanna Arendt," 87; Honohan, "Concept of Freedom," 41.

88. Cf. Button, "Arendt, Rawls, and Public Reason," 258–59.

Arendt insists on the importance of public spaces for the flourishing of the human condition. The public sphere is a space of appearance, where one's participation through speech and action allow one to take part in public debates and in the organization of the city. To be human, Arendt writes, is to be free in public, which means to act and speak in ways that are virtuous and which matter in the public world. Public freedom requires spaces where our actions are attended to, considered, and taken seriously enough to merit a response. In this way, the freedom of the citizen manifested through virtue becomes an exemplar for others to act in a similar way. Thus, if religion is not as a dogma or belief or worldview, but a virtue, as Thomas Aquinas understands it, one can argue that religious virtue makes its appearance in the public sphere either by commanding other virtues that have an essential public character (such as courage, political prudence, justice, responsibility in regard to civic obligations, all of which may be characterized as public virtue), or by itself, in the external acts of the virtue of religion that have consequences on the political sphere, such as oaths, public allegiance, and a host of other concepts and practices that modernity categorizes as political. One can argue, then, that the place of religion in the public square is truly that of virtuous action, which properly belongs to freedom, as Hannah Arendt argues.

The public sphere is not a fixed notion, but an open field which depends on the manifestations of the human person through speech and virtuous action. Religious virtue, then, when present, is ineluctably a part of one's own distinctive personal identity, and as a consequence will find a public expression, either indirectly or directly, whenever and wherever people act politically. Thus, from Arendt's point of view, it would be inhuman to locate one's religious virtue as part of one's "nonpublic identity," as Rawls does when talking about religious and moral conceptions.[89] This, in fact, was for Arendt the basic error of all materialism in politics, for it is impossible for man not to disclose himself as subject, as a distinct and unique person. To do otherwise, "if indeed it could ever be done, would mean to transform men into something they are not; to deny, on the other hand, that this disclosure is real and has consequences of its own is simply unrealistic."[90] And this is what Rawls intends when he attempts to separate his concept of religion from public life. Religious virtue is a disclosure of man's freedom and identity, which will bear consequences on the public sphere. Even if Arendt did not hold a notion of the religious as virtue,[91] her

---

89. Cf. Rawls, JF, 241.
90. Arendt, HC, 183.
91. She critically assessed the turn to religious "absolutes" during various political

conceptions of the public realm and political freedom provide a new insight into issues related to religious freedom, and one cannot but welcome what she has to offer in this respect.

Thus, having devoted the first chapters to present the debates on the place of religion in the pluralistic secular liberal state, and on the justification of religious freedom, and having found that there is incoherence and lack of clarity in the use these authors make of the notions of religion, freedom, and the public square, we set out to explore deeper into the meaning of these concepts. As the previous chapter focused on the notion of "religion" and its location within the public square, this present chapter has dealt with Hanna Arendt's notion of political freedom, that is, freedom as the stage for virtue. It is time now to present in the following chapter a new perspective on religious freedom and the place of religion in the public square, a perspective that draws from Aquinas's notion of the virtue of religion and Arendt's notion of freedom as a stage for virtue. My intention, in employing these notions, is to provide a way that will help us elucidate the meaning of religion and freedom in discussions related to religious freedom and the place of religion in the public square.

---

founding moments. See Arendt, *On Revolution*, ch. 5.

CHAPTER 5

Religious Freedom and the Public Realm

WE HAVE DEALT IN the previous chapters with issues such as the debate on the place of religion in the public square, the definitions and justifications of religious freedom, the understanding of religious freedom as tolerance, freedom as immunity from coercion, and the use of "religion" as a category. All these issues have made it clear that there is a need to clearly define the terms or notions employed in the discussion, which as a consequence will lead us to adopt a new perspective on religious freedom and the place of religion in the public square, a perspective which should avoid misunderstandings and unnecessary dichotomies (religion vs secularism, private vs public, religious or dogmatic reasoning vs secular reasoning).

We concluded in chapter 3 that the modern notion of religion as a category ought to be dropped, for it not only does not help to clarify what falls into the realm of religious freedom, creating unnecessary debates, but also creates a false problem regarding the place of "religion" in the public square.

In chapter 4, we saw how Hanna Arendt claimed that freedom is made manifest as virtuous action. According to her, there is an intimate connection between freedom and virtue. This allows us, then, to connect the notion of freedom to an understanding of "religion" that has been long forgotten: religion as a virtue. Such was the vision of Thomas Aquinas, who in a groundbreaking exposition, considered religion in a novel way. Combining the insight of both Arendt and Aquinas will hopefully lead us, then, to a new understanding on the meaning of religious freedom and its place in the public square. Thus, the aim of this chapter will be to see how the notions of freedom as a phenomenon of virtuosity, and religion as virtue, offer us a new perspective on the way we talk about religious freedom and its place in the public square.

In the first place, we will see how Arendt's notion of political freedom, and Aquinas's notion of religion as a virtue, provide for a new understanding of religious freedom. In the second place, I will explore the connection between the public realm and the practice of virtue. In the third place, the debate on religious freedom will be located within the context of the debate on the place of "religion" in the public square by identifying the proper stages that belong to the practice of the virtue of religion in connection with political freedom. Finally, in the fourth place, I will address the issue of religious freedom as a human right in light of the new understanding of religion as a virtue.

A New Understanding of Religious Freedom

As we saw in the previous chapter, Hanna Arendt articulated a philosophical concept of freedom that is distinct from independence or mastery. Her concept of freedom, rather than a phenomenon of the will, appears as a phenomenon of virtuosity. True freedom is manifested mainly in virtuous action, in company with others, within the context of a common public space. Thus, this connection between freedom and virtue is, for Arendt, the substance of politics. In this consists the political experience of freedom, a freedom experienced not within ourselves but in our dealings with others.

In chapter 2, we argued that religious freedom cannot mean tolerance as permission, for it implies that religious exercise is a mere favour or privilege granted by the state. One could argue that once religious acts are tolerated, they will enjoy a certain immunity from external coercion. However, there is a problem here, for immunity from coercion does not signify real political freedom. Political freedom, for Arendt, has to do with the practice of virtue, that is, of those virtues that have a public character, perfect the agent and his actions, and are an example for others to follow.

There is a solution, then, to the problems that follow from considering religious freedom as tolerance, and freedom as immunity from coercion: it is found in Aquinas's treatment of the virtue of religion. As we have seen on chapter 2, none of the definitions or justifications on religious freedom presented talk about "religion" in terms of virtue. This approach from Aquinas's perspective, then, will help us find a more useful meaning of religious freedom, for the modern notion religion as a category should be dropped as unsatisfactory. At the same time, the connection that Arendt makes between freedom as related to political life and virtue is of great help when trying to find a proper understanding of religious freedom. The virtue of religion and freedom go hand by hand. Arendt's notion of freedom as a stage for virtue, and Thomas Aquinas's notion of religion as a virtue are the ones, I will argue in this chapter, that best help us elucidate contemporary issues on religious freedom and the place of religion in the public square. Thus, my hope is that in offering this new understanding of religious freedom as freedom to practice the acts of the virtue of religion in their respective stage will offer the right tools to overcome the problems that the contemporary debates on religious freedom and the place of religion in the public square face.

One of the most problematic issues in the present time has to do with the "place" of "religion" in the public square. Freedom as virtue, for Arendt, needs a stage where to appear. This space of appearance must continually be recreated by action, whenever actors gather together for the purpose of discussing and deliberating about matters of public concern. Religion as virtue also needs a stage for its acts to take place. For example, the act of worship always needs a stage where to appear in order to excite devotion in the will of the faithful. Freedom of religion, then, refers to the appearance of religiously virtuous action in the public square, either through actions that are properly religious (such as the proffering of oaths), or through other virtues under the command of the virtue of religion that have a public character and a direct impact on the public political life.

Once one understands religion as a virtue, it follows that religious freedom acquires the character of acting in a virtuously religious way by freely manifesting a relation towards the divine through one's actions.[1] It is its character of a virtuous act that unites religion with freedom. Without freedom there is no virtue, for virtuous actions are always performed in the context of freedom.

The question here is in what those acts consist, and to what performing stage they belong to. These acts might be interior or exterior acts of the virtue of religion itself, or acts of other virtues commanded by the virtue of religion, some of which may have a public character, such as political prudence. Regarding the interior acts of religion, they can usually be performed without hindrance from others, for they properly take place within the interiority of one's soul, such as acts of prayer and devotion. On the other hand, the external acts of religion, which are ordained to the internal acts of prayer and devotion, have the characteristic that they can be observed by others, and for that reason one may argue in favor of a political right to religious freedom as long as these acts take place within their proper stage. Thus, it will be important to identify the proper stage of each religious act, for it may seem out of order to claim protection for certain acts if they are

---

1. At the same time, we have to discard the notion of truth from the notion of "religion." The intellectual consent to truth will certainly have an impact on religious virtue, for the practice of this virtue will depend on a correct understanding of the divine. However, being religious is not about imposing one's truth or faith, either in public or in private. That, be it virtuous or not, is something else, not an act of the virtue of "religion."

being performed in a stage that is not their own. This means that one should beware of equating a structurally and formally-abstractly external act of the virtue of religion to an actual act of religion.[2]

In regard to the acts of other virtues that are being commanded by the virtue of religion, it will be important that these virtuous acts be protected as well, for one cannot restrain certain actions in the public square depending on whether the person is acting by orienting his actions to God or not (such as the acts of virtue that are commanded by the virtue of religion). Thus, a judge who practices the virtue of religion will be commanded by this virtue to impart justice with fairness, and leaving his religious motivation aside would entail to split his personality.[3] No one would deny the benefits that would follow if public officials were all persons of virtue, and virtue includes not only justice or prudence, but also religion. However, it does not mean that we should classify as religious freedom the protection of the acts of these virtues under the command of religion. As seen on chapter 3, when talking about the proper setting of the different acts of religion, we argued that the fact that these virtuous acts belonging to other virtues are commanded by the virtue of religion does not transform the nature of the acts themselves. The point is that, for the religious person, those acts that have an impact on the political life of society may in fact be commanded by the virtue of religion, and for that reason it is necessary to protect religious freedom as the freedom to flourish through the practice of virtue. One should also be aware, however, that acts that seem to belong to religion may not be truly acts of religion, and that this virtue may also command acts that may not fully fall under the understanding of virtue. For that reason, it is important to discern these cases guided by the principles of what truly con-

---

2. An example of this misstep took place when Pope Benedict visited Washington, DC in 2008. A Christian sect walked to the midst of the Catholic gathering holding large banners and using loud speakers, quoting Bible verses on the Antichrist and referring them to the Pope. To counteract their preaching, a charismatic Catholic group encircled the members of the Christian sect singing worship songs to out-loud the other group. Both groups were performing acts that in their own nature would be qualified as formally belonging to the virtue of religion. However, these acts were not taking place in their respective setting. They obviously belonged to a different stage, so that the time and place were not the appropriate ones, and for that reason, these circumstances changed the nature of the acts. It follows that, if both groups were led out and expelled from the event, that would not constitute a violation of their religious freedom, for even if what they were doing would seem to be a religious act, the way and setting in which these acts were performed turned these acts into something else, not precisely acts belonging to the virtue of religion.

3. One can argue, then, that it is to go against the religious freedom of a public official to remove him from public office due to his practice of religion, as when, for example, a candidate to public office is heavily criticized because he attends Sunday mass.

stitutes an act of virtue. On the other hand, true acts of virtue manifested in the public political square need not be guided or under the command of the virtue of religion for them to take place.

From this perspective, then, religious freedom has to do with the freedom to act prompted by religious virtue within the context of a common public space, be it in acts of religion themselves, or in the practice of public virtues under the command of the virtue of religion. Now, since religious freedom takes place within the context of the common public space, it will also be important to note the proper spaces or stages of the different acts of the virtue of religion in connection with religious freedom. I will develop this point later in this chapter, but in order to do so, I will treat first the relationship between the practice of virtue and the public square, to then locate the acts of the virtue of religion within their own stages. This will help us in establishing the proper stage of religious freedom.

Public Life and the Practice of Virtue

As seen in the previous chapter, the original experience of freedom in ancient Greece and Rome, according to Hanna Arendt, took place within the realm of politics, which gave origin to the notion of political freedom, that is, freedom as a phenomenon of virtuosity that takes place in a public stage or space as a politically guaranteed public field of activity.[4] Virtuous action is essentially public, for it has an inherent tendency to disclose the agent together with the act, and for that reason, "action needs for its full appearance the shining brightness we once called glory, and which is possible only in the public realm."[5] Thus, the public sphere is the space or stage of certain virtuous actions that has been politically guaranteed in order for citizens to perfect themselves. This is the reason of politics, for when men enjoy political freedom through virtuous action, they constitute the political realm. And at the same time, it is through these virtuous actions that freedom becomes a reality.[6]

With respect to Aquinas, he states that the goal of every government is the common good, and the end of the multitude gathered together is to live virtuously. Being in public is about being good, and virtue is the proper way to achieving this end. It is not always about being free, for true freedom expresses itself in works of virtue. Thus, there is a strong resemblance between Arendt and Aquinas. However, for Aquinas, the public realm is distinct

---

4. Cf. Arendt, "Freedom and Politics," 192.
5. Arendt, *HC*, 160.
6. Arendt, "What Is Freedom?," 154–55.

from the practice of virtue, for the practice of virtue is not always public, as for example in the case of the essential acts of the virtue of religion, such as prayer and devotion.

In his *De regno*, Aquinas states that the goal of man in this life will also be the goal of the multitude that is governed. The role of government, then, is to create the conditions for the multitude to acquire such good and persevere in its possession. Now, since the goal of man is to attain the possession of God by means of virtue, this will also be the end of the multitude. What is of interest for our purpose here, is that the means for man to attain this is through works of virtue, from which it follows that the goal of the multitude will be to live virtuously in order to reach the ultimate end. Aquinas is certainly talking from a theological perspective since the virtues he refers to are the theological and infused virtues. However, since grace presupposes nature, it is necessary that men be virtuous from a natural perspective as well. And this is the aspect that is of interest to us here, dealing with a philosophical issue.[7] Then, Thomas continues to show that, even if the end of the individual is to acquire virtue, this would not be possible unless he lived in community with others. The end of the community, then, is to live in a virtuous way, in order to attain the ultimate end, which is fruition of God.[8]

An in his *S. Th.* I–II, q. 92, a. 1, ad 3, Thomas affirms that the common good of the state cannot flourish, unless the citizens be virtuous, at least those whose business it is to govern.[9] This is especially true regarding political prudence, "which is directed to the common good of the state or kingdom."[10] However, for Aquinas, prudence belongs not only to those that govern, but also to those that are ruled. Following Aristotle, Thomas states in II–II, q. 47, a. 12 that: "there are two kinds of political prudence, one of which is legislative and belongs to rulers, while the other retains the common name political, and is about individual actions. Now it belongs also to subjects to perform these individual actions."[11] Prudence is in the practical intellect, therefore,

---

7. Aquinas, *Regno*, bk. 1, ch. 15.

8. Cf. Aquinas, *Regno*, bk. 1, ch. 15.

9. Cf. Aquinas, *S. Th.*, I–II, q. 92, a. 1, ad 3.

10. Aquinas, *S. Th.*, II–II, q. 47, a. 11. In II–II, q. 50, Aquinas changes his vocabulary, and the kind of prudence designated as political here will receive the definitive name of "royal or regnative prudence" in a. 1.

11. Aquinas, *S. Th.*, II–II, q. 47, a. 12, s. c. Later, in II–II, q. 50, a. 2, this kind of prudence will retain the name of "political." By doing so, Aquinas departs from Aristotle's understanding of political prudence. Aristotle assigns two parts to political prudence: "νομοθετική" which has the function of making laws; and "πολιτική" which is subordinated to the first type, and its task is to apply laws to particular cases by means of decrees. Aquinas will take this distinction from Aristotle; however, following the vocabulary of Pseudo-Andronicus of Rhode, Thomas distinguishes between

Thomas states that: "Since . . . every man, for as much as he is rational, has a share in ruling according to the judgment of reason, he is proportionately competent to have prudence."[12] Thomas also talks about "regnative prudence" in II–II, q. 50, a. 1, as the art of governing the multitude, which belongs to the one in charge of the community, especially in the act of commanding. For that reason, it is a special and more perfect kind of prudence, for it is not at the service of a particular end, but rather at the service of human life in its totality. The special end of regnative prudence is the common good, and thus, it specifies a special kind of prudence.[13] In II–II, q. 50, a. 2, Thomas presents "political prudence," which is the kind of prudence that belongs to the subject as a subject. This kind of political prudence presented here, then, refers to the rectitude of government required in those that are subject to the one who governs, so that they may direct themselves in obeying their superiors.[14] It is in the act of obeying a superior, then, that one makes use of political prudence, as it is directed to the common good.[15]

Arendt's and Aquinas's vision of the goal of politics and of the multitude living together differs in regard to what the ultimate end is. However, they coincide in that virtue plays a central role in the life of citizens, and therefore, in the multitude to be governed. Thus, when religious freedom is understood as freedom as a phenomenon of religious virtue, it will be easier to see the role and place that religion as virtue takes within society, and in the public square. Thus, one can already see that religious freedom will demand the creation of conditions and protection for the practice of religious virtue.

One of the advantages of this approach is that it will help us overcome the problems that arise when trying to reach an overlapping consensus in a

---

"royal prudence," and "political prudence," assigning to them different roles than the ones noted by Aristotle. See Aristotle, *Nicomachean Ethics*, bk. VI, ch. 8–9. Thomas acknowledges his departure from Aristotle in II–II, q. 50, a. 1, ad 3. See also Deman, "Prudence," 282 (n. 92), and 317 (n. 156). Aristotle did not attribute his notion of prudence (φρόνησιF) to slaves either, for he considered it to be a virtue of command and a sign of the practical perfection of human reason. In his own presentation of political prudence, Aquinas departs from Aristotle, and thus we see in this a vigorous affirmation of the indelible human dignity present in all men. See Aristotle, *Politics*, bk. III, ch. 4; Aquinas, *S. Th.*, II–II, q. 50, a. 2.

12. Aquinas, *S. Th.*, II–II, q. 47, a. 12.
13. Cf. Aquinas, *S. Th.*, II–II, q. 50, a. 1.
14. Cf. Aquinas, *S. Th.*, II–II, q. 50, a. 2. Aquinas borrows the name form Aristotle, giving it a whole new meaning. What Thomas had called political prudence in II–II, q. 47, a. 11, is the equivalent now in q. 50, a. 1 of regnative prudence. See also Aquinas, *In Politicorum*, bk. III, lect. 3.
15. Cf. Aquinas, *S. Th.*, II–II, q. 50, a. 2, ad 3.

pluralistic society. It will not be possible to reach a consensus regarding the faith upon which a pluralistic society should be modeled, but it is possible instead to argue and open a public discussion on freedom as ordered to the practice of virtue, including religious virtue, which commands all other virtues, such as the ones that have a social and public impact. And the result does not necessarily have to be a consensus.[16]

In this context, one can argue that the governmental creation of legal dispositions and protection of the conditions favorable to the fostering of virtue, among which we find religion, should take the form of assisting those communities to flourish that are most properly fitted by nature for forming persons in the way of virtue and knowledge, such as familial and religious communities, and educational institutions given their form and end in organic relation with such communities.[17] For Aquinas, in fact, there should be two intentions in the lawgiver when making a law. In the first place, his intention is to lead men to virtue by the precepts of the law. In the second place, his intention is brought to bear on the matter itself of the precept, that is, in commanding that which leads and creates a disposition to an act of virtue.[18] Thomas very firmly states that the goal of the legislator is to make virtuous citizens. It is no surprise, then, that Aquinas views the entire existence of human law in the light of the desirability to become virtuous. He states in his S. Th. I–II, q. 95, a. 1:

> Man has a natural aptitude for virtue; but the perfection of virtue must be acquired by man by means of some kind of training. . . . Now it is difficult to see how man could suffice for himself in the matter of this training: since the perfection of virtue consists chiefly in withdrawing man from undue pleasures, to which above all man is inclined, and especially the young, who are more capable of being trained. Consequently a man needs to receive this training from another, whereby to arrive at the perfection of virtue. . . . But since some are found to be depraved, and prone to vice, and not easily amenable to words, it was necessary for such to be restrained from evil by force and fear, in order that, at least, they might desist from evil-doing,

---

16. However, the fact that it may be impossible to reach an overlapping consensus does not mean that questions regarding metaphysical and religious truth should be avoided, for it is the essential condition that these questions be kept alive at the heart of the legal political order in order to have a true vision of man and a just protection of human rights.

17. Schlinder offers a similar perspective, but with a different understanding of what religious freedom is. See Schlinder and Healy, *Freedom, Truth, and Human Dignity*, 153.

18. Cf. Aquinas, *S. Th.*, I–II, q. 100, a. 9, ad 2.

and leave others in peace, and that they themselves, by being habituated in this way, might be brought to do willingly what hitherto they did from fear, and thus become virtuous. Now this kind of training, which compels through fear of punishment, is the discipline of laws. Therefore in order that man might have peace and virtue, it was necessary for laws to be framed.[19]

Virtue, then, is the end of the law. This is also seen in S. Th. I–II, q. 96, a. 3, ad 2, where Thomas deals with an objection that held that the acts of the virtues could not be commanded by law, because the acts of the virtues presuppose the existence of the virtues, and virtue is the goal, end, of law.[20] In his reply, Thomas affirms that we must distinguish between the two ways of performing an act commanded by the law, that is, as proceeding from the virtue, and as merely performing the material act that the virtue requires. All the law can oblige is the latter, but the former is the end of the law. The goal, then, is that through the repetition of material acts of virtue, one may acquire the habit, and thus, the virtuous man is the end of the law. Thomas states:

> An act is said to be an act of virtue in two ways. First, from the fact that a man does something virtuous; thus, the act of justice is to do what is right, and an act of fortitude is to do brave things: and in this way law prescribes certain acts of virtue. Secondly an act of virtue is when a man does a virtuous thing in a way in which a virtuous man does it. Such an act always proceeds from virtue: and it does not come under a precept of law, but is the end at which every lawgiver aims.[21]

Regarding the virtue of religion and its connection to the law, Thomas speaks of religious practice as pertaining to the natural law, and thus, to offer sacrifice is presented by him explicitly as a duty decreed by natural law, and which he therefore sees it as altogether appropriate that the human political community enact positive laws in this regard. In his S. Th., I–II, q. 99, a. 3, Aquinas speaks of the different points of view of human and divine law in directing matters of divine worship, which belong to the virtue of religion. He states that, while the divine law is instituted chiefly in order to direct men to God, human law is instituted chiefly in order to direct men in relation to one another. Nevertheless, he states:

> Human laws have not concerned themselves with the institution of anything relating to divine worship except as affecting

---

19. Aquinas, S. Th., I–II, q. 95, a. 1.
20. Cf. Aquinas, S. Th., I–II, q. 96, a. 3, obj. 2.
21. Aquinas, S. Th., I–II, q. 96, a. 3, ad 2.

the common good of mankind: and for this reason they have devised many institutions relating to divine matters, according as it seemed expedient for the formation of human morals; as may be seen in the rites of the Gentiles.[22]

Religion as a virtue, then, plays a crucial role in the formation of virtuous members of society, and for that reason it also falls under the protection of human laws. Thus, if man is set on the road to virtue through law, religion as a virtue cannot be left aside in the constitution of a perfect society, which requires also, according to Aquinas, that those who govern be religiously virtuous as well.[23] For that reason, it is important that "religion" be considered as a virtue in matters dealing with religious freedom and the place of religion in the public square.

John C. Murray, as seen in chapter 2, insists on a negative notion of religious freedom, that is, as immunity from all external coercion. He even highlights this aspect as the essential element of religious freedom, for, according to him, the very question of religious freedom concerns the limits of public power in religious matters.[24] However, even though it is an important aspect, the limit of public power is a consequence that follows from a deeper foundation. Man enjoys immunity from coercion by reason of his relation to a higher being, manifested in the practice of the virtue of religion. Another way, and probably a more accurate way, to express this aspect of immunity, is to speak of an individual's or a religious community's freedom from subordination to the political powers in order to flourish in a religiously virtuous way without political interference, other than providing the conditions in political life for the practice of virtue, especially those public virtuous acts that are related to or commanded by the virtue of religion.[25] If it was otherwise, so that there should be total immunity regardless of the acts of religion, how can we explain the fact that there are limitations to the right, especially when it affects the common good? When religion is seen under the light of virtue, then we can discern better into what counts as religious virtue versus a perversion of religion, manifested through vicious acts, which therefore may be banned for the good of society.

Now that we have presented the connection between virtue and politics, and the place of virtue in the public square, it is time to locate the proper stage for religious freedom. The question is to see whether the acts

22. Aquinas, *S. Th.*, I–II, q. 99, a. 3.
23. Cf. Aquinas, *S. Th.*, II–II, q. 122, a. 2.
24. Cf. Murray, "Arguments," 238–41.
25. David Novak, for example, employs the expression "freedom from subordination." See Novak, *In Defense of Religious Liberty*, ix.

of the virtue of religion take place within the context of the common public space. For that reason, in this next section I will identify the proper space or stage of the virtue of religion in connection with religious freedom.

Religious Freedom in the Public Square

Arendt rightly argues that the notion of public space is not a fixed notion. The standard of what should be considered as "public" really varies across historical and institutional circumstances, and therefore it is essential to politics to keep that standard open to a variety of concerns and voices, including questions of religious faith. Things which are worthy to be talked about in public, for Arendt, belong in the public realm. These matters the location where these discussions take place change constantly in different historical moments.[26] Among the many historical examples of public matters, we can cite the public debate on the divinity of Christ which deeply divided the Roman Empire at the time of the Arian heresy in the 3rd and 4th centuries, the Investiture Controversy in the 12th and 13th centuries, which also carried political and social consequences, the sale of the indulgences and the Protestant Reformation in the sixteenth century, and its aftermath during the civil wars of configuration of the nation-states, which led to the public debate on tolerance and freedom of conscience, the debate on religious freedom and other human rights following the horrors of totalitarian regimes in the twentieth century. These were all issues that historically were worthy to be talked about in public, and which rightly belonged in the realm of the public, for its consequences affected the shape and configuration of politics and society, and the way people lived their lives.

In the last 30 years there has been a radical shift in reconsidering the relationship between politics and "religion," which has triggered a revision of theories about secularization, about the prevalence of religion in the life of modern communities, and about the need to establish the possible dependence of politics on religion. As a consequence, there has come to the fore the debate on the place of "religion" in the public square within the context of secularism, and more recently, the debate on religious freedom. Thus, Arendt was right when she affirmed that the status of the "public" is an open field, a constitutive feature of a free political life in common with others.[27]

One of the main problems with the current debates on the place of religion in the public square and on religious freedom, is that the notions of "religion" and "public square" seem to have no connection at all. It is not

26. Cf. Arendt, "On Hannah Arendt," 316.
27. Cf. Arendt, "What Is Existential Philosophy?," 186–87.

only that "religion" as a category ought to be dropped, but when religion is taken as a system of belief, then the issue here should be defined instead as the way in which a faith or belief system shapes society in a secular world. It is in this context that the problems that arise by reason of multiculturalism should be framed, when it is not just one but many dogmatic views seeking to shape the cultural and political spheres.

The notion of religion as a virtue, then, offers a better understanding in relation to both the public square and religious freedom, for here we are talking about actions which by their own nature take place within a stage. Political freedom manifests itself as a phenomenon of virtuosity on the public stage, and thus it is necessary to identify the proper stage of each act of the virtue of religion and of those virtues under its command. Only then will we be able to better situate the problem of religion in the public square and the status and protection that should be acknowledged to the civil right to religious freedom. At the same time, one needs to secure the idea of the public realm, and differentiate the public realm from the practice of virtue, for not all virtues enjoy a public character. One will have to identify those aspects of religious virtue that bear on the public, and proceed from that point on. Thus, I will now proceed to identify the proper stage or stages that belong to the different acts of the virtue of religion, both interior and exterior, in order to consequently throw light on issues of religious freedom as a political right. It makes a big difference whether certain acts take place within the heart or mind of the believers, in the privacy of their home, in the church as a liturgical space, within the social community, or in the common public political sphere.

In chapter 3, I presented four different stages where the exercise of the virtue of religion takes place. It is these acts and their proper stages that will offer the criteria for religious freedom.

The first and proper stage of the virtue of religion is within the interior life of the soul, where the internal acts of prayer and devotion take place. These are the essential acts of the virtue of religion. Man has a right to perform these interior acts, moved not by coercion but by his free will, as virtuous acts are free by nature. Thomas states:

> This cult of God is called religion [*religio*], because in some way man binds [from *religare*] himself by such acts, so that he will not wander away from God, and also because man feels that he is obligated by some sort of natural prompting to offer, in his own way, reverence to God, from whom comes man's being and is the principle of all goodness.[28]

28. Aquinas, *SCG*, bk. 3, ch. 119.

There is no coercion possible against these acts, for they are internal, and therefore the freedom that man enjoys in the practice of the essential acts of the virtue of religion cannot be taken away. However, man still needs the time and repose to be able to devote himself to these actions, and the freedom to perform his religious duties without being hindered by others, even in the privacy of his home.

These acts can also be manifested externally, in a way that they can be seen or heard by others. It can take the form of vocal prayer, or the form of other external acts of religion. Thus, by reason of his obligation to offer reverence to God, man has a duty to perform these actions, in the first place, privately, and secondarily, within other stages, such as at a church or other public places. Now, the obligation of the individual to offer reverence to God is already fulfilled in the interiority of the soul. However, the community of the faithful may desire to get together to pray, adore, and offer God the worship that is his due. For that reason, religious freedom has to do not just with the individual that is virtuous (potentially), but also with the community of such individuals. It is in regard to religious institutions that the community may need to contact political authorities regarding certain activities, such as permission to build a place for worship. Now, the building of a place to worship is not in itself a right, for one could worship God in different ways and places, and for that reason, there may be certain legal regulations regarding the place and time where these external acts of religion can take place (such as getting a city permit for a building destined for religious worship), or regarding certain acts which are not necessarily religious manifestations (such as a special celebration on public grounds, or for a religious procession to take place through the streets of the city). Nevertheless, governments should accommodate these requests from recognized religious organizations as long as they strictly belong to the virtue of religion, for the law should never discourage any action that is related to virtue, since the end of the law, as Aquinas states, is to form virtuous men.[29]

The second stage where acts of religion take place is within the liturgical performing stage, that is, in the community of the church (or temple, synagogue, mosque, etc.). One can locate here the secondary acts of religion

29. Cf. Aquinas, S. Th., I–II, q. 96, a. 3, ad 2. Laws differ in different states or nations, but generally a religious organization must meet certain criteria to be considered as such: a distinct legal existence; a recognized creed and form of worship; a definite and distinct ecclesiastical government; a formal code of doctrine and discipline; a religious history; members that are not associated with any other church or denomination; ordained ministers who have completed specific studies; a literature of its own; established places of worship; regular congregations; regular religious services; Sunday schools for religious teaching of children; schools that educate its ministers. Again, these criteria are heavily influenced by a modern notion of religion as a category.

which by nature are exterior, and which are ordained to the inner realm. Even though the internal acts of religion take precedence over the external rites, the external rites are not expendable or superfluous, for, as Aquinas states, "the human mind, in order to be united to God, needs to be guided by the sensible world."[30] The right to freely perform acts of the virtue of religion on this stage is the freedom that the members of the community of the faithful enjoy in order to gather, offer God his due honor, and worship together in their house of prayer.

The third stage on which the acts of the virtue of religion take place has to do with the physical spaces where the church operates and fulfills its mission. Thus, the acts of the virtue of religion that belong here, such as the offering of first-fruits and tithing or almsgiving, are directed to secure a physical space, build houses of prayer, and to support monetarily the liturgical life. These acts are also ordered to the social community, such as serving the poor on the streets, caring for the sick, and educating children. It is within the community that these acts, for Aquinas, have a public character, for they are directed to the good of the community, and are seen and heard by others, so that others are encouraged to do the same.

The goal of these acts of the virtue of religion is to support the works of the liturgy primarily, but also those actions related to the social community, and which have a direct impact on society. This does not mean, however, that acts that are ordered to care for the sick and the poor, educate children, care for orphans, or the elderly, are in themselves acts of religion. In contemporary debates on religious freedom, many advocates of this civil right make the mistake of including these and many other activities under the banner of religious freedom as if these acts were acts of religion themselves. The reason for this confusion is that an unclear notion of "religion" as belief system is being employed in the understanding of religious freedom, a belief or faith by reason of which people devote themselves to certain charitable acts. It is an act of religion to support these actions insofar as they aid in helping people get closer to God, but the acts themselves, even though when prompted by the virtue of religion, are not acts of religion themselves.[31] Therefore, to claim that one's acts should be protected by religious freedom is to stretch this right into a field that is not its own. Nevertheless, the virtue of religion is the motor behind many works that have a social impact in our community, and as such these acts relieve society and the government from the burden to care for those in need, provide a more efficient and cheaper

---

30. Aquinas, *S. Th.*, II–II, q. 81, a. 7.
31. This is something I will clarify more extensively in the following chapter.

education, and as Aquinas affirms, these religious institutions are "expedient for the formation of human habits."[32]

Religious freedom for the individuals involved in these activities means that they, motivated by the virtue of religion, freely engage in these works. Thus, no government should interfere with the conditions for these activities to take place, and instead must protect these individuals against any form of coercion.[33] Religious persons should also enjoy the freedom to enter public spaces in order to be able to fulfill their desire to care for others in regards not just to their spiritual, but also their physical well-being. At the same time, no government should compel these religious persons to offer services or carry out activities that are in contradiction to their beliefs, or either face heavy fines.[34]

The fourth stage on which some acts of the virtue of religion take place is on the political public forum. There are certain acts that belong to the virtue of religion which help people towards the common good, such as oaths, swearing, and the invocation of God's name. These are public acts in the modern sense of the term, for they take plae within the public political sphere and its public institutions, and are the basis of the political pact, such as swearing in office for a president or prime minister, oaths when testifying before the court, invoking God's name before starting sessions at Congress or Parliament, etc.[35] These are all acts that Aquinas assigns to the virtue of religion properly.

The virtue of religion also commands the acts of other virtues, some of which bear a direct impact on the common public sphere, the sphere of politics. According to Aquinas, "Every deed, in so far as it is done in God's

---

32. Aquinas, *S. Th.*, I–II, q. 99, a. 3.

33. Individuals usually perform these activities within private institutions. The activities carried out in the name of these institutions, then, should be acknowledged, protected, and the participation of citizens encouraged, such as when any donations to these institutions is tax-deductible given the charitable character of the organization. However, once again, these activities may not necessarily be acts of religion themselves, so that their violation may not necessarily be a violation of religious freedom. Thus, to force the workers of a Catholic adoption agency to offer children in adoption to gay couples, or otherwise face fines or being shut down, is properly a violation of their freedom of conscience, not their religious freedom, for the acts themselves being performed are not acts of religion, even if motivated by this virtue. What is proper of the virtue of religion, here, is the monetary support of the works of the institution, in the first place, and then, to command the acts of other virtues in the exercise of their functions.

34. As when the institutions where they serve lose their tax-exempt status, which will discourage citizens from aiding these charitable organizations.

35. Cf. Prodi, *Sacramento del potere*, 11.

honor, belongs to religion, not as eliciting, but as commanding."[36] As seen above, Aquinas states that religion has two kinds of acts. Some are its proper and immediate acts, which it elicits, and by which man is directed to God alone, such as prayer, sacrifices, adoration and the like. Religion also has other acts which it produces through the medium of the virtues which it commands, directing them to the honor of God.[37] The reason why religion commands the acts of other virtues, some of which have a public character, is that the virtue which is concerned with the end commands the virtues which are concerned with the means.[38] It is in this sense, then, that the virtue of religion has a particular impact on the sphere of common public life, for religious citizens will be motivated by religious virtue in the performance of other virtues that have to do with political life, such as political prudence, courage, justice, etc. For Aquinas, the virtue of religion was not a separate sphere of concern and activity, but permeated all the institutions and activities of medieval Christendom.[39] Thus, holiness, which encompasses all of the good works that a person performs, either in private or in public, is in a certain way, for Aquinas, the same as the virtue of religion, since it has an impact on the person's performance in the public stage, for there is no act that can be disconnected from sanctity.[40] As mentioned in chapter 3, when the acts of the virtue of religion structure a person's life, that person will bring all of his virtuous actions to bear on that, including the virtuous actions performed in the public stage, such as justice, temperance, honesty, fortitude, and political prudence. Viewed from this perspective, it is undeniable that religion as a virtue has an impact on the public political life of a community. The restriction of religious virtue regarding its external elements, and especially its influence on other virtues, will have consequences on the way that citizens enjoy their capacity to exercise political freedom. A restriction on the religious freedom of citizens will mean that their political freedom is compromised, for freedom is inherent to the practice of virtue, including religiously virtuous acts.

Thus, when religion is considered as a virtue, and as such, as a manifestation of freedom through a virtuous act, it becomes clear that any prohibition on the part of the state of religious acts that are properly virtuous

36. Aquinas, *S. Th.*, II–II, q. 81, a. 4, ad 2.
37. Cf. Aquinas, *S. Th.*, II–II, q. 81, a. 1, ad 1.
38. Cf. Aquinas, *S. Th.*, II–II, q. 81, a. 1, ad 1.
39. Cf. Cavanaugh, *Myth*, 68.
40. Cf. Aquinas, *S. Th.*, II–II, q. 81, a. 8. The difference between the two is that the virtue of religion does not differ essentially from sanctity, but differs only logically, in that religion refers to communal and individual rites that offer worship to God, while holiness refers to these and the works of all the other virtues as commanded by religion.

will be a violation of a fundamental way in which human beings flourish through the fulfillment of something they consider a duty. And in regard to those virtuous acts which bear on the public sphere, any kind of restriction will mean a denial of one of the most important ways in which freedom is manifested in the public political sphere. There is no virtue without the ability to perform these acts freely. Some virtues, such as courage, political prudence, and justice, always manifest themselves in a public context. In the case of a religious man, these virtues are commanded by the virtue of religion. It is especially in these instances, then, that religion as a virtue makes itself present in the public square, that is, though the virtuous actions that properly belong to the public sphere. It would be a contradiction to split man's virtuous action in order to leave religious virtue outside of the political realm. It is religious virtue that potentially guides the public allegiance of religious citizens, makes them honor their civic obligation, guides them in justice and public virtue, and a host of other concepts and practices that modernity categorizes as political. Religious freedom, then, has a direct impact on the political freedom of citizens, a freedom that allows them to act in the public sphere through acts of virtue, and religion is one of them, in its own acts and in the acts of other virtues which it commands.[41]

Thomas Aquinas's notion of religion as a virtue signifies the highest expression of a notion which, according to Agamben, developed out of the heart of the political pact which gave origin to our political institutions. As seen in chapter 3, Prodi argues that there is in Western Christian culture a dual belonging between religion and politics, which is testified by the role of the oath.[42] One may argue that a decline in the practice of religious virtue will inevitably lead to a decline of political institutions, for the oath, one of the acts of religion, is the "basis of the political pact in the history of the West."[43] And it is a fact that the oath will decline if the name of God is withdrawn from language and from public debates.

This is the political import of religious freedom, and another reason why it should be legally protected. Religious virtue has had a central function in the formation of our Western Christian civilization. To affirm that the religious is just a matter of private belief and practice, may undermine the very being of man as a political animal, for if the decline of religious virtue and of the oath is irreversible, it will only lead to a political crisis unknown

---

41. One could also argue, at the same time, that rejecting the religious freedom of citizens will inevitably have negative consequences on political institutions, especially in relation to the role of the oath, as shown by the work of Paolo Prodi and Giorgio Agamben. See Prodi, *Sacramento del Potere*; Agamben, *SL*.

42. Cf. Prodi, *Sacramento del Potere*, 522.

43. Prodi, *Sacramento del Potere*, 11.

to Western civilization, according to Agamben.[44] The oath, which is an act of religion, is what sustains the structure of political society. Thus, the decline of religious virtue implies the decline of the force and efficacy of the oath, and as a consequence, of political society as a whole.

A solution to the debate on the place of religion in the public square, then, will be the consideration of religion as virtue and its proper spheres or spaces of actions, some of which are located within the public political square. As Arendt argues that freedom is the reason of politics, we can well say that the actions or practice of the virtue of religion, which commands the acts of other virtues that have public significance, is at the core of the freedom of religious citizens, and that freedom is at the core of the religious act, for virtuous actions are by its own nature always free. Therefore, a true understanding of religion as virtue in the public square will help us overcome the difficulties found when religion is treated as a worldview, or belief, or a kind of reasoning which clashes with secular reasoning. Religion is a virtue and as such it cannot be left aside from any aspect of man and society, be it private or public. At the same time, religion as a virtue has its own proper stages of action, while, as a commanding virtue, it also belongs to the exercise of the public virtues that are required in political life. In the religious man, religious virtue is intrinsic to the actions that he performs for the common good of society, and it is as such that religion as virtue makes itself present.

Furthermore, this novel understanding of the terms used in the expression "religious freedom" will help us clarify what we are arguing for when we argue in favor of this right. Aquinas's notion of religion as virtue and its deviations (vices) offers a valuable guideline insofar as the public is concerned, and what should the limits of the civil right to religious freedom be.[45] Certain acts that are deemed religious do not bear any rational character, and

---

44. Cf. Agamben, *SL*, 1. He states: "In keeping with its central function, the irreversible decline of the oath in our time can only correspond, according to Prodi, to a 'crisis in which the very being of man as a political animal is at stake' (Prodi, *Sacramento del Potere*, 11). If we are today 'the first generations who, notwithstanding the presence of some forms and liturgies from the past live our own collective life without the oath as a solemn and total, sacredly anchored bond to a political body,' (ibid.) this means, then, that we find ourselves, without being conscious of it, on the threshold of 'a new form of political association' (ibid.), whose reality and meaning we have yet to recognize."

45. Cf. Aquinas, *S. Th.*, II–II, qq. 92–100. For Aquinas's presentation of the deviations of the virtue of religion, see his treatment of the vice of superstition (q. 92), which is opposed to the virtue of religion by excess, and includes undue worship of the true God (q. 93), idolatry (q. 94), divinations (q. 95), and superstition in observances (q. 96). Aquinas's treatment of the vice of irreligion, which is opposed to the virtue of religion by deficiency, includes temptation of God (q. 97), perjury (q. 98), sacrilege (q. 99) and simony (q. 100).

are dangerous or deadly in themselves, such as certain irrational, harmful, and dangerous practices performed in the name of "religion," the practice of human sacrifices, the use of drugs in rituals, etc. These practices do have social consequences, and for that reason they should be restricted, not only for the sake of peace and order, but because in themselves they entail an order against reason. Considering religion as a virtue, then, will offer a better guideline to address issues like these. It will help us distinguish actions that properly belong to the realm of virtue from those that are irrational, and which therefore should be banned. This will also open up space for discussion on arguments that bear on the ethics of citizens, and it will help guide public discussions about beliefs and religious practices, on what does belong to religious virtue as such, and what belongs to different realms such as conscience, cultural practices, etc.

Religious Freedom as a Human Right

It is time now to talk about religious freedom as a human right. We have to keep in mind, however, that we are dealing now with a new vision of what "religion" means, that is, religion as a virtue. A human right to religious freedom from this perspective, then, refers to the duty that man has to practice acts of religion within their proper space. It is only within the proper space of each act of religion that man may claim a right to act accordingly. In this section, then, we will see whether Aquinas's writings allow for a conception of human rights, and whether his notion of virtuous action gives room for a consideration of human rights.

Thomas Aquinas's strong defense of the human person has led some modern scholars to argue that he was, in fact, a defender of a specific set of natural human rights.[46] In this line, some argue that it is possible to connect the doctrine of human rights with Aquinas's doctrine of natural law.[47] However, authors have taken different views on the issue, so that while some negate any connection between Aquinas and modern human rights altogether,[48]

---

46. See, for example, Beuchot, *Derechos Humanos*; Beuchot, *Fundamentación Filosófica*; Beuchot, *Historia y Filosofía*; García López, *Derechos Humanos*.

47. See Maritain, *Rights of Man*; Maritain, *Man and the State*; McInerny, "Natural Law and Human Rights"; Finnis, *Natural Law*; Molano, "Ley Natural y Derechos Humanos"; Fortin, "New Rights"; Veatch, "Natural Law"; Veatch, *HR*.

48. According to Brian Tierney and Ernest Fortin, for example, Thomas Aquinas did not have a theory of natural rights. See Tierney, "Natural Rights," 67. According to Fortin, no medieval writer either before or after Aquinas ever tried to elaborate such a theory. See Fortin, "Individual Rights," 91; Fortin, "New Rights," 602. This has led some authors, such as Michel Villey, Leo Strauss, and Ralph MacInerny to affirm that

others see a connection with some qualifications,[49] or a plain connection or progression from Aquinas to contemporary human rights' theory.[50] It is not my intention to explore here the different answers found in recent scholarship.[51] Suffice to say that this is actually a quite complex issue, since what we now call "human rights" was a concept foreign to Thomas.

However, Aquinas does talk about *ius*, "right," in different contexts. I would like to mention two instances here.[52] In the first place, Thomas Aquinas often uses the word *ius*, "right," to refer both to what is right to have or receive, and what is right to do.[53] In the second place, Aquinas also uses the word *ius* in a sense that makes right personal. That is, Thomas not only speaks of what is right, but he also speaks of what is a person's right. An example of this is found on *S. Th.* I–II, q. 96, a. 3, where he speaks of protecting the right of a friend:

> All the objects of virtues can be referred either to the private good of an individual, or to the common good of the multitude: Thus matters of fortitude may be achieved either for the safety of the state, or for upholding the rights of a friend, and in like manner with the other virtues.[54]

---

contemporary human rights correspond to the natural rights of Modern iusnaturalism (such as Grotius, Pufendorf, and Rousseau), but not to Classical iusnaturalism (such as Aristotle, Justinian, and Thomas Aquinas). See Villey, *Questions*; Strauss, *Natural Right*; McInerny, "Natural Law and Human Rights." See also Stanley I. Benn in Edwards, *Encyclopedia of Philosophy*, vol. 7, 195; Weinreb, "Natural Law and Rights," 278.

49. See Syse, *Natural Law*, 122–23. In this line, Mauricio Beuchot is of the opinion that human rights can be grounded on a Thomistic notion of natural right through the work of the School of Salamanca, in 16th century Spain. Beuchot, *Fundamentación filosófica*; Beuchot, *Historia y filosofía*. Blandine Barret-Kriegel is of the same opinion. Cf. Barret-Kriegel, *Les Droits*, 47.

50. Jacques Maritain and John Finnis, on the other hand, affirm that contemporary human rights are connected with Aquinas's notion of natural law and the modern conception of natural rights. According to their view, there is no radical break, but rather a progression between Aristotle, Aquinas's natural law teaching, their modern expression in a teaching of natural rights (Richard Hooker and John Locke), and the *Universal Declaration of Human Rights* of 1948. Cf. Finnis, *Natural Law*, 198. On this line, see also MacDonald, "Natural Rights."

51. For this debate, as it currently stands, see Tierney, "Old Problems"; Finnis, "Aquinas on *Ius*," 407–10; Kries, "In Defense of Fortin," 411–13; Zuckert, "Response to Brian Tierney"; Tierney, "Author's Rejoinder."

52. For more examples of Aquinas use of *ius*, see Budziszewski, *Companion to the Commentary*, 138–39.

53. See Aquinas, *S. Th.*, I–II, q. 95, a. 4.

54. Aquinas, *S. Th.*, I–II, q. 96, a. 3.

This example of a virtuous act that bears on a private good, that is, protecting my friend's rights, underlines the law's recognition of the fact that individuals do have rights, and therefore, that defending them is not at odds with the common good. Now, the point is whether we can talk about virtuous action as a duty, and therefore, as a right that has to be uphold.

It was mentioned above that virtuous actions are always by nature free acts. That means that the agent is the origin, the cause, and the possessor of his own actions, in the sense that he is responsible and accountable for his own acts. As Arendt wrote, it is through these virtuous actions that freedom becomes a reality, "tangible in words which can be heard, in deeds which can be seen, and in events which are talked about, remembered, and turned into stories before they are finally incorporated into the great storybook of human history."[55] Now, virtuous acts that take place in "public" means "that everything that appears in public can be seen and heard by everybody and has the widest possible publicity."[56] For that reason one is always accountable for his own acts. Thus, when Aquinas talks about the difference between "royal and politic" rule and "despotic" rule, he affirms that all have "something of their own," that is, a right, a power, a faculty to resist the orders of him who commands.[57] There are other passages in Aquinas's work that suggest that human beings ought to have such an ability, that a certain constitutional respect is due to them just because they are persons rather than things, individual rational substances endowed by God with free will and moral capacities.[58] When talking about political prudence, for example, on II–II, q. 50, a. 2, Aquinas affirms that as a subject, one may not be competent to appreciate the necessities of the common good, which inspire the order of a superior. However, since the subject is a human being, one is responsible for the action to be performed, and this is the case even in slaves. Thus, one cannot pass along to the superior a responsibility that is bound to one's rational nature, since each person has the obligation to verify whether the order one has received is worthy of being carried out.[59]

55. Arendt, "What Is Freedom?," 154–55.
56. Arendt, *HC*, 50.
57. Cf. Aquinas, *S. Th.*, I, q. 81, a. 3, ad 2.
58. Cf. Budziszewski, *Companion to the Commentary*, 140. He affirms: "Because of this dignity, the best human government requires an element of democracy (Question 105, Article 1). Because of it, subjects may sometimes—in fact must sometimes—disobey unjust laws (Question 96, Article 4). Because of it, not only individuals but even their licit forms of association enjoy certain privileges that no human ruler may abridge. And because of it, the Divine governor Himself, whose law is always just and who must not be disobeyed, rules us, His images, not as He rules the animals, but through the participation of our minds (Question 91, Article 2)."
59. Cf. Aquinas, *S. Th.*, II–II, q. 50, a. 2.

We can affirm, therefore, that man ought to be responsible and accountable for his own acts. At the same time, by reason of his rationality, man ought to act in a virtuous way, that is, in a way that befits his human nature and dignity. It is by reason of man's dignity, then, that his freedom to act in a virtuous way should be respected. As a consequence, we could well elaborate a list of human rights based on virtuous acts. My interest here, however, is centered on the ability to perform acts of the virtue of religion as a human right.

Now, one of the fundamental questions when one is confronted with claims resting on human rights is: Why should they be respected? How to justify individual rights? One may appeal to the fundamental law of a nation. However, how are these positive laws justified? In order to justify that virtuous actions should be protected, one has to establish that there is in each human being a duty to attain his own perfection.

Henry Veatch, in his *Human Rights: Fact or Fancy?* (1985), affirms that, as there are good and objective standards of artistic excellence or skill, there are also objective standards of a properly moral excellence.[60] Following Aristotle, he affirms that the good is that at which all things aim in order to attain their proper perfection. And in the case of man, this search for perfection should be identified with the practical life of man as possessing reason.[61] We can also say that man's perfection is attained through virtuous living. Now, Veatch highlights four features of Aristotle's account which provides the criteria for determining just what the good for man is, that is, his natural end or *telos*: activity, practical reason, choice, and liberty. These four elements, Veatch argues, are important guides in the foundation of human rights.

In the first place, the Aristotelian ultimate end should be understood as the activity of "living well," that is, behaving "in a way that best befits a human being."[62] It entails managing our various needs and desires, and using the goods that correspond to them "wisely and intelligently and as they ought to be used and employed."[63]

In the second place, the ultimate end consists "not just of living but in living intelligently,"[64] that is, bringing the order of reason to bear upon "our

---

60. Cf. Veatch, *HR*, 72.

61. Cf. Veatch, *HR*, 77–78. Veatch offers a long text from Aristotle, *Nicomachean Ethics*, bk. I, l. 1, 1094a; and l. 7, 97a–b.

62. Veatch, *HR*, 79.

63. Veatch, *HR*, 80.

64. Veatch, *HR*, 81.

day-by-day decisions and choices."[65] One can have at his own disposal all the goods necessary to live well, and still not take advantage of such goods in an intelligent way. This is when practical reason plays an important role, for "man's characteristic activity must consist of the practical exercise or use of reason."[66] Veatch affirms: "The morally good man is one who knows what should be done and whose judgment can therefore be relied upon in the day-by-day circumstances of our lives, when we have to decide whether we ought or ought not to do this or that."[67]

The third criterion, according to Veatch, is "the matter of choice," for living well is also a question of choice. When it comes to making a choice, one must know how to bring one's own desires into harmony with the requirements of practical reason. Aristotle assigned this task to the moral virtues. And here we can point out the important role to the virtue of religion, for it will potentially have an essential impact through some of its acts that belong to the public sphere, and by commanding those virtues that have a public character. Veatch states: "We need also to cultivate the moral virtues, which are virtues not of knowledge but of choice, and as a result of which our choices and desires and preferences will, we hope, be made to accord with our better judgment."[68] Thus, the person will be better disposed to choose in a particular case to do what his better judgment tells him he ought to do.[69]

The fourth feature that pertains to a good life, according to Veatch, is "the individual human being's own personal freedom and autonomy in the living of his life."[70] Without one's personal effort, it would be impossible to ever attain one's natural end.

Thus, these four elements are important guides in the foundation of human rights. Veatch argues that since human beings are ordered by nature to an appropriate end or goal of human perfection, it is now possible to determine what these moral rules are that human beings must observe if they are to become what they naturally ought to be. It is in this specific sense, then, that moral laws are also natural laws. They are laws in view of an end, laws that one has to recognize and deliberately put into practice and consciously abide by them.[71]

65. Veatch, *HR*, 82.
66. Veatch, *HR*, 81.
67. Veatch, *HR*, 82–83.
68. Veatch, *HR*, 83.
69. Cf. Veatch, *HR*, 84.
70. Veatch, *HR*, 84.
71. Cf. Veatch, *HR*, 85.

Veatch also analyzes the intimate relationship that there is between man's good and his social nature, and the connection between the common good of the community and the individual good of each member of the community. He concludes that the demands of the common good should be understood as a necessary means for the attainment of individual happiness, as both of these are connected.[72]

Thus, based on Aristotelian ethics, Veatch argues that the end of an individual's life must be his own perfection or fulfillment as a human person. Now, this concern that one has in achieving one's happiness "would scarcely seem to imply that the human individual, as thus bent on achieving his own happiness, could claim any right to such happiness or even the pursuit of happiness."[73] Now, are human rights possible and justifiable as being things men have by nature? Or do these rights exist only insofar as men are in a *polis*?

According to Veatch, as a political animal, man's natural end will be not simply his own personal good but the common good. And the common good, considered as an end, is no more than an intermediate end, for the ultimate end is the good of each and all alike who are within the *polis*. However, from the mere fact that man's end as an individual is the common good, not less than its own good, it does not follow that one therefore has any natural rights as against one's fellow citizens or they as against one.[74]

Veatch stresses the duty that the individual perceives himself to be under to pursue his natural end. This is an end that everyone shares and understands through the experience of one's own natural needs and requirements. Each of one's own actions and conduct is ultimately governed in consideration of one's duties toward oneself. Veatch affirms: "Because man's natural end is determined for him by nature, that end will be obligatory, and in consequence a person's every action and his entire behavior will need to be governed by a regard for his duties toward himself."[75]

Thus, Veatch elaborates an explanation of human rights based on man's duties. One has to think of rights as a consequence of duties that one has towards oneself. Man knows his, and others' natural end not as a mere desire but as a duty. He therefore is led to recognize as rights all the means that prove to be necessary for each person, in different circumstances, to do what he and anyone else recognizes that he must do. When one recognizes that someone else has the duty to do a certain thing, because anyone in his place

---

72. Cf. Veatch, *HR*, 113–51.
73. Veatch, *HR*, 151–52.
74. Cf. Veatch, *HR*, 153.
75. Veatch, *HR*, 164.

would have the same duty to do it, one should also recognize that the means necessary in order to attain the goal are in some sense due to him. He argues, then, that the prior duty towards oneself generates rights. And by following Aristotle's characterization of the final end, Veatch identifies the rights to life, liberty, property, and political rights as the means necessary to fulfill one's duty toward oneself.[76] To this list I would add the right to virtuous action, which is the proper manifestation of man's freedom.

We could well argue that the right to perform acts of virtue is strictly derived from man's natural human duty to become and be truly human. Veatch states: "Our individual rights . . . can be derived from the duties that are incumbent upon us as individuals."[77] And once individual rights are established, the principle of universality takes over: given that one has rights based on the duty and obligation one has to oneself, so also does every other person have a similar right based on the like duties that he has to himself.[78] Thus, according to Veatch's account, the only important thing that everyone has by nature is the natural end, and the good man is capable of recognizing it. Therefore, neither life, nor liberty, nor property can be thought of as something that is ready-made or prearranged by nature for everyone in the same way. Rather, the virtuous man who recognizes everyone's ultimate end in its full meaning will understand that he somehow has the right to those conditions of life, freedom and property without which he cannot become truly free to know and pursue his end.

Finally, Veatch concludes his treatment of rights by showing the relationship between the common good and the rights of individuals. The twofold responsibility of every community is to promote the common good, and to protect individual citizens in their rights. Do these two functions come into conflict with one another? Can the community "make demands upon an individual's life, liberty, and property for the purpose, not of furthering the individual's own good but of furthering the common good, that is, the good of each and all?"[79] Since, according to Veatch, there is no opposition between the common good and one's own human fulfillment, for the demands of the common good should be understood as a necessary means for the attainment of individual happiness, everyone has "an obligation to contribute his fair share to the common enterprise of the *polis* and of the community, the achievement of the common good by the *polis* being no less

---

76. Cf. Veatch, *HR*, 163–64.
77. Veatch, *HR*, 168.
78. Cf. Veatch, *HR*, 168.
79. Veatch, *HR*, 206.

an integral part of any human being's natural end than is his achieving his own perfection as an individual rational animal."[80]

To conclude this section, then, we can affirm that virtuous acts do contribute in man's becoming truly human. Thus, there is a duty to act in a virtuous way. Now, regarding the virtue of religion, there is, following Aquinas, a duty that man needs to fulfill in order to reach perfection. Thomas states that, following natural reason, man can discern from his inclinations what is right and good for him.[81] Among these things that are right and good, natural reason decrees to man, in accordance with natural inclination, that he show submission and honor to that which is above him, and that he do so in a way that accords with human nature. The performance of these acts Aquinas assigns to the virtue of religion. Thus, for example, using material things and gestures as offerings to God, and offering sacrifice, is for Aquinas naturally right.[82] It is through acts of the virtue of religion, then, that man fulfills that duty that is prescribed by natural reason in regard to the divine.

All men, in Aquinas's eyes, enjoy human dignity as persons, for man is endowed with reason and free will, and therefore bears personal responsibility for his actions. Men are impelled by nature, and therefore bound by a moral obligation, to seek their own perfection. It is only as such that man dignifies himself. And this is done through works of virtue, among which we find the virtue of religion. For that reason, we can argue that, from a Thomistic perspective, religious freedom has its foundation in the very nature of the human person, so that all men must enjoy the freedom to perform virtuous acts related to religion in a manner in keeping with man's own nature, that is, enjoying immunity from external coercion as well as psychological freedom.

Conclusion

This chapter has aimed at offering a new perspective on religious freedom and the place of religion in the public square. The novel understanding of both freedom and the virtue of religion offered in the previous two chapters give us a better grasp of what is meant by the term religious freedom, and the proper location or stages of the acts of religious virtue and of the virtues it commands, some of which have an important public character. At the same time, as it can be deduced from the previous chapters, it is imperative to move from a belief-based to a virtue-based notion of religion, and as a

80. Veatch, *HR*, 205.
81. Cf. Aquinas, *S. Th.*, I–II, q. 94, a. 2.
82. Cf. Aquinas, *S. Th.*, II–II, q. 85, a. 1.

consequence to a new conception of religious freedom that sees religion as being freely lived through virtuous actions.[83] This approach, which takes Aquinas's perspective of "religion" in terms of virtue, and Arendt's notion of freedom as related to political life and virtue, results in what I believe is a stronger notion of religious freedom.

Man has the obligation to perform acts that belong to the virtue of religion, and therefore it follows that he has a right to do so. These acts are both internal and external. Man is also social by nature, and therefore he also enjoys the right to associate with others in pursuing goals that are in line with the common good of society. Since the true practice of religion belongs to a virtue, men have the right to associate with others with respect to the performance of external acts of the virtue of religion. These external acts of religion, because they are acts of a virtue, and as long as they are performed in their proper stage, will never perturb the order of society or attempt against its common good. Instead, the practice of religious virtue favors the common good since, as mentioned above, it is religious virtue that potentially guides religious people in regard to their public allegiance, makes them honor their civic obligations, guides them in justice, public virtue, and in other concepts and practices that modernity categorizes as political.

We also affirmed, following Arendt, that political freedom manifests itself as a phenomenon of virtuosity on the public stage, and thus it was necessary to identify the proper stage of each act of the virtue of religion and of those virtues under its command, especially virtues that enjoy a public character. The acts of the virtue of religion take place on four different stages: within the heart or mind of the believer and the privacy of his home, within the church as a liturgical space, within the social community, and finally, within the common public political sphere. In issues of religious freedom and on the place of religion in the public square, then, it is important to identify the proper stage of the act of religion being addressed in each case, for certain acts of religion enjoy a public character that other acts of religion do not. There are also certain acts of other virtues, such as political prudence, justice, and courage, that in themselves have a public character, and may be commanded by the virtue of religion. The virtue of religion, then, makes itself present in the public political forum through some of its external acts, and through the acts of other virtues that it may command.

At the same time, issues of faith and belief do not have to do with issues of religious freedom properly, but rather with freedom of conscience

---

83. Beaman, for example, distinguishes between notions of belied-based and practice-based religion. He sees the importance of moving beyond a notion of religion as belief. Cf. Beaman, "Is Religious Freedom Impossible?," 272.

and the way in which faith shapes society, culture, and politics. This is something that needs to be clarified, for religion should rather be understood as a virtue. It is the acts of this virtue that religious freedom properly protects. The understanding of "religion" as a belief system should be entirely abandoned in issues of religious freedom, for here we are running the risk of extending the protection of religious freedom to actions that are not properly religious, even when they involve one's own faith or belief. These are rather matters of conscience, and it is under the banner of freedom of conscience that they should be debated.

We can conclude by saying that the acknowledgement of religious freedom implies that, legally, the state should create the space and the conditions in order that freedom as religious virtue can appear, so that men may follow that which they perceive as a duty.[84]

Finally, the notion of religion as a virtue offers a better understanding in relation to questions on the place of religion in the public square and on religious freedom, for here we are talking about actions which by their own nature take place on a given stage, some in the privacy of one's own conscience, others on the public political forum, and which by their virtuous character are easier to identify, protect, encourage, and distinguish from false "religious" vicious acts. We must say, once again, that religion as a virtue has its own proper stages of action, while, as a commanding virtue, it also belongs to the exercise of the public virtues that are required in political life, for in the religious man, religious virtue is intrinsic to the actions that he performs for the common good of society.

At the same time, the virtue of religion is distinct from faith. Even though in the religious believer it is his faith that motivates his acts of religion, they are not the same, so that the protection of one's acts motivated by faith belongs rather to freedom of conscience. It is important to stress this fact, for many contemporary debates on religious freedom have been involved with issues that properly belong to a different category. When religion is understood as a virtue, the issues under debate become clearer, religious freedom is strengthened as a civil right, and matters of faith and

---

84. Ahdar and Leigh note that historically speaking, religious liberty was conceived not in terms of choice, but in terms of duty. Religious freedom was a freedom given to fulfil a duty. Cf. Ahdar and Leigh, *Religious Freedom*, 62. In the United States, Sanders notes how the framers of the American Constitution made little or no mention of "autonomy" or "choice" in their arguments for religious liberty. Rather, Sandel affirms: "Madison and Jefferson understood religious liberty as the right to exercise religious duties according to the dictates of conscience, not the right to choose religious beliefs. In fact, their argument for religious liberty relies heavily on the assumption that beliefs are not a matter of choice." See Sandel, "Religious Liberty," 610.

religious belief are offered a better place for their defense, for they belong rather to the sphere of freedom of conscience.

CONCLUSION

Religious Freedom from a New Perspective

THE NEW PERSPECTIVE ON religious freedom offered on this book will be considered in light of a few contemporary examples that make it evident there is a problematic understanding of religion, religious freedom, and the public square. At the same time, the analysis of these contemporary cases will be a test to the new meaning of religious freedom offered in this book, especially in comparison to contemporary theories presented in the first chapters. This will help us see whether this redefinition of religious freedom signifies a new development and a better solution to contemporary debates.

In the first place, I will consider this new perspective of religious freedom in light of the understanding of religion as a belief system which in recent scholarship has called for a new way of reasoning: public reason. This is what Rawls proposed, calling for a separation of "religion" from public debates due to the potentially coercive dimensions of religious and other comprehensive truth claims under the conditions of pluralism. I will bring in here the U.S. Supreme Court case *Zubik v. Burwell*, in order to see to what extent this separation of "religion" constitutes a violation of religious freedom.

In the second place, I will come back to the problems that may follow from considering religious freedom as a matter of conscience. This is what follows from treating religion as a system of belief. What those who advocate for this view do not seem to see is that, by doing so, the right to religious freedom is undermined. If one includes matters of conscience under religious freedom, or reduces it to these issues, the consequence, then, is that there is really no need for this right, for that is already covered by freedom of conscience. It is imperative, then, to distinguish between matters of consciences and issues that truly have to do with religion in order to uphold this right. An efficient and good way to do this is by considering religion as a virtue.

In the third place, this new understanding of religious freedom will make it clearer why we are not talking about religious tolerance, for virtue will be the guideline to discern and distinguish rational from irrational behavior, and virtuous from vicious acts. Thus, an understanding of religion as virtue provides a powerful argument for the protection of what is truly religious, while at the same time offering the tools to discern, prevent, and restrict actions that might be harmful to individuals or society, and which should never be considered as religious in the first place.

In the fourth place, I will refer to religious freedom and issues related to public spaces. As seen above, religious virtue makes its presence in the public square through some of its acts, and through the public acts of the virtues it commands. It is important to make this distinction in order to clarify the different aspects of debates centered on "religion" in the public square, such as the presence of religious symbols, the wearing of religious garments and symbols, religious monuments displayed on public property, etc.

Finally, in the fifth place, I will point out a few items in relation to where we should go next in terms of philosophical research, for there is still more to be done in the field of religious freedom and on the place of religion in the public square.

Religious Freedom and Public Discourse

In 2012, a mandate from the United States Department of Health and Human Services (HHS) triggered a new wave of court cases, arguments, and studies on religious freedom.

The HHS mandate established that employers must provide contraception, abortifacients, and sterilization as part of their insurance packages, in evident violation of religious institutions' beliefs, or pay heavy fines which would make it almost impossible for these institutions to operate.[1] This move resulted in what is now the prominent Supreme Court case *Zubik v. Burwell*, on whether religious institutions other than churches should be exempt from the contraceptive mandate. The plaintiffs in this case all agreed that the Obama Administration's mandate is burdensome, and that

---

1. In doing so, Wiker argues, the main target of the HHS mandate was the Catholic Church, which rejects contraception, abortion, and sterilization. It is very suspicious that there are exemptions for large corporations such as Exxon, Visa, large municipalities like the City of New York and even the government's own military healthcare, Tricare, for convenience or financial reasons. In fact, one third of Americans don't have plans subject to the government's mandate. Cf. Wiker, *Worshipping the State*, 12–13.

the government shouldn't be in the business of violating the free exercise of one's deepest-held religious beliefs.[2]

The Little Sisters of the Poor were denied an exemption to the mandate on the grounds that their activity of caring for the elderly is not religious enough. The Little Sisters, in turn, told the government that it has no right to tell them what is and is not against their religious beliefs, for their faith prohibits them from giving into the government's demands regarding that particular issue. The Little Sisters cannot in good conscience authorize their health plans to provide these services, like the day-after pill. At the same time, it made no sense for the government to make the Little Sisters provide those services, since they can be easily obtained through the government's own exchanges. In reply, the government said the Little Sisters were not religious enough to be exempt, and insisted that the mandate exemption apply only to churches and church-controlled ministries. That meant that within the boundaries of religious acts one is exempted, but when it comes to education, healthcare, and other fields in which churches operate, they are not considered as "religious." Thus, the government redefines religious institutions as entities that hire and serve mostly people of their own "religion."[3] Benjamin Wiker argues that, with this move, the mandate has proven to be a redefinition of what it means to be "religious" as well.[4]

After promising that the Little Sisters's religious beliefs would be protected, the government created a new regulation requiring the Little Sisters to change their healthcare plan to offer services that violate Catholic teaching. The government argued that since it offered to reimburse the costs of the services it wants the Little Sisters to provide, they should have no moral objection to offering them. The Little Sisters replied that this is not about money, but conscience, and thus they should not be forced to change their healthcare plan to offer services they have a moral objection to, while at the same time those services could be provided more effectively through the government's healthcare exchange. It is important to note that the Little Sisters were not trying to prevent the government from providing these services. They only objected to the government's insisting the Little Sisters provide them, against their religious beliefs. They argued that there are many easy solutions that

---

2. The plaintiffs, however, disagreed at points as to why. Many evangelical Christians objected in every case to abortion-causing drugs or devices, but not necessarily to contraception itself. The Little Sisters of the Poor and other Catholic groups conscientiously objected to all artificial contraception.

3. The so-called HHS religious exemption would effectively nullify the religious exemption traditionally afforded such institutions as Catholic social service agencies, hospitals, and colleges.

4. Cf. Wiker, *Worshipping the State*, 12–13.

protect the Little Sisters's religious freedom and the right of the government to offer these services to women who want them.[5]

In May 2016, the U.S. Supreme Court handed down a unanimous ruling, remanding the case of the Little Sisters of the Poor and other petitioners back to the lower courts to pursue an accommodation. Thus, the Supreme Court decided that the government cannot fine and penalize these groups for objecting to the Administration's demand that they authorize contraceptive coverage for their ministry's employees.

Throughout the process, the Little Sisters of the Poor and other petitioners had to make use of religiously based arguments in order to defend themselves from a mandate that, if followed, would have meant a violation of their faith and conscience. This fact is of crucial importance; however, it has been overlooked when analyzing this case in relation to religious freedom. At the same time, the Sisters argued that the government is redefining the notion of "religion," and what it means to be "religious." This is another important aspect, and often overlooked.

As we have seen in chapter 1, Rawls developed a notion of public reason that, out of a concern for the potentially coercive dimensions of religious and other comprehensive truth claims under the conditions of pluralism, encourages only certain modes of argumentation (such as secular reasons) in an effort to maximize the formation and stability of democratic majorities on fundamental questions of justice. At the same time, Rawls's attempt to accommodate religious arguments into his doctrine of political liberalism shows that he was aware that it would be unfair to leave religious motivations aside when discussing public policy. The notion of "religion" employed by Rawls, however, refers to a dogma or comprehensive view which has no ultimate influence in the public political forum. Thus, a Supreme Court justice, a legislator, or a candidate for public office cannot base his decisions on religious reasoning. For Rawls, religious reasons must be translated into secular ones, so that they be understood by, and acceptable to, the general population. At the same time, Rawls argues that in special circumstances, as when citizens are making coercive decisions on constitutional essentials and matters of basic justice, they will be bound by a duty to support only those policies that can in fact be justified by public reason alone, and therefore they will either have to translate their arguments or restrain their reasoning. Thus, citizens *qua* citizens are free to justify their political views in terms of whatever religious

---

5. For example, rather than trying to force religious plans to offer these services, the government could simply ask insurers to offer independent coverage to any women who want it, or the government could provide these services through the Affordable Care Act (ACA) healthcare exchange to any employees who want them but can't get them through employer plans.

or secular worldviews they choose, except when they come to the public political forum regarding coercive decisions.

Now, given the context of pluralism and different views present in society, will the demand to translate one's religious arguments into secular ones be a breach of one's religious freedom? Not necessarily, except when religious groups or individuals are being targeted by a certain coercive law or mandate, and may not be able to offer any other than religious arguments for their stance. This is the case of institutons or businesses forced to provide access to contraceptives or abortions in their benefits plans, or forced to take part in acts that they consider immoral, such as performing or assisting to an abortion, a gay union ceremony, etc. As mentioned above, not all religious institutions and individuals have acquired a strong philosophical foundation to show the reasonableness of their faith, and therefore are not equipped to offer secular reasons for their beliefs and opinions regarding public policy.

In my view, the *Zubik v. Burwell* Supreme Court case is properly a case of freedom of conscience rather than a matter of religious freedom. However, were one to apply Rawls's view on the matter, it is worth asking whether this case could be considered as a case of religious freedom were the defendants not allowed to provide religious arguments to defend their position. One of the problems with Rawls's theory is that he seems to have missed the possibility that one day the state, judges, or legislators, employing purely secular reasoning, may impose coercive laws on religious citizens or institutions, against which these citizens or institution may only have arguments based on their faith or belief system to offer in their defense. Thus, a problem arises when certain laws not only violate the conscience of individuals and the regulations of religious institutions, but when these same individuals or institutions are not able to argue their reasons for not accepting a mandate other than based on their faith and the ethical norms that spring from it. From a Catholic perspective, one could argue that reason and natural morality offer arguments that are supportive of revelation.[6] However, this is not the case with all religious institutions or movements, and for that reason it is argued that one should be mindful of religious groups that will not be able to provide secular reasons for their arguments in the public political forum. The question is, what should be done in favor of these groups when coercive laws are applied to them? Should dogmatic statements be allowed to play a role in the political public square, at least in regard to coercive laws that mandate something that is contrary to a groups'

---

6. In fact, in Catholic theology one can find natural or secular reasons to give for most measures supported by revelation.

belief or restrict or forbid their work and actions? However, this may lead in some cases to exceptions or permissions that are not in line with the common good of society, as when a religious group appeals to the faith or belief they hold in order to justify acts that they deem to be religious but which objectively are an attempt to the order, norms, and morals of the community, such as the use of drugs in "religious" rituals, or the practice of human sacrifices, torture, or other forms that strictly constitute violations of human dignity. But what about those religious groups that argue for protection from certain coercive laws with respect to actions that do not attempt against the common good? One may argue that here we are facing a deficiency in theories that, while trying to accommodate religious argument in public discourse, restrict the areas in which discourse based on a belief system can be manifested. These religious citizens will see themselves as being seriously disadvantaged by an ideal of citizenship and lawmaking that requires the justifications for coercive laws to be ones which all citizens could reasonably be expected to agree, and which requires arguments and deliberation advanced in favor of such laws to meet this standard. The religious reasons offered on their defense will seem opaque to many, for these are not reasons which others can reasonably be expected to agree, and therefore they do not meet the standard of public reason. One could also argue, then, that there are grounds to state that public reason liberalism should be more open to religious voices, reasons, arguments, and deliberations. Thus, from this point of view, the neutrality requirement advocated by Rawls and other liberal political philosophers leaves out those reasons arising from religious beliefs from public deliberation and lawmaking. Consequently, those reasons are not only unavailable to make laws, but they are also unavailable to justify an adjustment to laws that run afoul of these religious beliefs. It seems that these theories, then, fail in showing how an individual or institution, employing religious arguments, will argue opposition to a law, such as the HHS mandate requiring that businesses and institutions such as hospitals and universities provide free contraceptives to their employees. The problem I want to point to, then, is that arguments made from the point of view of neutrality, or secular reasoning, or in view of reaching a consensus, may not be available to the members of certain religious groups or institutions. If one were to follow these principles, there is no reason for adjusting general laws. But what about those individuals that do not agree with these liberal principles? Thus, against this position, one could also argue that if a citizen or institution has a defeater for a law, it is impermissible that the citizen or institution be coerced by that law, so that it must either be repealed or reformed in order to make accommodations for religious citizens and institutions.[7] The main question, then, is, how should one proceed in a situation like this?

One of the problems here is that the distinction between "public" and "religious" reasons is not helpful, for reason is always reason, and therefore there are not such religious non-public reasons or secular reasons. And we have to insist on that with persistence: as long as an argument proceeds from reasoning, and is sound and true in its premises, it does not really matter whether it be secular or religious or neutral anymore, for it will be an argument of reason, and as such it does not need any "religious" or "secular" connotation whatsoever. The problem, however, is that in many instances of what is considered to be a "religious" argument, we may instead be dealing with dogmatic statements or propositions, which clearly are not reasons, and therefore cannot be considered to be an argument. And it is for this reason that such argument has no place in the public political square, that is, because arguments like these are not arguments at all. Their only function is to work as argument stoppers and nothing more in a public discussion. And here we may be facing a serious problem if we are to uphold religious freedom as a human right, for the debate seems to stall on exactly this point, unless we introduce new criteria into the debate in order to progress to a solution. Thus, whether "religious" arguments have a place or not in the public square is something that should be left aside really, for the wording itself is misleading. If "religion" deserves a place in the public political square, a better device has to be found in order to make a sound argument. It is in this context that the new understanding of religion as a virtue may be an efficient way to reach an answer to all the questions the debate has arisen. It may not fit within liberal secular theories, yet it is nevertheless illuminating regarding the present debate.

Another problem we have already noted is the connection between "religion" and other acts performed by religious institutions, such as education and healthcare. If religion were understood as a virtue, it would be easier to establish the different aspects of the debate. In the first place, there is the religious faith that motivates the acts of religious virtue, and the conscientious denial to perform certain acts or offer certain services. In the second place, there is a religious virtue which commands the acts of other virtues, some of which have an impact in the public square. The Little Sisters of the Poor object that, in conscience, they cannot give in to the demands of the government, for doing so would be contrary to their faith. The government is violating their freedom of conscience in forcing them to act against their faith, or either pay heavy fines, or even shut down the services their institution provides to those

---

7. On this see Vallier; Tollefsen, "Basis of Liberalism."

in need. Now, since the services they provide are a response to their faith and their belief to serve Christ in others, we can argue that it is religious virtue that commands all these actions. The acts themselves, however, even if virtuous acts, are not in themselves acts of the virtue of religion. One may argue that trying to prevent them from acting in this way would not be a direct violation of their religious freedom. Still, preventing the Sisters to perform virtuous acts is a grave violation of their freedom. These virtues acts, which are potentially commanded by the virtue of religion in the religious person, belong to the stage of those actions ordered to the social community. Religious virtue makes its appearance on this stage by commanding acts of other virtues. Thus, the government, instead of restricting their action, should rather create the conditions for these activities to take place, and protect them against any form of coercion that attempts against their mission, both within their community and in society. Now, were the members of a religious institution denied their freedom to act under the command of the virtue of religion, this would mean a violation of their religious freedom in relation to its third stage of action. And this is what is taking place with the Little Sisters of the Poor.

The Little Sisters of the Poor have argued that, in this case, the government is redefining the notion of "religion," and what it means to be "religious." However, there has been no clear definition of "religion" in the first place, and no distinction has been made between a faith or belief which prohibits certain actions and a virtue of religion which commands the acts of virtues which are not properly "religious." Clarifying these aspects will help us distinguish matters that properly belong to freedom of conscience from matters which belong to issues of religious freedom, as well as identifying the place granted to arguments based on faith or belief regarding coercive decisions in the public square.

Thus, we can see here that the understanding of religion as a virtue offered in this book, and of religious freedom as a stage where religious virtue is played out, offers a better solution to the debate on the place of religion in the public square than the theories proposed by Rawls, Habermas, Taylor, and others. These authors have offered valuable insights; yet, their solutions may have developed around asking the wrong question about religion. This might be the reason why there has been a repeated failure to agree, to reach any satisfying answer, or even make progress towards one.

If the issue at play with the members of a religious institution has to do with works of virtue, then it is obvious that if freedom is manifested through virtuous acts, then they should be respected and left alone to do the work they are devoted to, for these are works of virtue potentially commanded by religious virtue. Now, if those acts which are supposedly "religious acts" do not objectively bear the character of virtuous acts, but are rather irrational or vicious in their own nature, then these acts can well be penalized for the sake of the common good and the protection of all citizens, especially if these vicious acts attempt against human dignity.[8] For Aquinas, the purpose of human law is to lead men to virtue, and thus, from this perspective, the rule of virtue should be the guiding principle in issues where the acts of the members of a religious group are questioned.[9] At the same time, by centering the public discussion around issues of virtue or vice, and not on "secular" or "religious" arguments, it will be possible to open up a discussion that will be more fruitful in the end, as no one in his right mind will deny that a life of virtue is more conducive to the common good of the *polis*.

Religious Freedom and Freedom of Conscience

It is a widespread view, as Thomas Reese holds, that "religious freedom includes the right to change one's religion or belief without coercion."[10] It is true that one's decision to belong to a certain religious tradition or to another, or to hold certain religious beliefs, should be protected. Yet, in this instance, religion is equated to faith and religious knowledge, and therefore religious freedom is understood as the freedom to believe. And these are two different things, unless one understands religion to be a system of beliefs, a notion which should be dropped, as seen above.

Religious freedom and freedom of conscience are not the same reality. Conscience as such, in Thomas Aquinas's view, is not part of the virtue of religion. Conscience is not an instance of the human person; rather it refers to an act of judgment of practical reason by which the human person recognizes the moral quality of a concrete act he is planning to perform, is actually doing, or has done in the past.[11] According to Aquinas, as an act of our practical intellect, conscience consists in applying our science, our knowledge, to a specific action. It is the judgment by which we apply the light of the first principles of the moral order to each one of our actions, proffering a judgment regarding their goodness or malice,

---

8. For Aquinas, laws are framed for the common good of all citizens. See Aquinas, *S. Th.*, I–II, q. 96, a. 1. Now, according to Aquinas, since human law is framed for human beings most of which are not perfect in virtue, it follows that human laws do not forbid all vices, only the more grievous ones, from which it is possible for the majority to abstain, and those vices that injure others, for without their prohibition it would not be possible to maintain human society. Cf. Aquinas, *S. Th.*, I–II, q. 96, a. 2.

9. Cf. Aquinas, *S. Th.*, I–II, q. 96, a. 2, ad 2.

10. Reese, "Religious Freedom".

11. Cf. Aquinas, *S. Th.*, I, q. 79, a. 13.

their order to the last end, or their lack of order.[12] Freedom of conscience, then, is understood in the sense that one cannot be forced to act against a judgment or rational conviction that doing or omitting something is right or wrong, for to do so would go against the precept that one must do good and avoid evil. Even though some argue that freedom of conscience is one of the most compelling justifications for religious freedom understood as the freedom to fulfill obligations, especially sacred duties, that flow from an authority higher than the state,[13] we are here talking about different things that need to be clarified and distinguished.

The Little Sister's case may be a good example of the need to distinguish between issues of conscience and those of religion. Another issue that has arisen in recent years has to do with religious freedom and same-sex unions.[14] Once the United States Supreme Court redefined marriage in *Obergefell*, the Court announced that it would hear cases about the extent to which private parties may be forced to embrace this new vision of marriage. One of the most prominent case involves Jack Phillips, a Colorado baker who declined to bake a wedding cake for a same-sex wedding reception.[15] He argues that there is no need to coerce artists to employ their abilities in ways contrary to their religious beliefs. The question for the Supreme Court to settle is whether the government should force the baker to make cakes for activities that contradict his faith, such as gay unions.

What we have to distinguish here, once again, is the baker's faith, which he does not want to betray by acting against his conscience, and the acts that he performs at work, which, as a religious believer, he offers to God, so that he sees his faith as encompassing all of the aspects of his life. This certainly involves acts of virtue, which may potentially be commanded by religious virtue. However, the baker's denial to make the cake really belongs to issues of conscience, not of religious freedom. The baker should seek protection under freedom of conscience, which includes a presumption of a right to inaction, to be free to refuse to participate in that which one's conscience forbids.

Anderson denounces that "some liberals are trying to drastically narrow the natural right to the free exercise of religion by redefining it as the freedom of worship." The result, according to him, is that religious freedom

---

12. Cf. Aquinas, *S. Th.*, I, q. 79, a. 13.

13. Cf. Hertzke, *Religious Freedom*, 6. As Cardinal Newman puts it, conscience "has rights because it has duties." See his "Letter to the Duke of Norfolk," quoted in Chaput, *Render unto Caesar*, 148.

14. See Laycock et al., *Emerging Conflicts*.

15. On this, see Anderson, "Threat to Religious Liberty"; Blake, "Cakes and Consciences."

"will be reduced to Sunday-morning piety confined to a chapel."[16] However, the answer to attacks against one's own actions motivated by faith does not consist in trying to include these actions under the banner of "religion."[17] A stronger case would be made by distinguishing the issues at play, clarifying the notions employed, and defending one's rights of conscience and religion as distinct issues. Only by doing so will one be able to avoid what Anderson fears: "The Little Sisters of the Poor will be free to worship how they want in their chapel, but will be forced to comply with the HHS mandate."[18] Thus, by separating and distinguishing the issues at play, the Little Sisters of the Poor will enjoy both the freedom to practice religious virtue and be able to perform, in relation to their mission, the acts of other virtues commanded by religion, while at the same time enjoying a right to inaction, and refuse to participate in offering services which their conscience forbids.

Finally, it is important to stress that the acts of virtues commanded by religion have their own internal principles and have nothing to do with religion or faith. That means that being a good doctor, or teacher, or caregiver does not depend on whether one has faith or the act is being commanded by the virtue of religion. The virtue of religion will certainly have a great influence in that one will probably offer his best in order to complete the task, but the act itself is distinct from the virtue of religion or faith. Thus, the fact that one may be a good doctor, or teacher, or caregiver is not by reason of one's own faith or virtue of religion, but due to the internal principles at play in a given virtue. In commanding the acts of other virtues, the virtue of religion directs these acts to the honor of God, but does not make them an act of the virtue of religion! Therefore, we can apply to the work of the Little Sisters this comment by Thomas Aquinas with respect to elicited and commanded acts of virtue: "To visit the fatherless and widows in their tribulation is an act of religion as commanding, and an act of mercy as eliciting; and to keep oneself unspotted from this world is an act of religion

---

16. Anderson, "Threat to Religious Liberty".

17. Clear as it may sound, Anderson's solution does not belong properly to the realm of religious freedom, but to freedom of conscience. It is here that it acquires a powerful tone. He states: "To adequately defend religious liberty, then, we must defend religion and work to spread it. In other words, we must evangelize. This takes many forms. Parents and pastors need to form their children and congregants in the truth. Spreading the faith to others—and helping them see the reasonableness of our beliefs—is likewise essential." In Anderson, "Threat to Religious Liberty." See how the notion of "religion" employed by Anderson is equal to "truth," "faith," and "reasonable belief" which should be spread. It is a confusing notion of "religion" which misleads Anderson in dealing with a case that properly should be argued from the perspective of freedom of conscience.

18. Anderson, "Threat to Religious Liberty."

as commanding, but of temperance or of some similar virtue as eliciting."[19] Therefore, while the members of Little Sisters certainly are an example of acts of mercy and temperance, among other virtues, all of which are probably commanded by the virtue of religion, these acts in themselves are not acts of the virtue of religion. For that reason, to try to make a case in their defense by assigning all of their works of mercy to "religion" will certainly not help in providing a good defense of their work, even if their practice of the virtue of religion is exemplar.

Religious Freedom and Tolerance

One of the main problems that follow from defining religion as a belief system or comprehensive view is that, when it comes to religious freedom, there is an assumption that it lies within the power of government to choose the content of a belief or a religious conviction in order to decide which "religions" are worthy of special protection and which not. Those that are found worthy, in turn, will be tolerated and granted freedom from external coercion.

If religion is considered as the exercise of a virtue, which in turn is a manifestation of true freedom, then there is no place for tolerance in relation to the efforts man makes to be virtuous, for this is always something positive and fullfilling. It is clear, as seen in chapter 2, that religious freedom and tolerance are not one and the same thing. Even more, religious freedom is not a matter of accommodation or toleration by the state, for it is the state that has to protect and promote initiatives that create the conditions for the practice of virtue. For that reason, it is necessary that the virtuous acts in order to practice religion be legally and politically protected, not because the state may allow these actions, but rather because it is the requirement of freedom to appear in the public sphere through virtuous action, and the virtue religion is one of these manifestations, in its own acts, and by commanding the acts of other virtues that have a public character and are ordered to the common good of the community. One should not speak of tolerance, then, when dealing with issues of religious freedom.

The practice of religion as a virtue is something that belongs to human beings as rational and free beings, and therefore it is ontologically prior to the state. That means that there is no room for a "tolerance" understanding of religious freedom, and even less for an understanding of religious freedom as permission on behalf of the state. The state has to ensure there is a stage for agents to perform freely and in a virtuous way. Religious freedom

19. Aquinas, *S. Th.*, II–II, q. 81, a. 1, ad 1.

is not a privilege granted by the state. However, when it comes to fellow citizens living in a pluralistic society, one can talk about a respect conception of toleration. Religious practices that are a consequence of trying to be religiously virtuous may be an object of tolerance for those who choose to exercise the virtue of religion in different ways. One should note, however, that most people trying to be religious have not yet achieved the habit of religion in a perfect way, that is, in a way that every one of their acts is truly an act of virtue, and this applies to the practice of all other virtues as well. And this is another reason why some acts may be the object of tolerance in a respectful way, especially for those that have not yet achieved the virtue of religion. One can also talk of tolerance regarding vicious practices that are opposed to the virtue of religion, like superstition or idolatry, or the attitude of those who choose not to practice the virtue of religion at all. These acts may be tolerated for the sake of peace.[20] Thus, these acts would fall under tolerance, and not under religious freedom.

Instead of tolerance as permission on the part of the state, then, one could argue that the state is there to create the conditions that are favorable to the fostering of the practice of the virtue of religion.[21] These conditions should be in place for the sake of fostering virtuous action, and not just as immunity from external coercion when it comes to the practice of religious virtue. At the same time, understanding "religion" as virtuous practice will provide a better guideline when it comes to discerning the nature of certain actions that might resemble religious virtue, but which truly are not acts of religion. It is these actions that the state may tolerate as permission, as long as they are not disruptive or dangerous to the common good and the morals and good customs of society.

The authority of the state is limited not in the sense that man is to be immune from external coercion in matters of conscience and religion, but in the sense that man enjoys a political freedom in order to reach self-perfection through virtue, and therefore the state is there to lay out the conditions for this to take place. It is in the household, in the family, that man begins this long way towards perfection, and thus, the purpose of governmental authority is always and everywhere to assist, not to replace, the authority of this community grounded in the nature of every human being.

Is there a limit to religious freedom, then? If religion is seen as a virtue, and the issues at stake are properly identified and defined, then one can

20. See Aquinas's thought on not punishing all vices in Aquinas, *S. Th.*, I–II, q. 96, a. 2.

21. This is an issue that goes beyond the topic of my book, but which certainly needs to be addressed in the future, once the proper meanings of religion, freedom, and the public square are established.

argue that there are no limitations, for as long as one remains in the realm of virtue, by their own nature these actions will contribute to promote the common good of society. When contemporary legal documents on religious freedom talk about the limits to this right, they imply actions which by their own nature are disordered, out of place, or perverse in themselves, and which should be restricted. However, these acts do not belong to the realm of religious virtue. Thus, an understanding of religion as virtue provides a powerful argument for the protection of what is truly religious, while at the same time offering the tools to discern, prevent, and restrict actions that might be harmful to individuals or society, and which should never be considered as religious in the first place.

This understanding of religious freedom does not eliminate tolerance. It will be needed in certain cases for the sake of peace, or for other reasons. Thus, in order to see more clearly this distinction between tolerance and religious freedom, and to see the need of understanding virtue as religion, I will present here the U.S. Supreme Court's decision regarding the Native American Church, which uses peyote, a hallucinogenic drug, in its religious rituals.

All international documents on religious freedom agree that, in the exercise of this right, everyone shall be subject to certain limitations as determined by the law in order to respect the rights of others, their human dignity, and to meet the just requirements of morality, public order and the general welfare in a democratic society.[22] This freedom in religious matters is therefore not unlimited. However, every time a restriction is placed on a religious act, there is in most cases disagreement as to why place or not place a restriction, for there is no guiding principle with respect to what it is that may damage the dignity of others, or not meet the just requirements of morality, public order, and the general welfare of society. In cases where the practice of human sacrifices is involved, it is clear that these things are deeply wrong and should not be tolerated in the name of religious freedom. However, there are other cases that have caused great debate and disagreement, such as the U.S. Supreme Court decision regarding the Native American Church, which uses peyote in its religious rituals.[23] This hallucinogenic drug is dangerously addictive, and for that reason its use was forbidden in the state of Oregon, even if within sacramental use.[24]

Alfred Leo Smith and Galen Black were counselors at a private drug rehabilitation clinic and members of the Native American Church. They were

---

22. See, for example, United Nations, *Human Rights*, 6.
23. See *Oregon v. Smith*, 494 U.S. 872 (1990).
24. Cf. Ore. Rev. Stat. § 475.992 (4) (1987).

fired because they had ingested peyote as part of their religious ceremonies. Intentional possession of peyote was a crime under Oregon law. The counselors filed a claim for unemployment compensation with the state, but the claim was denied because the reason for their dismissal was deemed work-related misconduct. The Oregon Court of Appeals reversed that ruling, holding that denying them unemployment benefits for their religious use of peyote violated their right to exercise their religion. The Oregon Supreme Court agreed, based in that the state's justification for withholding the benefits was outweighed by the burden imposed on the employees' exercise of their religion. The state appealed to the United States Supreme Court, again arguing that denying the unemployment benefits was proper because possession of peyote was a crime under Oregon law. Thus, the case required the Supreme Court to decide whether the Free Exercise Clause of the First Amendment permits the state of Oregon to include religiously inspired peyote use within the reach of its general criminal prohibition on use of that drug, and thus permits the state to deny unemployment benefits to persons dismissed from their jobs because of such religiously inspired use.

The Supreme Court argued that since the state prohibition is not specifically directed at their religious practice, the free exercise of religion was not violated, for an individual's religious belief does not excuse him from compliance with an otherwise valid law prohibiting conduct that the state is free to regulate.[25] At the same time, since the law in question applies generally to everyone, the government no longer has to show a compelling state interest for denying religious exemptions.

The decision was considered to be "disastrous" for many, for, following the Supreme Court's reasoning, Oregon cannot pass a law stating that Native Americans are prohibited from using peyote, but it could accomplish the same result by prohibiting the use of peyote by everyone. Thus, more than sixty religious and civil liberties groups joined forces to restore the compelling interest test by getting Congress to pass the Religious Freedom Restoration act of 1993, which insisted that the Court's decision was wrong. Congress declared that no regulation that interferes with a religious practice is permitted, however innocent and nondiscriminating its purpose, unless there is a compelling rather than simply an ordinary need for regulation, that is, unless the regulation is necessary to prevent

---

25. On a side note, we can see here how there are two different uses of "religion": as belief and as exercise. The majority opinion stated: "The 'exercise of religion' often involves not only belief and profession but the performance of (or abstention from) physical acts: assembling with others for a worship service, participating in sacramental use of bread and wine, proselytizing, abstaining from certain foods or certain modes of transportation." See *Oregon v. Smith*.

some emergency or grave danger.[26] Thus, the state of Oregon revised its law concerning peyote use.[27]

The action taken by Congress also caused disagreement, for the general right to religious freedom does not protect the religious use of a banned hallucinogenic drug when that use threatens general damage to the community.[28] Thus, even though the Court's majority opinion may not have proceeded according to the best analytical framework in order to conclude so, it was nevertheless right as a matter of morality, and Congress wrong, for, according to Dworkin, "religions may be forced to restrict their practices so as to obey rational, nondiscriminatory laws that do not display less than equal concern for them."[29]

If religious freedom is understood as the exercise of religious virtue on a protected stage or sphere, then matters would be easier to identify. Acts that are considered to be religiously doubtful would have to pass the "virtue" test in order to require an exemption. Since virtue implies acting according to reason, which is common to all human beings, what religious freedom entails should be something on which reasonable people of goodwill across the religious and political spectrums should agree on.

Religious Freedom and Public Spaces

I have argued above that the case brought to the Supreme Court by the Little Sisters of the Poor and others is properly a case of freedom of conscience, rather than of religious freedom. It is their faith that prevents them from providing services which they consider immoral. They can still pray, be devout, attend and hold their own religious ceremonies. However, there is truth in their insistence not to separate their work with the elderly from

---

26. See U.S. Senate and House of Representatives, "Religious Freedom Restoration Act."

27. On the revised Oregon law on religious use of peyote, see *Ore. Rev. Stat.* § 475.752 (4) (2016). It states: "In any prosecution under this section for manufacture, possession or delivery of that plant of the genus Lophophora commonly known as peyote, it is an affirmative defense that the peyote is being used or is intended for use: (a) In connection with the good faith practice of a religious belief; (b) As directly associated with religiously done practices; and (c) In a manner that is not dangerous to the health of the user or others who are in the proximity of the user."

28. Many commentators have called the Religious Freedom Restoration Act of 1993 perhaps the most unconstitutional statute in the history of the United States. See, for example, Dworkin, *Religion without God*, 125–26, 34–36; Eisgruber and Sager, "Unconstitutional," 437; Magarian, "Religious Freedom"; Graglia, "Boerne v. Flores," 675; Gressman, "RFRA."

29. Dworkin, *Religion without God*, 136.

faith and what they understand to be religious. The same can be said regarding the many instances in which Catholic adoption agencies have had to close their doors due to regulations that mandate that they could not discriminate in assigning children only to heterosexual couples, or cases in which these agencies stopped receiving government funds due to this policy. The representatives of these agencies have argued that, because their member's faith forbids same-sex unions, the government's policy discriminates against them on religious grounds, and that therefore their religious freedom is being infringed. The government has replied that an exemption from its rules for these Catholic agencies would discriminate in their favor against other agencies that might have their own reasons, not grounded on faith, for refusing adoption to same-sex couples.

Thomas Aquinas argues, in his S. Th. II–II, q. 94, a. 1, ad 1, that religion as a virtue is taken as an outward expression of faith, for it is motivated by true faith,[30] and in S. Th. II–II, q. 81, a. 5, ad 1, he goes even further, and states that the theological virtues of faith, hope, and charity cause the act of religion by their command, since these virtues have God as their proper object. Thus, since religion performs certain deeds directed to God, religion may be commanded by these higher virtues. The principle at play here is the same one by which the virtue of religion may command the acts of all other virtues directing them to the honor of God: "The power or virtue whose action deals with an end, moves by its command the power or virtue whose action deals with matters directed to that end."[31] Thus, one may argue that it would be a violation of religious freedom were the government, through certain restrictive laws, to not allow religious organizations and their members to carry on the kind of work and the acts of virtue (such as works of mercy or education) which they consider as being commanded by the virtue of religion, and which has a direct impact on citizens or on the public square itself. The government would make a grave mistake if it were to exempt religious institutions regarding a coercive mandate only within the boundaries of religious acts. The reason for this is that there are other fields in which the members of religious institutions operate, even when these works and acts of virtue are not acts of the virtue of religion itself. As already mentioned, these actions are indeed potentially commanded by the virtue of religion, and therefore, individuals would be prevented from attaining this virtue in its fullness were they restricted or prevented from acting under the guidance of faith and the command of the virtue of religion.

---

30. Aquinas, S. Th., II–II, q. 94, a. 1, ad 1. See: "Religion is not faith, but a manifestation of faith through exterior signs."

31. See Aquinas, S. Th., II–II, q. 81, a. 5, ad 1.

It is interesting to note, as well, that religion as a virtue, for Aquinas, is commanded not just by faith, but also by hope and charity. There is a contemporary secular fixation on centering the debate on issues of faith, when the fact is that religion is also motivated by hope and charity!

As seen above, one of the ways in which religion is present in the public square and enjoys public relevance is by commanding the acts of other virtues that have a public character. Neuhaus denounced and challenged the naked public square, where "religion" had no place in it, for it belonged inside the four walls of a house of worship. For Neuhaus, it is wrong to see religion as a merely private affair with no public relevance. Yet, since Neuhaus did not offer a clear understanding of what he meant by religion, his solution did not have the tools to distinguish the different aspects of the debate and foresee a feasible solution. Thus, this new understanding of religious freedom, in which religion is taken as a virtue, will offer a better guideline to situations in which the place of "religion" is being challenged in the public square. At the same time, the notion of the "public square" is a notion that changes over time. In short, the public square is a place of meeting, and history has seen many kinds of meeting places: the Greek Council of Areopagus, the Roman Forum, the cathedrals in the Middle Ages, the plazas at the heart of Spanish towns, parks, legislative halls and courthouses, zoning boards and city council meetings, schools and sports facilities, and so many other physical spaces that may also be considered part of the public square. The public square is not a monolithic reality, but a place that symbolizes the free encounter of peoples and ideas that is at the heart of civil society. Thus, it is the space in which people gather together as citizens and members of society, leaving for a moment the privacy of their homes, to discuss matters that affect the inhabitants of a town, nation, or even the world. It is an ever-changing reality, so that issues of public importance are discussed nowadays even via the Internet, through websites, blogs, and social media, in addition to the older means of television and radio. No one will deny that each of these methods of communication has impacted the political arena.

Any discussion on the place of religion in the public square should be aware that the notion of "religion" as a political and theological category is a confusing and unclear notion, which ought to be dropped in favor of more distinct realities, such as belief systems, issues of conscience, cultural symbols, cultural garments, and virtue.[32] This will help clarify what it is that one is talking about in these debates, for most discussions on "religion" in the public

---

32. As an example of the struggle to identify whether the issue of religious garments belongs to religious freedom or equality, and the understanding of religious attire as an expression of "religion," see Vickers, "Religious Freedom."

square deal with a host of different issues that properly do not have to do with "religion" itself. Discussions, for example, are centered on issues such as "religious discourse" in politics, or the view that faith should or should not shape the different aspects of society, politics, and the ways we live and interact with one another, or issues related to the display of religious symbols in the public square, such as the presence of a crucifix in public lands, courthouses or schools, or the wearing of crosses, veils, head covers, and other religious garments, or government funding of faith-based organizations, or the regulation and coercive laws regarding institutions that are devoted to works of mercy (such as the Supreme Court case regarding the Little Sisters of the Poor) or education (as when ministries of education mandate that certain issues be taught in religious schools in violation of the believer's conscience). If proper distinctions were made, it would be easier to discern where the discussion of these issues properly belongs to.

In the United States, in 2003, there was a prominent case involving Judge Roy Moore from Alabama, who refused to obey official court orders to remove a monument of the Ten Commandments from the front of the Alabama courthouse. This order had followed the lawsuit actions by the ACLU of Alabama and the Americans United for Separation of Church and State, who argued that the monument amounted to an official state endorsement of "religion." Moore countered that, instead, the monument honored the Ten Commandments as the moral foundation of Western law.[33] The action taken by the ACLU is clearly an example of a debate misguided by an unclear concept of "religion."[34] According to the ACLU's understanding of religion, it includes a moral code, such as the Ten Commandments, and probably a belief system as well, for it was argued that by displaying the monument the state endorsed "religion." Thus, one may argue against this that a monument like that does not have anything to do with the place of "religion" in the public square. The placement of the monument may be challenged by the ACLU, but under different terms. The same can be said regarding the disputes over seasonal religious displays. Each year as the winter holidays approach, Americans across the country debate the

33. Cf. Broadway, "Decalogue Displays." The Ten Commandments controversy set off a wave of similar disputes across the United States. In February of 2004, the City Council voted that the Ten Commandments monument in Plattsmouth, Nebraska, must be torn down. The following month, a City Council in Minnesota arrived at the same verdict. In April of 2004 the city of Redlands, California, agreed to remove a cross from its official seal due to pressure from the ACLU.

34. In a more coherent verdict, a court ruled on June of 2003 that a Ten Commandments plaque that had been hanging for eighty-three years on the facade of the Chester County, Pennsylvania, courthouse did not constitute an official endorsement of religion, and therefore, it may remain there for the sake of historical preservation.

appropriateness of the government sponsoring, or even permitting, the display of Christmas nativity scenes, Hanukkah menorahs, and other religious holiday symbols on public property. The debate centers once again on the state's promotion of "religion," and the presence of "religion" in the public square.[35] A defined and clear notion of religion as virtue would avoid the confusion created along these issues, and would offer a more efficient tool to those who defend the display of religious symbols in public grounds, as well as to those who oppose them. In any debate, great progress is made when both parties are able to clearly articulate the issues at play. Without this, the debate will never move forward.

The Future of Religious Freedom

To conclude this book, I will point out a few items in relation to where we should go next in terms of philosophical research, for there is still a lot to be done.

The solution to the debate on religious freedom and the place of religion in the public square provided in this work is centered on a new understanding of "religion" as virtue. However, since it is individual persons that are the agents of virtue, and can be qualified as virtuous, there is still work to be done with respect to those businesses organized as corporations which claim are touched with a religious character. One could argue, for example, that a corporation is an association of free persons, and that for many legal purposes a corporation has the standing of a person.[36] Yet, it is always individuals that perform acts of virtues, so that even when a religious institution claims it does a lot of good works for the poor, it is always the members of such institutions in their day-to-day dedication that bring these good acts to completion.

From a legal-philosophical perspective, a new perspective should be taken regarding the notion of "religion" employed in legal documents, constitutions, amendments, and international documents. In chapter 2, we noted how legal definitions of religious freedom seem to fail to present a coherent notion of what is meant by "religion." One side of the debate, in fact, argues that "religion" cannot be reduced to a body of "beliefs" with no claims to truth, while the other side argues that no claim is to be taken seriously by anyone who does not share those beliefs. However, as we have argued in this book, religion has to do not with beliefs, or opinions, or truths, but rather with virtue. Thus, it is imperative to review all legal documents

---

35. One may probably speak of cultural issues instead.
36. Cf. Arkes, "Recasting Religious Freedom," 45.

that deal with "religion," and redefine the terms employed, for an unclear understanding of what is meant by the notion of religion will only help perpetuate the confusion, and, what is worse, not be of service when it comes to resolving real issues and administering justice.

This consideration of the civil right to religious freedom, where religion is understood as a virtue, has opened the door to a consideration of human rights from the aspect of virtue. This is something that should be explored and applied to different areas that traditionally have been protected as rights, such as justice, marriage, family, and education. One can argue that, since it is through works of virtue that man flourishes and finds his own fulfillment, virtues act as guiding principles in what should be offered protection as truly belonging to our human nature. Virtue will offer a guide, then, in what should or should not be considered a human right. Another advantage that a systematic treatment of virtues as foundation for human rights would offer is that it would avoid the criticism made by skeptics of human rights that there have been no real grounds for speaking of rights in a way that is independent of the contingent conjunction of political expediency and institutional convenience.[37]

There is also the question on God and the possibility of opening a public debate on the existence and nature of God from a philosophical perspective.[38] From all the public discussions that can take place around religion as virtue, the problem of God is, for Aquinas, central to the debate. The reason is that Aquinas argues that the more a person possesses a proper understanding of God, and acts accordingly, the greater his ability to practice the virtue of religion in a more adequate way. For to Aquinas, man is totally and absolutely dependent on God,[39] and this is what demands the virtue of religion in man.[40] It is this orientation to God, then, that is the mark of the virtue of religion, and since the virtue of religion has such an important impact on the public life of citizens, it seems that it is not out of place to open a public debate about the knowledge of the true God.[41]

37. Cf. Bhuta, "Concepts of Religious Freedom," 10; Geuss, *History and Illusion*, 149.

38. Tony Blair has in fact advocated for a political debate that includes a serious discussion on religion based on mutual dialogue on all parts involved: religious, secular, and political people. See Blair, "Protecting Religious Freedom should be a Priority for All Democracies," 7.

39. Cf. Aquinas, *SCG*, bk. 3, ch. 119.

40. Thomas also states that "man is not ordained to the body politic, according to all that he is and has; and so it does not follow that every action of his acquires merit or demerit in relation to the body politic. But all that man is, and can, and has, must be referred to God." In Aquinas, *S. Th.*, I–II, q. 21, a. 4, ad 3.

41. Joseph Ratzinger states: "In any question concerning man and the world, the

The reason why we can explore the philosophical possibility regarding a public debate on God within the public realm is that, according to Lawrence Dewan, all men have access to a natural knowledge of God. He in fact talks about a spontaneous knowledge of God.[42] Thomas acknowledges that there is certain knowledge of God had by almost all, which is the result of a natural, instantaneous reasoning process.[43] The common man might not be conscious of the number of distinct steps that are actually involved in the reasoning, for it seems like the simple vision of a total situation. It will be the work of the metaphysician to show the number and nature of the intermediate steps, which certify the conclusions of the reasoning process.[44] Therefore, it will be important to explore how, for Aquinas, the existence of God is naturally known to all. Needless to say, this kind of knowledge is according to man's rational nature, and therefore, the existence of God is a conclusion naturally reasoned to, so that if anyone denies the existence of God, it stems from a moral disorder. It is this natural knowledge, the product of a spontaneous natural inference, that allows us to suggest a public debate about knowledge of the true God, which will have consequences on the way we see the virtue of religion, and the guidelines to be followed in issues related to religious freedom.

Finally, I invite all those working on issues related to religious freedom and the place of religion in the public square to review the perspective from where they have been debating, and question the terminology employed in the debates, especially the meaning of "religion." What I propose here is that once religion is understood as a virtue, it is easier to see its relationship to freedom, the public square, and questions of faith and conscience.

It is my hope that by now it will be clear that a redefinition of the concepts used in debates regarding religious freedom and the place of religion in the public square is necessary. This new approach, however, is meant not to subvert a fixed position, but rather it is offered as carrying forward new developments that will allow us to overcome the impasse into which contemporary discussions have been sidetracked.

---

question about the Divinity is always included as the preliminary and really basic question. No one can understand the world at all, no one can live his life rightly, so long as the question about the Divinity remains unanswered. Indeed, the very heart of the great cultures is that they interpret the world by setting in order their relationship to the Divinity." See Ratzinger, *Truth and Tolerance*, 61.

42. Cf. Dewan, "Moral Order," 206–12.

43. See, for example, the text quoted above from Aquinas, *S. Th.*, I, q. 2, a. 1, ad 1. Thomas does admit that in our natural knowledge of beatitude as the end of life there is included a sort of knowledge of God as himself beatitude. According to Dewan, this is a sort of innate knowledge that God exists. Cf. Dewan, "Moral Order," 126–27.

44. As an example, see Aquinas, *SCG*, bk. 3, ch. 38.

Bibliography

Agamben, Giorgio. *Il Sacramento del Linguaggio: Archeologia del Giuramento*. Roma: Laterza, 2008.

Ahdar, Rex, and Ian Leigh. "Is Establishment Consistent with Religious Freedom?" *MLJ* 49 (2003–2004) 635–82.

———. *Religious Freedom in the Liberal State*. 2nd ed. Oxford: Oxford University Press, 2005.

Allen, Prudence. "Where Is Our Conscience? Aquinas and Modern and Contemporary Philosophers." *IPQ* 44:3 (2004) 335–72.

Anderson, Ryan T. "The Continuing Threat to Religious Liberty." *National Review*, August 3, 2017. https://www.nationalreview.com/2017/08/religious-liberty-under-attack/.

———. *Truth Overruled: The Future of Marriage and Religious Freedom*. Washington, DC: Regnery, 2015.

André–Vincent, Philippe I. *La Liberté Religieuse: Droit Fondamental*. Paris: Téqui, 1976.

Aquinas, Thomas. *Contra Doctrinam Retrahentium a Religione*. Leonine edition 41C. Rome: Ad Sanctae Sabinae, 1969.

———. *Contra Impugnantes Dei Cultum et Religionem*. Leonine edition 41A. Rome: Ad Sanctae Sabinae, 1970.

———. *De Regno ad Regem Cypri*. Leonine edition vol. 42. Rome: Editori di San Tommaso, 1979.

———. *In Octo Libros Politicorum Aristotelis Expositio*. Rome: Marietti, 1966.

———. *In Psalmos*. Stuttgart–Bad Cannstadt: Frommann–Hoolzbog, 1980.

———. *Quaestiones de Quodlibet* (qq. 7–11). Leonine edition 25, 1. Paris: Cerf, 1996.

———. "Quaestiones Disputatae de Virtutibus in Communi." In *Quaestiones Disputatae*, edited by E. Odetto. Rome: Marietti, 1965.

———. *Scriptum super Libros Sententiarum Magistri Petri Lombardi*. 4 vols. Paris: Lethielleux, 1929.

———. *Summa Contra Gentiles*. Rome: Herder, 1934.

———. *Summa Theologiae*. Leonine edition 4–12. Rome: Propaganda Fide, 1882–1906.

———. *Super Boetium de Trinitate*. Leonine edition 50. Paris: Cerf, 1992.

———. *Super Epistolam ad Ephesios Lectura*. Rome: Marietti, 1953.

———. *Super Epistolam ad Titum Lectura*. Rome: Marietti, 1953.

———. *Super Evangelium S. Ioannis Lectura*. Rome: Marietti, 1972.

———. *Super Primam Epistolam ad Corinthios Lectura*. Rome: Marietti, 1953.
———. *Super Primam Epistolam ad Thessalonicenses Lectura*. Rome: Marietti, 1953.
Arendt, Hannah. *Between Past and Future: Eight Exercises in Political Thought*. New York: Penguin, 2006.
———. *Eichmann in Jerusalem: A Report on the Banality of Evil*. New York: Penguin, 2006.
———. "Freedom and Politics." In *Freedom and Serfdom*, edited by A. Hunold, 191–217. Dordrecht: Riedel, 1961.
———. "Freedom and Politics: A Lecture." *CR* 14:1 (1960) 28–46.
———. *The Human Condition*. Chicago: University of Chicago Press, 1958.
———. *The Life of the Mind*. Vol. 2. Willing, NY: Harcourt, 1978.
———. *Men in Dark Times*. New York: Harcourt, 1968.
———. "On Hannah Arendt." In *Hannah Arendt: The Recovery of the Public World*, edited by M. A. Hill, 301–39. New York: St. Martin's, 1979.
———. *On Revolution*. New York: Viking, 1963.
———. "Reflections on Little Rock." *Dissent* (1959) 45–56.
———. "Truth and Politics." In *Between Past and Future: Eight Exercises in Political Thought*. New York: Penguin, 2006.
———. "What Is Existential Philosophy?" In *Essays in Understanding: 1930–1954*, edited by Jerome Kohn, 163–87. New York: Harcourt, 1994.
———. "What Is Freedom?" In *Between Past and Future*, 143–71. New York: Penguin, 1961.
Arendt, Hannah, and Ronald Beiner. *Lectures on Kant's Political Philosophy*. Brighton: Harvester, 1982.
Aristotle. *Metaphysics*. Books 1–9. Translated by Hugh Tredennick. Cambridge, MA: Harvard University Press, 1989.
———. *The Nicomachean Ethics*. Translated by H. Rackham. Cambridge, MA: Harvard University Press, 1982.
———. *Politics*. Translated by H. Rackham. Cambridge, MA: Harvard University Press, 1998.
———. *Posterior Analytics*. Translated by Hugh Tredennick. Cambridge, MA: Harvard University Press, 1966.
Arkes, Hadley. "Recasting Religious Freedom." *FT*, June–July 2014, 45–51.
Asad, Talal. "Reading a Modern Classic: W. C. Smith's 'The Meaning and End of Religion.'" *HR* 40:3 (2001) 205–22.
Balagangadhara, S. N. *"The Heathen in His Blindness . . .": Asia, the West, and the Dynamic of Religion*. Leiden: Brill, 1994.
Barnett, Laura. *Freedom of Religion and Religious Symbols in the Public Sphere*. Ottawa: Parliamentary Information, 2013.
Barret-Kriegel, Blandine. *Les Droits de L'homme et le Droit Naturel*. Paris: Presses Universitaires France, 1986.
Baubérot, Jean. "The Place of Religion in Public Life: The Lay Approach." In *Facilitating Freedom of Religion or Belief*, edited by W. Cole Durham et al., 441–53. Leiden: Nijhoff, 2004.
Beaman, Lori G. "Is Religious Freedom Impossible in Canada?" *LCH* 8:2 (2012) 266–84.
———. "'It Was All Slightly Unreal': What's Wrong with Tolerance and Accommodation in the Adjudication of Religious Freedom?" *CJWL* 23:2 (2011) 442–63.

Beek, A. van de, et al. *Freedom of Religion*. Leiden: Brill, 2010.
Beiner, Ronald. *Civil Religion: A Dialogue in the History of Political Philosophy*. Cambridge: Cambridge University Press, 2011.
Bellah, Robert N. "Civil Religion in America." In *American Civil Religion*, edited by Donald E. Jones and Russell E. Richey, 21–44. San Francisco: Mellen Research University Press, 1990.
Benhabib, Seyla. "Models of Public Space: Hannah Arendt, the Liberal Tradition and Jürgen Habermas." In *Habermas and the Public Sphere*, edited by Craig Calhoun, 73–98. Cambridge, MA: MIT Press, 1992.
Benson, Iain T. "The Freedom of Conscience and Religion in Canada: Challenges and Opportunities." *EILR* 21 (2007) 111–66.
———. "Notes towards a (Re)Definition of the Secular." *UBCLR* 33 (1999–2000) 519–50.
Benveniste, Émile. "L'expression du Serment dans la Grèce Ancienne." *RHR* (1948) 81–94.
Berger, Adolf. *Encyclopedic Dictionary of Roman Law*. Philadelphia: American Philosophical Society, 1953.
Berger, Benjamin L. "Law's Religion: Rendering Culture." *OHJL* 45:2 (2007) 277–314.
Berger, Peter L. *The Desecularization of the World*. Washington, DC: Ethics and Public Policy Centre, 1999.
Berman, Harold J. "Religious Freedom and the Challenge of the Modern State." *ELJ* 39 (1990) 149–64. Also published in *Articles of Faith, Articles of Peace: The Religious Liberty Clauses and the American Public Philosophy*, edited by J. D. Hunter and O. Guinness, 40–53. Washington, DC: Brookings Institution, 1990.
Bernstein, J. M. "Forgetting Isaac: Faith and the Philosophical Impossibility of a Postsecular Society." In *Habermas and Religion*, edited by Craig J. Calhoun et al., 154–75. Cambridge: Polity, 2013.
Beuchot, Mauricio. *Derechos Humanos: Historia y Filosofía*. México, D.F.: Fontamara, 1999.
———. *Los Derechos Humanos y su Fundamentación Filosófica*. Guadalajara: Universidad Iberoamericana, 1997.
———. *Filosofía y Derechos Humanos*. Mexico, D.F.: Siglo XXI, 1993.
Beyer, Peter. "Defining Religion in Cross-National Perspective: Identity and Difference in Official Conceptions." In *Defining Religion: Investigating the Boundaries between the Sacred and the Secular*, edited by Arthur L. Greil and David G. Bromley, 163–88. Oxford: JAI, 2003.
Bhuta, Nehal. "Two Concepts of Religious Freedom in the European Court of Human Rights." *SAQ* 113:1 (December 21, 2014) 9–35.
Bienert, Walther. *Martin Luther und die Juden*. Frankfurt: Evangelisches Verlagswerk, 1982.
Blackford, Russell. *Freedom of Religion and the Secular State*. Hoboken, NJ: Wiley-Blackwell, 2011.
Blair, Tony. "Protecting Religious Freedom Should Be a Priority for All Democracies." *RFIA* 10:3 (2012) 5–9.
Blake, Nathanael. "Cakes and Consciences: The Case of Jack Phillips and Masterpiece Cakeshop." *PD*, 2017. http://www.thepublicdiscourse.com/2017/07/19699/.

Böckenförde, Ernst-Wolfgang. "The Rise of the State as a Process of Secularisation." In *State, Society, and Liberty: Studies in Political Theory and Constitutional Law*, 26–48. Oxford: Berg, 1991.

Bohman, James. "A Postsecular Global Order? The Pluralism of Forms of Life and Communicative Freedom." In *Habermas and Religion*, edited by Craig J. Calhoun et al., 179–202. Cambridge: Polity, 2013.

Bossy, John. *Christianity in the West, 1400–1700*. Oxford: Oxford University Press, 1985.

———. "Some Elementary Forms of Durkheim." *PP* 95 (1982) 3–18.

Bourdin, Ceslas Bernard. "Religious Freedom and the Separation of Church and State: A Lesson from Post-Revolutionary France." In *Philosophical Psychology*, edited by Craig Steven Titus, 108–49. Arlington, VA: IPS, 2009.

Bouwsma, William J. *Concordia Mundi: The Career and Thought of Guillaume Postel, 1510–1581*. Cambridge, MA: Harvard University Press, 1957.

Bradley, Gerard V. "The Judicial Experiment with Privatizing Religion." *LLR* 1:1 (2006) 17–35.

———. "The Public Square: Naked No More?" In *The Naked Public Square Reconsidered*, edited by Christopher Wolfe, 1–31. Wilmington, DE: ISI, 2009.

Bradley Lewis, V. "Natural Right and the Problem of Public Reason." In *Natural Moral Law in Contemporary Society*, edited by Holger Zaborowski, 195–234. Washington, DC: CUA Press, 2010.

Bremmer, Jan N. *Greek Religion*. Oxford: Oxford University Press, 1994.

Brennan, Shauna, James Gillespie, Daniel Mascaro, and Howard Mulligan. "Constitutional Law: Establishment Clause Scrutiny of a Nativity Scene Display." *NDLR* 62:1 (December 1986) 114.

Bretherton, Luke. *Christianity and Contemporary Politics: The Conditions and Possibilities of Faithful Witness*. Malden, MA: Wiley-Blackwell, 2010.

Bridges, Thomas. *The Culture of Citizenship: Inventing Postmodern Civic Culture*. Albany: SUNY Press, 1994.

Broadway, Bill. "A New Judgment Day for Decalogue Displays." *Washington Post*, October 23, 2004, B09.

Brook, Angus. "Faith: The Basis of Justice." *HJ* 56:3 (2015) 361–72.

Brown, Wendy, and Rainer Forst. *The Power of Tolerance: A Debate*. New York: Columbia University Press, 2014.

Buckingham, Janet Epp. *Fighting over God: A Legal and Political History of Religious Freedom in Canada*. Montréal and Kingston: McGill-Queen's University Press, 2014.

Budziszewski, J. *Companion to the Commentary*. New York: Cambridge University Press, 2014.

Button, Mark. "Arendt, Rawls, and Public Reason." *STP* 31:2 (2005) 257–80.

Calhoun, Craig J. "Rethinking Secularism." *HR* 12 (2010) 35–48.

Calhoun, Craig J., et al. *Rethinking Secularism*. New York: Oxford University Press, 2011.

Calhoun, Craig J., Eduardo Mendieta, and Jonathan VanAntwerpen, editors. *Habermas and Religion*. Cambridge: Polity, 2013.

Campillo, Antonio. "Animal Político. Aristóteles, Arendt y Nosotros." *RF* 39:2 (2013) 169–88.

Canovan, Margaret. *Hannah Arendt: A Reinterpretation of Her Political Thought*. Cambridge: Cambridge University Press, 1992.

Caruso, Anthony J. "Hubris and the HHS Mandate." *LQ* 81:3 (2014) 204–8.
Casanova, José. "Exploring the Postsecular: Three Meanings of the Secular and Their Possible Transcendence." In *Habermas and Religion*, edited by Craig J. Calhoun et al., 27–48. Cambridge: Polity, 2013.
———. "Immigration and the New Religious Pluralism." In *Democracy and the New Religious Pluralism*, edited by Thomas F. Banchoff, 59–84. Oxford: Oxford University Press, 2007.
———. *Public Religions in the Modern World*. Chicago: University of Chicago Press, 1994.
———. "Rethinking Secularization: A Global Comparative Perspective." *HR* 8 (2006) 7–22.
———. "The Secular, Secularizations, Secularisms." In *Rethinking Secularism*, edited by Craig J. Calhoun et al., 54–74. New York: Oxford University Press, 2011.
Cavanaugh, William T. "A Fire Strong Enough to Consume the House: The Wars of Religion and the Rise of the State." *Modern Theology* 11:4 (1995) 397–420.
———. *The Myth of Religious Violence: Secular Ideology and the Roots of Modern Conflict*. Oxford: Oxford University Press, 2009.
———. "Religious Violence as Modern Myth." *PT* 15:6 (2014) 486–502.
Chaput, Charles J. *Render unto Caesar*. New York: Doubleday, 2008.
Chidester, David. "Colonialism." In *Guide to the Study of Religion*, edited by Willi Braun and Russell T. McCutcheon, 423–37. London: Cassell, 2000.
———. *Empire of Religion: Imperialism and Comparative Religion*. Chicago: University of Chicago Press, 2014.
Cicero, Marcus Tullius. *De Natura Deorum*. Translated by H. Rackham. Cambridge: Harvard University Press, 1933.
———. *De Officiis*. Translated by Walter Miller. Cambridge, MA: Harvard University Press, 1913.
———. *De Oratore*. Translated by H. Rackham. Cambridge, MA: Harvard University Press, 1948.
———. *On Moral Ends*. Translated by Raphael Woolf. Cambridge: Cambridge University Press, 2001.
Claflin, Charlotte Isabel. "The Inscription of Dvenos." *CP* 22:4 (1927) 418–20.
Cohen, Richard S. *Beyond Enlightenment: Buddhism, Religion, Modernity*. New York: Routledge, 2006.
———. "Why Study Indian Buddhism?" In *The Invention of Religion: Rethinking Belief in Politics and History*, edited by Derek R. Peterson and Darren R. Walhof, 19–36. New Brunswick, NJ: Rutgers University Press, 2002.
Colliard, Claude Albert. *La Déclaration des Droits de L'homme et du Citoyen de 1789, ses Origines-sa Pérennité*. Paris: Documentation Française, 1990.
Council of Europe. *European Convention for the Protection of Human Rights and Fundamental Freedoms*. Amended ed. Strasbourg: European Court of Human Rights, 2010.
Cristi, Marcela. *From Civil to Political Religion: The Intersection of Culture, Religion and Politics*. Waterloo, ON: Wilfrid Laurier University Press, 2001.
Cusa, Nicolas de. "De Pace Fidei." Translated by John P. Dolan. In *Unity and Reform: Selected Writings of Nicholas de Cusa*, edited by John P. Dolan. Notre Dame, IN: University of Notre Dame Press, 1962.

Dandekar, R. N. "Hinduism." In *Historia Religionum: Handbook for the History of Religions*, edited by E. Jouco Bleeker and Geo Widengren, 237–345. Leiden: Brill, 1969.
Deman, Thomas. "La Prudence." In *Saint Thomas D'Aquin. Somme Théologique: La Prudence*, edited by Thomas Deman, 247–373. Paris: Descleé, 1949.
Derrida, Jacques, and Gianni Vattimo. *La Religion*. Paris: Seuil, 1996.
Dewan, Lawrence. *Form and Being: Studies in Thomistic Metaphysics*. Washington, DC: CUA Press, 2006.
———. "The Foundations of Human Rights." *SE* 62:2–3 (2010) 227–36.
———. "Jacques Maritain, St. Thomas, and the Philosophy of Religion." In *Wisdom, Law, and Virtue*, 349–58. New York: Fordham University Press, 2008.
———. "Philosophy and Spirituality: Cultivating a Virtue." In *Wisdom, Law, and Virtue*, 358–64. New York: Fordham University Press, 2008.
———. "St. Thomas and the Divinity of the Common Good." In *Ressourcement Thomism: Sacred Doctrine, the Sacraments, and the Moral Life*, edited by Reinhard Hütter and Matthew Levering, 211–33. Washington, DC: CUA Press, 2010.
———. "St. Thomas and the Ontology of Prayer." In *Wisdom, Law, and Virtue*, 365–73. New York: Fordham University Press, 2008.
———. "St. Thomas, John Finnis, and the Political Good." In *Wisdom, Law, and Virtue*, 279–311. New York: Fordham University Press, 2008.
———. "St. Thomas, Our Natural Lights, and the Moral Order." In *Wisdom, Law, and Virtue*, 199–212. New York: Fordham University Press, 2008.
———. "Wisdom and Human Life: The Natural and the Supernatural." In *Wisdom, Law, and Virtue*, 7–31. New York: Fordham University Press, 2008.
Dreisbach, Daniel L. *Thomas Jefferson and the Wall of Separation between Church and State*. New York: New York University Press, 2002.
Dubuisson, Daniel. *The Western Construction of Religion: Myths, Knowledge, and Ideology*. Baltimore, MD: Johns Hopkins University Press, 2003.
Dulles, Avery Cardinal. "John Paul II on Religious Freedom: Themes from Vatican II." *The Thomist* 65:2 (2001) 161–78.
Dumézil, G. *Idées Romaines*. Paris: Gallimard, 1969.
Durham, et al. *Facilitating Freedom of Religion or Belief*. Leiden: Nijhoff, 2004.
Durham, et al. "Definition of Religion." In *Religious Organizations in the United States*, edited by W. Cole Durham and James A. Serritella, 3–32. Durham: Carolina Academic Press, 2006.
Durkheim, Émile. *The Elementary Forms of Religious Life*. Translated by Carol Cosman. Oxford: Oxford University Press, 2001.
Dworkin, Ronald. *Freedom's Law: The Moral Reading of the American Constitution*. Cambridge, MA: Harvard University Press, 1996.
———. *Religion without God*. Cambridge, Massachusetts: Harvard University Press, 2013.
Edwards, Paul, editor. *The Encyclopedia of Philosophy*. 8 vols. New York: Macmillan, 1967.
Ehler, Sidney Z., and John B. Morrall, editors. *Church and State through the Centuries: A Collection of Historic Documents with Commentaries*. New York: Biblo and Tannen, 1988.
Eisgruber, Christopher L., and Lawrence G. Sager. "Why the Religious Freedom Restoration Act Is Unconstitutional." *NULR* 69:3 (1994) 437–60.

Engel, Christoph. "Law as a Precondition for Religious Freedom." In *Universal Rights in a World of Diversity*, edited by Mary Ann Glendon and Hans Zacher, 393–412. Vatican City: Pontifical Academy of Social Sciences, 2012.
Erasmus, Desiderius. *The Manual of the Christian Knight*. London: Methuen, 1905.
Evans, Malcolm D. "Historical Analysis of Freedom of Religion or Belief as a Technique for Resolving Religious Conflict." In *Facilitating Freedom of Religion or Belief*, edited by W. Cole Durham et al., 1–17. Leiden: Nijhoff, 2004.
———. *Religious Liberty and International Law in Europe*. New York: Cambridge University Press, 1997.
Falkeid, Unn. *The Avignon Papacy Contested: An Intellectual History from Dante to Catherine of Siena*. Cambridge, MA: Harvard University Press, 2017.
Feuerbach, Ludwig. *Vorlesungen über das Wesen der Religion, nebst Zusätzen und Anmerkungen*. Berlin: Akademie-Verlag, 1967.
Finnis, John. "Aquinas on Ius and Hart on Rights: A Response to Tierney." *RP* 64:3 (2002) 407–10.
———. *Natural Law and Natural Rights*. 5th ed. Oxford: Clarendon, 1988.
———. "Telling the Truth about God and Man in a Pluralist Society: Economy or Explication?" In *The Naked Public Square Reconsidered*, edited by Christopher Wolfe, 111–25. Wilmington, DE: ISI, 2009.
Fitzgerald, Timothy. *The Ideology of Religious Studies*. New York: Oxford University Press, 2000.
———. "A Response to Saler, Benavides, and Korom." *RSR* 27:2 (2001).
Forst, Rainer. *Justification and Critique: Towards a Critical Theory of Politics*. Cambridge: Polity, 2014.
———. *Toleranz im Konflikt*. Frankfurt: Suhrkamp, 2003. English translation: *Toleration in Conflict: Past and Present*. Translated by Ciaran Cronin. Cambridge: Cambridge University Press, 2013.
Fortin, Ernest L. "The New Rights Theory and the Natural Law." *RP* 44:4 (1982) 590–612.
———. "On the Presumed Medieval Origin of Individual Rights." In *Final Causality in Nature and Human Affairs*, edited by Richard F. Hassing, 86–106. Washington, DC: CUA Press, 1997.
Gaius. *Gai Institutiones*. Oxford: Clarendon, 1904.
Galston, William A. "Religious Pluralism and the Limits of Public Reason." In *The Naked Public Square Reconsidered*, edited by Christopher Wolfe, 151–64. Wilmington, DE: ISI, 2009.
Gamwell, Franklin I. *The Meaning of Religious Freedom: Modern Politics and the Democratic Resolution*. Albany, NY: SUNY Press, 1995.
García López, Jesús. *Los Derechos Humanos en Santo Tomás de aquí*. Pamplona: Universidad de Navarra, 1979.
Garnsey, Peter. "Religious Toleration in Classical Antiquity." In *Persecution and Toleration*, edited by W. J. Sheils, 1–28. Oxford: Blackwell, 1984.
Gauchet, Marcel. *La Révolution des Droits de L'homme*. Paris: Gallimard, 1989.
Gaylord, Scott W. "For-Profit Corporations, Free Exercise, and the HHS Mandate." *Washington University Law Review* 91 (2013) 589–658.
Geertz, Clifford. *The Interpretation of Cultures: Selected Essays*. New York: Basic Books, 1973.

Gentile, Emilio. *Politics as Religion*. Translated by George Staunton. Princeton, NJ: Princeton University Press, 2006.

———. *The Sacralization of Politics in Fascist Italy*. Cambridge, MA: Harvard University Press, 1996.

George, Robert P. *Conscience and Its Enemies: Confronting the Dogmas of Liberal Secularism*. Wilmington, DE: ISI, 2013.

Geuss, Raymond. *History and Illusion in Politics*. New York: Cambridge University Press, 2001.

———. *Public Goods, Private Goods*. Princeton, NJ: Princeton University Press, 2001.

Glendon, Mary Ann. "The Naked Public Square Today: A Secular Public Square?" In *The Naked Public Square Reconsidered*, edited by Christopher Wolfe. Wilmington, DE: ISI, 2009.

Glotz, G. "Iusirandum." In *Dictionaire des Antiquités Grecques et Romaines*, edited by C. Daremberg and E. Saglio. Paris: Hachette, 1900.

Graglia, Lino A. "City of Boerne v. Flores: An Essay on the Invalidation of the Religious Freedom Restoration Act." *MLJ* 68 (1998).

Gressman, Eugene. "RFRA: A Comedy of Necessary and Proper Errors." *CLR* 21 (1999) 507–38.

Habermas, Jürgen. "Natural Law and Revolution." Translated by J. Viertel. In *Theory and Practice*, 82–120. London: Heinemann, 1974.

———. "The Political: The Rational Meaning of a Questionable Inheritance of Political Theology." In *The Power of Religion in the Public Sphere*, edited by Eduardo Mendieta and Jonathan VanAntwerpen, 15–34. New York: Columbia University Press, 2011.

———. "Popular Sovereignty as Procedure." In *Between Facts and Norms*, 463–90. Cambridge, MA: MIT Press, 1996.

———. "Religion in the Public Sphere." *EJP* 14:1 (2006) 1–25.

———. "Reply to My Critics." Translated by Ciaran Cronin. In *Habermas and Religion*, edited by Craig J. Calhoun et al., 347–90. Cambridge: Polity, 2013.

———. *The Structural Transformation of the Public Sphere: An Inquiry into a Category of Bourgeois Society*. Translated by Thomas Burger and Frederick Lawrence. Cambridge, MA: MIT Press, 1989.

———. *The Theory of Communicative Action*. 2 vols. Boston: Beacon Press, 1984.

———. *Zwischen Naturalismus und Religion: Philosophische Aufsätze*. Frankfurt am Main: Suhrkamp, 2005. English trans.: *Between Naturalism and Religion: Philosophical Essays*. Cambridge: Polity, 2008.

Habermas, Jürgen, and Eduardo Mendieta. "A Postsecular World Society? On the Philosophical Significance of Postsecular Consciousness and the Multicultural World Society an Interview with Jürgen Habermas." *SSRC*, http://blogs.ssrc.org/tif/2010/02/03/a-postsecular-world-society/.

Harrison, Peter. *'Religion' and the Religions in the English Enlightenment*. Cambridge: Cambridge University Press, 1990.

Hegel, Georg Wilhelm Friedrich. *Die Positivität der christlichen Religion*. Frankfurt am Main: Suhrkamp, 1986.

———. *Vorlesungen über die Philosophie der Religion*. Hamburg: F. Meiner, 1993.

Herrera Lima, María. "The Anxiety of Contingency: Religion in a Secular Age." In *Habermas and Religion*, edited by Craig J. Calhoun et al., 49–71. Cambridge: Polity, 2013.

Hertzke, Allen D. *The Future of Religious Freedom: Global Challenges.* New York: Oxford University Press, 2013.
Hesiod. *Theogony.* Translated by M. L. West. Oxford: Clarendon Press, 1997.
Hirzel, R. *Der Eid: Ein Beitrag zur seine Geschichte.* Leipzig: Hirzel, 1902.
Hittinger, Russell. "Dignitatis Humanae, Religious Liberty, and Ecclesiastical Self-Government." *GWLR* 68 (1999–2000) 1035–58.
Honohan, Iseult. "Hannah Arendt's Concept of Freedom." *IPJ* 4:1/2 (1987) 41–62.
Hvithamar, Annika, Margit Warburg, and Brian Arly Jacobsen. *Holy Nations and Global Identities: Civil Religion, Nationalism, and Globalisation.* Leiden: Brill, 2009.
Isomae, Jun'ich. "Deconstructing 'Japanese Religion': A Historical Survey." *JJRS* 32:2 (2005) 235–48.
Jaeger, Werner. *Paideia: The Ideals of Greek Culture.* Translated by Gilbert Highet. 3 vols. 2nd ed. New York: Oxford University Press, 1945.
Jeffries Jr., John, and James Ryan. "A Political History of the Establishment Clause." *MLR* 100 (2001) 279–370.
Jellinek, Georg. *The Declaration of the Rights of Man and of Citizens: A Contribution to Modern Constitutional History.* Translated by M. Farrand. Westport, CT: Hyperion, 1979.
Josephson, Jason. "When Buddhism Became a 'Religion.'" *JJRS* 33:1 (2006) 143–68.
Kamen, Henry. *The Rise of Toleration.* New York: McGraw-Hill, 1967.
Kant, Immanuel. "An Answer to the Question: What Is Enlightenment?" Translated by Mary Gregor. In *Kant, Practical Philosophy,* edited by Mary Gregor, 11–22. Cambridge: Cambridge University Press, 1996.
Kateb, George. *Hannah Arendt: Politics, Conscience, Evil.* Oxford: Robertson, 1984.
Kauper, Paul G. "Legal Aspects of Religious Liberty." In *Religious Liberty,* edited by Cedric W. Tilberg, 23–59. New York: Lutheran Church in America, 1968.
Kozinski, Thaddeus J. *The Political Problem of Religious Pluralism.* Lanham, MD: Lexington, 2010.
Kries, Douglas. "In Defense of Fortin." *Review of Politics* 64:3 (2002) 411–13.
Lafont, Cristina. "Religion and the Public Sphere: What Are the Deliberative Obligations of Democratic Citizenship?" In *Habermas and Religion,* edited by Craig J. Calhoun et al., 230–48. Cambridge: Polity, 2013.
Lara, María Pía. "Is the Postsecular a Return to Political Theology?". In *Habermas and Religion,* edited by Craig J. Calhoun et al., 72–91. Cambridge: Polity, 2013.
Laycock, Douglas, Anthony R. Picarello, and Robin Fretwell Wilson. *Same-Sex Marriage and Religious Liberty: Emerging Conflicts.* Lanham, MD: Rowman & Littlefield, 2008.
Lecler, Joseph. *Toleration and the Reformation.* 2 vols. New York: Association Press, 1960.
Leiter, Brian. *Why Tolerate Religion?* Princeton, NJ: Princeton University Press, 2013.
Lerner, Natan. "The Nature and Minimum Standards of Freedom of Religion or Belief." In *Facilitating Freedom of Religion or Belief,* edited by W. Cole Durham, et al., 63–83. Leiden: Nijhoff, 2004.
Lewin, Eyal. *Comparative Perspectives on Civil Religion, Nationalism, and Political Influence.* Hershey, PA: ISR, 2017.
Lindholm, Tore. "Philosophical and Religious Justifications of Freedom of Religion or Belief." In *Facilitating Freedom of Religion or Belief,* edited by W. Cole Durham, et al., 20–61. Leiden: Nijhoff, 2004.

Lobato, Abelardo. "Lo Sacro y la Religión en Santo Tomás de aquí." *DC* 1:2 (2006) 138–53.
Locke, John. *An Essay concerning Human Understanding*. Oxford: Clarendon, 1979.
———. *A Letter concerning Toleration*. Translated by James Tully. Indianapolis: Hackett, 1983.
Loy, David R. "The Religion of the Market." *JAAR* 65:2 (1997) 275–90.
Lübbe, Hermann. "Religion and Politics in Processes of Modernisation." *TMPR* 6:1 (2005) 53–70.
Luther, Martin. "Before the Diet at Worms (18 April 1521)." In *The World's Famous Orations*, edited by W. J. Bryan. New York: Funk and Wagnalls, 1906.
———. *De Captivitate Babylonica Ecclesiae Praeludium* (1520). Weimar: Hermann Böhlaus Nachfolger, 1914.
Lycurgus. *Minor Attic Orators*. Translated by O. J. Burtt. Vol. 2. Cambridge: Harvard University Press, 1962.
MacDonald, Margaret. "Natural Rights." *PAS* (1946–47) 40–60.
Macedo, Stephen. "Toleration and Fundamentalism." In *A Companion to Contemporary Political Philosophy*, edited by R. E. Goodin and P. Pettit, 622–28. Oxford: Blackwell, 1993.
Magarian, Gregory P. "How to Apply the Religious Freedom Restoration Act to Federal Law without Violating the Constitution." *MLR* 99:8 (2001) 1903–98.
Maier, Hans. *Totalitarianism and Political Religions*. London: Routledge, 2004.
Maritain, Jacques. *The Rights of Man and Natural Law*. New York: Scribner, 1947.
———. *Man and the State*. Chicago: University of Chicago Press, 1951.
Marty, Martin E., and Jonathan Moore. *Politics, Religion, and the Common Good*. San Francisco: Jossey-Bass, 2000.
Masuzawa, Tomoko. *The Invention of World Religions, or, How European Universalism Was Preserved in the Language of Pluralism*. Chicago: University of Chicago Press, 2005.
McCoy, Richard C. *Alterations of State: Sacred Kingship in the English Reformation*. New York: Columbia University Press, 2002.
McCutcheon, Russell T. *Manufacturing Religion: The Discourse on Sui Generis Religion and the Politics of Nostalgia*. New York: Oxford University Press, 1997.
McInerny, Ralph. "Natural Law and Human Rights." *AJJ* 36:1 (1991) 1–14.
Meinvielle, Julio. "La Declaración Conciliar Sobre Libertad Religiosa y la Doctrina Tradicional." In *De Lamennais a Maritain*, 215–33. Buenos Aires: Ediciones Theoría, 1967.
Mendieta, Eduardo, and Jonathan VanAntwerpen, editors. *The Power of Religion in the Public Sphere*. New York: Columbia University Press, 2011.
Mendus, Susan. *Toleration and the Limits of Liberalism*. Basingstoke, Hampshire: Macmillan, 1989.
Morariu, Mihaela. "Public and Private in the Anthropology of Hannah Arendt." *Agathos* 2:2 (2011) 146–50.
Münkler, Herfried. "Politisches Denken in der Zeit der Reformation." In *Pipers Handbuch der politischen Ideen*, edited by I. Fetscher and H. Münkler, vol. 2, 615–83. Munich: Piper, 1993.
Murray, John Courtney. "Arguments for the Human Right to Religious Freedom." In *Religious Liberty*, edited by J. Leon Hooper, 229–44. Louisville: John Knox, 1993.

———. "The Declaration on Religious Freedom." In *Vatican II: An Interfaith Appraisal*, edited by John Miller 565–76. Notre Dame: Associated Press, 1966.

———. "Declaration on Religious Freedom: Commentary." In *American Participation at the Second Vatican Council*, edited by Vincent A. Yzermans, 668–76. New York: Sheed and Ward, 1967.

———. "The Issue of Church and State at Vatican II." *TS* 27 (1966) 580–606.

———. *The Problem of Religious Freedom*. Westminster, MD: Newman, 1965.

———. *Religious Liberty: Catholic Struggles with Pluralism*. Louisville: John Knox, 1993.

———, editor. *Religious Liberty, an End and a Beginning: The Declaration on Religious Freedom, an Ecumenical Discussion*. New York: Macmillan, 1966.

———. *We Hold These Truths: Catholic Reflections on the American Proposition*. New York: Sheed and Ward, 1960.

Murray, John Courtney, editor. *Religious Liberty: An End and a Beginning: The Declaration on Religious Freedom, an Ecumenical Discussion*. New York: Macmillan, 1966.

Neal, Patrick. "Is Political Liberalism Hostile to Religion?" In *Reflections on Rawls: An Assessment of His Legacy*, edited by Shaun P. Young, 153–77. Surrey: Ashgate, 2009.

———. "Three Readings of Political Liberalism: Rawls, Maritain and Crick." *JPI* 5:2 (2000) 225–46.

Nestle, Eberhard, Erwin Nestle, Kurt Aland, and Barbara Aland. *Novum Testamentum Graece*. 27th rev. ed. Stuttgart: Deutsche Bibelgesellschaft, 1996.

Neuhaus, Richard John. "C. S. Lewis in the Public Square." *FT*, December 1998, 30.

———. "The Idea of Moral Progress." *FT*, August 1999, 21.

———. *The Naked Public Square: Religion and Democracy in America*. Grand Rapids: Eerdmans, 1984.

———. "A New Order of Religious Freedom." *FT*, February 1992, 13–17.

———. "Religious Liberty: Freedom of Conscience." *VSD* 52 (1986) 607–8.

Novak, David. *In Defense of Religious Liberty*. Wilmington, DE: ISI, 2009.

O'Reilly, Kevin E. "The Significance of Worship in the Thought of Thomas Aquinas." *IPQ* 53:4 (2013) 453–62.

Parsons, Gerald. *Perspectives on Civil Religion*. Aldershot: Ashgate, 2002.

Philo of Alexandria. *Allegorical Interpretations of Genesis II and III*. Translated by F. H. Colson and G. H. Whitaker. New York: Putnam, 1929.

———. *On the Birth of Abel and the Sacrifices Offered by Him and by His Brother, Cain*. Translated by F. H. Colson and G. H. Whitaker. New York: Putnam, 1929.

Pieper, Josef. *Living the Truth*. San Francisco: Ignatius, 1989.

Pitkin, Hannah Fenichel. "Justice: On Relating Public and Private.'" *PT* 9 (1981) 327–52.

Prodi, Paolo. *Il Sacramento del Potere*. Bologna: Il Mulino, 1992.

Pyysiäinen, Ilkka. "Buddhism, Religion, and the Concept of 'God.'" *Numen* 50:2 (2003) 147–71.

Ratzinger, Joseph. *Truth and Tolerance: Christian Belief and World Religions*. San Francisco: Ignatius, 2004.

Rawls, John. "The Idea of an Overlapping Consensus." *OJLS* 7:1 (1987) 1–25.

———. "The Idea of Public Reason Revisited." *UCLR* 64:3 (1997) 765–807.

———. *Justice as Fairness: A Restatement*. Cambridge, MA: Harvard University Press, 2001.

———. "Justice as Fairness: Political Not Metaphysical." *PPA* 14:3 (1985) 223–51.

———. *The Law of Peoples*. Cambridge, MA: Harvard University Press, 1999.
———. *Political Liberalism*. Expanded ed. New York: Columbia University Press, 2005.
———. *A Theory of Justice*. Cambridge, MA: Harvard University Press, 1971.
Reese, Thomas. "Religious Freedom Is a Fundamental Human Right." *NCR*, May 16, 2014. https://www.ncronline.org/blogs/faith-and-justice/religious-freedom-fundamental-human-right.
Reeves, Thomas C. *The Empty Church: Does Organized Religion Matter Anymore?* New York: Simon & Schuster, 1998.
———. *The Empty Church: The Suicide of Liberal Christianity*. New York: Free Press, 1996.
Reno, R. R. "Neuhaus, the Liberal." *FT*, August–September 2016, 6–7.
Rials, Stéphane, editor. *La Déclaration des Droits de L'homme et du Citoyen*. Paris: Hachette, 1988.
Rico, Herminio. *John Paul II and the Legacy of Dignitatis Humanae*. Washington, DC: Georgetown University Press, 2002.
Rossano, Matt J. "Religion on Which the Devout and Skeptic Can Agree." *Zygon* 42:2 (2007) 301–16.
Rousseau, Jean-Jacques. *The Social Contract*. Translated by Willmoore Kendall. South Bend, IN: Gateway, 1954.
Sandel, Michael J. "Religious Liberty—Freedom of Conscience or Freedom of Choice." *ULR* 1989:3 (1989) 597–616.
Schleiermacher, Friedrich. *Über die Religion: Reden an die Gebildeten unter ihren Verächtern*. Hamburg: Meiner, 2004.
Schlinder, David. "Freedom, Truth, and Human Dignity: An Interpretation of Dignitatis Humanae on the Right to Religious Liberty." *Communio* 40 (2013) 208–316.
Schlinder, David, and Nicholas J. Healy. *Freedom, Truth, and Human Dignity*. Grand Rapids: Eerdmans, 2015.
Seneca, Lucius Annaeus. *Seneca's Letters to Lucilius*. Translated by Edward Phillips Barker. 2 vols. Oxford: Clarendon, 1932.
Sheldon, Garrett Ward, and Daniel L. Dreisbach. *Religion and Political Culture in Jefferson's Virginia*. Lanham, MD: Rowman & Littlefield, 2000.
Skinner, Quentin. *The Foundations of Modern Political Thought*. Vol. 2: *The Age of Reformation*. Cambridge: Cambridge University Press, 1978.
Smith, Christian. *The Secular Revolution: Power, Interests, and Conflict in the Secularization of American Public Life*. Berkeley: University of California Press, 2003.
Smith, Jonathan Z. "Religion, Religions, Religious." In *Critical Terms for Religious Studies*, edited by Mark C. Taylor, 269–84. Chicago: University of Chicago Press, 1998.
Smith, Rogers M. "Revelation and Democratic Responsibilities: A Comment on Finnis." In *The Naked Public Square Reconsidered*, edited by Christopher Wolfe, 127–39. Wilmington, DE: ISI, 2009.
———. *Stories of Peoplehood: The Politics and Morals of Political Membership*. New York: Cambridge University Press, 2003.
Smith, Steven B. "Toleration and the Skepticism of Religion in Spinoza's Tractatus Theologico-Politicus." In *Early Modern Skepticism and the Origins of Toleration*, edited by A. Levine, 127–46. Lanham, MD: Lexington, 1999.

Smith, Wilfred Cantwell. *The Meaning and End of Religion: A New Approach to the Religious Traditions of Mankind.* New York: Macmillan, 1963.
Sölle, Dorothee. "Thou Shalt Have No Other Jeans before Me." In *Observations on the Spiritual Situation of the Age,* edited by Jürgen Habermas. Cambridge, MA: MIT Press, 1984.
Sommerstein, Alan H., Andrew J. Bayliss, and Isabelle C. Torrance. *Oaths and Swearing in Ancient Greece.* Berlin: de Gruyter, 2014.
Staal, Frits. *Rules without Meaning: Ritual, Mantras, and the Human Sciences.* New York: Peter Lang, 1989.
Stow, Kenneth R. *Alienated Minority: The Jews of Medieval Latin Europe.* Cambridge, MA: Harvard University Press, 1992.
Strauss, Leo. *Natural Right and History.* Chicago: University of Chicago, 1950.
———. *Spinoza's Critique of Religion.* Translated by E. M. Sinclair. Chicago: University of Chicago Press, 1997.
Syse, Henrik. *Natural Law, Religion, and Rights.* South Bend, IN: St. Augustine's, 2007.
Tahzib, Bahiyyih G. *Freedom of Religion or Belief: Ensuring Effective International Legal Protection.* The Hague: Nijhoff, 1996.
Tal, Uriel. *Religion, Politics and Ideology in the Third Reich: Selected Essays.* New York: Routledge, 2004.
Taylor, Charles. "The Meaning of Secularism." *HR* 12 (2010) 23–34.
———. *A Secular Age.* Cambridge, MA: Harvard University Press, 2007.
———. "Why We Need a Radical Redefinition of Secularism." In *The Power of Religion in the Public Sphere,* edited by Eduardo Mendieta and Jonathan VanAntwerpen, 34–59. New York: Columbia University Press, 2011.
Tertullian. *Ad Scapulam.* Edited by J. P. Migne. Paris: Imprimerie Catholique, 1879.
———. *Apologeticus adversus Gentes pro Christianis.* Edited by J. P. Migne. Paris: Imprimerie Catholique, 1879.
Thomas, Y. "Corpus aut Ossa aut Cineres: La Chose Religieuse et le Commerce." *Micrologus* 7 (1999) 73–112.
Tierney, Brian. "Author's Rejoinder." *RP* 64:3 (2002) 416–20.
———. "Natural Law and Natural Rights: Old Problems and Recent Approaches." *RP* 64:3 (2002) 389–406.
———. "Natural Rights in the Thirteenth Century: A Quaestio of Henry of Ghent." *Speculum* 67:1 (1992) 58–68.
Tollefsen, Christopher. "Harm, Neutrality, or Truth: What Is the Basis of Liberalism?" *PD,* April 2017. http://www.thepublicdiscourse.com/2017/04/19032/.
Torfs, Rik. "Contractual Religious Freedom." In *Freedom of Religion,* edited by A. van de Beek, et al., 141–54. Leiden: Brill, 2010.
Troeltsch, Ernst. *The Social Teaching of the Christian Churches.* Louisville: John Knox, 1992.
Tutino, Stefania. *Shadows of Doubt: Language and Truth in Post-Reformation Catholic Culture.* New York: Oxford University Press, 2014.
U. S. Senate and House of Representatives. "Religious Freedom Restoration Act of 1993." *JCS* 36:2 (1994) 451–53.
Ulpian. *The Commentaries of Gaius and the Rules of Ulpian.* Translated by J. T. Abdy and Brian Walker. Cambridge: Cambridge University Press, 1885.
United Nations. *Human Rights: A Compilation of International Instruments.* 6th ed. New York: United Nations, 2002.

———. "International Covenant on Civil and Political Rights. Adopted by the General Assembly of the United Nations on 19 December 1966." In *Treaty Series*, 171–86. New York: United Nations, 1976.

United States Federal Government. *The Constitution of the United States of America and Selected Writings of the Founding Fathers*. New York: Barnes & Noble, 2012.

———. *The Constitution of the United States with the Declaration of Independence*. New York, NY: Castle, 2014.

———. *The Declaration of Independence. The Articles of Confederation. The Constitution of the United States*. New York: Oxford University Press, 1917.

Vallier, Kevin. *Liberal Politics and Public Faith: Beyond Separation*. New York: Routledge, 2014.

Van der Vyver, Johan David, and John Witte, editors. *Religious Human Rights in Global Perspective: Religious Perspectives*. The Hague: Nijhoff, 1996.

Vatican Council II. *Declaration on Religious Freedom* (*Dignitatis Humanae*). Boston: Daughters of Saint Paul, 1965.

Veatch, Henry Babcock. *Human Rights: Fact or Fancy?* Baton Rouge: Louisiana State University Press, 1985.

———. "Natural Law: Dead or Alive?" *LL* 1:4 (1978) 7–31.

Vermeulen, B. P. "The Freedom of Religion in Article 9 of the European Convention of Human Rights: Historical Roots and Today's Dilemmas." In *Freedom of Religion*, edited by A. van de Beek, et al., 9–29. Leiden: Brill, 2010.

Vickers, Lucy. "Religious Freedom: Expressing Religion, Attire, and Public Spaces." *JLP* 22 (2013–2014) 591–612.

Villey, Michel. *Questions de Saint Thomas sur le Droit et la Politique*. Paris: Presses Universitaires France, 1987.

Voegelin, Erich. *Political Religions*. Lewiston, NY: Mellen, 1986.

Voltaire. *Treatise on Tolerance*. Translated by Simon Harvey and Brian Masters. New York: Cambridge University Press, 2000.

Waggoner, Michael D. "Religious Freedom and the Eye of the Beholder." *RE* 41:3 (2014) 233–34.

Ward, Graham. *True Religion*. Malden, MA: Blackwell, 2003.

Weed, Ronald L., and John von Heyking. *Civil Religion in Political Thought: Its Perennial Questions and Enduring Relevance in North America*. Washington, DC: CUA Press, 2010.

Weightman, Simon. "Hinduism." In *A Handbook of Living Religions*, edited by John R. Hinnells, 191–236. Harmondsworth: Penguin, 1984.

Weinreb, Lloyd L. "Natural Law and Rights." In *Natural Law Theory: Contemporary Essays*, edited by Robert P. George, 278–308. Oxford: Oxford University Press, 1992.

Wenger, Tisa J. "The God-in-the-Constitution Controversy: American Secularisms in Historical Perspective." In *Comparative Secularisms in a Global Age*, edited by Linell E. Cady and Elizabeth Shakman Hurd, 87–105. New York: Palgrave Macmillan, 2010.

Wiker, Benjamin. *Worshipping the State: How Liberalism Became Our State Religion*. Washington, DC: Regnery, 2013.

Williams, Edward J. "The Emergence of the Secular Nation-State and Latin American Catholicism." *CP* 5:2 (1973) 261–77.

Wilson, Bryan R. *Religion in Sociological Perspective*. New York: Oxford University Press, 1982.
Winham, Ilya. "Rereading Hanna Arendt's 'What Is Freedom?'" *Theoria* 6 (2012) 84–106.
Wolfe, Christopher. *Natural Law Liberalism*. New York: Cambridge University Press, 2006.
Wolterstorff, Nicholas. "An Engagement with Jürgen Habermas on Postmetaphysical Philosophy, Religion, and Political Dialogue." In *Habermas and Religion*, edited by Craig J. Calhoun et al., 92–111. Cambridge: Polity, 2013.
———. "The Role of Religion in Decision and Discussion of Political Issues." In *Religion in the Public Square*, edited by R. Audi and N. Wolterstorff, 67–120. Lanham, MD: Rowman & Littlefield, 1997.
Young, Iris Marion. *Justice and the Politics of Difference*. Princeton, NJ: Princeton University Press, 1990.
Zagorin, Perez. *How the Idea of Religious Toleration Came to the West*. Princeton, NJ: Princeton University Press, 2003.
Zuckert, Michael P. "Response to Brian Tierney." *RP* 64:3 (2002) 414–15.

Index

ACLU, 275
adoption, 2, 21, 242n33, 273
adoration, 155, 157, 163, 166, 167, 179, 182, 243
Agamben, Giorgio, 5, 141–53, 172, 189, 244, 255
Aquinas, Thomas. *See* Thomas Aquinas
Arendt, Hannah, 5, 6, 73, 204–27, 228, 229, 230, 232, 234, 238, 245, 248, 254
Aristotle, 148, 157, 174, 202n329, 215, 216, 222, 233, 234n11, 247n48, 247n50, 249, 250, 252
Augustine, 78, 160, 205

belief, 2, 5, 6, 7, 16, 20, 21, 25, 29, 34–41, 43, 46–49, 52, 53, 58, 60–63, 68, 70–73, 77n7, 82, 84, 89–94, 99–110, 118, 120–23, 131–40, 142, 146, 153, 159, 161, 184–201, 226, 239, 241–46, 253–59, 261–62, 264–68, 271–72, 274–76
Benedict XVI. *See* Ratzinger, Joseph
Buddhism, 191–96, 201, 202

Casanova, José, 2n4, 4, 8, 9n6, 42–49, 66, 68, 70
Catholicism, 194, 199
Cavanaugh, William T., 180n219, 183–85, 187–88, 190, 192–93, 195, 199, 200, 202
Christ, 115n132, 179, 200, 238, 264

Christianity, 10–11, 48, 78n9, 161, 183, 185–87, 189, 191–95, 197–98, 202
Cicero, 67, 76, 144, 148n38, 151–52, 162, 173, 174
circumcision, 2
coercion, 15, 25, 28, 71, 77n7, 98, 100, 101, 106–10, 113–14, 118–19, 121–22, 126–33, 137, 206, 214, 228–29, 237, 239, 240, 242, 253, 264–65, 268–69
common good, 14, 24, 25, 26, 113, 121, 124, 127, 139, 170, 174, 175, 178, 179, 181, 222, 234, 237, 242, 245, 247, 248, 251, 252, 254, 255, 262, 265, 268, 269, 270, 272
Communism, 196, 199n318
community, 29, 36, 54, 88, 94, 97, 98, 99, 101, 102, 103, 105, 108, 109, 116, 117, 124, 165, 166, 167, 174, 175, 176, 177, 178, 180, 181, 182, 191, 197, 199, 200, 209, 218n64, 219, 220, 222, 233, 234, 236, 237, 239, 240, 241, 243, 251, 252, 254, 262, 264, 268
conscience, 2, 4, 6, 32, 36, 40, 67, 72, 77, 78, 79, 80, 81,, 82, 85, 87, 99, 100, 115, 117, 118, 120, 121, 124, 125, 126, 127, 130–34, , 186, 199, 246, 255, 257, 259, 260, 261, 263, 266, 267, 269, 274, 275, 278

INDEX

consensus, 12–18, 20,23–24, 26, 53, 72, 73, 105, 150n44, 219, 224, 234, 235, 262
Constantine, 78
constitution, 8, 11, 20, 50, 51, 62, 82, 86, 87, 97, 99, 100n97, 103, 109–10, 122, 123, 143, 161, 181, 215n47, 217, 237, 255n84, 276
courage, 180, 211, 212, 213, 221, 226, 243, 244, 254
culture, 1, 10, 14, 15, 17–19, 30–34, 39, 43, 50, 60n208, 65, 67, 68, 72, 111, 142, 144, 154, 183, 190, 191, 196n209, 201, 202, 224, 244, 255, 278n41
Cusa, Nicolas de, 183, 184

Derrida, Jacques, 49n166, 191
devotion, 5, 70, 141, 155, 160, 162–64, 166, 176, 177, 180, 182, 221, 230, 233, 239
Dewan, Lawrence, 155n73, 165, 167–69, 180n215, 278
dignity, 2, 79, 80, 107, 112–19, 127–30, 173, 177n202, 234n11, 248n58, 249, 253, 262, 265, 270
divine providence. *See* providence

Erasmus, 79
ethnicity, 30

Fascism, 198, 199n318
faith, 2, 11, 16, 21, 22, 38, 51–53, 56, 59, 61, 62, 67, 70n236, 71, 76, 77, 78, 79, 80–83, 94, 96, 98, 99, 102, 104, 105, 110, 120, 121, 135, 144, 145, 149, 153, 156, 161, 173n182, 174, 175, 177, 179, 184–87, 191, 194, 195, 198, 199, , 224, 235, 238, 239, 254, 255, 259, 260, 261, 262, 263, 264, 265, 266 267, 272, 273–75, 278
Feuerbach, Ludwig, 189
freedom 79, 205–6, 209–14, 219–27
freedom of conscience, 2, 4, 6, 67, 77, 78–82, 85n39, 86–87, 98–110, 115–39, 186, 238, 242, 246, 254–56, 257–61, 263–78
freedom of religion. *See* religious freedom.

Gentile, Emilio, 198–99
God, 32, 45, 61, 67, 77, 79, 80, 81, 84, 85n39, 98, 111, 113–20, 122, 128, 133, 136, 139, 143–93, 196, 199, 224, 231, , 233, 239, 240–48, 253, 266, 267, 273, 277, 278
goodness, 163, 164, 182, 213, 221, 239, 265
government, 2, 10, 11, 19, 23, 27, 28, 29, 30, 39, 40, 48, 52, 60, 69, 84, 96, 98n95, 99, 100, 103, 109, 112, 116, 117, 123, 124, 130, 135, 138, 141, 159, 162n162, 175, 179, 193, 199, 210, 217, 232, 233, 234, 235, 240, 241, 242, 248n58, 258n1, 259, 260, 263, 264, 266, 268, 269, 271, 273, 275, 276
Greece, 142, 143, 153, 204–213, 232

Habermas, Jürgen, 4, 7, 8, 41, 42, 43, 44, 46, 49–60, 64, 65, 66, 69, 74, 205n4, 224n84, 264
Hegel, 85n42, 189
Hinduism, 191, 192, 201
history, 1, 4, 15, 26, 45, 74, 75, 76, 77, 79, 81, 83, 85, 87, 89, 90 91, 137, 140, 183, 189, 201, 205, 210, 213, 222, 223, 240n29, 244, 248, 272n28,274
Hooker, Richard, 186n245, 247n50
human flourishing, 46, 72
human nature, 98, 99, 105, 107, 112–17, 120, 124, 128, 129, 130, 157, 159, 167, 168n141, 183, 218, 226, 244, 249, 250, 251, 253, 265, 268, 269, 272, 277
human person. *See* human nature
human reason, 15, 16
human right, 2, 3, 6, 51, 64, 76, 77, 82, 84n37, 86–89, 95, 98, 101, 103, 104, 105, 107, 111–14, 120–24,

126, 137, 138, 229, 235n16, 238, 247, 249, 250, 251, 263, 277
humanism, 79, 80, 196

independence, 80, 86, 135, 136, 225, 229
injustice, 33, 116, 180
intolerance, 4, 75, 78n10, 83, 84n37, 85, 88, 103, 108, 137
Islam, 10n6, 161, 183, 185, 190n272, 191, 194, 200, 201, 202

Judaism, 161, 183, 200, 201, 202
justice, 6, 12–18, 20–22, 24, 27, 66, 129, 144, 148, 155–60, 173–75, 180, 181, 212, 223, 226, 231, 236, 243, 244, 254, 260, 277

Kant, Immanuel, 16, 65, 86, 92
Kateb, George, 213, 214

language, 1, 11, 41, 49n166, 53, 54, 55, 56, 60, 64, 65, 69–71, 141–53, 172, 185, 190, 202, 244
law, 2, 5, 6, 10, 11, 19, 25, 28, 32n98, 34, 39, 50, 54, 60, 64, 68, 71, 72, 74, 82n28, 88, 89n61, 91, 99, 100, 104, 105, 106, 108, 109, 113, 118, 122, 127, 131n198, 136, 141–45, 147–54, 158, 167, 168, 170, 171, 173, 181, 187n258, 207, 214, , 233n11, 235–37, 240, 246–50, 261, 262, 265, 270–73, 275
legislation, 21, 64
liberalism, 2, 12–17, 22n57, 23–27, 42n135, 65, 67, 68n236, 84n37, 85, 119, 198n314, 208, 260, 262
Little Sisters of the Poor, 141n2, 259, 260–64, 267, 268, 272, 275
liturgy, 177, 179, 241
Locke, John, 84, 89, 186, 187, 247
Luther, Martin, 80–82
Lutheranism 81, 83, 184

man. *See* human nature
Maritain, Jacques, 247n50
multiculturalism, 1, 44, 239
Müntzer, Thomas, 80n23

Murray, John Courtney, 97–101, 111, 112, 121–32, 204, 214, 237
Muslim. *See* Islam

nationalism, 192n284
Native American Church, 270
natural law, 127, 131n198, 158, 157, 168, 170, 171, 181, 236, 246, 247n50, 250
Nazism, 198, 199
Neuhaus, Richard John, 7, 8, 11n11, 30–42, 47, 66–68, 70, 72, 274
New Testament, 67, 191

oath, 5, 70, 141–55, 163, 171–75, 179, 180, 211, 212, 226, 230, 242, 244, 245
overlapping consensus, 12–18, 20, 23, 24, 26, 72, 73, 219, 224, 234, 235n16

peyote, 270–72
pluralism, 2, 7, 8, 12–17, 24, 27–30, 35, 38, 50, 52, 59, 60, 61, 63, 64, 65, 69–72, 101, 105, 184, 214, 219, 223, 257, 260, 261
political freedom, 206–9, 217
political liberalism. *See* liberalism
political prudence, 157, 180, 221, 226, 233n11, 234, 243, 244, 248, 254
postsecularism, 7, 8, 42–46, 49–60, 66, 68, 73
prayer, 5, 11n13, 36, 38, 67, 70, 120, 141, 155, 162–65, 175–78, 180, 182, 221, 230, 233, 239, 240, 241, 243
Protestantism, 9, 10, 15, 45n146, 79, 80n23, 81–83, 85n39, 137, 185, 194
providence, 165n124
prudence, 231, 233, 234
public reason, 5, 12–13, 18–23, 24–25, 27, 260, 263
public square, 3–74, 75, 89, 100, 101, 104–113, 123n160, 136, 140, 154, 155, 157, 161, 166, 175–81, 187, 188, 190, 192, 195, 200, 201, 203, 204–227, 228–56, 257, 258, 260, 261, 263, 264, 268, 269n21, 272–76, 278

Ratzinger, Joseph, v, 231n2, 277n41
Rawls, John, 4, 8, 12–30, 38, 41, 49n166, 50, 52, 53, 55, 57, 58, 60, 64–71, 74, 91, 102, 196n299, 219, 223, 224, 226, 257, 260–62, 264
Reese, Thomas, 102, 265
religion, 7–74, 140–203
religious freedom, 2–12, 15, 18, 20, 22, 24, 26–30, 32, 44, 52, 60, 62, 67, 69–74, 75–139, 140, 141, 166, 181, 190, 194, 200, 202, 204, 214, 225, 227, 228–56, 257–78
religious liberty. *See* religious freedom
revolution, 62, 82, 84, 85, 86, 87n51, 88n54, 89, 188, 215
rite, 145, 147, 150, 154, 159, 160, 161, 162, 180n218, 183, 184, 192, 193, 237, 241, 243n40,
Rome, 137, 142–54, 200n323, 204, 213, 232
Rousseau, Jean-Jacques, 88n54, 187, 210n29, 247n48

sacrifice, 77, 94, 95, 151, 152, 155, 157, 167–69, 178, 179, 182, 236, 243, 246, 253, 262, 270
Schleiermacher, Friedrich, 188
Schlinder, David, 75, 111, 112, 114, 115, 117, 119, 120n153, 123, 130n195, 131n198, 204, 235n17
Satanism, 2
secularization. *See* secularism
secularism, 4, 7–12, 23, 31, 34, 36, 42–49, 52, 59, 60–69, 187, 201, 228, 238
Seneca, 76
slavery, 208n16, 211n33, 234n11, 248
society, 1, 3, 4, 10,, 13, 14, 15, 16, 17, 18, 19, 20, 21, 23, 25, 27, 28, 29, 30, 33, 35, 38, 40, 41, 42n135, 43, 44, 45, 47, 50, 51, 52, 56, 59, 60, 61, 62, 68n236, 69, 72, 73, 78, 86, 91, 92, 96, 98, 99, 100–102, 104–6, 110, 113, 116, 117, 121, 122–25, 127–29, 131, 135, 137–39, 159, 161, 170, 174, 175, 178, 179, 181, 187, 188n162, 191, 198, 205, 208, 209, 215, 219, 231, 234, 235, 237–39, 241, 245, 254, 255, 258, 261, 262, 264, 265n8, 269, 270, 274, 275
Strauss, Leo, 246n48
Supreme Court, 10, 11, 12n13, 19, 22, 32, 65, 74, 135n215, 141n2, 257, 258, 260, 261, 266, 270, 271, 272, 275

Taylor, Charles, 4, 7, 8, 10, 11, 41, 42, 43, 44, 49, 60–65, 66, 68–70, 74, 195, 264
Tertullian, 77
Thomas Aquinas, 5, 141, 154–82, 183n233, 203, 207n10, 211, 228–29, 232–37, 240, 241, 242, 243, 244, 245, 246, 247, 248, 253, 254, 265, 266, 267, 273, 274, 277, 278
Tierney, Brian, 246n48
tithing, 5, 142, 155, 163, 167, 170, 178, 179, 182, 241
tolerance, 2, 4, 9, 60, 74, 75, 76–81, 84, 85n39, 86, 88n57, 89–97, 137, 138, 228, 229, 238, 258, 268–72
toleration. *See* tolerance
truth, 14, 16, 17, 21, 22, 27, 28, 31, 34n104, 35, 39, 54n183, 58, 68, 69, 73, 79, 81, 86, 88, 90, 98, 101, 107, 110, 112, 113, 114–16, 117,118, 119, 120, 121, 122, 123, 124, 125, 126–27, 128, 129, 130, 131, 136, 142, 145, 147, 148n38, 149, 150, 153, 158, 159n91, 172, 174, 184, 186, 191, 207, 230n1, 235n16, 257, 260, 267n17, 272, 276

United Nations, 88, 89, 103, 107, 108

Vatican Council II, 103, 106–7, 111, 119, 122, 123–24
Veatch, Henry Babcock, 249–53
vice, 6, 161, 235, 245, 265, 269n20

violence, 2, 36, 66, 87, 206, 207, 213n40
virtue, 5, 6, 15, 22n55, 34, 35, 76n1, 96, 141, 142, 145, 149n38, 155–81, 182, 188, 190, 202, 203, 204, 209, 211, 212, 213, 214, 219, 221, 223, 224, 226–47, 249, 250, 252–55, 258, 263–70, 272–74, 276–78

Voltaire, 85
vow, 5 142, 155, 161n105, 163, 167, 170–71, 175, 177, 178, 182

war, 1, 9, 15, 26, 29, 30n87, 79, 82–83, 88, 89, 103, 215n47
Western Civilization, 8n2, 142, 154, 190, 244, 245

www.ingramcontent.com/pod-product-compliance
Lightning Source LLC
Chambersburg PA
CBHW061431300426
44114CB00014B/1631